MARKETING FOR NONPROFIT ORGANIZATIONS

PHILIP KOTLER
Northwestern University

PRENTICE-HALL, INC.
Englewood Cliffs, New Jersey

Library of Congress Cataloging in Publication Data

KOTLER, PHILIP.
    Marketing for nonprofit organizations.

    Includes bibliographical references.
    1. Marketing.   2. Corporations, Nonprofit.
3. Marketing—Case studies.   I. Title.
HF5415.K6312   658.8   74-16052
ISBN   0-13-556084-5

Printed in the United States of America

10   9   8   7   6   5

Prentice-Hall International, Inc., *London*
Prentice-Hall of Australia, Pty. Ltd., *Sydney*
Prentice-Hall of Canada, Ltd., *Toronto*
Prentice-Hall of India Private Limited, *New Delhi*
Prentice-Hall of Japan, Inc., *Tokyo*

This book is dedicated to my Mother and Father who provided my first introduction to a nonprofit organization.

Contents

Preface

In recent years, marketing has become a subject of growing interest to managers of public and private nonprofit organizations. The concepts, tools, and models that have worked so effectively to manage products and services in the profit sector are becoming increasingly relevant to the management of products and services in the nonprofit sector. Nonprofit organizations face a host of problems that would be analyzed as straightforward marketing problems if found in the profit sector. Museums and symphonies have a difficult time attracting sufficient funds to carry on their cultural activities. Blood banks find it hard to enlist enough donors. Churches are having difficulties attracting and maintaining active members. Many colleges face serious problems in attracting a sufficient number of qualified students. Police departments are hampered by a poor image in many communities. Family planners face formidable problems in selling the idea of "zero population growth." Safety councils seek more effective ways to persuade motorists to wear their safety belts. National parks such as Yellowstone are plagued with overdemand and are seeking ways to discourage or "demarket" the parks. There is hardly a public or private nonprofit organization in existence that is not faced with some problems stemming from its relations to its markets.

But what is marketing? As used in this book, *marketing is the effective management by an organization of its exchange relations with its various markets and publics.* All organizations operate in an environment of one or more markets and publics. A university operates in a student market, a faculty market, a donor market, and a public opinion market. A political party operates in a voter market, a contributor market, and an interest group market. Each market is made up of significant subgroups called market segments with particular needs, perceptions, and preferences. The organization has goals with respect to each significant market or market segment. Marketing is the organization's undertaking of analysis, planning, implementation, and control to achieve its exchange objectives with its target markets.

Through decades of working in business markets, marketers have formulated a conceptual system that yields systematic insight into the structure and dynamics of market exchanges. Concepts such as market segmentation, market positioning, marketing mix, channels of distribution, and logistical systems, among others, serve to organize the analysis of any marketing problem. The application of these concepts to the problems of nonprofit organizations has already proven its value in a relatively short period of time.[1]

At the same time, the transposition of a conceptual system from one domain (the profit sector) to another (the nonprofit sector) poses a number of challenges that call for new creative conceptualization. The concepts of product, price, promotion, and distribution, which are employed by profit-sector marketers, have to be redefined for maximum relevance to all organizations. The concepts of markets and exchange processes must be generalized. The concept of profit maximization must be translated into benefit-cost maximization so that marketing models can be applied fruitfully in the nonprofit sector.

The purpose of this book is, precisely, to broaden and apply the conceptual system of marketing to the marketing problems of nonprofit organizations. Although there is a growing number of articles describing specific applications of marketing concepts to specific problems in the nonprofit area, no comprehensive text exists on the subject. All the existing marketing texts, including those by the author,[2] deal specifically with marketing institutions and practices found in the private-for-profit sector. This makes it difficult for nonprofit organization managers—public administrators, educators, museum directors, hospital administrators, family planners, religious leaders, foundation directors, social activists, urban

---

[1] See the collection of articles in the *Journal of Marketing*, July 1971.

[2] Philip Kotler, *Marketing Management: Analysis, Planning, and Control*, 2nd ed. (Englewood Cliffs, N.J.: Prentice-Hall, Inc., 1972); and *Marketing Decision Making: A Model Building Approach* (New York: Holt, Rinehart and Winston, Inc., 1971).

planners, and others—to gain a direct and comprehensive idea of marketing that is relevant to their types of organizations. This book hopes to provide the needed introduction to marketing for these administrators.

The book is divided into five parts and a section of cases. Part I (Conceptualizing Marketing) explains the nature, role, and relevance of marketing to nonprofit organizations. Part II (Analyzing the Market) describes the major concepts and tools available to the organization to help it understand its markets and potential strategies. Part III (Determining the Marketing Program) discusses the four major instruments—product, price, place, and promotion—that constitute the organization's strategic and tactical means for relating to its markets. Part IV (Administering the Marketing Program) takes up the question of the internal administration of the marketing function to achieve efficient organization, information, planning, and control. Finally, Part V (Applications) examines the marketing problems, opportunities, and solutions found in such specific nonprofit areas as health, education, public service, and politics.

This book is the result of a happy association with extremely creative and valued colleagues in the Marketing Department of the Graduate School of Management at Northwestern University. Professor Sidney J. Levy was the first person to stimulate members of our department to the awareness that marketing behavior is manifest in a wide range of situations far beyond the conventional exchange of goods and services for money. Professor Gerald Zaltman carried out some studies of the use of marketing concepts in promoting causes in the fields of health and family planning. Other colleagues in the department were helpful in their suggestions and criticism of the "broadened concept of marketing" as it evolved. Doctoral students, including Reinhard Angelmar, Paul Bloom, Nikhilesh Dholakia, Bernard Dubois, Ira Kaufman, Eduardo Roberto, Avraham Shama, Ronald Stiff, Steven Thrasher, and Richard Yalch, carried on investigations of the broadened concept in various nonprofit settings and offered critical comments on the manuscript. The enthusiasm and suggestions of Masters' students assured the author of the relevance of his effort. Helpful manuscript reviews were provided generously by Professors John U. Farley (Columbia), Ronald Frank and Paul E. Green (Wharton), Michael Ray (Stanford), and Benson Shapiro (Harvard). Paul Bloom developed the end-of-chapter questions and materials to help the reader test his understanding of the concepts. Finally, the meticulous secretarial assistance of Edith Bass and Marion Davis made this manuscript a reality. To all these persons, the author extends his deep-felt gratitude.

PHILIP KOTLER
Northwestern University

PART

I Conceptualizing
Marketing

1 The Concept of Marketing

We shall not cease from exploration
And the end of all our exploring
Will be to arrive where we started
And know the place for the first time.

T. S. ELIOT [1]

Consider the following problems facing nonprofit organizations:

The Massachusetts Institute of Technology experienced a substantial decline in applicants in the early 1970s. In 1972, applications for the freshman class were down 20 percent. The director of admissions cited such factors as the swing of interest away from engineering, the rising cost of an M.I.T. education, increased competition from state universities, and a widespread impression that M.I.T. is hard to get into and hard to stay in; therefore it does not pay to apply.[2] M.I.T. faced a classic marketing problem—that of maintaining the demand for its services.

The Michael Reese hospital of Chicago is located in a changing neighborhood. It has traditionally served a primarily white affluent clientele

3

but in recent years has been losing many of its patients and doctors to the suburbs. Some administrators want the hospital to reorient its services to the new clientele surrounding the hospital and other administrators are urging the hospital to consider relocating in the suburbs, where their former patients have moved. This hospital is facing a basic decision on its markets and services.

Amtrak is a semigovernmental corporation set up in May 1971 to take over many of the railway passenger services in the U.S. and bring passenger railway service back to a high standard of efficiency and comfort. It continues to face tough problems in getting enough resources from Congress, in getting railway union cooperation, and in drawing commuters back to the railroads. These problems will severely test Amtrak's skill as a marketer.

The U.S. Peace Corps has found it increasingly hard to recruit idealistic young Americans with specific skills, such as engineering, business, and farming. It must find a way to market the Peace Corps in the face of a low budget and a lukewarm public and Congressional attitude toward the Peace Corps.[3]

The Addiction Research Foundation of Ontario, Canada, carries on educational, research, and rehabilitation programs in the area of alcoholism and addiction. It allocates a $7 million budget toward a large variety of activities and is very uncertain of the results. It needs guidance as to how to be more effective in selling people on the harmful effect of alcohol and hard drugs. It wants to find a way to be more effective in social marketing.[4]

Each of these problems involves an organization's relationship to one or more markets and publics. In each case, the organization is seeking to alter the amount or type of exchange it has with specific other publics. Whenever an organization is trying to expand or modify its exchange relations with others, it is facing a marketing problem.

Administrators in nonprofit organizations—university presidents, hospital administrators, government officials, museum directors, religious leaders, to name a few—are increasingly becoming aware of the potential relevance of the marketing discipline to solving their problems. Yet they approach marketing with some skepticism because it has the image of being exclusively a tool for use in commercial businesses and one highly identified with selling and promoting, concerning which nonprofit administrators normally feel uncomfortable. Producing and selling a breakfast cereal is one thing and running a hospital or a university is another. The administrator of a not-for-profit organization understandably says "show me." The burden of proof of the relevance of marketing to nonprofit organizations is on the shoulders of the marketer.

Actually, such administrators often ask the following questions about marketing:

1. What is marketing?
2. Are there different styles of marketing?
3. Why should an administrator of a nonprofit organization be interested in marketing?
4. Is marketing ethical for nonprofit organizations?
5. How does one acquire an understanding of marketing?

We shall comment on these questions in the following paragraphs.

WHAT IS MARKETING?

Every organization is a purposeful coalescence of people, materials, and facilities seeking to accomplish some purpose in the outside world. To survive and succeed, the organization must (1) attract sufficient resources, (2) convert these resources into products, services, and ideas, and (3) distribute these outputs to various consuming publics. These three tasks are normally carried on in a framework of voluntarism by the cooperating parties. The organization does not resort to force to attract resources, convert them, or distribute them. Nor does it ask for selfless giving. It relies mainly on offering and exchanging values to the different parties of sufficient incentive to elicit their cooperation. In short, it relies on *exchange mechanisms* rather than *threat systems* on the one hand or *love systems* on the other.[5]

Exchange is the central concept underlying marketing. It calls for the offering of value to someone in exchange for value. Through exchanges, various social units—individuals, small groups, organizations, whole nations—attain the inputs they need. By giving up something, they acquire something else in return. This something else is normally more valued than that which is given up, which explains the motivation for exchange.

A professional marketer is someone who is very good at *understanding, planning, and managing exchanges*. He knows how to research and understand the needs of the other party; to design a valued offering to meet these needs; to communicate the offer effectively; and to present it in a good place and under timely circumstances. All of this is summarized in the following definition of marketing:

> Marketing is the analysis, planning, implementation, and control of carefully formulated programs designed to bring about voluntary exchanges of values with target markets for the purpose of achieving organizational objectives. It relies heavily on designing the organization's offering in terms of the target markets' needs and desires, and on using effective pricing, communication, and distribution to inform, motivate, and service the markets.

Several things should be noted about this definition of marketing.

First, marketing is defined as a managerial process involving analysis, planning, implementation, and control. Marketing can also be looked at as a social process in which the material needs of a society are identified, expanded, and served by a set of institutions.[6] However, we will not use the social process view of marketing in this book. That view is appropriate for those interested in social values and public policy but less relevant to managers and administrators facing very practical marketing problems.

Second, marketing manifests itself in carefully formulated programs, not just random actions to achieve desired responses. If a charity organization simply asks a group of volunteers to go out and collect money, this is not a program and is likely to produce disappointing revenue. The volunteers are without direction as to whom to call on, what to say about the organization, and how much to ask for. Their effort is more like selling than marketing. Marketing takes place before any selling takes place and manifests itself in carefully formulated plans and programs.

Third, marketing seeks to bring about voluntary exchanges of values. Marketers seek a response from another party, but it is not a response to be obtained by any means or at any price. Marketing is the philosophical alternative to force. The marketer seeks to offer benefits to the target market of sufficient attractiveness to produce a voluntary exchange. A museum seeking members, for example, tries to design a set of benefits that are appealing to potential members.

Fourth, marketing means the selection of target markets rather than a quixotic attempt to win every market and be all things to all men. A symphony orchestra in need of funding does not send letters to all citizens. Rather it buys mailing lists containing the names of people who, because of educational, income, or other characteristics, are more prone to support the local symphony orchestra. Marketers routinely try to distinguish among possible market segments and concentrate on those segments with the highest potential response to the cause.

Fifth, the purpose of marketing is to achieve organizational objectives. In the commercial sector, the major objective is profit. In the noncommercial sector, the major objective is often stated in public interest terms: a park district wishes to expand the recreational services and opportunities available to the public; the National Safety Council wants to bring down the death and accident rate in the nation; and the city health department wants to enhance the level and distribution of health in the community. Effective marketing planning requires being very specific about the target objectives.

Sixth, marketing relies on designing the organization's offering in terms of the target market's needs and desires rather than in terms of the seller's personal tastes. Marketing is a democratic rather than an elitist technology. It holds that efforts are likely to fail that try to impose on a market a product, service, or idea that is not matched to the market's tastes or desires. In the commercial world, companies that design products they feel are good for the market without consulting the market beforehand often find they have few customers. In the noncommercial sector, the same thing holds true. Local governments that design playgrounds or toll roads without studying the public's attitudes often find the subsequent level of public usage disappointing. Effective marketing is user-oriented, not seller-oriented.

Seventh, marketing utilizes and blends a set of tools called the *marketing mix*—product design, pricing, communication, and distribution. Too often the public equates marketing with only one of its tools such as advertising. But marketing is oriented toward producing results, and this requires a broad conception of all the factors influencing buying behavior. A church, for example, may do no advertising and yet attract a large following because of other elements appealing to the public's needs.

ARE THERE DIFFERENT STYLES OF MARKETING?

The definition that was advanced of marketing is compatible with a whole range of marketing styles seen in the commercial and noncommercial sectors. There is no such thing as one marketing style. Every organization chooses a style of marketing that is compatible with its goals and self-concept.

Aggressive Marketing

At one extreme is the marketing style known as aggressive, or hard-sell marketing. This is practiced by many business firms in the United States in such industries as automobiles, packaged goods, appliances, and toiletries and cosmetics. These firms have expensive, highly automated production lines that must be kept running to cover their costs. The result is that product comes out continuously and must be sold. These companies attempt to design desirable products and make accurate predictions as to demand, but they still make errors and also face competitors. This situation compels them to make a heavy investment in promotion and selling to generate a sufficient level of demand to avoid excess inventories or employee layoffs. These firms allocate a large budget to sales-producing investments, such as advertising, large sales forces, and sales promotions.

Nor is aggressive marketing limited to the industries mentioned. It pops up in very unexpected places, especially when the gap between sales expectations and sales realizations widens. Many encyclopedia and Bible-selling companies, including the most respected ones, resort to high-pressure marketing tactics to sell their books. Many land development companies wine and dine prospects, fly them out to the land sites, and exert great pressure on them to sign the purchase agreement. Some major public accounting firms, which are forbidden by the accounting profession's Code of Professional Ethics from using direct solicitation or advertising, nevertheless conduct themselves in an aggressive way to get new clients, including glad-handing, wining and dining, sharp pricing and discounting, slick brochures, partner bonuses for new clients, and occasional bad-mouthing about competitive firms. Even the family planning effort in certain developing nations is characterized by hard-sell tactics including offers of transistor radios or pots and pans to get as many persons as possible to adopt family planning practices.

Minimal Marketing

At the other extreme of marketing styles is that known as minimal or no-sell marketing. Organizations practicing minimal marketing do not consciously perform a marketing function and assume that demand will grow for their product simply because they are offering it, or offering it well. Many hospitals assume that there will be an adequate number of patients for their beds simply because of the growing population and the availability of their services. Many universities assume that there will be an adequate number of student applicants for the same reasons. They think, "Why should one have to sell a worthwhile service?"

Some organizations use a more subtle logic that displaces in their mind the need for an active form of marketing. They concentrate on producing a high-quality product or service. In their minds, a high-quality offering will (1) retain present clients and (2) lead to favorable client word-of-mouth that will bring in new clients. Thus they rely on one marketing variable, product or service design, to do the whole job: this is the sense in which they practice minimal marketing. The reasoning is fallacious. First, all the firms may decide to produce a high-quality offering, in which case the buyers will have no basis for preference. Second, buyers may not really be sensitive to quality variations. Third, if some of the firms undertake a more aggressive marketing program, then the firm practicing minimal marketing will be at a disadvantage.

Balanced Marketing

In between the two extreme marketing styles lies a third style known as balanced marketing. The other two styles of marketing rely heavily on a single marketing element: aggressive marketing relies heavily on *promotion;* minimal marketing relies heavily on *product.* Balanced marketing seeks to blend effectively all the elements of the marketing mix in a way that would contribute to high product adoption and high consumer satisfaction. It is a style of marketing that meets the tastes and needs of most nonprofit organizations.

WHY SHOULD A NONPROFIT ORGANIZATION
BE INTERESTED IN MARKETING?

By now it should be clear that nonprofit organizations are involved in marketing whether or not they are conscious of it. They are involved in various markets and use certain operating principles in dealing with each market. These operating principles define their marketing. The issue is not one of whether or not nonprofit organizations should get involved in marketing, but rather how thoughtful they should be at it.

The basic reason a nonprofit organization should be interested in formal marketing principles is that they will enable the organization to be more effective in achieving its objectives. Organizations in a free society depend upon voluntary exchanges to accomplish their objectives. Resources must be attracted, employees must be stimulated, customers must be found. The designing of proper incentives is a key step in stimulating these exchanges. Marketing is the applied science most concerned with managing exchanges effectively and efficiently.

Marketing is designed to render two specific benefits to its practitioners:

1. Improved satisfaction of the target market

Marketing places a great emphasis on measuring the needs and desires of the target market. If the organization has not done this, or does not do it well, the clients are apt to be poorly served. This results in high customer turnover or bad word-of-mouth which ultimately hurts the organization. The apathy or low morale of many college students, for example, stems from the failure of some universities to be sufficiently sensitive to their needs and desires. Such universities ultimately find it difficult to attract new students and adequate alumni support.

2. Improved efficiency in marketing activities

Marketing places a great emphasis on the scientific formulation and handling of activities involving product development, pricing, communication, and distribution. Many nonprofit organizations make these decisions with insufficient knowledge resulting in either more cost for the given impact or less impact for the given cost. Because the funds of non-profit organizations are often inadequate and tenuous, it behooves the administrator to achieve the maximal efficiency and effectiveness in marketing activities.

These benefits of bringing marketing thought into an organization are not without some cost. The administrator may properly be concerned with the question of whether a marketing orientation would require adding a large staff that he cannot afford and that would offset the benefits. This would not necessarily be the case. A marketing orientation is essentially two things. First, it is an *attitude* on the part of the administrators and employees that their job is to understand their clients' needs and to satisfy them. This attitude can be brought into an organization without much cost and should lead strongly at least to the first benefit—that is, improved customer satisfaction. This is the experience of a city automobile license bureau which for many years treated the citizens in a highly bureaucratic fashion, resulting in many complaints both to the license bureau and to local legislators. After the license bureau put its employees through training programs to create friendlier service, the complaints stopped and citizens reported how pleased they were in dealing with the organization.

The other aspect of a marketing orientation is that it is *technical knowledge* about how various marketing variables perform separately and together in influencing the market. This knowledge is brought into the organization at a real price, such as paying the salaries of an advertising manager, a new product development manager, or a marketing researcher. Even here, the organization can scale the costs to its budget through such measures as contracting for consulting services when needed or using volunteer services by professionals. Universities, churches, and medical charities are in a good position to draw on technical marketing experience from their own members who are heavily identified with their causes, at very little cost.

IS MARKETING ETHICAL?

Marketing activity has raised ethical questions dating back to ancient times. Philosophers such as Plato, Aristotle, and Aquinas thought of merchants as unproductive and acquisitive. Merchants were seen as taking advantage of helpless customers through buying "cheap" and selling "dear." In modern times, marketers are accused of getting people to buy what they do not want. Customers are seen as victims of high-pressure and sometimes deceptive selling.[7]

The time-honored professions such as medicine and law are touchy about marketing activity and have adopted codes of professional ethics that proscribe client solicitation. Activities such as advertising, sales promotion, discounting, bad-mouthing, and personal selling are enjoined at the risk of losing one's license to practice. In this way, the public cannot accuse these professionals of attempting to create more business than the "natural" level of need for their services. Further, the ban allows the practitioners to think of themselves as "professional people" and not at all engaged in anything as crass as business activity.

Many nonprofit organizations come close to the professions in their attitude toward marketing. Universities for a long time assiduously avoided advertising for students.[8] Hospitals are careful not to promote themselves as superior to other hospitals. Churches try not to compete directly for membership. These and other institutions exhibit a traditional minimal marketing attitude.

Administrators of nonprofit organizations feel that they must proceed cautiously with marketing activity lest their publics challenge them. Three types of criticism are anticipated.

1. Marketing wastes the public's money

A frequent criticism of marketing activities is that they add expense to the organization's operations. For example, in 1971 the U.S. Army spent $10.7 million on advertising in a thirteen-week period in an effort to increase army enlistments, and this upset many people.[9] Similarly, the U.S. Postal System increased its salary expense in establishing a marketing department within the postal service. Many people carefully watch the marketing expenses of charitable organizations to make sure that they do not get out of line with the amount of money being raised.

All organizations must watch their expenses carefully. For-profit firms must be careful because their profit performance will be judged by their stockholders and affect future support. Nonprofit organizations must be careful because their funds are limited and subject to scrutiny by donors, legislators, and taxpayers. Nonprofit organizations owe their publics an explanation of the benefits they are seeking to create through marketing activity. They should not overspend and they should not underspend. Nonprofit organizations are probably more prone to underspend than overspend on marketing. If the U.S. Army needs a certain number of recruits, $10 million spent on national television is probably the most efficient way to proceed. The issue should not be the absolute cost but the relative cost per 1,000 new recruits. If the U.S. Postal System needs to develop new and viable mail services for its users, its expenditure on marketing research, planning, testing, and promotion are proper if this expenditure yields a reasonable return. Yet it is important for administrators in nonprofit organizations to take into account the public's feelings about marketing and be prepared to explain the expected benefits from the planned expenditure level.

2. Marketing activity is intrusive

A second criticism about marketing activity is that it often pries into personal affairs. The marketing researcher goes into homes and asks people about their likes and dislikes, their perceptions, their incomes, and other personal matters. For example, a health clinic sent out researchers to study the fears of married men about vasectomies (male sterilization) in order to formulate a more effective information campaign. There is a widespread concern, however, that if various government agencies started doing a lot of marketing research, the information might eventually be used against individual citizens or in mass propaganda. Citizens also dislike the fact that their tax money is being spent to do the research.

Ironically, the motive for marketing research is primarily to learn the needs and wants of people and their attitude toward the organization's current products so that the organization can deliver greater satisfaction to its target publics. At the same time, organizations must show a sensitivity to the public's feelings for privacy.[10]

3. Marketing is manipulative

A third criticism is that organizations will use marketing to manipulate the target market. Many smokers resented the anti-smoking ads put out by the American Cancer Society as trying to manipulate them through fear appeals. Some congressmen were upset with the report that the Interior Department planned to spend more money on a high-powered campaign to tout itself and "its photogenic boss." [11] Image ads by police departments are seen by some citizens as manipulative.

Administrators should be sensitive to the possible charge of manipulation when they implement a marketing program. In the majority of cases, the nonprofit organization is seeking some public good for which there is widespread consensus and it is using proper means. In other cases, the charge of manipulation may be justified and such efforts, unless they are checked, will bring a "black eye" to the organization and to marketing.

HOW DOES ONE ACQUIRE AN UNDERSTANDING OF MARKETING?

Administrators and students who feel that a marketing perspective would be useful in nonprofit organizations face the problem of acquiring the necessary knowledge. In looking for source material, they confront the fact that current marketing textbooks deal primarily if not exclusively with the private-for-profit sector. These textbooks devote most of their pages to the problems faced by large consumer firms that are producing goods such as toothpaste and automobiles for the mass market. Some space is devoted to the problems of industrial marketers who try to place raw materials and heavy machinery with corporate customers. Relatively little space is devoted to the marketing of services such as insurance, banking, hotel accommodations, or restaurants. Virtually no attention is paid to the marketing of public services. As a result, the nonprofit administrator or student finds the study of marketing from a standard text somewhat frustrating. He feels that the text gives too much treatment to goods and not enough to services. He feels that the text pays too much attention to the profit motive and not enough to the service motive. He feels that the text devotes too much space to wholesaling, mass retailing institutions, and physical distribution, which figure less importantly in the marketing of services.

The basic concepts of the marketing discipline are the same for profit and nonprofit organizations but the most relevant ones for the nonprofit organization tend to be obscured in the standard text. The purpose of this book is to bring together those concepts, methods, and applications that are of the most utility to nonprofit administrators, even recognizing here, however, that each nonprofit organization will have particular needs that cannot all be satisfied by one text.

SUMMARY

Marketing, far from being a management tool of exclusive interest to business establishments, has great relevance to the problems and challenges facing the nonprofit organization. All organizations depend upon exchange relations to attract resources that they need, to convert them into useful products and services, and to distribute them efficiently to target markets. Marketing is a systematic approach to planning and achieving desired exchange relations with other groups. Marketing is concerned with developing, maintaining, and/or regulating exchange relations involving products, services, organizations, persons, places, or causes.

At the same time, styles of marketing vary from aggressive to minimal to balanced marketing. Aggressive marketing emphasizes promotion as an element in the marketing mix; minimal marketing emphasizes product; and balanced marketing blends all elements into an effective mix that brings about high transactional efficiency and consumer satisfaction.

When systematic marketing is introduced into an organization, two distinct benefits may be achieved. First, the organization may increase the satisfaction that it delivers to the target market as a result of understanding its needs better and developing better-matched products and services. Second, the organization may improve the efficiency of marketing activities through a better knowledge of how to formulate prices, communications, and distribution.

Finally, the administrator is concerned with ethical questions raised by marketing. Critics may charge that marketing is a waste of money, that it is intrusive, and that it is manipulative. It is important for administrators to be sensitive to these criticisms and avoid marketing practices or expenditures that cannot be defended. At the same time, marketing is an efficient way of accomplishing communication and distribution tasks facing organizations; it researches people's attitudes primarily to serve them better; and it usually advances causes that are in the public interest.

NOTES

1. From "Little Gidding" in *Four Quartets* by T. S. Eliot (copyright 1943 by T. S. Eliot, copyright 1971 by Esme Valerie Eliot); and in *Collected Poems 1909–1962* by T. S. Eliot. Reprinted by permission of Harcourt Brace Jovanovich, Inc., and Faber and Faber, Ltd., Publishers.

2. "Admissions: Still in the Downswing," *Technology Review* (May 1972), p. 71.

3. See the teaching case called *The Peace Corps* (Boston, Mass.: Harvard Business School, 1970).

4. See the teaching case called *The Addiction Research Foundation of Ontario* (London, Ontario: The University of Western Ontario, 1970).

5. Kenneth Boulding, *A Primer on Social Dynamics* (New York: Free Press, 1970).

6. For a comparison of the managerial and social process definition of marketing, see Daniel J. Sweeney, "Marketing: Management Technology or Social Process?" *Journal of Marketing* (October 1972), pp. 3–10.

7. The major critics in this connection are Vance Packard, *The Hidden Persuaders* (New York: Pocket Books, Inc., 1957); John Kenneth Galbraith, *The Affluent Society* (Boston: Houghton Mifflin Co., 1958) and *The New Industrial State* (Boston: Houghton Mifflin Co., 1967); and Herbert Marcuse, *One-Dimensional Man* (Boston: The Beacon Press, 1964).

8. There were notable exceptions however. See Scott M. Cutlip, " 'Advertising' Higher Education: The Early Years of College Public Relations," *College & University Journal* (Fall 1970), pp. 21–28.

9. "Advertising the Army," *New Republic,* October 2, 1971, p. 10.

10. The American Marketing Association has published a Code of Ethics for Marketing Research. A good discussion of ethical perspectives and problems in marketing research is found in C. Merle Crawford, "Attitudes of Marketing Executives Toward Ethics in Marketing Research," *Journal of Marketing* (April 1970), pp. 46–52.

11. Jack Anderson, " 'Blow Your Horn Louder,' Interior Department Told," *Chicago Daily News,* September 28, 1971, p. 13.

QUESTIONS

1. There are many nonprofit organizations that are practicing, either intentionally or unintentionally, *minimal* marketing. Choose a nonprofit organization you are familiar with that is practicing minimal marketing and state briefly how this organization could benefit from adopting a *balanced* marketing style.

2. How would you answer the mayor (or city manager) of your local community if he made the following statement? "I'd like to use marketing in managing our community's affairs, but I simply can't afford it. If I were to go out and hire a few marketing specialists, do a little advertising for our public services, and conduct regular surveys to find out what's bothering people, the citizens of this community would have my head. They'd say I was wasting the public's money."

3. The chief of police in a large city is worried about the poor relations his force has with citizens in black and Spanish-speaking communities. The chief believes in marketing and would like to conduct a survey of the people in these communities to get information about their security needs and their feelings toward his force. This information could help him correct a deteriorating situation. But because the people in these communities dislike and distrust the police, cooperation with a survey is likely to be minimal. What can the chief do to get the information he needs?

4. Develop a set of axioms that would allow one to distinguish marketing activity from other activities.

5. What are the basic similarities and differences between profit-making organizations and nonprofit organizations?

6. The executive director of a private philanthropic organization saw an advertisement for a book entitled *Marketing for Nonprofit Organizations.* He decided against ordering a copy because his business is to give away money, not to market anything. Would you agree that a private philanthropic organization has no need to understand marketing concepts?

7. It is possible to classify organizations into four types by specifying whether they are private or public and whether they are profit or nonprofit. Thus there are *private profit organizations, public profit organizations, private nonprofit organizations,* and *public nonprofit organizations.* Supply examples of each type of organization. Do you see any differences between a private profit organization and a public profit organization? Prepare a rationale for marketing for each of these organization types.

2　Publics, Markets, and the Concept of Exchange

*There is no group in America that can withstand
the force of an aroused public opinion.*

FRANKLIN D. ROOSEVELT

The previous chapter attempted to establish the relevance of marketing to all organizations. This does not mean that all organizations face the same marketing problems or use the same marketing strategies. Even within the commercial sector, marketing problems and strategies vary between industries and even within firms within the same industry. The same variation can be expected in the nonprofit sector, especially given the vastly different types of organizations that fall within this category. The purpose of this chapter is to consider the nature of the marketing challenge facing different types of nonprofit organizations.

Organizations can be looked at in many ways. The sociologist sees an organization as a set of people occupying roles and statuses. The political scientist sees an organization as a set of power relations among persons. The economist sees the organization as a set of people attempting to maximize their utilities.

The marketer, too, brings a special perspective to organizations. He is primarily interested in the relations between the organization and its various markets and publics. He is interested in understanding what the organization exchanges with each public; i.e., what each party gives and gets. He is interested in the motivations underlying their transactions and the satisfaction received.

To understand the types of marketing problems faced by organizations we first have to examine the concept of a *public*, the concept of a *market*, and then the concept of *exchange*. We will then be in a position to classify different types of nonprofit organizations in a marketing-relevant way.

THE CONCEPT OF A PUBLIC

Every organization operates in an environment of publics. We define a public in the following way:

A *public* is a distinct group of people and/or organizations that have an actual or a potential interest and/or impact on an organization.

It is fairly easy to list the various publics that surround any particular organization. Consider a university. Figure 2-1 shows sixteen major publics with which a university deals. The publics include groups within the university (faculty, staff), groups supporting the university (alumni, foundations), groups consuming the university's offerings (students), and groups regulating the university (government agencies).

Classifying Publics by Function

It would be helpful to find a way to classify the various publics of an organization that would show their functional relations to the organization. The classification should be exhaustive so that important publics are not overlooked. Figure 2-2 offers such a classification.

An organization is viewed as a resource-conversion machine in which the *internal publics* of the organization take the resources of certain *input publics* and convert them into useful products that are carried by *agent publics* to designated *consuming publics*. Let us look at the various publics more closely.

The first input public of an organization is its *supporters*, those who lend it resources (money, time, encouragement). Using the example of

FIGURE 2-1
The University and Its Publics

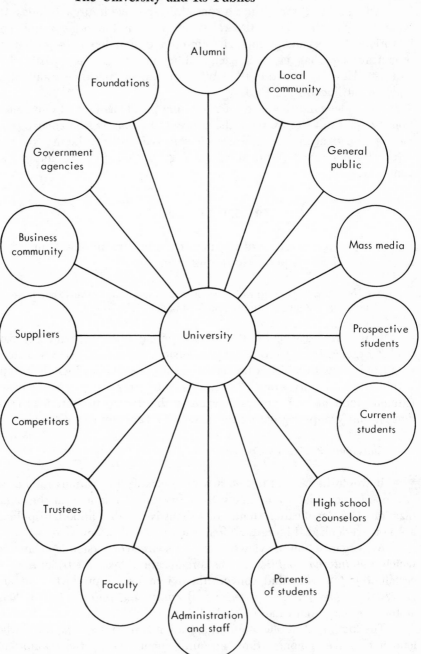

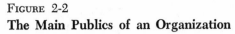

FIGURE 2-2

The Main Publics of an Organization

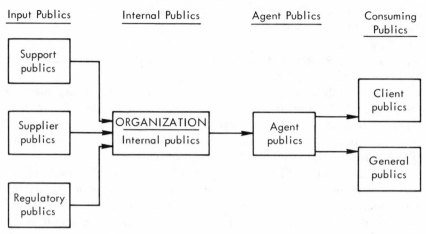

a private university, the supporters would consist of the alumni, foundations, and the business community. The second input public is other *suppliers,* those who sell it material goods and services. The suppliers of a university would consist of material, machine, and service suppliers. The third input public consists of *regulatory organizations* that input rules of conduct. The regulatory publics of a university include federal, state, and local legislatures and agencies.

These inputs are processed by the *internal publics* of the organization. The main internal publics of a university, for example, are its trustees, faculty, and staff.

The products may be distributed through *agents* or directly to the consuming publics. In the case of the university, agent publics include the mass media and high school counselors. Teachers, besides being an internal public of the organization, may also be considered agents.

Finally, the consuming publics consist of two main groups. The first group comprise the direct consumers of the product, called the *client publics.* The main client publics of a university are prospective students, current students, and business firms (who hire graduates). Then there are several indirect consumers of the organization's output, called *general publics.* In the case of the university, its general publics include local publics, the mass public, parents of students, and competitive publics.

It should be noted that a particular public may function in more than one way in relation to an organization. Thus some government agencies may act as regulatory publics and others as supporter publics.

Business firms may relate as supporters, suppliers, and consumers of an organization. The classification of publics into these seven types is proposed as having heuristic value in bringing to mind the main groups relating to an organization.

Classifying Publics by Level of Involvement with the Organization

Not all publics are equally active or important to an organization. Some, such as a university's current students and faculty, are very active. Others, such as the parents of current students and the general public, are passive. Others, such as aborigines and infants, are not publics of the university by any stretch of the imagination.

An organization faces three types of publics on the basis of the amount of mutual interest that might exist. A *reciprocal public* is a public that is interested in the organization, with the organization also interested in them. Students are a reciprocal public of a university. A *sought public* is a public that the organization is interested in but that is not necessarily interested in the organization. A group of wealthy individuals who are not currently donors to a university may be a *sought public*. Finally, an *unwelcome public* is a public that is interested in the organization but in whom the organization is not interested. A group of nonstudents living near the university who use the university's facilities may be viewed by the university as an unwelcome public. In all three cases, the organization enjoys a certain relation to each public and may wish to shape this relation in further ways.

Interrelations of the Various Publics

The publics are related not only to the organization but also to each other in many important ways. A particular public may have a great deal of influence on the attitudes and behavior of other publics toward the organization. Consider a university whose students are highly satisfied. Their enthusiasm will be transmitted to their parents and to friends back home who might be potential students. Their enthusiasm will have a reinforcing effect on the faculty who will feel that their teaching is effective. Their enthusiasm will affect the future level of support they will give to the school as alumni. Thus the satisfaction felt by students will influence the attitudes and behavior of other university publics.

Likewise, the dissatisfaction of a particular public will affect the attitudes of other publics. Suppose current students are highly dissatisfied with the university over some policy. If the students choose to act, they have several recourses. These recourses are suggested in Figure 2-3. First, they may go directly to the university (administration, trustees, faculty)

FIGURE 2-3

**Dynamic Relations between a University
and its Publics**

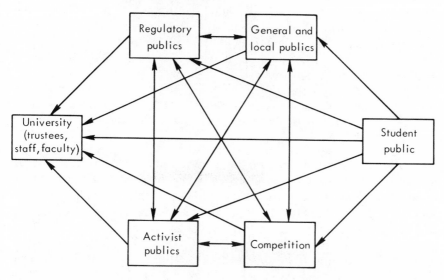

and try to negotiate a better policy. Second, they may attempt to win the sympathy of the general public as an effective pressure to bring on the university. Third, they may attempt to get the government to intervene. Fourth, they may solicit the support of various activist publics. Fifth, they might give up, leave the university, and go over to competitors. Thus, publics that are passive in one period might suddenly be spurred into action in another period because of sympathy with the grievance of a particular public.

From the organization's point of view, it is important to set up relations with its valued publics that produce satisfaction. The organization's task is to consider what benefits to offer each of its valued publics in exchange for their valued resources and support. Once an organization begins to think seriously about cultivating the support of a public, it is beginning to think of that public as a *market*, a group to whom it will attempt to offer benefits in exchange for valued resources.

THE CONCEPT OF A MARKET

What then, is a market and what is its relationship to a public? The term "market" has a different origin than the term "public," and yet has several affinities with it.

From the point of view of an organization, a market is *a potential arena for the trading of resources.* For an organization to operate, it must acquire resources through trading other resources. The organization goes to the financial market to obtain capital; to the labor market to obtain employees; to the raw material market to obtain raw materials; to the construction market to obtain plant; to the buyer market to obtain customers; and so on. In each case, it must offer something to the market to receive in return the resources it seeks. For this reason, we define a market in the following way:

> A *market* is a distinct group of people and/or organizations that have resources which they want to exchange, or might conceivably exchange, for distinct benefits.

We can now see the affinities between a market and a public. A public is any group that has an actual or potential interest or impact on an organization. If the organization wishes to attract certain resources from that public through offering a set of benefits in exchange, then the organization is taking a marketing viewpoint toward that public. Once the organization starts thinking in terms of *trading values* with that public, it is viewing that public as a market. It is engaged in trying to determine the best marketing approach to that public.

THE CONCEPT OF EXCHANGE

An organization that is seeking to acquire a particular set of resources has various options available, only one of which is *exchange.*

Its first option is *self-production.* Suppose an organization wishes to acquire fuel to heat its building. Self-production takes place if the members of the organization go and search for fuel supplies in nature and bring them back.

Its second option is *theft.* The organization can find a stockpile of fuel that belongs to someone else and attempt to steal it.

Its third option is *force.* The organization can approach the party owning the fuel and use force or threat of force to obtain the fuel.

Its fourth option is *beggary.* The organization can approach the party owning the fuel and plead for some share as a charitable gesture.

Its fifth option is *exchange.* The organization can approach the party owning the fuel and offer it a set of values or benefits in exchange for the fuel.

Marketing is concerned with the last approach to the acquisition of resources, that of exchange. Exchange stands as an alternative to self-production, theft, force, and beggary. Exchange requires two conditions: [1]

1. There are two parties.
2. Each has something that might be valued by the other party.

If one of the parties has nothing that is valued by the other party, exchange cannot take place. Therefore it is important to understand what things have value.

Value is rooted in human wants. A want is a felt deficiency on the part of an organism. This felt deficiency produces an uncomfortable state of tension in the organism and a wish to act. The organism will perceive certain things outside itself that would satisfy its want. These things have value to the organism.

Suppose one party wants to attract a resource of another party. To do this, it must be able to offer values to the other party. Before it can do this, it must understand the other party's needs. It must figure out what it has that might satisfy the other party's wants.

There are three categories of things that might satisfy the want of the other party. The first category is *goods*. Goods are *objects* that are capable of satisfying certain wants. The second category is *services*. Services are *acts* that the person might perform that might satisfy the needs of the other party. Services involve time, energy, and/or skill. The third category is *money*. Money is a generalized store of value that can be offered to another party which he can exchange against goods and services that he might want.

Analyzing Exchange Flows

Whenever two social units are engaged in exchange, it is useful to develop a diagram or map showing what is actually or potentially being exchanged between the two parties. Figure 2-4 presents five familiar exchange situations.

The first, diagrammed in Figure 2-4A, describes the classic commercial transaction. There are two parties designated respectively as *buyer* and *seller*. The seller offers things of value to the buyer in the form of goods and/or services. The buyer offers money in exchange. It is important to note that the designations "buyer" and "seller" are somewhat arbitrary, for we might also say that the party with money is offering to "sell" his money for goods. In fact, if both parties were exchanging goods, a condition known as *barter*, we could not easily distinguish the buyer from the seller. In this case, both could be called *traders*. In any event, two parties partake in a commercial transaction because each

Figure 2-4
Examples of Exchange Transactions

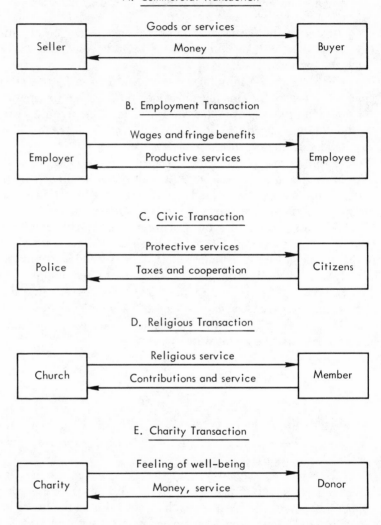

A. Commercial Transaction

| Seller | → Goods or services → | Buyer |

B. Employment Transaction

| Employer | → Wages and fringe benefits → | Employee |

C. Civic Transaction

| Police | → Protective services → | Citizens |

D. Religious Transaction

| Church | → Religious service → | Member |

E. Charity Transaction

| Charity | → Feeling of well-being → | Donor |

sees himself as better off after the exchange. The buyer expects more satisfaction from the good than from other uses to which he can put the money; and the seller has obtained a desired profit through the sale.

Another basic economic exchange is that between the employer and the employee (Figure 2-4B). The employee offers productive services (made up of time, energy, and skill) to the employer; in exchange, he receives a wage and fringe benefits. There is also an overlay of psychological exchanges (not shown) in this relationship, such as fear, respect, loyalty, and so on.

A third type of exchange occurs between a local police department and the local citizens (Figure 2-4C). The local police department offers the citizens protective services; in exchange, the citizens provide taxes and cooperation. There is a question of how voluntary this transaction is, but we shall assume for the present that a social contract is voluntarily entered into between the police and the citizens.

A fourth exchange occurs between a church and its members (Figure 2-4D). The church offers its members religious services and experiences; in exchange, the members offer the church contributions and support.

A fifth exchange occurs between a charity and donors (Figure 2-4E). The charity offers the donor a sense of good conscience or wellbeing in return for the donor's time, money, or other donations.

We will now examine three specific exchange situations in more detail.

The U.S. Peace Corps and the Student Market

Each year the U.S. Peace Corps seeks to attract graduating students with Masters degrees in Business Administration to join it instead of immediately taking a job with industry.[2] The Peace Corps receives requests from countries abroad for business-trained volunteers and tries to honor these requests.

The Peace Corps, however, finds it very difficult to compete with industry for able business graduates. Industry offers an attractive job paying $13,000 or more a year with career advancement opportunities, a paid vacation, and residence in the United States. The Peace Corps offers an uncertain position in a developing nation at low pay with no career opportunities and under hard living conditions. Under these circumstances, how can the Peace Corps hope to attract any business school graduates?

The answer lies in target marketing and in improving the exchange values it can offer to volunteers. By "target marketing" we mean that there should be more concentration on efforts to reach the more idealistic students. They may learn of these students through asking deans or through poster campaigns using idealistic appeals.

Next the Peace Corps must think of ways to improve its economic offer relative to competitors. The following possibilities should be considered. The Peace Corps could

1. Raise the pay nearer to $13,000 a year;
2. Tell the potential volunteer exactly what his overseas assignment would be instead of leaving this to chance;
3. Guarantee the returning volunteer a job in industry by getting several major firms to agree to preferential hiring and promotion of Peace Corps returnees;
4. Tie in a month-long paid vacation in England or France as an added incentive;
5. Establish comfortable overseas living quarters for M.B.A. volunteers so they need not face hard living;
6. Offer to introduce the volunteers to the most important businessmen in the host country so that they can expand their acquaintances and experiences.

In addition, the Peace Corps could use appeals based on its position as a humanitarian organization. Many business school graduates would like an opportunity to make a worthwhile contribution. Idealistic students may have doubts about whether they will achieve this doing conventional things like selling soap or automobiles. The Peace Corps can emphasize the feeling of being worthwhile and making an important contribution. Furthermore, Peace Corps volunteers can be pictured as very special members of a very special group. Their advertisement might read: "Most graduates do the easy thing and take a job with industry. The Peace Corps is an elite corps of men and women whose training, aptitude, and world-wide experience uniquely prepares them for any challenge."

These are some of the ways suggested by exchange analysis to make the Peace Corps job more attractive to M.B.A. students. It is difficult to know which ones would have the most incentive value without consumer research into the motivations and perceptions of business school students. Exchange analysis followed by consumer research is a potent way of determining the package of values that would be most effective in bringing about the desired market response.

The Health Maintenance Organization and the Physician Market

In a message to Congress in 1971, President Nixon proposed support for a new type of health organization called a Health Maintenance Organization (HMO). An HMO is set up as a prepaid plan of health care delivery provided by a group of physicians. One of the original HMOs, the Kaiser Foundation Health Plan, issues contracts to groups and individuals at an average cost of $150 per member annually. This covers the member for office visits, hospitalization, X-ray, laboratory, prescription drugs, and other medical services. If a large network of HMOs can be established throughout the country, it would be a way of stabilizing the cost of health care to the average family.

In order to start a successful HMO, there are two requirements. First, the HMO must attract enough doctors to join it or else it is doomed to failure. Second, it must attract enough groups and individuals to join it. Let us consider the doctor-attraction problem, because often it is the more difficult marketing task.

The HMO is asking physicians to give up their private and lucrative practice in exchange for a fixed salary and slightly better working hours. This exchange is not very appealing to most physicians. They are their own bosses in their private practice and can make a great deal of money; in an HMO, they are salaried employees and may be subject to a lot of supervision from others. It would seem that promoters of the HMO concept face a formidable marketing problem.

HMO marketers should attempt to develop a full list of the possible benefits and costs for physicians who might join an HMO. Table 2-1 shows a comprehensive list of benefits and costs as they may appear to a physician. These benefits and costs can provide the basis for formulating a recruitment program. It is wise to present both the benefits and costs to prospective physicians. The purpose is to recruit physicians who will be happy in the HMO. It would be short-sighted to attract physicians by minimizing the disadvantages and later find them disgruntled and frustrated.

Recruitment can be increased by directing recruitment effort toward the best prospects, those for whom the values of affiliation would be highest. Physician segmentation by age, stage of practice, and attitudes would reveal the best prospect segments. It is easier to attract new physicians, physicians coming out of the armed services, and socially concerned physicians than older physicians with large and lucrative practices. The HMO benefits would be tailored to the different physician segments being sought.

The Fire Department and the Citizen Market

A fire truck speeds at three in the morning to a two-alarm blaze in a home, arrives three minutes after the call, and successfully extinguishes the fire. The firemen have been awakened from a sound sleep and take some personal risk in fighting the fire, and now it is over. The homeowners sometimes thank the firemen. In other cases, they complain that the firemen glutted the house with more water than was necessary. The firemen fill out a report and return wearily to the station.

Is this an exchange process? It seems more like a one-way flow of

Table 2-1

Benefits and Costs for Physician Affiliation with an HMO

Benefits

Better hours for work week and vacation
No set-up costs for office, equipment, or client seeking
Association and consultation with professional colleagues
Opportunities for research
Full array of modern medicine
No need to worry about business or administrative details
Ability to prescribe what is medically appropriate without worrying inordinately
   about the cost
Personal satisfaction in helping solve health-care delivery problems
Can work full time or part time for the HMO

Costs

Less freedom (lay interference, closer scrutiny, less control)
Absence of personal-professional relationship
Professional dissatisfaction in seeing healthy patients
The system is socialistic
Less money than private practice
Less prestige than private practice
Pressure from the AMA and other societies

---

value. The firemen undertook great effort and personal risk to put out a fire. What did they get in return? Did they do it for the gratitude? They certainly would not have done it for the complaints. Why did they speed so fast and work so hard?

To understand this, we must recognize that the exchange process between the firemen and the homeowners fails to depict the full exchange relationship. In this case, there is a third party, the local government, that enters into an exchange relation with the citizens on the one hand and with the fire department on the other. Figure 2-5 presents a fuller picture of these exchange relations. The citizen pays taxes to the government. Part of these taxes help the government support a fire department. The fire department, in exchange for the jobs and money it receives, provides a service back to the citizens, and a promise of service back to the government. If the fire department grows lax or inefficient, it risks losing money from the government and gets less appreciation from the citizens. The citizens may start protesting their taxes to the government. So part of the reason that the firemen perform so well is to insure the continuity of their jobs and the growth of their income.

FIGURE 2-5

A Map of Fire Department-Citizen Exchange Relations

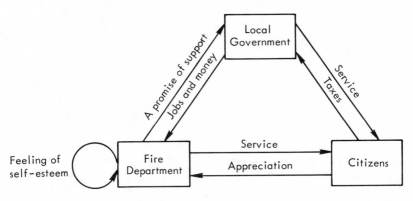

There is also a self-exchange process going on within the minds of the firemen. A fireman has a need for community approval and esteem; he also wants to avoid guilt for doing a poor job. To get positive feelings about himself, he must perform well.

Analyzing the exchanges in this way makes it easier for the head of the fire department to motivate his men ("employee marketing"). It suggests some of the factors that could be used by any public administrator to get his staff to serve the public with more enthusiasm and sensitivity.

CLASSIFICATION OF ORGANIZATIONS

Having examined the concepts of publics, markets, and exchanges, we are now ready to classify organizations in a way that is relevant to marketing.

Organizations come into being to render a certain service to one or more groups or publics. In each case, we can identify a particular public that is supposed to be the main beneficiary of the organization's activities. Blau and Scott have suggested a useful classification of organizations based on the main beneficiary.[3] *Business concerns* are defined as those organizations whose main beneficiaries are *owners; service organizations* benefit mainly their *clients; mutual benefit associations* benefit mainly their *members;* and *commonweal organizations* benefit mainly the *public at large.* Table 2-2 lists some well-known examples of each type of organization.

Let us examine each type of organization more closely.

TABLE 2-2

Four Main Types of Organizations *

Organization	Main Beneficiary	Examples
Business concerns	Owners	Industrial firms, mail-order houses, wholesale and retail stores, banks, insurance companies and other private-for-profit organizations
Service organizations	Clients	Social welfare agencies, hospitals, schools, legal aid societies, mental health clinics, museums
Mutual benefit associations	Members	Political parties, unions, fraternal associations, clubs, veterans' organizations, professional associations, and religious sects
Commonweal organizations	Public at large	State Department, Bureau of Internal Revenue, military services, police and fire departments, philanthropic foundations

* Table prepared from prose description in Peter M. Blau and W. Richard Scott, *Formal Organizations* (San Francisco: Chandler Publishing Co., 1962), pp. 45–58.

Business Concerns

Business concerns are organizations that carry on the main economic work of society. They are organized systems of men, machines, materials, and money that produce, distribute, and facilitate the flow of economic goods and services.

In a private enterprise economy, business firms are set up by private individuals with capital for the purpose of making a profit. They undertake high effort and risk in the hope of producing a profit for themselves. Thus they are the formal beneficiaries of the activities of business concerns. At the same time, they make a profit by serving the needs of a group of customers. These customers are also beneficiaries of the business concern. Figure 2-6A shows the business concern at the center of these two key groups. The business concern receives the capital of owners, uses this capital to produce goods and services, sells these goods and services to customers for money, and returns this money to the owners in the form of dividends.

A fuller picture would show other groups that are beneficiaries of the business concern's activities. Such groups include workers, lenders, and suppliers. These groups also pose exchange problems to the business concern although historically, marketers have given most of their attention to the exchange relations between the private business firm and its customers. Under a broadened concept of marketing, the business concern can be seen as using the principles of exchange in its relations to all of its markets and publics.

Service Organizations

Service organizations have a different structure of exchange relations compared with business concerns. Figure 2-6B shows the service

FIGURE 2-6

Exchange Relations of Four Main Types of Organizations

A. Business Concern

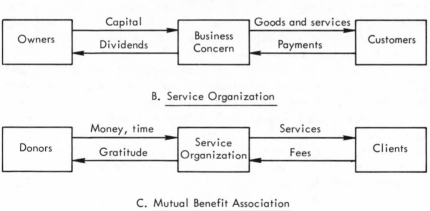

B. Service Organization

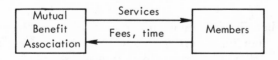

C. Mutual Benefit Association

D. Commonweal Organization

organization as relating to two main markets, clients and donors. The clients comprise the group receiving the services of the organization, in return for which they sometimes pay fees. The fees rarely cover the costs of providing the services and the deficit must be made up by raising money from another public, the donors. It may appear that the donors are not in an exchange relation with the organization, that they make a one-way presentation of gifts to the organization. But their giving does yield a return to them in the form of feelings which have a positive value, which reduce one or more needs they have. A given donor may experience a feeling that some unfortunate people will be better off as a result of his gift, or that the society will be safer, or that he is a worthwhile and unselfish person. These feelings are his return payment. The organization must be capable of returning these feelings to him. If the organization were very weak at stimulating these positive feelings in donors, it would soon lose its donors.

Thus, the service organization must work effectively in at least two markets. It must undertake the following tasks in the client market: determine its target clients, identify their needs, develop services matched to their needs, arrange for the availability of these services, and communicate these services to the target clients. Client-related marketing problems stem from the fact that service organizations sometimes face too much demand, at other times too little demand, and sometimes demand of the wrong kind, all of which require marketing planning and effort. With respect to the donor market, the service organization must similarly identify the potential donors, appraise their motivations, develop rewarding relationships, and keep them informed. The major marketing challenge is to develop sufficient funds for the service organization through competing effectively for donor interest and attention against a very large number of other service organizations which are also seeking support from the same donors.

Mutual Benefit Associations

Mutual benefit associations are organized by a group of persons to create benefits not for others so much as for themselves. The benefits may be social, religious, or protective. Typical examples of such organizations are churches and trade unions. Thus the mutual benefit association is characterized by one major exchange relation, that between the organization (officers and staff) and the members. This exchange relation is depicted in Figure 2-6C. The organization offers services to the members and receives financial support and volunteer services in return.

The mutual benefit association exemplifies the marketing problems facing an organization with respect to developing and maintaining its own supporters. A church, for example, must attract a sufficient number of members, keep them coming to services, keep them giving generously to support the church and the community, and so on. This work is carried on by such committees as the membership committee, the social program committee, and the finance committee. These committees require a good understanding of the membership's needs, desires, and attitudes if they are to achieve their goals.

A mutual benefit association also deals with other publics as part of seeking to satisfy its main market—its own members. Thus a trade union, in attempting to gain company recognition, must market itself to the management and to the general public as well as to the workers. After it achieves recognition, it carries on a formal continuous exchange relation with companies, signified by contracts, bargaining, and mutual dealing. In the meantime, the officers of the trade union must continue to sensitively serve and satisfy the membership to avoid revolts or lack of support when it comes to union-management showdowns.

Commonweal Organizations

Commonweal organizations (e.g., license bureaus, police departments, and so on) are created by the public to serve the interests of the public at large. They are analogous to mutual benefit associations when projected to a community or national scale. They differ from mutual benefit associations in often being involuntary, in occasionally being restrictive or repressive, and in being psychologically at more distance from the public than a smaller mutual benefit association is to a member. Nevertheless, like the mutual benefit association, the commonweal organization is characterized by one major exchange loop, that between the commonweal organization and the general public. This is depicted in Figure 2-6D. The organization offers services to the public and receives taxes (a compulsory payment) in exchange.

It might seem that a marketing orientation is less relevant to a commonweal organization because its financial basis is guaranteed and it has a monopoly of power. The classic literature on bureaucracy originated to describe such organizations because they could maintain power while showing little or no client sensitivity. But the ability of bureaucratic organizations to shrug public opinion is more limited than commonly suggested, and the more enlightened commonweal organizations recognize that they can achieve their goals more efficiently through a marketing orientation. Those that satisfy their constituencies increase their chances of being more effective in their other markets, such as the legislature and public opinion market.

Concluding Observations

In asserting that all of these organizations face marketing problems, we are not trying to say that the essence of these organizations
is marketing, or that they constitute marketing enterprises. We cannot
even say this about a business firm. Instead we are saying that the conceptual system known as marketing can be applied effectively to a class
of problems facing all organizations and yields useful insights and strategies. We do not want to confuse marketing phenomena with marketing
logic. We do not see marketing as a specific set of institutions and exchanges but rather as a conceptual system about exchanges and transactions that helps analyze, explain, and control them.

The hypothesis is advanced that marketing thinking is useful in all
four types of organizations. Marketing is already entrenched in *business
concerns* as a widely recognized function. Even here, it should be noted,
it first achieved explicit recognition in the consumer goods area, moved
later into the industrial goods area, and is now receiving strong attention
in the commercial services area. Marketing will become more important
in *service organization* thinking because of the close analogy between
customers-for-profit and clients-for-service. Then it will receive more
attention in *mutual benefit associations* as these organizations face increasing problems of attracting and holding members relative to growing competitive uses of members' time and changing values. Finally,
marketing is entering the thinking of *commonweal organizations* as they
increasingly recognize that the quality of service they render their publics
affects the amount of public support and the size of their budget.

SUMMARY

Under the marketing concept, the proper starting point
for marketing planning is to understand and map the organization's
major publics and markets. A public is defined as a distinct group of
people and/or organizations that have an actual or a potential interest
and/or impact on an organization. The publics surrounding an organization were classified into seven types: support publics, supplier publics,
regulatory publics, internal publics, agent publics, client publics, and
general publics. These publics are interrelated to each other in important
ways. When a public becomes valued by an organization, it becomes a
target market for which the organization undertakes marketing planning
and communications. A market is any group which an organization sees

as having valued resources that it would like to obtain by offering organizational resources in exchange.

Organizations differ considerably in their main market relations. A business concern deals with a customer market with which there is an exchange of goods and services for money, and a market of owners with which there is an exchange of capital for dividends. A service organization also deals with two markets—a client market with which there is an exchange of services for fees or attendance, and a donor market with which there is an exchange of money and time for gratitude. A mutual benefit organization has one major market—the members—with whom it exchanges services for fees, time, and energy. A commonweal organization also has one major market—the public—with whom it exchanges services for taxes. All of these organizations also participate in other markets such as the labor market, the capital market, and the supplies market.

NOTES

1. For a fuller treatment of the conditions of exchange, see the author's "A Generic Concept of Marketing," *Journal of Marketing* (April 1972), pp. 46–54.

2. See the teaching case called *The Peace Corps* (Boston, Mass.: Harvard Business School, 1970).

3. Peter M. Blau and W. Richard Scott, *Formal Organization* (San Francisco, Calif.: Chandler Publishing Co., 1962), pp. 45–58.

QUESTIONS

1. Is marriage an exchange process? Is courtship exchange? Does one market oneself to one's spouse or steady date?

2. Develop a diagram similar to Figure 2-1 showing the publics of a hospital.

3. How could a consumer group express dissatisfaction with the products, advertising, and selling tactics of an automobile company?

4. A group of supporters of the Equal (Women's) Rights Amendment is seeking to get the legislature of a Southern state to ratify the amendment. Identify the publics and markets this group must deal with and suggest what they might be able to offer to their markets in exchange for ratification.

5. Do you accept the distinction between a market and a public—that a market is a public looked at with a certain intent?

6. What do you think of the concept of self-marketing? Can it be applied to dieting, smoking, drinking, and studying? Work out a self-marketing plan.

7. The economics department at a prestigious private university has a reputation for having one of the best Ph.D. programs in the country. Graduates of the program are placed in the finest schools and are considered to be superior economists. However, in the past few years, the department has been having trouble recruiting Ph.D. students. A shortage of funds has allowed the department to offer only small amounts of financial aid to only a few prospective students each year, and many of these prospects have been going to schools that offer more aid. What can the department offer to prospective students instead of financial aid?

3 The Responsive Organization

I respect kindness to human beings first of all, and kindness to animals. I don't respect the law; I have a total irreverence for anything connected with society except that which makes the roads safer, the beer stronger, the food cheaper, and old men and old women warmer in the winter and happier in the summer.

BRENDAN BEHAN

Many organizations view marketing as essentially a tactical activity designed to help the organization improve its effectiveness in attracting resources and customers. They think that this job is accomplished by adding a marketing director and a small staff who carry out the necessary planning and doing. They think that this staff can be added and be effective without making any changes in the rest of the organization. The organization continues to produce the same products and services for the same customers and the job of the marketing staff is to help promote or sell them.

This view of marketing is of course wrong. If marketing is to be effective, it calls for more than a new function or department. It calls for a new orientation for the organization. Marketing is more than a set of add-on activities. It amounts to a whole new attitude toward the organization's various publics and missions. It is the thoroughgoing adoption of this new orientation that produces the major benefits of better survival and growth for the organization and satisfaction for its customers.

This chapter attempts to describe the special qualities of a marketing orientation and how it can be implemented. First we shall develop a picture of a bureaucratic organization, which is at the far extreme from a marketing organization. We shall then contrast four different degrees of responsiveness of an organization to its clients. Then we shall describe the earmarks of an organization that is market-oriented and that practices the marketing concept. Finally, we shall indicate the steps that an organization must take to move from a nonmarketing orientation to a full marketing orientation.

THE BUREAUCRATIC ORGANIZATION

We shall draw a picture of the bureaucratic organization in order to emphasize the radical change that is implied by a marketing orientation.

Organizations come into being to accomplish some purpose. The founders are clear-minded about the organization's mission and they often pursue it with single-minded dedication. The new hospital is organized to serve the sick; the public school, to provide education and job skills to the young; the new church, to minister to the spiritual needs of the community. The original founders are spirited, dedicated, and customer-oriented.

The organization that meets the needs of its customers grows and prospers. As it grows, it becomes more complex and multipurposed. It takes on additional responsibilities to its customers, employees, agents, suppliers, and other publics. The organization has to serve well not only the original client group that prompted its creation but also the various internal and external groups that derive their income or symbolic status from the organization. Interest groups form around the organization. Top management faces the task of harmonizing often incompatible goals and interests. Much of its energy turns inward. Its management members grow increasingly self-serving; that is, their purpose becomes to maintain the organization and their jobs at any cost. Spontaneous job relations are replaced by careful job descriptions and hierarchical chains of command. Relations with outside groups are routinized by rule-bound behavior. The organization develops an officialdom that shows an impersonal face to the world. The officials exhibit care and caution instead of daring and innovativeness. They feel safest in maintaining traditional policies, procedures, and products.

Bureaucracy is the tendency of organizations to routinize their operations, replace personal judgment with impersonal policies, specialize the job of every employee, create a rigid hierarchy of command, and convert the organization into an efficient machine.[1] The bureaucrat is not concerned with innovation, with problems outside his specific authority, with qualifying human factors. He will serve people as long as their problems fall within the limits of his jurisdiction. People's problems are defined in terms of how the bureaucratic organization is set up rather than having the organization set up to respond to people's problems. Questions of structure dominate questions of substance; means dominate ends.

Essentially, the organization becomes extremely efficient in serving the original market purpose. But here comes the weakness. The world and the markets are continuously changing while the organization stands still. New needs emerge, new interest groups appear, new stages are reached in the economy, law, technology, and culture. The organization becomes increasingly maladapted to its environment. It appears to its publics to be increasingly unresponsive to their needs. There is a creeping tendency toward organizational unresponsiveness:

> Organizations show a tendency over time toward lessening responsiveness to their clients' current needs because they tend to overspecialize their staff and operations to meet efficiently the old needs.

Many examples of organizational unresponsiveness can be cited. In the automobile business, the Big Three—General Motors, Ford, and Chrysler—continued for several years to produce large cars in spite of the growing interest of American car-buyers in small cars. The Big Three were not quite ready to curtail the manufacture of the cars they knew best. Similarly, *Life* magazine continued its old format as a picture magazine although people were increasingly gratifying their visual needs through the new medium of television. *Life* failed because it did not modify its format to meet new needs in the marketplace.

Examples of unresponsive organizations abound even more in the nonprofit area because many of these types of organizations do not face active competition or depend for their continuity on active customer support through purchase. The present budgetary crisis among private universities is due in part to overconfidence in their product and their failure to see new forms of competition and "customer" needs emerging. Many hospitals are in financial trouble today because of their unresponsiveness to new developments that make it desirable to coordinate their services with surrounding hospitals, install tighter fiscal control on equipment purchases, and so on. Many police departments continue to use methods of relating to citizens that show neither respect nor sensitivity for their needs or interests.

TOWARD A RESPONSIVE ORGANIZATION

For analytical purposes, it is possible to classify organizations into four groups according to their level of organizational responsiveness.

The Unresponsive Organization

An unresponsive organization is the extreme opposite of a market-oriented organization. It has two characteristics:

1. It does nothing to measure the needs, perceptions, preferences, or satisfaction of its constituent publics.
2. It makes it difficult for its constituent publics to place inquiries, complaints, suggestion, or opinions.

This kind of organization either assumes that it knows what its publics need and feel or that their needs and feelings do not matter. It sees no reason to consult with consumers nor make it easy for them to supply voluntary information or suggestions. The images that come to mind are monarchies that operate to serve the king's, not the people's interests; or the prison that cares little for the needs, feelings, or opinions of the inmates. Business monopolies that are highly insulated from public control are able to proceed with very little concern for customer needs or tastes. Organizations facing a high and continuous demand for their services can also be quite unresponsive. Hospitals and universities, as has been noted, have until recently done very little to study or learn the attitudes of their customers—patients and students, respectively—because they were receiving more customers than they could handle. In general, the most unresponsive organizations tend to be those in a sovereign, monopoly, or high demand position that is somehow insulated from popular control.

Such an unresponsive organization brings about a host of undesirable consequences. The products and services are usually poor or shoddy. Citizens or customers become frustrated and dissatisfied. Their dissatisfaction leads to rebellion or apathy. Ultimately, the organization may seal its own doom because of attack or withdrawal by the citizens.

The Casually Responsive Organization

The casually responsive organization differs from the unresponsive organization in two ways:

1. It shows an interest in learning about consumer needs, perceptions, preferences, and satisfaction.
2. It encourages consumers to submit inquiries, complaints, suggestions, and opinions.

When American universities began to experience a decline in student applications in the early seventies, they began to pay more attention to their students and publics. College administrators who formerly were largely oriented toward problems of hiring faculty, scheduling classes, and running efficient administrative services—the earmarks of the bureaucratic mentality—now began to listen more to the students. They left their doors open, made occasional surprise appearances in the student lounge, encouraged suggestions from students, and created faculty-student committees. These steps converted the university organization into being informally responsive.

This conversion tends to create a better feeling in the organization's customers. It is the first step in building a better partnership between the served and the serving. Whether or not the increased customer satisfaction continues depends on whether the organization merely makes a show of listening or actually undertakes to do something about what it hears. It may merely offer a semblance of openness and interest without intending to use the results in any way. It sooner or later becomes apparent to the consumers that this is a public relations ploy. It can lead to greater strain because of rising consumer expectations than when the organization was completely unresponsive. For the consumers have awakened, coalesced, and feel a sense of power and united purpose. If their voices fall on deaf ears, they resent the organization and may prepare to force it into greater responsiveness.

The Highly Responsive Organization

The problem with the casually responsive organization is that it collects its information very informally and therefore may be slow to learn of important developments and may not really be receiving representative information. As a result, it will be slow to react and may not react to the right problem. A highly responsive organization differs from a casually responsive organization in three ways:

1. It shows a keen interest in learning about the needs, perceptions, preferences, and satisfaction of its constituents and relies on systematic information-collection procedures such as formal opinion surveys and consumer panels.
2. It encourages its constituents to submit inquiries, complaints, suggestions, and opinions and creates formal systems to facilitate this, such as suggestion boxes, comment cards, ombudsmen, and consumer committees.
3. It sifts the incoming information and takes positive steps where called for to adjust products, services, organizational policies, and procedures.

Large progressive business firms such as Sears, Procter & Gamble, General Mills, and General Electric have gone the furthest in adopting the operating characteristics of a highly responsive organization. Sears, for example, conducts periodic surveys to learn what consumers are thinking about various Sears product lines and overall Sears quality and service. It uses the information to chart an attitude index to see if there are developing problems requiring attention. Sears also runs a complaint department and public information department. Several large firms are developing committees of consumer representatives for a direct give-and-take with management. These organizations feel that they cannot afford to serve the customer's needs less than optimally. They take the incoming information seriously and make the necessary adjustments in products, services, and procedures.

Nonprofit organizations are typically not in a highly responsive mode for dealing with their constituent publics. Virtually no university takes a periodic survey of its students' desires and attitudes. Municipalities do not regularly poll their citizens to know how they stand on public issues. Many legislators do not survey their constituencies in formal ways. Many hospitals are casual about collecting patient feedback on their services.

What are the consequences of introducing highly responsive systems in an organization? Presumably they will result in a better adjustment of the organization's products and services to the customers' changing needs. The result is likely to be the delivery of a higher level of satisfaction to the constituent publics.

The Fully Responsive Organization

The highly responsive organization is free to accept or reject complaints and suggestions from its constituent publics on the basis of judging their validity and considering whether change can be effected. The public proposes and the organization disposes. It is still a situation of "us" and "them." A fully responsive organization overcomes this distinction by accepting its publics as voting members. The characteristics of this type of organization are that

1. It formally audits at regular intervals the needs, perceptions, preferences, and satisfaction of its constituents publics.
2. It encourages its constituent public to participate actively in the affairs of the organization and to vent through formal and informal systems their complaints, suggestions, and opinions.
3. It wholeheartedly accepts the will of the organization's members as expressed through the ballot box or their representatives.

Among examples of fully responsive organizations, at least in principle, are local town democracies, churches, trade unions, and democratic nation-states. The organization is seen as existing for and serving the interests of the citizen-members. There is no question of the organization going off on its own course to pursue goals that are not in the interest of its members. The organization shows an extreme interest in measuring the will of the members and responding to their wishes and needs.

When these principles are fulfilled, the expectation is that the citizen-members will be highly involved, enthusiastic, and satisfied. They will be well-informed about issues and ready to lend their support and energy. The products and services of the organization will be constantly adjusted to serve the changing interests and needs of the constituents.

Occasionally a traditional organization proposes to treat a specific group of consumers as members. A Canadian university recently was searching for ways to build a more active alumni association. Just sending out newsletters about the school did not suffice to build up alumni pride or interest. It developed the idea of conferring membership status to its alumni, with certain privileges and voting rights on certain issues. Suddenly this group became alive with interest in the school. This gesture proved very meaningful to the alumni, who had hitherto felt that the university was simply using them for their money.

THE MARKETING CONCEPT

The concept of a responsive organization has been articulated in the marketing literature in a doctrine known as "the marketing concept." The marketing concept was first formulated in the 1950s in the context of business firms. It has gone through many expositions, refinements and extensions.[2] Its applicability to all organizations is increasingly being recognized.

The marketing concept was formulated as an alternative to previous and prevailing orientations of business. The modern business organization has passed through a production orientation, a sales orientation, and most recently a marketing orientation.

Production Orientation

Production orientations arose in scarcity economies. In a scarcity economy, incomes are low and people spend all their energy trying to satisfy their basic needs for food, clothing, and shelter. Business firms concentrate on the problem of finding ways to increase their output and efficiency. The product needs of people are well-defined. There is no need for marketing research or advertising. There is not much concern with measuring customer satisfaction because there are always a lot of customers around. Products are kept simple and occasionally product quality is scaled down in order to increase profits. There is a feeling that the firm's product will continue in demand forever and there will always be plentiful customers. The firm concentrates on finding ways to increase output and reduce costs—hence the name "production orientation."

It is clear that many nonprofit organizations also exhibit this orientation. They feel that they have a good product; that it is basically needed; that it will always be in demand. The organization spends its energy concentrating on how to produce this product—public education, medical services, garbage collection, police protection—in the most efficient way. Little effort is made to sense the satisfaction of the using publics or examine their latest needs.

Sales Orientation

As an economy grows affluent, citizens obtain enough of what they need in the way of basic products. They have surplus resources to buy additional goods appealing to their personal tastes or fancies. Business firms face high uncertainty about what level of demand to expect. They are anxious to use all their production capacity. They begin to invest heavily in sales stimulation devices—branding, packaging, advertising, promotion, product styling and features, easy credit. A great effort is made to get people to accept what the company is producing. The customer is viewed as someone who can be cajoled into wanting the product, given sufficient promotion and enticement.

This is summarized succinctly in the sales concept:

The sales concept is a *product orientation* backed by *selling and promoting* aimed at generating *high sales* as the key to achieving *high profits*.

The following premises underlie this concept:

1. The main task of the firm is to get sufficient sales for its products.
2. The customer can be induced to buy through various sales-stimulating devices.
3. The customer will probably come back again and even if he does not, there are many other customers out there.

The sales concept is practiced by auto dealers, insurance salesmen, encyclopedia salesmen, and many others who have a fixed product and assigned quotas. Once the auto industry, for example, designs its car for the year, about the only thing it can do for the rest of the year is to tout the auto's virtues and try to get the public to buy it. So much is invested in the design, facilities, inventory, and labor force that the industry feels justified in practicing the sales concept.

The sales concept is also well-known in the nonprofit area. A political party, once it has chosen its candidate, spends the rest of its time, like any sales-oriented organization, trying to get people to like him and vote for him. After he is elected, the new official and his administration continue to take a sales-oriented view toward the citizens. There is little measurement of what the public wants and a lot of propagandistic effort to get the public to accept policies that the administration wants. Many fund-raising organizations also practice the sales concept. They believe strongly in a cause and spend a great deal of time not in listening, but in propagandizing for their product to make it look like the most important cause a person can support.

The major risk that organizations take in practicing the sales concept is that their offering will grow outmoded or their credibility strained. By not watching carefully the evolving needs of the market, their product or service may grow increasingly irrelevant and increasingly difficult to sell. They will face the need to increase their investment in sales stimulation still further with diminishing results. Furthermore, the offering will not produce the expected satisfaction. Buyers will increasingly distrust future messages. They will speak badly of the offering to others. They will see the organization as using them, rather than serving them.

Marketing Orientation

In the mid-1950s, a growing number of major American firms began to perceive the limitations of the sales concept as a plank for doing business. They began to recognize that firms would do better if they tried to serve a need rather than to sell a product. They began to see their customers as real people who were trying to satisfy real needs. The firm's job was to find out these needs and organize a product line and program that would satisfy these needs. It would be easier to sell what the market wanted than to get the market to buy what the firm wanted to sell. Companies began to invest heavily in consumer research to measure consumer needs and satisfaction.

The marketing concept is summarized in the following statement:

> The marketing concept is a *consumers' needs orientation* backed by *integrated marketing* aimed at generating *consumer satisfaction* as the key to satisfying *organizational goals*.

The major foundations of the marketing concept are discussed below.

Consumers' Needs Orientation. The marketing concept calls for a basic reorientation of the company from looking inward toward its products to looking outward toward the consumers' needs. According to Levitt,

> Selling focuses on the needs of the seller; marketing on the needs of the buyer. Selling is preoccupied with the seller's need to convert his product into cash; marketing with the idea of satisfying the needs of the customer by means of the product and the whole cluster of things associated with creating, delivering and finally consuming it.[3]

The call for a consumer orientation has been expressed in many different ways:

> We're not the boss; the consumer is. What the consumer wants, the consumer gets. . . .
> Under the marketing concept, the customer is at the top of the organization chart.
> A company should prefer a franchise over a market to a franchise over a plant.
> Look at the company through the customer's eyes.
> Instead of trying to market what is easiest for us to make, we must find out much more about what the consumer is willing to buy. In other words, we must apply our creativeness more intelligently to *people*, and their wants and needs, rather than to *products*.[4]

Integrated Marketing. The second pillar of the marketing concept is integrated marketing. Many organizations agree that a major purpose of an organization is to serve customers, but they fail nevertheless to take the necessary organizational steps to implement the marketing concept.

Integrated marketing means that the various departments in the organization recognize that the actions they take, and not just the actions of the sales and marketing people, have a profound effect on the organization's ability to create, retain, and satisfy customers. If the admissions department of a hospital is slow and perfunctory, if the food department serves bad food, and if the receivables department insists on immediate payment by the patient, all other efforts to cultivate the patient's good-will may be cancelled. Some means must be developed to coordinate the customer impacts of all the departments. This can be accomplished partly by educating other departments to "think customer" and partly by setting up liaison committees to solve interdepartmental coordination problems.

Consumer Satisfaction. The third pillar in the marketing concept is that the telling factor in the organization's long-run success is the amount of satisfaction it generates in its customers and publics. To the extent that consumers are able to choose among sellers, they will give their greatest support and loyalty to the seller who gives them the most satisfaction. Therefore the seller must strive to help consumers solve their real prob-lems in a better way than competitors.

There is some ambiguity in the concept of consumer satisfaction, especially if we distinguish between short-run consumer satisfaction and long-run consumer welfare. The original marketing concept emphasized "giving the customer what he wants" without making any social judg-ments about his wants. This includes supplying him with cigarettes, large fuel-consuming automobiles, one-way bottles, detergents, tasty but non-nutritious food, and whatever else gave him convenience and satisfaction. But as the consumer of the sixties happily increased his goods, he de-creased his supply of clean air, clean water, and nutritious foods. Busi-ness catered to the consumer's short-run satisfaction but not to his long-run welfare. Some consumers began to get suspicious of this in the late sixties and to raise questions about whether the corporations were serving their long-run interests. Some argued that organizations have an obligation to publicize the ill effects and dangers of the product as well as the attractive features, leaving if for the consumers to be the ultimate judge. Furthermore, the growing shortages of national resources required business to rethink its "cowboy" attitude toward the economy. This has led some marketers to reformulate the marketing concept into the societal marketing concept:

> The societal marketing concept is a consumers' needs orientation backed by integrated marketing aimed at generating consumer satisfaction *and long-run consumer welfare* as the key to satisfying organizational goals.

The addition of long-run consumer welfare does not change the marketing concept but rather raises it to a broader concept of serving well one's markets and society. The underlying premises of the societal marketing concept are that

1. The main purpose of an organization is to create satisfied and healthy customers and to contribute to the quality of life.

2. The organization must search for products that combine high appeal and high benefit to consumers. It must provide information on the proper use of the product to maximize the benefits the consumer receives.

3. Consumers will patronize those organizations that are perceived to be genuinely concerned with their immediate satisfaction and long-run welfare. This is because (a) consumers are intelligent; (b) they prefer organizations that treat them humanely and that show social responsibility; (c) they talk to each other about which products and organizations are good; and (d) they are increasingly represented by consumer advocates and agencies who call attention to the organizations that fail to do a good job.

What the modern marketing concept says in essence is that the modern organization exists to serve its markets. It receives its validation from the marketplace—that is, from the groups it serves and affects. It is production for the sake of consumption, not consumption for the sake of production. The marketing concept is a philosophy about the relations an organization should have with its markets and publics. It is essentially antibureaucratic, anti-production-oriented, and anti-sales-oriented. It calls for a highly responsive organization as defined earlier. The organization seeks to sense, serve, and satisfy its markets and publics, and through this makes its contribution to increasing the well-being of society.

IMPLEMENTING THE MARKETING CONCEPT

Administrators who like the spirit of the marketing concept and the emphasis it places on serving the consumer and society are often eager to install it in their organizations. Yet this is not easy to do. This is evident because of the widespread lip service that the concept receives among business leaders and the fact that much practice belies the concept. Some of this is due to insincerity; but a great part of it is due to serious, but not insurmountable, implementation problems.

Installing the marketing concept calls for major commitments and changes in the organization. As noted by Edward S. McKay, a long-time marketing consultant:

It may require drastic and upsetting changes in organization. It usually demands new approaches to planning. It may set in motion a series of appraisals that will disclose surprising weaknesses in performance, distressing needs for modification of operating practices, and unexpected gaps, conflicts, or obsolescence in basic policies. Without doubt, it will call for reorientation of business philosophy and for the reversal of some long-established attitudes. These changes will not be easy to implement. Objectives, obstacles, resistance, and deep-rooted habits will have to be overcome. Frequently, even difficult and painful restaffing programs are necessary before any real progress can be made in implementing the concept.[5]

For these reasons, top management must think and plan very carefully about how to bring a viable marketing orientation into their organization. Based on the experience of many organizations, the following steps will be crucial in introducing this orientation.[6] They will be illustrated for a hypothetical postal system which has hitherto been very production-oriented.

Need for Preplanning

The first step calls for the top management of the postal system to thoroughly study and understand the marketing concept before making a commitment. It should try to visualize what systems would have to be changed, what groups would be affected, and what programs would help smooth the way to the desired change. Some of the following things will emerge:

1. The postal system would add a marketing research department with the responsibility of studying and measuring current and changing customer needs. This department will come up with recommendations that will call for new services to be added and certain old services to be dropped. This will hurt certain interests in the organization and they can be expected to object.
2. The postal system may want to introduce a new-products department to develop, launch, and manage new services. This department, along with the marketing research department, will add costs that may be objected to by the financial officer of the postal system. Also, there may be objections from some legislators and taxpayers.
3. The postal system is likely to increase its advertising expenditures to make users aware of new services. Yet this increased expense may be objected to by the financial officer and legislators and taxpayers.
4. The employees who deal directly with customers will have to be trained to show more interest in the customer and his needs. At the present time, they are well-protected by civil service and their union. The postal system is not able to fire employees who are insolent or indifferent to their customers. It can try to be more careful in hiring customer-oriented employees, but even here screening criteria might be interpreted as discriminatory by the union or unhired individuals.
5. The mail-handling employees who have little customer contact will want to know what a marketing orientation will do to their jobs and schedules.

This analysis shows to top management some of the major issues they will face in attempting to install a highly customer-oriented service.

One would ordinarily not expect to face resistance in trying to make an organization serve the public interest better, but change is very painful to groups, and resistance can be expected.

Management should avoid announcing prematurely a public commitment to a marketing orientation (or customer service orientation, if this term is more acceptable). Instead it should call in representatives of the various departments, outline the nature and need for the marketing concept, and solicit their views. It will be helpful to hear how the various departments state their interests and reservations and to know how much cooperation can be expected in advance. If the new orientation is seen to be beneficial by the majority of departments, the others will soon fall in line because of the weight of opinion. If the new orientation is seen as threatening and objectionable by a majority of departments, management must be prepared to use its authority or to postpone plans for installing this concept until a better climate develops. Even then, management may consider introducing the concept in a less total way, by creating only a marketing research department for the present, or an employee training program, and eventually adding new stages of marketing activity as the timing is right, without committing the organization to a totally new, strange, and possibly threatening orientation.

Top Management Sponsorship

When the problems have been thought through and the climate seems right, and some plans have been laid for the installation of the concept, the chief executive of the organization can announce and explain the new orientation, its benefits to the public and to the organization's own employees and management, and the implementation plan. The statement should be presented in a series of meetings and also should be in writing and broadly circulated throughout the organization. At this time, the chief executive should also announce the establishment of a department and officer who will be in charge of the marketing activities and marketing orientation of the organization. In business organizations, the department is normally called the marketing department and the officer is called the vice-president of marketing. In the postal system, the person might be called the director of marketing, and in other organizations, such as universities or hospitals, the person might be called the director of development. In any event, there can be no marketing progress without the appointment of a high-level person responsible for working with the chief executive to bring the marketing orientation into the organization. He must be high-level and of equal status with the officers in charge of finance, operations, and personnel in order that (1) they are shown that this position is of equal importance with theirs; and

(b) to insure that the marketing officer has ready access to the other officers so that he can bring in the marketing perspective when needed. The selection of this person must be carefully made and will be crucial to the ultimate success of the marketing orientation.

The chief marketing officer has two jobs to perform. The first, and easier one, is to integrate and coordinate the organization's various market-impinging activities so that they have a unified impact. His department should coordinate market forecasting, marketing research, advertising, personal selling, promotion, and customer service. He will manage these activities either directly or through managers, depending on the size of the organization. The main point is that these activities can work at cross-purposes if they are not coordinated. Suppose the advertising department of the postal system placed ads announcing a new service, but the sales department was too busy with other commitments to handle the inquiries that arose. Or suppose the market forecasters estimated a great increase in the use of the mail services beyond the postal system's current capacity, and the advertising department in the meantime started a campaign to stimulate more people to use the postal service, thus straining the system's capacity even further. These contradictory actions by various marketing units must be avoided. They can be avoided by the creation of a market-ing department, or at least a marketing committee.

The chief marketing officer's other job is to deal with the finance, operations, and personnel departments on a regular basis and try to edu-cate them to the value and benefits of a customer point of view. He should stress the advantages of a customer orientation not only for the ultimate customer but for each department in the organization. Thus an improvement in the accuracy of demand forecasting will allow the opera-tions manager to plan personnel, material, and facility needs more ac-curately. It will allow the finance officer to have a more accurate picture of the cash flow that will come into the organization. The chief marketing officer must show that a customer orientation will lead to greater customer satisfaction, fewer complaints to legislators, and more financial support from legislators.

Education and Training Programs

Implementing a marketing orientation will take time and call for a series of education and training programs throughout the organization. Those involved in marketing will want to attend courses for updating their knowledge of marketing concepts and techniques. Other groups in the organization, such as employees in contact with the public, will need training programs and periodic communications showing the benefits of a customer orientation to the organization, the public, and themselves.

New employees must be trained in the concept; many of the older employees forget it. There is a tendency toward creeping unresponsiveness. The employees, during periods of high demand, lose some of their concern with customers' needs. This is why the chief marketing officer must exist, to behave as the customer conscience of the organization against the many tendencies to forget the customers' interest.

SUMMARY

Marketing means more than installing a few activities in an organization such as marketing research, advertising, and customer service. If these activities are to mean anything, they must be part and parcel of an overall orientation adopted by the organization known as the marketing orientation.

Organizations normally start out with a clear purpose to serve some class of human needs. Over time, they add new activities and concerns and become inwardly oriented. The early charisma is routinized and the organization becomes rule-bound, officialdom emerges, and efficiency in the production of existing products and services becomes paramount. The organization grows increasingly unresponsive to emerging needs and trends.

The degree of an organization's unresponsiveness varies across organizations. At one extreme is the unresponsive organization that neither studies its customers' needs nor makes it easy for them to place inquiries, complaints, suggestions, or opinions. A casually responsive organization is one that is interested in hearing the opinions of its publics as they casually flow in. A highly responsive organization is one that uses formal methods of collecting representative opinion, encourages spontaneous inflows of information, and attempts to adapt its products, programs, and policies in line with the sounder suggestions. Finally, a fully responsive organization is one that accepts its customers as members and abides by their will in its product and market decisions.

The marketing concept was formulated in the mid-1950s by large business firms to overcome the limitations of unresponsive organizations. It arose out of the ashes of two previous orientations, the production orientation and the sales orientation. A production orientation characterizes organizations that spend their major energy on improving the output or reducing the cost of whatever they are producing, with little or no regard for the customer's evolving needs; it usually is practiced by organizations in sovereign, monopoly, or high-demand situations. A sales orientation characterizes organizations that spend their major energy in trying to convince the public to want and buy their current goods; it usually is practiced in the early stages of an affluent economy. The sales orientation ultimately leads to a consumer credibility gap and products that are poorly adapted to market needs. The marketing orientation then emerges as a new platform for the organization, one in which it sees its role to be identifying and serving the evolving needs of its customers and publics. The marketing concept calls for a consumer needs orientation, integrated marketing, and consumer satisfaction. The purpose of the organization under the marketing concept is "profit" through service.

Installing the marketing concept in an organization is not a simple matter. Some interest groups will be affected and they will resist or attempt to sabotage the concept. Its introduction requires careful understanding and preplanning by management; top-level sponsorship and organization; and continuous training and education.

NOTES

1. The characteristics of bureaucracy were first set down by Max Weber at the turn of the century. See his *Essays in Sociology,* ed. and transl. H. H. Gerth and C. Wright Mills (New York: Oxford University Press, 1946). An excellent modern analysis is found in Anthony Downs, *Inside Bureaucracy* (Boston: Little, Brown and Co., 1967).

2. The marketing concept has been described in many ways. For additional readings, see John B. McKitterick, "What is the Marketing Management Concept?" *The Frontiers of Marketing Thought and Action* (Chicago: American Marketing Association, 1957), pp. 71–82; Fred J. Borch, "The Marketing Philosophy as a Way of Business Life," *The Marketing Concept: Its Meaning to Management,* Marketing Series, no. 99 (New York: American Management Association, 1957), pp. 3–5; Arthur F. Felton, "Making the Marketing Concept Work," *Harvard Business Review* (March–April 1959), pp. 117–27; and Robert J. Keith, "The Marketing Revolution," *Journal of Marketing* (January 1960), pp. 35–38.

3. Theodore Levitt, "Marketing Myopia," *Harvard Business Review* (July–August 1960), pp. 45–56.

4. Charles G. Mortimer, "The Creative Factor in Marketing," *Fifteenth Annual Parlin Memorial Lecture,* Philadelphia Chapter, American Marketing Association, May 13, 1959.

5. Edward S. McKay, *The Marketing Mystique* (New York: American Management Association, 1972), p. 22.

6. This discussion is based on McKay, *The Marketing Mystique,* pp. 22–30, and also on the author's experience.

QUESTIONS

1. The conductor of a symphony orchestra states: "If we adopt a marketing orientation and give the audiences just what they want to hear, we'd be putting on some pretty uninteresting performances. We'd

never get a chance to play anything new and daring." Should the conductor adopt the marketing concept?

2. Can an organization be *overly* responsive?

3. How can you tell if consumers are satisfied?

4. The state consumer protection office in a major city is swamped with telephone calls from irate consumers who have been gypped or swindled in rather small transactions. The office feels that it can utilize its scarce resources best by prosecuting cases of larger magnitude that affect numerous consumers. What should the office do about the phone calls?

5. A marketing orientation seems to suggest in the minds of some that an organization should go all out to please the customer. Is it a fair interpretation of a fully responsive organization that it thinks the customer is always right?

6. "The marketing concept provides marketers with an excuse for acting against society's interests." Comment and discuss.

7. The marketing viewpoint calls for an organization to "benefitize" its offering to the target audience. Consider the following types of benefits: *immediate personal benefits, long-run personal benefits, immediate social benefits,* and *long-run social benefits.* Assume a family planning agency is trying to market birth control to a group of poor people. Describe a benefit of each type that might be used in the appeal. Rank the four benefits in order of their likely motivational strength.

4 Marketing Method

When the Chinese write the word "crisis," they do so in two characters, one meaning danger, the other opportunity.

Chapter 1 established the relevance of marketing to the problems of nonprofit organizations. Chapter 2 introduced the basic concepts underlying the marketing discipline, those of publics, markets, and exchange. Chapter 3 described the philosophical orientation of marketing as seeking to bring about high organizational responsiveness to the organization's various publics.

We are now at a point in the discussion where it is appropriate to develop an overall view of marketing method. If an organization has a marketing problem, what method is brought to bear upon it? What variables does the marketer look at? What reasoning does he go through in seeking a solution? We are seeking in this chapter to understand the distinctive style of thinking of the marketer.

THE MARKETING AUDIT

The best way to convey the thinking style of the marketer is to imagine him being invited to perform a marketing audit by a nonprofit organization. A marketing audit is undertaken to assist management in evaluating the organization's markets, products, marketing programs, and overall marketing effectiveness. More formally,

A marketing audit is an independent examination of the entire marketing effort of an organization covering objectives, programs, implementation, organization, and control, for the purpose of determining and appraising what is being done and recommending what should be done in the future.

The usual reason for inviting a marketing audit is that the organization is facing a major problem stemming from its markets, products, or marketing methods. The marketer may start examining the specific problem or take it to be symptomatic of a larger problem. In the latter case, he will ask a comprehensive set of questions to attempt to understand the organization and its marketing weaknesses.[1]

The marketing audit consists of three parts. The first part calls for evaluating the *marketing environment* of the organization, specifically its markets, customers, competitors, and macroenvironment. The second part calls for evaluating the *marketing system* within the organization, specifically the organization's objectives, programs, implementation, and organization. The third part calls for evaluating the major areas of *marketing activity* in the organization, specifically its products, pricing, distribution, personal contact, advertising, publicity, and sales promotion.

This audit will reveal the major practices, problems, and opportunities facing the organization and will serve as a basis for more effective planning.

THE MARKETING ENVIRONMENT REVIEW

The first task of the marketer is to establish the status of the main environmental factors—markets, customers, competitors, and macroenvironmental forces—affecting the organization. The key questions are listed in Table 4-1 and discussed in the following paragraphs.

Markets

The marketer specifically starts by asking the organization to identify its major markets and publics. When this question is put to a business firm, it first states its consuming market. General Motors would define its major market as "all people who buy cars" and Volkswagen would define its major market as "all people who buy compact economy cars." These companies would also recognize other publics, such as stockholders, legislators, the local community, and the general public.

TABLE 4-1

A Systematic Marketing Audit

Part I. The Marketing Environment Review

   A. *Markets*

     1. Who are the organization's major markets and publics?

     2. What are the major market segments in each market?

     3. What are the present and expected future size and the characteristics of each market or market segment?

   B. *Customers*

     4. How do the customers and publics feel toward and see the organization?

     5. How do customers make their purchase or adoption decisions?

     6. What is the present and expected future state of customer needs and satisfaction?

   C. *Competitors*

     7. Who are the organization's major competitors?

     8. What trends can be foreseen in competition?

   D. *Macroenvironment*

     9. What are the main relevant developments with respect to demography, economy, technology, government, and culture that will affect the organization's situation?

The markets and publics surrounding a nonprofit organization are often more complex. A university might say that it operates in four markets: a student market, a faculty market, a research market, and a philanthropic market. It might add that the student market (or some other) is the most important. It might further add that it is not interested in all potential college students but "only the top students" or "largely students from our state." A hospital might say that it operates in four markets: the patient market, the doctor market, the nurse market, and the donor market. At a particular time, it may regard one or two of these markets as posing the greatest problem and give less attention to the other markets. It is important to get the organization to list the markets that it sees as important and the relative importance of each in the total scheme of the organization's objectives.

Each market in turn consists of distinguishable market segments. It is a central tenet of marketers that *market segmentation* is an essential step to analyzing and planning for markets. Organizations are not able to serve whole markets effectively and the organization is wise to choose a segment to serve, or at least differentiate its marketing programs for the different market segments it serves. Market segmentation itself is a sophisticated art; [2] and there are many ways to fruitfully segment a market. Markets can be segmented geographically, demographically, psycho-graphically, or behaviorally. Thus we can talk about "Eastern, Midwest-ern, Western, or Southern students," or "upper-, middle-, or lower-class students," or "high achiever versus low achiever students," or "quality-, price-, or service-sensitive students."

Information should also be gathered on the present and expected future size and characteristics of each important market and market seg-ment. M.I.T., for example, is interested in the expected number of stu-dents who will want to major in engineering for the next five years and who are able to afford a quality school. The Addiction Research Founda-tion of Ontario, Canada, is interested in the expected growth rate of dif-ferent types of drug addiction. This information has crucial implications for each organization's long-range planning.

Customers

The marketer will then want to understand the needs, perceptions, preferences, and satisfactions of each target market. Many nonprofit orga-nizations never conduct formal research into their market's knowledge, attitudes, or behavior; they rely on casual impressions and intuition. Con-sider the following case:

> The administrative officials of a suburban hospital thought that the local community was highly pleased with the hospital and its services. When the hospital proposed building a new wing, it was surprised to find the community raising all sorts of objections and lobbying the suburban officials not to permit the hospital's expansion. The administrators dis-covered that the local residents were not of one mind regarding the hospital's presence. Many thought the building was ugly. Many resented the noise of the sirens in the middle of the night. Many thought the hospital mainly served rich people coming from other suburbs. Many complained about the poor medical attention in the emergency room. These and other complaints came out during the zoning inquiry.

From this example it can be seen that there is a need on the part of the organization to know how it is seen by its various publics. Many non-profit organizations never formally research the minds of their publics.

Another area of inquiry is how well the organization understands the actual forces shaping the patronage and purchase decisions of buyers. Business firms spend a great deal of money in studies of consumer motiva-tion, information processing, and decision making. Most nonprofit orga-nizations are still in the stage of stereotyping their customers' behavior. Many charity organizations assume, without carefully researching "giving" motives or behavior, that donors give out of a feeling of altruism or under social pressure. Alternative motivational assumptions have quite different implications for the type of fund-raising campaign to run. If the organization believes social pressure is a key factor, it will rely on personal calls from acquaintances and possibly publishing how much each person gives. If it believes that feelings of fear lead to giving, it would develop an advertising campaign suggesting that anyone might be a victim unless enough people give to conquer the disease.

The marketer will also want to probe what is known about current and future needs and satisfaction levels in each market. Many organizations do a poor job of monitoring important changes occurring in customer requirements or satisfaction. The U.S. Postal Service for years overlooked growing businessman dissatisfaction with the quality of service, attitudes of personnel, and slowness of mail. As a result, many business users resorted to working through private mail-handling firms that offered speedy intracity and intercity distribution. This loss of business and other developments led to a reorganization of the U.S. Postal Service a few years ago that included the introduction of marketing, marketing research, and marketing training as formal responsibilities in the postal system.

Competitors

The marketer will want to know who the organization considers to be its major competitors. Three different forms of competition can be distinguished. The first is *generic competition* and refers to other broad product categories that might satisfy the same need. Thus generic competition to the Methodist church would include rock concerts, drugs, nature trips, transcendental meditation, and other experiences that may be emotionally uplifting to the participants. The second is *product-form competition* and refers to specific versions of the product that may be competitive with each other. Methodist religious service may be experienced in the church, in the home, or over broadcast media; these are competitive forms of the same service. Finally, the third is *enterprise competition*, which refers to specific organizations that are competitive producers of the same product or service. The Methodist church is in competition with Episcopalian, Lutheran, Presbyterian, and Baptist churches, and more remotely the Catholic church. The marketer must use these distinctions in his attempt to identify the major competitive marketing problems facing the organization.

The trends in competitive forces are important to note. For example, U.S. churchgoing peaked in 1955 with 49 percent of adults attending church in a typical week. It slipped to 40 percent in 1972.[3] The decline in churchgoing was even more pronounced among Roman Catholics, falling from 74 percent in 1955 to 57 percent in 1972. The major competition is coming from the conducting of in-home rather than in-church services, and the growing popularity of secular forms of gratification such as sports, television, and the movies.

Macroenvironment

The term "macroenvironment" describes the major forces and institutions surrounding and affecting the organization, its markets, and competitors. Five main forces can be distinguished: demography, economy, technology, government, and culture. These forces have a profound effect on the organization, while the reverse cannot be said.

The marketer is interested in how demographic developments will affect the ultimate size of the organization's markets and the demand for its products. The main demographic factors are the size of the population, its age distribution, trends in the birth and death rate, and its geographic distribution. For example, one private university ruefully concluded after analyzing the age distribution of the population that "the number of college enrollments will increase slowly in the Seventies and then decrease from 1982 until the end of the Eighties." Family planning organizations, environmental groups, park districts, and housing authorities also have an especially strong and direct interest in future demographic developments.

Economic forces have to be audited because they have a strong effect on the demand for the organization's product and the cost of providing it. Private universities expect rising tuitions to depress the demand for private education. In the meantime, they will face rising costs of faculty, library, building maintenance, and other services.

Technological developments have a great significance for possible new products and/or cost savings that alert institutions will want to watch. Universities are watching developments in computer-aided instruction and in cable television as alternative methods of delivering education. Hospitals are alert to new equipment that will increase their health-delivery capacity or reduce their costs.

Government developments are very difficult to predict but can have a profound effect on an organization. Universities have been plummeted into major budget crises overnight because of substantial reduction of government money for research and graduate student training. Philanthropic foundations have been uneasy about new laws passed or proposed that would affect their tax-exempt status. Public mass transit companies are placing a lot of hope on the granting of new federal appropriations to support them. The marketer will want to know the major contingencies in the government area that will affect the organization's future.

Finally, new cultural developments have to be anticipated. College enrollments shrank in the late sixties partly because of the emergence of a new value system among a small but growing group of young people who saw college education as irrelevant to their lives. Whether this anti-college sentiment grows or diminishes will make a great difference to the future demand for college education. Changing values and life styles have profound implications for family planning groups, ecology groups, consumer organizations, and other activist organizations.

The great need for organizations to anticipate the future has spurred the development of many firms offering forecasting services of various kinds. The most solid work is done in demographic forecasting, followed by economic forecasting. There is some recent progress in improving technological forecasting. As for political forecasting, there is little in the way of respectable theory to guide the prediction of major political events. And cultural forecasting is one of the most neglected and least developed of the forecasting arts.

THE MARKETING SYSTEM REVIEW

After the marketer assesses the role of marketing environment forces—markets, customers, competitors, and the macroenvironment—in creating threats and opportunities for the organization, he moves on to a series of questions that attempt to assess whether the organization is well-positioned in its environment. These questions are listed in Table 4-2.

Objectives

The first task is to ascertain the organization's long-run and short-run objectives. Business firms have generally adopted a "management-by-objectives" philosophy of business. Many nonprofit organizations, on the other hand, have a difficult time specifying their objectives beyond some pleasant-sounding public relations oriented statement. Universities want to "discover and disseminate knowledge," hospitals want to "relieve pain and suffering," and police departments want to "protect public health and safety." These are true and worthwhile goals but they do not go far enough in guiding the organization toward concrete relations to its environment.

Useful statements of objectives are characterized by two attributes. The first is the spelling out of a hierarchical set of objectives.[4] A hospital's basic objective is to deliver quality medical care to the community. Because it cannot be good at all things, it must set more specific objectives for various services to offer. These in turn suggest subsidiary objectives

TABLE 4-2

TABLE 4-2

A Systematic Marketing Audit (continued)

Part II. The Marketing System Review

A. *Objectives*
  10. What are the organization's long-run and short-run overall objectives and marketing objectives?
  11. Are the objectives stated in a clear hierarchical order and in a form that permits planning and measurement of achievement?
  12. Are the marketing objectives reasonable for the organization given its competitive position, resources, and opportunities?

B. *Program*
  13. What is the organization's core strategy for achieving its objectives, and is it likely to succeed?
  14. Is the organization allocating enough resources (or too many) to accomplish the marketing tasks?
  15. Are the marketing resources allocated optimally to the various markets, territories, and products of the organization?
  16. Are the marketing resources allocated optimally to the major elements of the marketing mix; i.e., product quality, personal contact, promotion, and distribution?

C. *Implementation*
  17. Does the organization develop an annual marketing plan? Is the planning procedure effective?
  18. Does the organization implement control procedure (monthly, quarterly, etc.) to insure that its annual plan objectives are being achieved?
  19. Does the organization carry out periodic studies to determine the contribution and effectiveness of various marketing activities?
  20. Does the organization have an adequate marketing information system to service the needs of managers for planning and controlling operations in various markets?

D. *Organization*
  21. Does the organization have a high-level marketing officer to analyze, plan, and implement the marketing work of the organization?
  22. Are the other persons directly involved in marketing activity able people? Is there a need for more training, incentives, supervision, or evaluation?
  23. Are the marketing responsibilities optimally structured to serve the needs of different marketing activities, products, markets, and territories?
  24. Do the organization's personnel understand and practice the marketing concept?

---

with respect to facilities, doctors, nurses, and so on, all hierarchically related to the more basic objectives of the organization.

The second attribute of well-formulated objectives is that they are numerically stated to the maximum extent possible so that subsequent accomplishment can be planned for and measured. There is a difference between whether a hospital states as its objective "to be a nationally prominent hospital in cancer research" or "to be rated as one of the top three cancer research hospitals in the nation within five years." The latter statement is very specific and more serviceable in policy making and results measurement.

The marketing audit should also raise the question of whether the core objectives are really appropriate for the organization given its position, resources, and opportunities. A small city hospital is deceiving itself if it adopts the objective "to be rated as one of the top three cancer research hospitals in the nation within five years." A medical charity raising $5 million a year may be deceiving itself if it believes that it can raise $100 million a year within two years. Objectives are not supposed to represent exercises in wishful thinking but rather the results of appropriately chosen goals for the organization given its environmental opportunities and constraints.

Program

The marketer will want to examine the current program that the organization has developed to achieve its objectives. Does the organization have a core strategy by which it expects to achieve its objectives? Is this core strategy likely to succeed? Very often, this question reveals that the organization has no core strategy, only faith that it will succeed by doing a good job. Consider the following case:

> Two private universities some years ago enjoyed about the same national ranking (somewhere in the 8th to 15th rank) and both at about the same time adopted the objective of advancing into the ranks of the top five private universities in the nation within ten years. One succeeded and the other did not. The one that succeeded developed a well-formulated strategy consisting of such steps as hiring a distinguished scholar in each major department who had a reputation for attracting money and other scholars; starting a research institute that would work closely with business firms; increasing its scholarship fund to attract top talented students; established a first-class development office and public relations department. This university identified each market important to the university (students, faculty, government, business, foundations) and developed a plan for becoming a strong factor in each market. The other university did none of these things and operated on the theory that if it hired generally good people, kept good control over funds, and reminded

alumni of their obligations to support the university, it would succeed. This university failed to achieve its objective because it failed to do any innovative thinking on how to build up public interest and respect. It also failed because it did not allocate enough resources to the marketing job that had to be done.

Many nonprofit organizations want to attract more funds and achieve more repute but show no willingness to spend the money necessary to accomplish these results. Every businessman knows that he has to spend money to make money. Marketing activities are highly productive and also costly. Many nonprofit organizations cut corners by hiring mediocre marketing personnel or carrying out these activities through volunteers or staff who are overworked. The result is that the objectives are not achieved and the organization grows cynical about the productivity of marketing investments. They think their marketing effort has failed whereas they really never tried it on the proper scale.

The marketer will want to examine whether current marketing resources are optimally allocated to the various markets, products, and territories of the organization. If a university has a poor-quality faculty, then marketing efforts to attract more students is misdirected. It will succeed in attracting these students in the short run but they will be disappointed by the quality of the faculty and turn around and bad-mouth the university to other prospective students. They will also give little as alumni to the university. The university will have to devote still more time and effort to attract qualified students and sufficient gifts from alumni. Much of this could be avoided if the university would spend more of its current money in upgrading the faculty.

Other signs of misallocations of marketing resources can also be spotted. One university regularly sent its recruiters to Ivy League universities in search of quality graduate students with very little success. This effort was doomed never to pay off until the school improved its national reputation by other steps. Another school ran an evening program that lost money and was losing students. A business firm would have either liquidated the program or made a concerted effort to improve it. The current expenditure was too much, given the results, and too little if real improvements were to be made.

The marketer is also interested in the mix of marketing tools used by the nonprofit organization. Medical charities, for example, try to raise money through a variety of activities, including national advertising, local advertising, direct mail, philanthropic solicitations, and door-to-door campaigns. The mix of activities is optimal if no reallocation of funds from one activity to another would increase the total revenue raised. Yet medical charities stick to a particular mix of marketing activities although their causes go through significant changes during their life cycles. When a medical charity first starts out, advertising is a very productive way to build up awareness of the organization at a low cost per thousand people. After the medical charity is well-established in the minds of people, it might profitably put more of its funds into direct mail solicitation using good mailing lists, because this provides people with an easy mechanism for giving money to a charity. Still later it might add door-to-door solicitation to build grassroots support. A marketer knows that every product and cause goes through a life cycle, and that the most productive mix of marketing investments varies through the stages of the product life cycle.

Implementation

Even when an organization has developed clear and sound objectives and a well-reasoned core strategy and program, it may fail to carry out the program in an effective way. Many programs fail because the proper systems are not installed to provide for effective implementation.

The first implementational requirement is a well-formulated procedure for annual marketing planning. Whereas *strategy* means that the top management of the organization has agreed upon some overall method of achieving its objectives, *planning* means that the organization takes concrete steps to translate the strategy into a set of targets and scheduled actions that are carried out by different persons in the organization. It is important to appraise whether the planning procedures are the best available. A number of organizations use *top-down planning*, in which the top administrators meet and develop objectives, strategies, programs, budgets, and quotas and then expect everyone to carry these out. Other organizations use *bottom-up planning*, in which meetings are held at different levels and everyone gets involved in goal setting and commitment. Still other organizations use *participative planning*, in which objectives are sent down by top management and plans are developed and sent up by lower management for approval. The latter two methods are finding growing favor among organizations because of the crucial need to gain the insight, enthusiasm, commitment, and understanding of all those in the organization who will be responsible for the objectives.

The marketer will also want to examine the controls used by the organization to make sure that the organization is advancing each period toward the goals it has set. At one extreme is the situation in which the organization designs an annual plan with no provision for control. The plan is dutifully filed in everyone's desk drawer and the staff goes about its business without any formal checks on the progress toward the objectives until the end of the year when it is too late. At the other extreme is the situation in which the organization engages in daily, weekly, or monthly checks on its progress toward the goals and introduces corrective action when necessary. Obviously plans do not mean much unless the organization arranges for concrete controls.

In addition to plan control, the organization should carry out periodic studies to determine the contribution and effectiveness of specific marketing activities. Is a regular evaluation made of the advertising program to determine what it is accomplishing and whether it can be improved? Is an evaluation made of the results being achieved through direct mail, personal contact, and so on? Does the organization know the "profitability" or value contribution of different products and services in its line?

A key factor in implementation is the quality of the marketing information system that the executives have to work with. This system in most nonprofit organizations is very primitive, because there is not much budget for investing in information acquisition, storage, analysis, and dissemination. Much of the crucial information is in people's heads, or in reports scattered throughout the organization. The computer, if there is one, is used mainly for payroll and accounting rather than also for information storage, retrieval, and analysis. This is in contrast with major business firms that have highly sophisticated information systems with advanced data banks, statistical banks, and model banks. There are exceptions of course. In the fund-raising area, several medical charities and universities have built advanced computerized information systems with which they can analyze the market potential of different giving groups and the effectiveness of different fund-raising methods.

Organization

The marketing effort of an organization can often be faulted on the grounds that the organization lacks competent marketing leadership, organization, or staff. Business firms have recognized the marketing function through the establishment of a formal marketing department headed by a marketing vice-president. Nonprofit organizations have recognized the financial function, operations function, and personnel function, but have been less ready to recognize the marketing function. Thus a university may not have a marketing department as such but has shadow marketing departments in the form of a development office (for fund raising), a public relations office (for publicity), and an admissions office (for student recruitment). Hospitals, museums, churches, public schools, and many other nonprofit organizations similarly will carry on their marketing operations through public relations departments, development offices, and education departments.

The major problem posed by the lack of a formal marketing department is that it goes with a lack of formal leadership responsible for planning marketing programs and making people in the organization enthusiastic about the marketing concept. Marketing is a sophisticated concept that must be practiced from top management down to the lowest employee to be fully effective. But is not likely to come into an organization as an attitude unless some center of marketing leadership, training, and planning is established.

Installing a marketing orientation requires that the top administrator understand and believe in the productivity of a marketing orientation. Some officer under him, whatever his title and formal role, must understand, accept, and be willing to act as the marketing consciousness in the organization. He must inject a marketing perspective in planning sessions. The marketing auditor will want to know whether some person who is high in the organization takes the marketing point of view and reminds others of their marketing opportunities and responsibilities.

The marketing auditor will want to appraise the competence of the members of the organization who are directly responsible for specific marketing activities, such as advertising, public relations, client service, product design, marketing research, and so on. Each of these activities is important and should not be left to incompetent or unmotivated management. A check should be made to find out whether there is a need for more training, incentives, supervision, or evaluation of these personnel.

An important question in business firms that have large marketing departments is whether the marketing effort is optimally structured to meet the needs of different marketing functions, products, customer groups, and territories. Marketing departments start out normally as a collection of marketing functions. When the organization's product line grows, the firm adds product managers, each of whom is responsible for a major product. Still later, the firm might add some market managers who are responsible for monitoring and planning for each important customer group. In the context of a university, product managers would include the deans of liberal arts, the evening program, the medical school, and so on. Market managers would include the deans of students, faculties, alumni, and so on. Each job position involves expense and an organization must review periodically the job positions to make sure they are optimal for handling the organization's marketing functions, customer groups, and products.

Even when the top administrators of an organization adopt the marketing concept, its success depends on a customer point of view being practiced by everyone in the organization. A major problem in universities is that many professors place research ahead of service to their students. In hospitals, nurses can be found who treat patients in a very perfunctory manner. The staff in many government agencies—license bureaus, tax departments, and police departments—treat citizens indifferently. In the past, museum and library personnel were often indifferent or hostile to visitors. The situation has a parallel in banking when the top bank officials adopted the marketing concept but the tellers and lending officers still made the customers feel like second-class citizens. The marketing auditor will want to appraise the degree to which the employees are oriented toward serving the interests of the organization's clients.

DETAILED MARKETING ACTIVITY REVIEW

The preceding questions were designed to establish the general configuration of marketing practices, problems, and opportunities facing the organization. They should be supplemented by assessments of how well the organization carries out specific marketing activities. Sometimes a marketing consultant is contacted because of a problem in a specific marketing area, such as low morale among door-to-door solicitors for a medical charity. The consultant will first look at the program for training, motivating, and supervising volunteers to see if it is at fault. Often the basic problem stems from some other factor. For example, the volunteers may be demoralized because the charitable cause and appeals are not potent against competitive causes. What appears to be the result of a weakness in volunteer training may actually stem from a poor product.

Table 4-3 lists the questions that the marketer would raise about the various elements in the marketing mix.

Products

The marketer asks management to describe the main products and lines produced by the organization. A hospital might view its major products to be health care, research, and education. An ecology group might see its major products as education, lobbying, and organizing. A social welfare agency might see its major products as counseling, education, and relief. In each case, specific programs may be organized around the major products.

The marketer wants to be sure that management understands the difference between the generic needs the organization is serving and the specific products it is offering. The cosmetics company is producing lipstick

TABLE 4-3

A Systematic Marketing Audit (continued)

Part III. Detailed Marketing Activity Review

A. *Products*
   25. What are the main products of the organization? What are the generic products?
   26. Should any products in the line be phased out?
   27. Should any products be added to the line?
   28. What is the general state of health of each product and the product mix as a whole?

B. *Price*
   29. To what extent are prices set on cost, demand, and/or competitive criteria?
   30. What would the likely response of demand be to higher or lower prices?
   31. How do customers psychologically interpret the price level?
   32. Does the organization use temporary price promotions, and how effective are they?

C. *Distribution*
   33. Are there alternative methods of distributing the product that would result in more service or less cost?
   34. Does the organization render adequate service along with product to its customers?

D. *Personal Contact*
   35. Is the sales force large enough to accomplish the organization's objectives?
   36. Is the sales force organized along the proper principles of specialization (territory, market, product)?
   37. Does the sales force show high morale, ability, and effort? Is it sufficiently trained and motivated?
   38. Are the procedures adequate for setting quotas and evaluating performances?

E. *Advertising*
   39. Does the organization adequately state its advertising objectives?
   40. Does the organization spend the right amount on advertising?
   41. Are the themes and copy effective?
   42. Are the media well-chosen?

F. *Publicity*
   43. Does the organization have a carefully formulated program of publicity?

G. *Sales Promotion*
   44. Are sales promotions used by the organization, and are they well-conceived?

---

but selling "hope." The symphony orchestra is producing music but supplying diversion. A church may think of its product as spiritual experience but members may think of the product as human fellowship. Organizations must keep their eyes on the basic needs the consumer is trying to gratify through the product. As these needs change, the alert organization will want to modify its products.

Some of the products may be weak and require either elimination or rehabilitation. One purpose of the product audit is precisely to detect such weak products. Another purpose is to determine whether any new products should be added to the line that are suggested by consumer need studies or by the actions of competitors in introducing these products. The marketer will also want to appraise the vitality of the product mix as a whole—to know whether it has a lot of viable products or is mainly composed of weak products.

Price

Business firms set their prices to maximize their profits. The theory of profit-maximizing pricing is well worked out and widely understood, requiring knowledge of the demand and cost functions for the product. Nonprofit organizations price according to other standards, such as covering costs, matching competition, subsidizing certain groups, and so on. A university sets its tuition with an eye on enrollment, the tuitions charged by other universities in its class, and its immediate revenue needs. Hospital pricing is very cost-oriented and has the additional parameter that most of the payment is not made by the immediate users but by secondary payers, such as medical insurance companies and local, state, and national governments. The question of the proper criteria for pricing in a nonprofit organization is a fascinating one on which considerably more work is needed.

Marketers are particularly interested in estimating the response of consumers to alternative price levels. This is commonly called the problem of estimating the price elasticity of demand. Toll road authorities would like to know how many drivers would be lost if the tolls were raised by a certain amount; the U.S. Postal System is similarly interested in the effect of higher postage rates on mail usage; the U.S. Army is interested in how many more recruits it could attract with a specified increase in take-home pay; some public mass transit systems are thinking of lowering their fares rather than raising them if they can attract enough riders.

Marketers have a lot of experience in estimating consumer response to price changes. The marketer is much more sensitive than the economist to the psychological overtones of price. Prices are not only an indicator of the rate of exchange but also communicators of a product's probable quality. If a list of tuitions charged by different colleges were shown to a group of people, they would probably take the tuitions to be an indicator of academic quality.

Nonprofit organizations will occasionally resort to price promotion to stimulate demand. One museum ran a campaign for new members offering a membership for the year for $10 instead of $15 if the person joined during the promotion period. A social psychologist suggested that the demand for medical checkups on the part of the poor might be stimulated by putting a high price tag on the service and then discounting it for the poor who took advantage that month. Marketers have worked long and hard in the area of price promotion—cents off, two-for-the-price-of-one, premiums, and so on—and can bring this expertise into nonprofit organizations.

Distribution

The marketer will want to examine how the organization distributes its products and whether improvements could be made in service level or cost. Business firms use quite complex channels and agents to distribute their products—brokers, jobbers, wholesalers, retailers, and so on. Many nonprofit organizations are in direct contact with their customers but even here many of the concepts in distribution can be used. For a nationwide door-to-door solicitation campaign, there is a tremendous problem of organizing channels reaching all the way to the individual households. There must be a coordination of state, city, and neighborhood organizations and all must be supplied with the appropriate training and materials for door-to-door solicitation. There are various questions on the number of levels of supervision, on channel motivation, and on evaluation that are similar to the channel problems faced by manufacturers.

The distribution channels must do a good job of providing the consumers with post-sale services. University alumni are usually organized into local chapters. The university must be sensitive to the various services and information needed by alumni. Membership organizations in general must work out a careful plan for providing quick, efficient, and thoughtful services to their members.

Personal Contact

Many nonprofit organizations reach clients through a network of agents, volunteers, and staff workers. An important question is whether enough personnel are engaged in client contact to help the organization achieve its objectives. One university had trouble attracting new applicants because it relied on one overworked admissions director traveling to scores of campuses and not having enough time to do the job required.

In large fund-raising organizations, there is a question of whether the fund raisers are organized according to the best principles of specialization. At one extreme, each fund raiser may have complete freedom to determine who to call on. At the other extreme, fund raisers might all be specialized: black fund raisers call on the black community, the organization's officers call on company presidents, and so on. Or the fund raisers can be organized by territory or product.

For people to be effective at personal contact work, they must be well-selected, trained, motivated, supervised, and evaluated. The techniques for this are well-known from years of work with sales forces in the commercial sector, and are readily applicable to those doing the contact work for nonprofit organizations. A cursory look at who does army recruiting at local army recruiting posts leaves the impression that much can be done to improve the selection, training and ability of army recruiters.

Large organizations go beyond training into establishing actual quotas for their sales forces and evaluating performances on the basis of the final percentage of quota realized. One family planning organization in the South has established quotas for its representatives on the number of new clients they should attract to the center each month, and they are given bonuses based on how successful they are.

Advertising

Advertising is an area of great waste for many organizations because they do not approach the instrument with sufficient understanding. Very often they do not correctly appraise the state of the market and the job to be done by advertising. The same advertising message is continued even after the market enters a new stage. For example, the Indian government carried on a campaign to make its people aware of the concept of family planning. The awareness-building campaign continued even after studies began to show that high awareness had been achieved and that people were now eager for information on how to practice family planning. Many nonprofit organizations fail to clarify the precise objectives they are trying to secure with their advertising, or make the mistake of choosing objectives inappropriate for advertising.[5]

Advertising, like other marketing tools, may be used too much or too little. Marketing professionals have developed theoretical models for attempting to establish the optimal level of advertising. Their expertise would be very relevant to advertising budget determination in nonprofit organizations.

Techniques for pre-testing and post-testing advertising themes and copy are available. Advertising agencies employ these techniques in the normal course of serving a client. They obtain estimates of readership and cost per thousand exposures. The client is also interested in the attitudinal and behavioral effects of the advertising. Recently some researchers developed a pre-testing technique for public service campaigns—particularly anti-drug-abuse campaigns—to use in determining whether or not the campaign would have the intended effects.[6]

Media selection for advertising campaigns has benefited enormously in recent years by much better demographic and readership data, the growing number of specifically targeted media, and the advances in computer programs that efficiently select media according to maximizing exposure or sales criteria.[7]

Publicity

Publicity is the development and dissemination of news and promotional material designed to bring favorable attention to a product, person, organization, place, or cause. It contrasts with advertising in that the message is carried in media (1) without payment to the media and 2) without explicit indication of the source. Many nonprofit organizations arrange for publicity for their activities. Someone on their staff or some hired public relations agency writes stories of human interest about the organization and attempts to get the media to use them. Publicity is an important means of informing the public and gaining attention, especially for organizations without the budget or inclination to use advertising. Various standards can be applied to appraising a publicity operation with respect to how much it is helping an organization accomplish its objectives.

Sales Promotion

Another instrument of growing interest to nonprofit organizations is sales promotion, defined as "those marketing activities, other than personal selling, advertising and publicity, that stimulate consumer purchasing and dealer effectiveness, such as displays, shows and exhibitions, demonstrations, and various nonrecurrent selling efforts not in the ordinary routine."[8] Various political cause groups, such as minority rights groups, consumerist groups, and environmental groups, rely heavily on setting up exhibits, passing out leaflets, marches or protests, and bringing attention to their cause in other ways. These activities are less costly to these organizations than advertising. Some nonprofit organizations have worked out fairly sophisticated sales promotion schemes for converting prospects. For example, family planners in many parts of the world offer incentives—transistor radios, costume jewelry, free bank accounts, etc.— to potential adopters of birth control measures. Many charity organizations put their own fund raisers into competition for large prizes—such as trips to Hawaii—for those who raise the most money.

SUMMARY

Marketing method describes the way that marketers think about relations between an organization and its markets. To illustrate the major marketing variables, we assumed that a marketer was called into an organization and asked to appraise its operations from a marketing point of view. His marketing audit would consist of three parts. First, he would evaluate the marketing environment of the organization, specifically its markets, customers, competitors, and macroenvironment. Second, he would evaluate the marketing system within the organization, specifically the organization's objectives, programs, implementation, and organization. Third, he would evaluate the major marketing activities of the organization, specifically its products, pricing, distribution, personal contact, advertising, publicity, and sales promotion. Reviewing these variables and their interrelations, the marketer would be in a good position to understand the marketing problems and opportunities facing the organization.

NOTES

1. These questions are drawn from the author's *Marketing Management: Analysis, Planning and Control* (Englewood Cliffs, N.J.: Prentice-Hall, Inc., 1967), Chapter 23; and from an article by Dr. Ernest A. Tirmann, "Should Your Marketing Be Audited?" *European Business* (Autumn 1971), pp. 49–56.

2. See Ronald E. Frank, William F. Massy, and Yoram Wind, *Market Segmentation* (Englewood Cliffs, N.J.: Prentice-Hall, Inc., 1972).

3. George Gallup, "Churchgoing Holds at 40 Percent," *Chicago Sun Times*, December 24, 1972, p. 13.

4. See Charles H. Granger, "The Hierarchy of Objectives," *Harvard Business Review* (May–June 1964), pp. 63–74.

5. See Russell H. Colley, ed., *Defining Advertising Goals* (New York: Association of National Advertisers, 1961).

6. See "Anti-Drug Abuse Ads Studied, Pretesting Technique Ready," *Marketing Science Institute Newsletter,* December 1973, p. 1.

7. One of the best mathematical media selection models is by John D. C. Little and Leonard M. Lodish, "A Media Planning Calculus," *Operations Research* (January–February 1969), pp. 1–35. Their model is called MEDIAC and handles in an analytical fashion a large number of marketing and advertising variables such as market segments, sales potentials, exposure probabilities, diminishing marginal response rates, forgetting, seasonality and cost discounts.

8. *Marketing Definitions: A Glossary of Marketing Terms,* compiled by the Committee on Definitions of the American Marketing Association, Ralph S. Alexander, Chairman (Chicago: American Marketing Association, 1960).

QUESTIONS

1. Should government agencies be required to submit to a periodic marketing audit in the same way that publicly held business firms are required to submit to a periodic accounting audit? Pick out a government agency and discuss what a marketing audit of this agency might reveal.

2. Identify the major competitors to an art museum.

3. The environmental protection agency of an industrialized state claims that its major objective is to "clean up the environment for the citizens of our state." What is wrong with this statement of objectives? Can you develop a better statement?

4. The Air Force Academy is having trouble recruiting and keeping high-quality students. What do you think a marketing audit of this organization would reveal?

PART

II

Analyzing
the Market

5 Marketing Problems
Facing Organizations*

On an island in the South Pacific there are no taxes, unemployment, crime, beggars, jazz bands, radios, or inhabitants.

Thus far, we have described marketing as a method applicable to all organizations in their dealings with their markets and publics. At any point in time, an organization is actively involved in a number of markets. In some of these markets, its relations may be quite satisfactory and in other markets, problematic. In the latter case, a variety of problems might exist. The organization might find that a particular market resists its offer, or is indifferent to its offer, or wants it at the wrong time, or wants more than the organization can supply. There are a host of factors that might lead to strained or unsatisfactory market relationships. It is very important to distinguish carefuly among different marketing problems. Each problem may call for a special blend of marketing concepts and skills. The purpose of this chapter is to describe eight

* This chapter was published earlier under the title "The Major Tasks of Marketing Management," *Journal of Marketing* (October 1973), pp. 42–49.

strategically different marketing problems that an organization might face in any of its markets.

OVERVIEW

The popular image of marketing is that it deals primarily with the problems of *creating* and *maintaining* a demand for something. This is too limited a view. *Marketing management may be viewed generically as the task of regulating the level, timing, and character of demand in one or more markets of the organization.*

The organization is assumed to form an idea of a desired level of transaction with a market. The *current demand level* may be below, equal to, or above the *desired demand level.* Four specific demand states make up *underdemand:* negative demand, no demand, latent demand, and faltering demand. Two specific demand states make up *adequate demand:* irregular demand and full demand. Finally, two demand states make up *overdemand:* overfull demand and unwholesome demand. These eight demand states are distinguished primarily with respect to the level of current demand in relation to desired demand; although two additional factors, the timing of demand (irregular demand) and the character of demand (unwholesome demand), are also important. The set of demand situations is fairly exhaustive and the order fairly continuous.

Each demand situation gives rise to the specific marketing task described in column 2 of Table 5-1. Negative demand results in efforts

TABLE 5-1
The Basic Marketing Tasks

Demand State	Marketing Task	Formal Name
I. Negative demand	Disabuse demand	Conversional marketing
II. No demand	Create demand	Stimulational marketing
III. Latent demand	Develop demand	Developmental marketing
IV. Faltering demand	Revitalize demand	Remarketing
V. Irregular demand	Synchronize demand	Synchromarketing
VI. Full demand	Maintain demand	Maintenance marketing
VII. Overfull demand	Reduce demand	Demarketing
VIII. Unwholesome demand	Destroy demand	Countermarketing

to disabuse it; no demand, in efforts to create demand; latent demand, in efforts to develop demand; and so on. Each of these tasks is given the more formal name shown in column 3.

All of these tasks require a managerial approach consisting of analysis, planning, implementation, organization, and control. Furthermore, they all utilize the two basic steps of marketing strategy development: defining the *target markets* and formulating a *marketing mix* out of the elements of product, price, promotion, and place. In these respects, all of marketing management has a unity, a core theory. At the same time, the eight tasks are not identical. They involve or emphasize different variables, different psychological theories, different managerial aptitudes. The eight tasks can give way to specialization. Some marketers may become especially skillful at developmental marketing, others at remarketing, others at maintenance marketing, and others at demarketing. Not all marketers are likely to be equally skilled at all tasks, which is one of the major points to be considered in assigning marketers to tasks.

A marketer in a given job may face all of these tasks as the product, service, or market moves through its life cycle. At the beginning of an offering's life, there may be only latent demand and the task is one of developmental marketing. In the stage of high growth, there may be overfull demand in relation to the organization's ability to produce, and some need for systematic demarketing. When facilities have been built up and demand reaches the maturity stage of the life cycle, the task may be primarily one of maintenance marketing. When demand begins to decline or falter, it may be time to face some basic questions on reshaping it, or remarketing. Finally, the offering may eventually fall into the category of being unwholesome either for the consumer or the organization, and someone may undertake steps to destroy demand by countermarketing.

Thus the task of marketing management is not simply to build demand but rather to regulate the level, timing, and character of demand for the organization's products and services in terms of its objectives at the time. In the discussion that follows, each of the basic marketing tasks is developed and illustrated.

NEGATIVE DEMAND

Negative demand is a state in which all or most of the important segments of the potential market dislike the product or service and in fact might conceivably pay a price to avoid it. Negative demand is worse than no demand. In the case of no demand, the potential market has no particular feelings about the product or service one way or another. In the case of negative demand, they actively dislike the product or service and take steps to avoid it.

Negative demand, far from being a rare condition, applies to a rather large number of products and services. Vegetarians feel negative demand for meats of all kinds. Many Americans feel negative demand for kidneys and sweetbreads. People have a negative demand for vaccinations, dental work, vasectomies, and gall bladder operations. A large number of travelers have a negative demand for air travel, and many others have a negative demand for rail travel. Places such as the North Pole and desert wastelands are in negative demand by travelers. Atheism, ex-convicts, military service, and even work are in negative demand by various groups.

The challenge of negative demand to marketing management, especially in the face of a positive supply, is to develop a plan that will cause demand to rise from negative to positive and eventually equal the positive supply level. We call this marketing task that of *conversional marketing*. Conversional marketing is one of the two most difficult marketing tasks a marketer might face (the other is countermarketing). The marketer faces a market that dislikes the offering. His chief task is to analyze the sources of the market's resistance; whether they lie largely in the area of *beliefs* about the offering, in the *values* touched upon by the offering, in the raw *feelings* engendered by the offering, or in the *cost* of acquiring the offering. If the beliefs are misfounded, they can be clarified through a communication program. If the person's values militate against the offering, it can be put in the framework of other possible values that are positive for the person. If negative feelings are aroused, they may be modifiable through group processes[1] or behavioral therapy.[2] If the costs of acquisition are too high, the marketer can take steps to bring down the real costs. The marketer will want to consider the cost of reducing resistance and whether some other marketing opportunity might be more attractive and less difficult.

NO DEMAND

There is a whole range of products and services for which there is no demand. Instead of people having negative or positive feelings toward an offering, they may be indifferent or uninterested. *No demand is a state in which all or important segments of a potential market are uninterested or indifferent to a particular offering.*

Three different categories of offerings are characterized by no demand. First, there are those familiar objects that are perceived as having no value. Examples would be urban junk such as disposable coke bottles, old barbed wire, and political buttons right after an election. Second, there are those familiar objects that are recognized to have value but not in the particular market. Examples would include boats in areas not near any water, snowmobiles in areas where it never snows, and burglar alarms in areas where there is no crime. Third, there are those objects which are unfamiliar or new and face a situation of no demand because the relevant market has no knowledge of the object. Examples include trinkets of all kinds that people might buy if exposed to but do not normally think about or desire.

The task of converting no demand into positive demand is called *stimulational marketing*. Stimulational marketing is a tough task because the marketer does not even start with a semblance of latent demand for the offering. He can proceed in three ways. One is to try to connect the product or service with some existing need in the marketplace. Thus antique dealers can attempt to stimulate interest in old barbed wire on the part of those who have a general need to collect things. The second is to alter the environment so that the offering becomes valued in that environment. Thus sellers of motor boats can attempt to stimulate interest in boats in a lakeless community by building an artificial lake. The third is to distribute information or the object itself in more places in the hope that people's lack of demand is really only a lack of exposure.

Stimulational marketing has drawn considerable attack from social critics. Because the consumer had no demand (not even latent demand), the marketer has intruded into his life as a manipulator, a propagandist, an exploiter. The target group had no interest in the offering until the marketer, using the whole apparatus of modern marketing, "seduced" or "bamboozled" the consumer into a purchase.

Two things, however, must be said in defense of stimulational marketing. The buyer does not buy because he is forced or coerced by the seller. He buys because he sees the transaction as creating more value for him than avoiding it. The product or service is now seen as related to some need which he does have. The basic need is not manufactured by the marketer. At most, it is stimulated, activated, given a direction and object for expression. Social critics would also have to hold that it is not right for organizations to attempt to activate people's needs.

This nonintervention thesis becomes more difficult in light of the positive benefits that stimulational marketing can confer. Stimulational marketing applies to efforts to get villagers in developing nations to take immunization shots to protect them from dreadful diseases; farmers to adopt better means of farming; mothers to improve their child-rearing practices; and teenagers to improve their nutritional habits. Stimulational marketing is also responsible for accelerating the adoption of many material inventions for which there was no initial market interest. Altogether, a blanket condemnation of stimulational marketing would consign many positive developments, along with the negative ones, to a state of limbo.

LATENT DEMAND

A state of *latent demand* exists *when a substantial number of people share a strong need for something which does not exist in the form of an actual product or service.* The latent demand represents an opportunity for the marketing innovator to develop the product or service that people have been wanting.

Examples of products and services in latent demand abound. A great number of cigarette smokers would like a good-tasting cigarette that does not yield nicotine and tars damaging to health. Such a product breakthrough would be an instant success, just as the first filter-tip cigarette won a sizable share of the market. Many people would like a car that promises substantially more safety and substantially less pollution than do existing cars. There is a strong latent demand for fast city roads, efficient trains, uncrowded national parks, unpolluted major cities, safe streets, and good television programs. When such products are finally developed and properly marketed, their market is assured.

The latent demand situation might seem not so much a problem in demand management as one in supply management. Yet it is thoroughly a marketing problem because the latent need must be recognized, the right product or service developed, the right price chosen, the right channels of distribution put together, and adequate and convincing product information disseminated. Such products as electric dishwashers and air conditioners were adopted slowly at first because people were not convinced that these products could do the job or were worth the price.

The process for effectively converting latent demand into actual demand is that of *developmental marketing.* The marketer must be an expert in identifying the prospective users of the offering who have the strongest latent demand and in coordinating all the marketing functions so as to develop the market in an orderly way.

In contrast to the substantial social criticism directed as stimulational marketing, most observers feel that developmental marketing is not only natural but highly desirable from a social point of view. Latent demand is the situation for which "the marketing concept" is most appropriate. It is not a question of creating desire but rather of finding it and serving it. The buyers and sellers have complementary interests. There is, however, one important qualification that has come to the surface in recent years. The sheer existence of a personal need may not be sufficient to justify its being served and satisfied. There are needs that people have which, if satisfied, are harmful to others or themselves through the spillover effects of consumption. Satisfying those *needs* may hurt a lot of people's *interests*. Thus it is no longer sufficient for a developmental marketer to say that his new product is justified because there is a real need for it. He may have to show that the need is salutary and the product will not lead to more social harm than private good.

FALTERING DEMAND

All kinds of products, services, places, organizations, and ideas eventually experience declining or *faltering demand*. *Faltering demand is a state in which the demand for a product or service is less than its former level and where further decline is expected in the absence of remedial efforts to revise the target market, offering, and/or marketing effort.*

For example, railway travel has been a service in steady decline for a number of years, and it is badly in need of imaginative remarketing. Many grand hotels have seen their clienteles thin out in the face of competition from bright new hotels with the most modern, though somewhat aseptic, facilities. The downtown areas of many large cities are in need of remarketing. Many popular entertainers and political candidates lose their following and badly need remarketing.

The challenge of faltering demand is revitalization, and the marketing task involved is *remarketing*. Remarketing is based on the premise that it is possible in many cases to start a new life cycle for a declining product or service. Remarketing is the search for new marketing propositions for relating the offering to its potential market.

Remarketing calls for a thorough reconsideration of the *target market, product features, and current marketing program.* The question of the appropriate *target market* is faced, for example, by the United Methodist Church.[3] Many of its congregations in the North have found themselves in changing neighborhoods in terms of a rapidly increasing black population. A congregation has two ways to respond. Many have closed their doors, sold the church building to a black congregation, and moved into all-white areas. Others have attempted integration in line with the church's policy of receiving individuals into church membership without regard to race, color, or national origin. Thus the individual Methodist congregations face a basic decision regarding the target market for their religious services. The decisions they make today will affect the size, character, and composition of their future membership.

The task of revising *product or service features* is faced by Amtrak, the semipublic corporation charged with the responsibility for revitalizing railway passenger travel. Amtrak's initial temptation was to carry on a massive advertising campaign to get people to try the trains again. However, this would have been fatal because it would have shown people how really bad train service and trains have become. It is a marketing axiom that the fastest way to kill a bad product is to advertise it. This accelerates the rate of trial and the rate of negative word-of-mouth which finally tolls the death knell on the product. Amtrak wisely decided that mass advertising should come *after* service improvement. A sharp distinction must be drawn between *cosmetic marketing*, which tries to advertise a new image without revising the offering, and *remarketing*, which calls for a thorough reconsideration and revision of all aspects of the offering and market that may affect sales.

The task of revising its marketing program was faced by the Florence Crittenton Anchorage Home for unwed mothers in Chicago.[4] The Home originally served the daughters of middle- and upper-class families who paid good fees to have their daughters cared for throughout their pregnancies. In recent years, the Home's maternity cases increasingly came from lower-income families who could not afford to pay the fees. Thus the Home's income was falling while its expenses were rising because of the general inflation. It had to resort for the first time to systematic fund raising; it went from a minimal marketing effort to an elaborate marketing program designed to raise sufficient funds to carry on its operations.

Remarketing is similar to the physician's job of curing a sick patient. It calls for good diagnosis and a long-term plan to build up the patient's health. In some ways, however, it might be charged that the skilled remarketer serves to slow down progress by trying to preserve the weaker species in the face of stronger competitors. There is some truth to this in that the offering in faltering demand would probably disappear or stagnate in the absence of creative marketing respiration. In some situations, perhaps the organization simply should take steps to adjust the supply downward to match the demand. On the other hand, when the faltering demand is due to poor marketing premises and not to natural forces, able remarketing can make a major contribution to saving the organization's assets.

IRREGULAR DEMAND

Very often an organization might be satisfied with the average level of demand but quite unsatisfied with its temporal pattern. Some seasons are marked by demand surging far beyond the supply capacity of an organization, and other seasons are marked by a wasteful underutilization of an organization's supply capacity. *Irregular demand is defined as a state in which the current timing pattern of demand is marked by seasonal or volatile fluctuations that depart from the timing pattern of supply.*

Many examples of irregular demand can be cited. In mass transit, much of the equipment is idle during the off-hours and in insufficient supply during the peak hours. Museums are undervisited during the weekdays and terribly overcrowded during the weekends. Hospital operating facilities are overbooked at the beginning of the week and underutilized toward the end of the week to meet physician preferences.

A less common version of the irregular demand situation is where supply is also variable and in fact fluctuates in a perverse way in relation to demand. For example, legal aid is more available to the poor in the summer (because of law students on vacations) but more in demand in the winter. Where demand and supply are both variable and move in opposite directions, the marketer has the option to attempt to (1) alter the supply pattern to fit the demand pattern, (2) alter the demand pattern to fit the natural supply pattern, or (3) alter both to some degree.

The marketing task of trying to resolve irregular demand is called *synchromarketing* because the effort is to bring the movements of demand and supply into better synchronization. Many marketing steps can be taken to alter the pattern of demand. For example, a museum that is undervisited on weekdays and overvisited on weekends could (a) shift most of the optional events to weekdays instead of weekends, (b) advertise only its weekday programs, (c) charge a higher admission price during the weekends. In some cases, a pattern of demand can be readily reshaped through simple switches in incentives·or promotion; in other cases, the reshaping may be achieved only after years of patient effort to alter habits and desires.

FULL DEMAND

The most desirable situation that a seller can face is that of full demand. *Full demand is a state in which the current level and timing of demand is equal to the desired level and timing of demand.* Various products and services achieve this condition from time to time. When this state is achieved, however, it is not a time for resting on one's laurels and doing simply automatic marketing. Market demand is subject to two erosive forces that might suddenly or gradually disrupt the equilibrium between demand and supply. One force is changing needs and tastes in the marketplace. The demand for engineering educations and church services have all undergone major declines because of changing market preferences. The other force is active competition. A condition of full demand is a signal inviting competitive attack. When a new product is doing well, new suppliers quickly move in and attempt to attract away some of the demand.

Thus the task of the marketer in the face of full demand is to maintain it. His job is *maintenance marketing*. This is essentially the task of the product manager whose product is highly successful. The task is not as challenging as other marketing tasks, such as conversional marketing or remarketing, in which creative new thinking must be given to the future of the product. However, maintenance marketing does call for maintaining efficiency in the carrying out of day-to-day marketing activities and eternal vigilance in monitoring possible new forces threatening demand erosion. The maintenance marketer is primarily concerned with tactical issues such as keeping the price right, keeping the quality up, and keeping the employees responsive to changing market needs.

OVERFULL DEMAND

Sometimes the demand for a product or service substantially begins to outpace the supply. Known as *overfull demand*, it is defined as *a state in which demand exceeds the level at which the marketer feels able or motivated to supply it*. It is essentially the reverse of the situation described earlier as faltering demand.

The task of reducing overfull demand is called *demarketing*. More formally, *demarketing deals with attempts to discourage customers in general or a certain class of customers in particular on either a temporary or permanent basis*.

There are two major types of demarketing situations: general demarketing and selective demarketing. *General demarketing* is undertaken by an organization when it wants to discourage overall demand for its offering. This can arise for two different reasons. First, it may have a *temporary shortage* of the product or service and want to get buyers to reduce their consumption. This situation was faced by various American cities beginning in 1973 as fuel supplies dried up. Second, the organization's offering may suffer from *chronic overpopularity*, and it may want to discourage permanently some demand rather than increase the size of its plant. This situation is faced by some small restaurants that suddenly are "discovered"; by the John F. Kennedy Center of the Arts in Washington, which draws larger crowds than it can handle, resulting in vandalism, damage to the property, and high cleaning bills; by certain tourist places, such as Hawaii, where the number of tourists has become excessive in terms of the objective of achieving a restful vacation; and by the Golden Gate Bridge in San Francisco, where authorities are urging motorists to reduce their use of the bridge. The Chinese mainland is engaged today in demarketing pork, a meat product that is historically more popular than beef in China but is in chronically short supply. U.S. electric power companies are demarketing certain uses of electricity because of the growing shortage of power generation facilities. Several of the far Western states are actively demarketing themselves as places to live because they are becoming overcrowded.[5]

Selective demarketing occurs when an organization does not wish to reduce everyone's demand but rather the demand coming from certain segments of the market. These segments or customer classes may be considered relatively unprofitable in themselves or undesirable in terms of their impact on other valued segments of the market. The seller may not be free to refuse sales outright, either as a matter of law or of public opinion, so he searches for other means to discourage demand from the unwanted customers.

Many examples could be cited. A renowned university wants to discourage marginal applicants because of all the paperwork and the wish to avoid rejecting so many applicants and creating bad feelings. A prepaid medical group practice wants to discourage its hypochondriac patients from running to them with every minor ailment. A police department wants to discourage nuisance calls so that its limited resources can be devoted to major crime prevention.

Demarketing largely calls for marketing in reverse. Instead of encouraging customers, it calls for the art of discouraging them. Prices may be raised, and product quality, service, promotion, and convenience reduced. The demarketer must have a thick skin because he is not going to be popular with certain groups. Some of the steps will appear to be unfair ways to ration a product or service. Some of the groups who are discriminated against may have just cause for complaint. Demarketing may be highly justified in some situations and ethically dubious in others.

UNWHOLESOME DEMAND

There are many products or services for which the demand may be judged unwholesome from the viewpoint of the customer's welfare, the public's welfare, or the supplier's welfare. *Unwholesome demand is a state in which any positive level of demand is felt to be excessive because of undesirable qualities associated with the offering.*

The task of trying to destroy the demand for something is called *countermarketing* or *unselling*. Whereas demarketing tries to reduce the demand without impugning the offering itself, countermarketing is an attempt to designate the offering as intrinsically unwholesome. The offering in question may be the organization's own product which it wishes to phase out, a competitor's product, or a third party's product which is regarded as socially undesirable.

Classic examples of unselling efforts have revolved around the so-called "vice" products: alcohol, cigarettes, and hard drugs. Various temperance groups mounted such an intense campaign that they succeeded in gaining the passage of the 18th Amendment banning the manufacture of alcoholic beverages. Antismoking groups managed to put enough pressure on the Surgeon General's office to get a law passed requiring cigarette manufacturers to add to each package the statement: "Warning: The Surgeon General Has Determined That Cigarette Smoking Is Dangerous to Your Health." They also sponsored many effective television commercials aimed at "unselling" the smoker. Later, they managed to get a law passed prohibiting cigarette advertising on television and radio. Anti-drug crusaders have sponsored advertising aimed at unselling the youth on the idea of drug usage.

Unselling appears in other contexts as well. Peace groups for years tried to unsell the Vietnam War. Population control groups have been trying to unsell the idea of large families. Nutrition groups have been trying to unsell the idea of eating pleasing but nutritionally poor foods. Environmental groups have been trying to unsell the idea of being careless with the environment as if it were inexhaustible.[6]

Unselling is the effort to accomplish the opposite of innovation. Whereas innovation is largely the attempt to add new things to the cultural inventory, unselling is the attempt to eliminate cultural artifacts or habits. It is an attempt to bring about the discontinuance of something. Whereas innovation usually ends with the act of adoption, unselling seeks to produce the act of disadoption. In the perspective of innovation theory,[7] unselling may be called the problem of *deinnovation*. Many of the concepts in innovation theory might be usable in reverse. The countermarketer attempts to identify the varying characteristics of the early, late, and laggard disadopters so that unselling effort can be aimed at them in this order. He also considers the characteristics of the product or service that will tend to facilitate unselling, such as relative disadvantage, incompatibility, complexity, indivisibility, and incommunicability.

At the same time, every effort to unsell something may also be viewed as an effort to sell something else. Those who attempt to unsell cigarette smoking are attempting to sell health; those who attempt to unsell large families are trying to sell small families; those who attempt to unsell the competitor's product are trying to increase the sales of their product. In fact, it is usually easier to sell something else. For example, instead of trying to unsell young people on drugs, the marketer can try to sell them on another way of achieving whatever they are seeking through drugs.

Efforts to turn off the demand for something can profitably draw on certain concepts and theories in psychology. In general, the effort is largely one of deconditioning or habit extinction theory. Instead of trying to build up a taste for something, the marketer is trying to break down a taste for something. Learning and reinforcement theory are suggestive in this connection. The marketer is trying to associate disgust, fear, disagreeableness, or shame with the use of the unwholesome object. He is trying to arouse unpleasant feelings in the potential or actual users of the product or service.

In addition to these psychological steps, the marketer also attempts to load the other marketing variables against the use of the unwholesome product or service. He tries to increase the real or perceived price. He tries to reduce the availability of the offering through reducing or destroying channels of distribution. He tries to find an alternative offering that is wholesome and that can be substituted for the current offering.

Clearly unselling is one of the most difficult and challenging marketing tasks. Unselling is an attempt to intervene in the lives and tastes of others. Unselling campaigns often backfire, as witness the popularity of X-rated movies and drugs whose evils are publicized. In its defense, however, two things must be said. First, unselling relies on exchange and communication approaches to bring about legal and/or public opinion changes. It is an alternative to violent social action. Second, unselling has as much social justification in a democracy as does selling. To set up a double standard where selling—say of alcohol and cigarettes—is allowable but unselling by those who object is not allowable would compromise the rights of free speech and orderly legislative due process.

SUMMARY

The marketer is a professional whose basic interest and skill lies in regulating the level, timing, and character of demand for a product, service, place, or idea. He faces up to eight different types of demand situations and plans accordingly. If demand is negative, it must be disabused (conversional marketing); if nonexistent, it must be created (stimulational marketing); if latent, it must be developed (developmental marketing); if faltering, it must be revitalized (remarketing); if irregular, it must be synchronized (synchromarketing); if full, it must be maintained (maintenance marketing); if overfull, it must be reduced (demarketing); and finally, if unwholesome, it must be destroyed (countermarketing). Each demand situation calls for a particular set of psychological concepts and marketing strategies and may give rise to task specialization. Managerial marketing deals with not just an effort to build or maintain demand but also with a variety of problems that an organization might face in its relation to a market.

NOTES

1. A classic discussion of alternative methods of modifying people's feelings is found in Kurt Lewin, "Group Decision and Social Change," in *Readings in Social Psychology*, Theodore M. Newcomb and Eugene L. Hartley, eds. (New York: Holt, Rinehart and Winston, Inc., 1952).

2. New behavioral therapies such as implosive therapy and systematic desensitization are discussed by Perry London, *Behavior Control* (New York: Harper and Row, 1969).

3. See the teaching case, "The United Methodist Church" (Boston: Harvard Business School, 1971).

4. "Watching Rebirth of a Maternity Home," *Chicago Sun Times*, November 21, 1972, Section Two, p. 1.

5. "The Great Wild Californicated West," *Time*, August 21, 1972, p. 15.

6. These causes form a large part of "social marketing" and are taken up in greater detail in Chapter 15.

7. See Everett M. Rogers, *Diffusion of Innovations* (New York: The Free Press, 1962).

QUESTIONS

1. The WCTU is an old organization that recently fought and lost what may have been its last battle. Over WCTU opposition, the city council of Evanston, Illinois—home of the WCTU's national headquarters—voted to allow liquor to be served in city restaurants. What would you advise the WCTU to do after this defeat?

2. Is it easy for the marketer to distinguish between no demand and latent demand?

3. A recent rash of murders at tourist hotels has almost completely cut off the tourist trade in the U.S. Virgin Islands. Some people feel that the murders have been racially motivated while others feel they have been motivated by economic considerations. What kind of marketing task does the tourist council of the islands face?

4. An army dentist who believes in "preventive dentistry" (flossing, gum massaging, fluoride treatments, frequent checkups, restorative work,

etc.) for the men in the service faces different marketing tasks. What are they?

5. A hospital in a large city does not know what to do about the enormous number of visitors it gets each day. The hospital's parking facilities cannot handle all the people, and patients, doctors, and nurses complain all the time about the noise the visitors create. What should the hospital do?

6. The American Cancer Society faces a rather full demand situation. The public is quite willing to donate funds to this organization. What kinds of things could happen to put the Society in another demand situation and what can be done to prevent this from happening?

7. In many museums there is a conflict between the education department and the curatorial staff. The education department would like to maximize the number of visitors on the theory that the museum exists to serve the cultural needs of the large public. The curatorial staff would like to minimize the number of museum visitors because they take curators' time away from scholarship and use up scarce funds on education that could go into acquisition. The education department in most museums has the upper hand today. If the curatorial staff gained more power and wanted to make the museum less responsive to the general public, what steps might it take to demarket the museum?

6 Market Structure Analysis

Though all men be made of one metal, yet they be not cast all in one mold.

JOHN LYLY

Let us assume that an organization is facing one of the marketing problems described in Chapter 5. Somehow it is unsatisfied with the transactions taking place in a particular market. It wants to build up, maintain, revitalize, or reduce demand. In order to be effective at this task, the organization will need first-hand knowledge of this market. It needs to analyze and grasp the market's structure and behavior. The task it faces is called *market analysis*. Market analysis is an essential prerequisite for effective marketing action.

Market analysis consists of two parts. The first part is called *market structure analysis*. Any market consisting of more than one member will have a structure insofar as the members have different needs, perceptions, and preferences. In most cases, the organization cannot serve the whole market with equal facility and must make a choice among the parts that it will serve. Market structure analysis consists of four steps. The first step is *market definition,* the determination of all the actual and potential members of the market. The second step is *market segmentation,* the identification of meaningfully different parts of the market. The third step is *market positioning,* the choice of the parts of the market to which the organization will relate. The fourth step is called *market orchestration,* the work of harmonizing the marketing program to the different market segments served by the organization. This chapter will deal with these four issues in market structure analysis.

The second part of market analysis is *consumer analysis.* Once an organization has taken a position in a market, it must maintain the most current information on the needs, perceptions, preferences, and satisfaction of the consumers in that market. This information is vital in developing marketing programs that will be effective in accomplishing the organization's goals. Consumer analysis is the subject of the following chapter.

MARKET DEFINITION

The first step facing an organization that is seeking to deal in a market is to define that market's boundaries. The market for a product or service does not consist of everybody. Not everyone is in the market for a university education, or day-care center services, or cancer treatment, or a job with a police department. Organizations offering these products and services must determine who is in the market.

We will start with the concept of a product. *Product* will be defined broadly *to include physical objects, services, persons, places, organizations, and ideas.* The particular product must be described specifically because this affects the size and composition of the market. If the product is defined as health service, then the market consists of everyone in the world. If the product is defined as a smokers' clinic, then the market consists of everyone who smokes. If the product is defined as a smokers' clinic that meets weekly on Tuesday evenings at the Passavant Hospital in Chicago, then the market consists of all smokers who might find this product accessible. If the product is defined as the same clinic charging $1,000 for treatment, then the market consists of all smokers who find this product accessible and the price acceptable. The more specifically the product is defined, the smaller is the market size. Also, the less attractively the product is defined, the smaller is the market size.

Now a product is something with want-satisfying attributes. For example, a smokers' clinic will provide smokers with the chance to gain better health, greater self-control, more harmonious family relations, and other benefits. We can ask who is in the market for this product—that is, who has a set of wants that may be satisfied by this product's attributes. We can imagine three possibilities and illustrate them using Venn diagrams (see Figure 6-1).[1] The circle on the left in each case represents the product's attributes and the circle on the right represents a particular person's wants. The first case shows no interaction between the product's attributes and the person's wants. There is nothing about the product that appeals to that person. If the product is a smokers' clinic, the person is either a nonsmoker or a smoker who has no interest in any of the benefits that might be attained through this product. Such a person is not in the market for the service of a smokers' clinic.

FIGURE 6-1

Defining a Person's Relation to a Product

A. No Market

Product's   Person's
attributes   wants

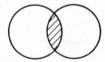

B. Potential Market

Product's   Person's
attributes   wants

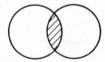

C. Actual Market

Product's   Person's
attributes   wants

The second case shows a small overlap in the want-satisfying attributes of the product and the wants of the person. This person is a member of the *potential market* for the services of this clinic in the sense that he is capable of becoming interested in acquiring or consuming it under the right circumstances.

The third case shows a major overlap in the product's attributes and the person's wants. This person is strongly attracted to the product and can be considered to be in the *actual market*.

Because different degrees of overlap might occur, the boundary between the potential and actual market is not easy to establish. We simply use the actual market to describe persons who are currently willing and ready to acquire or consume the product or are currently using it.

The degree-of-overlap test can be applied in principle to everyone in the population. Were this done, then the boundaries of a market would become readily apparent. Figure 6-2 illustrates the hypothetical

FIGURE 6-2
The Results of a Market Definition

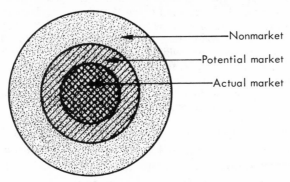

results of a market definition exercise. The total circle represents all possible people, each represented by a point. The market consists of the two inner circles, with the nonmarket consisting of the outer circle. The larger of the two inner circles represents the potential market. The smallest circle represents the actual market.

The relative size of the two inner circles would vary from situation to situation. Consider, for example, the market for police recruits. Because most people are not in the market for a police job, the outer nonmarket circle would be extremely large. The actual market circle would be very small and there would be a slightly larger circle of potential recruits who have never thought about being a policeman but who might become interested if they thought about the job and its benefits.

We have defined the market as consisting of those who have an actual or potential interest in the product. We must add a further requirement, that these persons also have resources desired by the organization which they might conceivably trade for the product. Returning to the police recruitment illustration, we can imagine a number of persons who might want to join a police force but cannot offer the resources wanted by the police department in exchange for the job. For example, an eighty-year-old man might want to join but would be ruled out because he cannot bring the needed level of energy to the job. In fact, police departments set up tight definitions of the resources they would accept in exchange for the job.

> The Austin, Texas, police department limits the market to persons who are between 21 and 35, weigh at least 140 pounds but are not excessively overweight, stand between 5'7" and 6'5", have 20-40 uncorrected vision, are in "good physical health," have a high school diploma, do not have any felony convictions, have "acceptable" profiles on the Minnesota Multiphasic Personality Inventory, and have "acceptable" scores on the General Knowledge and the Police Adaptability examinations. A 1968 recruitment campaign by the Austin Police Department attracted 556 interested persons for personal interviews. Following the personal interview, it was found that 160 were not qualified to take the examinations and 144 were not willing. Of the 282 who took the examination, 136 failed and 146 passed. However, 86 of those who passed the examinations were either eliminated by the background investigation or lack of interest or the fact that they took other jobs during the three or four weeks that the investigation usually takes.[2]

Thus a market for a given product is made up of all persons (and organizations) who might have a conceivable interest in a product and the right resources to exchange for the product. The market is delimited both by the person's ability to recognize want-satisfying attributes in the product and by the organization's delineation of the resources that it would accept in exchange for the product.

Most organizations offer a product line rather than a single product and therefore their total markets represent the union of all the markets for their separate products. Each new product increases the size of the total market facing the organization. The extent to which market size increases depends upon the degree of overlap between the existing and the new product. If the new product is very different from the existing products, then it will substantially increase the total market facing the organization.

To illustrate this, consider the market facing a college. Suppose the college teaches only one course, accounting. The market consists of all people who might be interested in studying accounting at this school and who could pay the necessary tuition. The situation is illustrated in Figure 6-3A. On the left is a box representing the organization, and a circle within the box representing its single product, accounting. On the right is a circle representing the market for accounting. Now suppose that the college adds other business courses, such as marketing and finance. Each separate course is of interest to a potential market but there is a great overlap in the potential markets because of the close interrelatedness of the courses. Figure 6-3B shows the market for this set of courses as a set of high overlapping circles. Now suppose the college adds a music department and an engineering department in addition to a business department. Because these programs provide widely different want satisfactions, they will appeal to widely different markets and each will add a substantial market potential to the school. Thus the size and composition of the market depends on the number of products offered by the organization and their heterogeneity.

MARKET SEGMENTATION

Suppose the organization has defined the market for some product it offers. It knows who is interested in the product (the actual market), who might be interested (the potential market), and who would not be interested (the nonmarket). It recognizes that those in the market do not all have the same intensity of interest in the product. Nor does the organization have the same intensity of interest in all the members of the market. As a result, the organization is interested in a further step after market definition. This step is called market segmentation and consists of *dividing the market into fairly homogeneous parts where any part may conceivably be selected as a market target to be reached with a distinct marketing mix.*

The importance of market segmentation cannot be overemphasized. An organization cannot attain any marketing efficiency if it treats the whole market as having equal product interest and equal resources. Some parts of the market will inevitably be more responsive to the product offer than others. A blood bank organization, for example, does not go after everyone just because everyone has blood. People vary in their readiness to donate blood and in the quality of their blood. The blood bank organization will want to appeal to those parts of the market that have the highest response and resource potential.

FIGURE 6-3
Market Size as a Function of Product Line

A. Single Product Offer

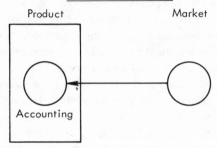

B. Product Line Homogeneity

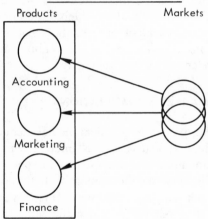

C. Product Line Heterogeneity

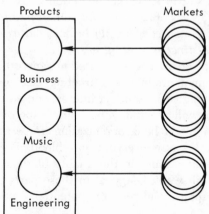

Determining Market Structure

There is no unique way to divide a market into segments. The *market structure* is the result of the particular variables used to analyze the market. These variables are called the segmenting variables.

This important point is illustrated in Figure 6-4. Figure 6-4A shows

FIGURE 6-4

Different Approaches to Market Segmentation

A. No market
segmentation

B. Complete market
segmentation

C. Market segmentation
by income classes
1, 2, and 3

D. Market segmentation
by age classes
a and b

E. Market segmentation
by income–age class

a hypothetical market consisting of six persons who share some need in common. If only the common need is considered, and no differences are recognized among the six members of the market, then the market would be conceived as homogeneous and without further structure. This means that the organization would relate to all six members of the market in the same fashion and make the same offer. There is no basis indicated for differential opportunity or marketing in this market.

At the other extreme, the organization can choose to see the six members of this market as all being different. This is shown in Figure 6-4B. The members may all differ from each other on only one segmenting variable, such as age, or on several variables in combination. Ultimately, they can be seen as different because each occupies a different physical space, even if no other differences are apparent. This view of the market results in a market structure consisting of six parts, equal to the number of members of the market. Each member of the market can be studied separately in terms of the benefits he is seeking and his resources. Normally, this degree of market segmentation is only justified where there are few members in the market and each is big and important to the organization. For example, many universities seeking money from foundations treat each of the major foundations as a quite separate entity, because each has different standards, resources, and procedures for making grants.

Most organizations do not find it worthwhile to study every individual member of the market and "customize" the product and marketing program to each buyer's needs and tastes. Instead, the organization generally searches for broad groupings of buyers who can be approached as separate segments. The organization may choose to deal with all these segments or to concentrate on one or a few of them.

Suppose the organization believes that income is a significant variable for conceptualizing the parts of the market. Figure 6-4C shows the market segmented into three income classes. A number (1, 2, or 3) is used to identify each buyer's income class. Lines are drawn around prospects in the same income class. Segmentation by income class results in three segments, the most numerous one being income class 1 in the illustration.

On the other hand, the organization may find pronounced differences in product interest between younger and older members of the market. In Figure 6-4D the same individuals are shown, except a letter (a or b) is used to indicate the buyer's age class. Segmentation of the market by age class results in two segments, both equal in size.

It may turn out that income and age class both count heavily on differentiating the buyer's behavior toward the product. The organization may find it desirable to partition the market according to those joint characteristics. In terms of the illustration, the market can be broken into the following six segments: 1a, 1b, 2a, 2b, 3a, and 3b. Figure 6-4E shows that segment 1a contains two buyers, segment 2a contains no buyers (a null segment), and each of the other segments contains one buyer. In general, as the market is segmented on the basis of a larger set of joint characteristics, the marketer creates smaller and more numerous segments. If the marketer tried to segment the market using all conceivable characteristics, he would soon arrive again at Figure 6-4(b), where each buyer would be a separate segment.

Thus we see that market segmentation is a creative conceptual art that results each time in some particular view of market structure. Often some particular market structure dominates the thinking of organizations that deal in that market, only to be upset in time by some fresh thinking that leads someone to conceive of the market structure in some new way, suggesting new opportunities for serving it and transacting with it.

Segmentation Variables

Because market structure depends on the choice of segmenting variables, it is critically important to appreciate the major variables that can be used for segmenting a market. Table 6-1 lists most of the important

TABLE 6-1

Major Segmentation Variables and their Typical Breakdowns

Variables	*Typical Breakdowns*
Geographic	
Region	Pacific; Mountain; West North Central; West South Central; East North Central; East South Central; South Atlantic; Middle Atlantic; New England
County size	A; B; C; D
City or S.M.S.A. size	Under 5,000–19,999; 20,000–49,999; 50,000–99,999; 100,000–249,999; 250,000–499,999; 500,000–999,-999; 1,000,000–3,999,999; 4,000,000 or over
Density	Urban; suburban; rural
Climate	Northern; Southern
Demographic	
Age	Under 6; 6–11; 12–17; 18–34; 35–49; 50–64; 65+
Sex	Male; female
Family size	1–2; 3–4; 5+
Family life cycle	Young, single; young, married, no children; young, married, youngest child under 6; young, married, youngest child 6 or over; older, married, with children; older, married, no children under 18; older, single; other
Income	Under $5,000; $5,000–$7,999; $8,000–$9,999; $10,000–$14,999; over $15,000
Occupation	Professional and technical; managers, officials, and proprietors; clerical, sales; craftsmen, foremen; operatives; farmers; retired; students, housewives; unemployed
Education	Grade school or less; some high school; graduated high school; some college; graduated college

TABLE 6-1
Continued

Variables	Typical Breakdowns
Religion	Catholic; Protestant; Jewish; other
Race	White; Negro; Oriental
Nationality	American; British; French; German; Eastern European; Scandinavian; Italian; Spanish; Latin American, Middle Eastern; Japanese and so on.
Social class	Lower-lower; upper-lower; lower-middle; middle-middle; upper-middle; lower-upper; upper-upper
Psychographic	
Life style	Swinger; status seeker; plain Joe; etc.
Personality	Compulsive; gregarious; conservative; ambitious; etc.
Benefits sought	Economy; convenience; dependability; prestige; etc.
User status	Nonuser; potential user; first-time user; regular user; ex-user
Usage rate	Light user; medium user; heavy user
Loyalty status	None; medium; strong; absolute
Readiness stage	Unaware; aware; informed; interested; desirous; intending to buy

variables and their major breakdowns. They fall into three major classes: geographic variables, demographic variables, and psychographic variables. Not all segmentation variables are appropriate for every market. Industrial markets are usually segmented on such bases as customer size, location, industrial classification, and usage rate. Consumer markets are usually segmented on such bases as income, age, and family size. Fund-raising markets are usually segmented on such bases as donor type, donor motive, and donor size. Political markets are usually segmented by voter age, income, occupation, and party affiliation.

The major bases for market segmentation have changed through time. The earliest segmentation variables were geographic; later, demographic variables came into general use; and most recently, psychographic variables. Here we will look more closely at each major category of segmentation variables.

Geographic Segmentation. A major form of segmentation is geographic, for which the market is subdivided into the different locations in which members of the market are found. The locations are signified by geographical units such as nations, states, counties, cities, or neighborhoods.

Geographic segmentation is undertaken because of the varying response potentials and costs of serving different market locations. Given the geographical structure of the market, the organization decides which part(s) it could serve best. A small hospital will cater to the local residents; a major research hospital will serve patients from all over the world. Most city museums solicit support and membership from the local citizens; a major museum such as the Smithsonian Institute in Washington, D.C. solicits membership from all parts of the country.

Demographic Segmentation. Another form of segmentation is demographic, in which the market is subdivided into different parts on the basis of demographic variables such as age, sex, family size, income, occupation, education, family life cycle, religion, nationality, or social class. The term "demographic" covers factors helpful in grouping large populations independent of product interests or psychological characteristics. Demographic variables have long been the most popular bases for distinguishing significant groupings in the marketplace. One reason is that consumer interest is often highly associated with demographic variables; another is that demographic variables are easier to recognize and measure than are most other types of variables.

For example, a family planning agency may be interested in segmenting the market for vasectomies. Suppose the organization's marketing research reveals three important demographic variables: age of male head of household, number of children, and level of income. Figure 6-5 shows a joint segmentation of the market according to these three variables. Each variable is subdivided into the number of levels deemed useful for analysis; the result is 27(=3 × 3 × 3) distinct segments. Every family belongs to one of these 27 segments. Having conceptualized the market structure in this way, the agency can proceed to determine each

Figure 6-5

**Segmentation of the Vasectomy Market
by Three Demographic Variables**

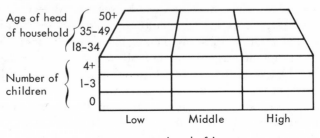

market segment's "buying" potential for vasectomies, the most appropriate segments to aim for, and the most effective marketing programs to use.

Psychographic Segmentation. The third category of segmentation variables is psychographic. Psychographic variables tend to refer more to the individual and his makeup, life style, attitudes, and behavior patterns. People within the same demographic group can exhibit vast differences in these variables. Psychographic factors are critical in the search for a significant structure to the market for the purpose of recognizing market opportunity or serving needs more effectively.

Life style refers to the distinctive mode of orientation an individual or group has toward consumption, work, and play. Such terms as "hippies," "swingers," "straights," and "jet-setters," are all descriptive of different life styles. Each life style group has a particular orientation toward clothes, work habits, time, space, friends, and recreations. The importance of life-style differences can be illustrated for a welfare agency. The poor can be said to consist of at least two life-style groups. One group accepts the culture of poverty. Another group works hard and saves as much as it can to escape from poverty. The job of a welfare agency is to differentiate between these two groups and design different programs for them.[3]

Personality may also be a useful variable for classifying the members of a market. In recruiting policemen, police departments attempt to screen out applicants whose personalities may be psychopathic. Propagandists for a fanatic cause attempt to target their message to the psychological type that Eric Hoffer calls "the true believer."[4] There is some evidence that persons who must achieve a high degree of order in their lives are highly subject to frustration and headaches, thus making them larger users of aspirins and other medical services.[5]

Benefits sought constitute another useful psychographic variable. The members of a market are typically looking for different benefits.[6] Some buyers look for one benefit in choosing a brand and others seek a particular *benefit bundle*.[7] The religious market can be benefit-segmented according to those seeking spiritual purity, salvation, good deeds, or sociability. The art market can be segmented according to those seeking peak esthetic experiences, cultural edification, or short-term diversion. An organization in these markets can attempt to offer all of these benefits to attract the largest number of consumers, or concentrate on offering one benefit in the extreme to develop a program of high satisfaction for that benefit segment.

User status is a segmentation of the market according to whether a person is a nonuser, potential user, ex-user, first-time user, or regular user of a product. This segmentation variable is helpful to anti-drug agencies in planning their education programs and campaigns. Much of their effort is directed at identifying potential users of hard drugs and discouraging them through information and persuasive campaigns. They also sponsor rehabilitation programs to help regular users who want to quit their habit. They utilize ex-users in various programs to add credibility to their effort.

User rate refers to the fact that users of a product vary in their amount of consumption per period from light to medium to heavy. Heavy users may constitute only a small percent of the numerical size of the market but account for a major percent of the unit volume consumed.[8] Marketers make a great effort to determine the demographic characteristics and media habits of the heavy users and aim their marketing programs at them. An anti-smoking campaign, for example, might be aimed at the heaviest smokers, a safe driving campaign may be aimed at those having the most accidents, and a family planning campaign may be aimed at those likely to have the most children.

Loyalty status describes the amount of loyalty a user has to a particular object. The amount of loyalty can range from zero to absolute. We find buyers who are absolutely loyal to a brand (such as Budweiser beer, Crest toothpaste, Cadillac automobiles); to an organization (such as IBM, the Republican Party, or Harvard University); to a place (such as New England or Southern California); and so on. A new organization in a market has to appraise the number of loyals, their distribution over the competing entities, and their degrees of loyalty, in order to assess its own opportunities and possible positioning. Loyalties change slowly and most organizations do not try to pull away those loyal to others but to build up a loyal group out of the nonloyals.

Finally, *stage of readiness* is also useful in segmenting a market. At any point of time, there is a particular distribution of people in various stages of readiness for buying the product. Some members of the potential market are unaware of the product; some aware; some informed; some interested; some desirous; and some intending to buy. The particular distribution of people over stages of readiness makes a big difference in planning the marketing program. Suppose the concept of an annual breast cancer detection examination is formulated by a health agency. The market is described at this point in Figure 6-6A. Most of the potential market is unaware of the concept. In this state, most of the marketing effort should go toward awareness-producing advertising and publicity using a simple message. If successful, the market will shift to the configuration shown in Figure 6-6B. At this point, the advertising should begin to use more copy to explain the nature and purpose of an annual examination and begin to target certain market segments such as the poor, with more message frequency. After more knowledge is generated

FIGURE 6-6
Stages of Market Readiness

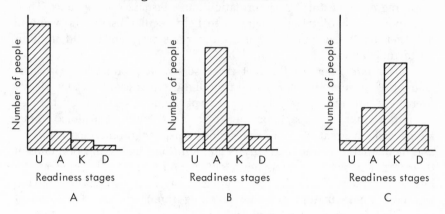

U = unaware, A = aware only, K = knowledgeable, D = desirous

(see Figure 6-6C), advertising should attempt to dramatize the benefits of taking an annual examination and the risks of not taking it, so as to move more people into a stage of desire. Facilities should also be readied for handling the large number of women who may be motivated to take the examination. In general, the marketing program must be adjusted to the changing market profile.

Alternative Strategies toward Market Segments

An organization can adopt one of three possible strategies toward a market in which it has an interest. These strategies are known as undifferentiated marketing, concentrated marketing, and differentiated marketing.

Undifferentiated marketing occurs when an organization decides to treat the whole market as homogeneous, focusing on what is common to all the members of the market rather than what is different; in this case the organization engages in no market segmentation. An example of this is "mass marketing," when an organization acts as if its offer has great and equal appeal to everyone. A politician who projects one message to everyone and tries to bend everyone to his views is doing undifferentiated marketing. A family planning organization that tries to convince everyone that one particular form of birth control is best is doing undifferentiated marketing. We will not say much about undifferentiated marketing because it is normally ineffective and misses the force of the modern marketing concept, which calls for paying close attention to market differences as a basis for achieving transactional success.

Concentrated marketing occurs when an organization decides to divide the market into meaningful segments and devote its major marketing effort to one segment. Instead of spreading itself thin in many parts of the market, it concentrates on serving a particular market segment well. Through concentrated marketing the organization usually achieves a strong following and standing in a particular market segment. It enjoys greater knowledge of the market segment's needs and behavior and it also achieves operating economies through specialization in production, distribution, and promotion. This type of marketing is done, for example, by a private museum that decides to concentrate only on African art; or an environmental group that concentrates only on the problem of noise pollution; or a private foundation that awards grants only to transportation researchers.

Differentiated marketing occurs when an organization decides to operate in two or more segments of the market and to design separate product and/or marketing programs for each. By doing this it hopes to attain a greater impact in each segment. It hopes that a deep position in several segments will increase the market's overall identification of the organization with the product field. It hopes for greater loyalty because its offerings are tailored to each segment's desires rather than the other way around. Differentiated marketing is practiced by a family planning agency that provides different birth control programs to meet the needs and desires of different segments of the market; and by a church that runs different programs tailored to teenagers, young adults, middle-aged adults, and senior citizens.

The actual choice of a marketing strategy depends on specific factors facing the organization. If the organization has *limited resources,* it will probably choose concentrated marketing because it does not have enough resources to relate to the whole market and/or to tailor special services for each segment. If the market is fairly *homogeneous* in its needs and desires, the organization will probably choose undifferentiated marketing because little would be gained by differentiated offerings. If the organization aspires to be a leader in several segments of the market, it will choose differentiated marketing. If *competitors* have already established dominance in all but a few segments of the market, the organization might try to concentrate its marketing in one of the remaining segments. Many organizations start out with a strategy of undifferentiated or concentrated marketing and if they are successful, evolve into a strategy of differentiated marketing.

If an organization decides on a strategy of concentrated marketing, it will have to determine the best segment of the market to concentrate on. Its problem is that of effective *market positioning*. It wants to locate a segment of the market that is relatively underserved and to which it can bring the necessary services and resources. If an organization decides on a strategy of undifferentiated or differentiated marketing, it will find that different market segments are often in conflict with each other. That is, the segments served are not compatible and pose a delicate problem for the organization. We can describe this as the problem of *market orchestration*. The problems of market positioning and market orchestration are described in the following sections.

MARKET POSITIONING

Market positioning occurs when an organization makes a careful study of the structure of a market in order to identify a viable niche in which to locate. Instead of being content to duplicate the style and efforts of other organizations in the market, it seeks a niche where it can make its own distinctive contribution. Market positioning for a new hospital means taking into account where existing hospitals are positioned in the array of health-care needs of the population and defining a distinctive role that it might play. Market positioning for an environmental action group means taking into account what other environmental action groups are doing and defining a distinctive contribution that it could make to the overall environmental cause. For a local political candidate, market positioning means taking into account the array of people's needs and the offerings of different candidates and then determining a viable position to assume in relation to the other candidates.

College Market Positioning: An Example

The positioning concept will be illustrated at greater length with an educational example. Suppose a new president takes over a small college in the Midwest that has not had a distinguished history. The college has coasted along each year, drawing just enough students and alumni contributions. Several vacancies on the faculty are about to occur. The president sees this as an opportunity to initiate a new phase in the college's history that would generate some educational excitement.

Discussions with a number of students lead him to believe that potential students see existing colleges along at least two dimensions. The first is the intellectual level of each college; the second is the amount of freedom each college offers the students to choose their own courses of study. These two dimensions are shown in Figure 6-7. The two dimensions are drawn perpendicularly to suggest that there is no necessary

Figure 6-7

Market Structure and Competitive Niches
of Small Midwestern Colleges

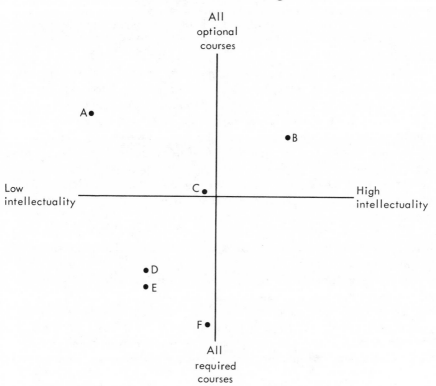

correlation seen between them. A third dimension could be added to the diagram by creating a three-dimensional space but here the diagram will be kept simple.

The diagram shows the competitive niches of various Midwest colleges in this market space. College A stands out as offering a program of low intellectual calibre and a high number of optional courses. It is commonly called "a snap school." College B offers mostly optional courses but is of high intellectual calibre. College C occupies a niche of middling intellectuality and optionality. It is highly predictable that an organization will be found near the center of any market axis to supply a middling amount of both dimensions. At the same time, College C probably has a less distinctive image precisely because it avoids extremes. Usually distinctiveness belongs to the schools that take extreme positions and define the market space by so doing.

Colleges D and E occupy roughly the same competitive niches, both offering a fairly traditional program (a good number of required courses) and a low to medium level of intellectual quality. In occupying the same niche, the two colleges share whatever demand exists in this market segment. If they both survive, it is because there is a strong demand level for this blend of educational offer. College F is somewhat distinctive in requiring all students to take the same program although it is of medium intellectual quality.

With this information, the president has managed to clarify the field of opportunities. The most striking revelation of this market structuring is the total absence of any college in the lower right quadrant, particularly at the extreme. This would be a college that offered a highly intellectual and fully specified program. It would be like the old college program of the University of Chicago under Robert M. Hutchins, in which all students had to take a fully specified general education. The bachelor's degree meant that they had read and examined the great ideas in each of several knowledge areas. A new college of this type would be uniquely positioned in the market.

There is, of course, an important question that must be researched before any decision is made; that is, whether or not there is a sufficient demand for this product. The fact that no college at the present time occupies this position could indicate that it is not a viable market niche. Of course, it also could mean that no college has perceived the opportunity. In either case, a college must do further research to test this product concept on a sample of prospective students. This must be supplemented by a study of the trends in educational curricula, student preferences, and the fortunes of this type of college in other parts of the country.

It must be added that the market structure analysis may also reveal other interesting opportunities. The map in Figure 6-7 really shows only the perceived positions of existing colleges and not the preference or demand densities on the part of college-bound students. Suppose we prepare another map showing densities of preference in this space.[9] These preference densities are shown as circles in Figure 6-8, the size of the circle being proportional to the level of demand for that type of product. The results are very revealing. For example:

1. College C is responding to the area of greatest demand. In fact, if college C is small, its chances for successful expansion are high. If it chooses to remain small, there is a viable opportunity for another college starting in this area and being successful.

2. The coexistence of colleges D and E in the same competitive niche is explained by a fairly large demand intensity in this position. The two colleges may so adequately supply this demand that there is no opportunity for a third college in this segment of the market.

FIGURE 6-8
Demand Intensity in the Market Space

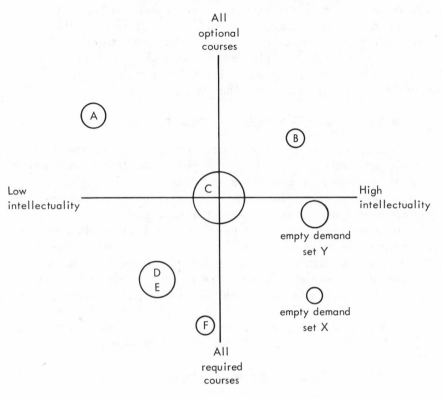

3. College F appears to serve a rather small market, and this may explain why the college is small and having trouble attracting a sufficient number of students. Not enough students want a preset program in a college of medium intellectual quality.

4. There is a viable demand (empty demand set X) where the president is thinking of positioning his college. However, it should also be noted that there is an even larger segment of students looking for a demanding intellectual program in which they are free to elect about half of the courses (empty demand set Y).

Thus the president must consider carefully at least three market opportunities: locating in the same position of C to take advantage of the strong demand, or locating in empty demand set X or Y. If the revamped college is to be a profit-maximizing organization, it should undertake further studies of these three opportunities and project the expected discounted cash flows that could be expected from the three market positions. It should consider whether demand intensities in these locations would widen or narrow over time, and whether other existing schools or new schools are likely to locate in these market positions. As a nonprofit institution however, it will try to satisfy other than profit criteria. It may want to carry out a benefit/cost analysis oriented to the social good, or it might simply want to give high priority to the desires and conceptions of the trustees with respect to what type of education they think should be supplied to this market.

Market Positioning with Respect to Other Publics

Market positioning has been analyzed on the assumption that the organization is trying to relate to one public and that its relations to other publics are a secondary concern. This is a fairly safe assumption to make in many cases. The organization can define its relations to other publics after it defines its relation to the main market.

In other cases, positioning must be done with simultaneous consideration of the major markets and publics. If a new college elects to be in position X, prospective students will see it clearly, but what are the implications for raising funds, recruiting faculty, getting media coverage, placing students in jobs, and so on? The college really has to position itself not in a single market space but in a multiple market space. Put another way, any position it takes with respect to one public will require compatible and viable positioning with respect to other publics.

MARKET ORCHESTRATION

If an organization decides to serve more than one market segment, it faces at least two additional questions. First, which market segments should be included? The organization must draw a boundary around those segments that it will include in its plans. This can be called the *target market range*. It is very important to include market segments that are compatible with each other—that is, that can be easily orchestrated.

The second question is how important should each segment be in the organization's total operations? Although several segments may be served, they are not all equal in attractiveness. The organization has to determine *segment representation ratios*—that is, desirable percentages of representation of the segments in the target market range.

The Concept of Target Market Range

The concept of target market range will be described for the case of a political candidate seeking a national office. Suppose this candidate analyzes the voter market and finds that it consists of the two major dimensions shown in Figure 6-9.[10] The horizontal axis is a dimension ranging from liberal to conservative voter tastes. The vertical axis is a dimension ranging from a preference for less versus more government involvement.

Suppose Candidate X's preferred position in this political space is shown by the dot in the lower left quadrant. That is, he takes a liberal position and favors a strong government role. If he wanted this to come across very clearly to the voters, he would position himself in this location at every opportunity and contrast his position with the other candidates, even those somewhat near him. This would be concentrated marketing. If voters voted purely on the basis of a candidate's position, he would win 100 percent of the votes in the immediate segment surrounding him. To the extent that voters were also influenced by the candidate's personality and experience, he would get somewhat less than all the votes in this segment. He would also get some votes in other segments depending upon how close he and competing candidates were located to each voter segment.

FIGURE 6-9
Candidate X's Target Orchestration

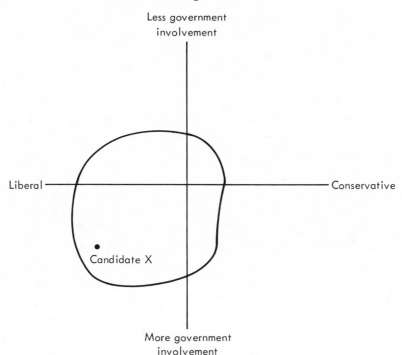

Now the candidate realizes that he will not win the election by simply winning nearly 100 percent of one segment. Whereas a profit-making firm might find that substantial sales in one segment would produce sufficient profits, a political candidate needs a plurality vote to win an election. The political candidate cannot afford a strategy of market concentration.

This immediately leads to the question of how much market space he will try to appeal to. Let us assume that he cannot afford to pursue the other extreme of undifferentiated marketing because (a) it will bring in some undesirable segments with whom he does not want to be associated and (b) it will so diffuse his image that no one will find the candidate highly to his liking. There is a great suspicion of the candidate who promises something to everyone. For these reasons, the candidate wants to appeal strongly and differentially to several segments.

The candidate must define the *range of market space* over which he will devote his effort. This range is illustrated as the almost-circular space in Figure 6-9. It covers several segments of the voter market while excluding other segments. For example, the candidate will try to draw some support from the mildly conservative and from the mildly anti-government voters. He will not, however, go after extreme conservative or anti-government voters. On the other hand, he will not try to appeal to the radicals or to those who want too much government involvement. In general, the range defines a feasible space of target segments given the candidate's background, objectives, and existing public image.

It should be noted that the candidate's ideal position is not necessarily in the exact center of the target market range. In fact, the target market range is not always a continuous set of neighboring segments. The candidate can conceivably go after select segments in different parts of the market space if some overall consistency can be established. For example, the election of Governor Walker of Illinois illustrates the choice of a noncontinuous target market range:

> The segments that Walker went after were the blue-collar suburbanites, seeking new forms of expression for their muted anger; the wealthier suburbanites, with an expanding appetite for independent politics; and the Downstaters, neglected and with a deep distrust of Chicago machine goings-on.

Before mass communications became so important in political contests, the politician had an easy time with this problem. The various voter segments were in relative isolation from each other and could be reached as individual segments by a candidate. He could attend a union meeting and say one thing and then attend a businessmen's luncheon and say the opposite thing. He could always claim that he was misquoted by the press if the contradiction was discovered and pointed out. In effect, he multiplied his product offerings. He represented a different product on each occasion, and each voter segment heard pretty much what they wanted. With the advent of radio, and more recently television, the candidate's statements became broadcasted rather than narrowcasted. Voters from various segments were now in the same audience at the same time. The candidate could not prevent "leakage" of his tailored message to unintended audiences. He was forced to become more vague about his real position because he needed to please a mass audience. Often he failed to please anyone very much.

Mass communications have reduced but not completely eliminated the ability of the candidate to use differentiated marketing. The candidate dresses differently for different audiences, emphasizes different issues, and sends different "representatives" to negotiate with the leaders of the various voter segments. He uses young people to reach youth, black leaders to reach black voters, and senior citizens to reach older voters. He does not make an equal effort to win each segment but instead establishes priorities and desired degrees of penetration based on the size and responsiveness of the various segments to his candidacy. He seeks to orchestrate a winning coalition. His job is to render multiple messages to the chosen market segments that have a coherent totality.

The Concept of the Segment Representation Ratios

Besides defining the target market range, the organization has to be specific about the degree to which each segment will be pursued. The organization has limited time and resources. Not all segments in the target market range are equally important or attractive. In the case of a politician, he will have to decide on how his time and resources will be allocated over the target segments. He wants to allocate his time in a way that will yield a plurality of votes from the whole market. He can try to attract most of the votes of a few segments or some of the votes from many segments. He has to determine the *segment representation ratios*.

It is not possible to portray these ratios on the two-dimensional diagram used to portray market space because this diagram does not indicate the numerical sizes of the different market segments. Another method of mapping will be used, that shown in Figure 6-10. Suppose the organization distinguishes three target segments—A, B, and C—making up its target market. The height of each bar represents the number of persons in each segment. Thus A is the smallest segment, B is a medium-sized segment, and C is the largest segment. The question is, what penetration percentage does the organization want to seek in each market segment, given its limited resources?

FIGURE 6-10
Three Patterns of Market Representation

A. Equal
Representation

B. Proportional
Representation

C. Disproportional
Representation

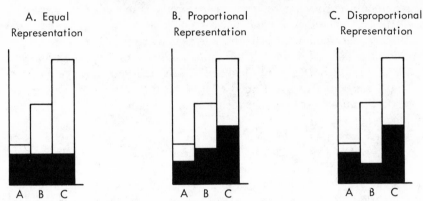

A   B   C   A   B   C   A   B   C

Three basic representation patterns are possible. The first pattern, that of equal representation, is shown in Figure 6-10A. An example would be a day camp that seeks an equal number of white, black, and oriental children.

Figure 6-10B illustrates a pattern of *proportional representation.* The organization decides to pursue a mix of customers proportional to their numbers in the population. Tenants in mixed-race apartment buildings and minority workers in factories often ask for proportional representation. Some universities strive to orchestrate a student body to be numerically proportional in important characteristics (sex, race, geography) to the larger society.

Finally, Figure 6-10C shows the pattern known as *disproportional representation,* in which the customer mix is based on objectives other than segment size considerations. For example, a city police force may deliberately recruit disproportionately more Irish policemen because of a historical tradition or preference, although other nationals are also recruited. Most organizations pursue a policy of disproportionate representation.

Divergence between Actual and Desired Customer Mix

We have examined the idea of an ideal customer mix by an organization. At any point in time, the actual customer mix may diverge from the ideal mix. Most organizations must accept the buyers that come to them. They may advertise mainly to one segment, but word-of-mouth may bring many customers from other segments. Thus a prestigious university will want to recruit only the ablest students but nevertheless will receive applications from less qualified students who would like to be admitted. This creates a lot of paperwork, cost, and hard feelings. The divergence between the university's ideal applicant profile and its actual applicant profile is wasteful to both parties.

The problem of an unsatisfactory customer mix is illustrated in Figure 6-11. The shaded figure shows the relative size of the three market

FIGURE 6-11
Actual (Shaded) Versus Desired (Dashed) Orchestration

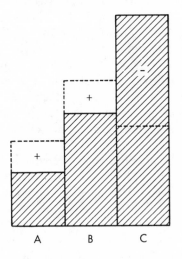

segments making up the current market. For concreteness, assume that this is a rapidly growing suburb. A (shaded) represents the current size of the upper class, B (shaded) the current size of the middle class, and C (shaded) the current size of the lower class. The town leaders are unhappy that the suburb is taking on a predominantly lower-class character. They prefer a different mix of the social classes, the one shown by the dashed line. They would like to attract more upper- and middle-class families and discourage lower-class families. This task calls for a mixture of stimulational marketing and demarketing efforts. Segments A and B must be attracted in greater numbers while segment C must be demarketed.

Problems in Market Orchestration

The orchestration problem is especially challenging for organizations whose customers are in face-to-face contact with each other. This is the situation facing hotels, restaurants, housing developments, and universities. A hotel, for example, is not equally happy with all customers who come to its doors. A fine hotel would not like to accommodate street prostitutes, truck drivers, criminals, acidheads, barefooted youth, rowdy individuals, and so on. It demarkets to those groups by its high prices, its signs, and actual steps toward physical exclusion.

Market orchestration faces a university in recruiting students. The university is not just seeking an able student body. It must make decisions on how many men and women it wants to attract, how many students from each major geographical part of the country, how many minority students, how many majors in different subjects that it offers, how many paying versus nonpaying students, and so on. The university is trying to build an attractive student community which in turn becomes part of its product to other prospective students who are trying to judge whether to apply and come to that university. An increasing number of universities are trying to build great diversity in the student body on the grounds that this will maximize the academic and social learning on the campus. At the same time, the student mix must be a workable one—that is, share a sufficiently common set of understandings and motivations so that they can interact fruitfully.

The problem of trying to cater to consumers who are not naturally compatible is serious. For example, the U.S. Army relaxed its rules about dress in order to attract a larger number of volunteers. As a result, the army contains a number of soldiers who represent the new life style: long hair, more casual manners, and so on. These soldiers come into conflict with the older type of soldiers who are straight, obedient, and immaculate. Each group is internally resentful of the other group. This makes for problems of morale and discipline. The orchestration is a strained one and it is difficult to create substantial satisfaction for the two parts of the market.

SUMMARY

Effective marketing action requires a prior analysis of the market—its structure and its behavior. Market structure analysis, the subject of this chapter, consists of four steps: market definition, market segmentation, market positioning, and market orchestration.

Market definition is the determination of the actual and potential members of the market for a given product, where product is defined broadly to include physical goods, services, organizations, persons, places, and ideas. A person may have no wants that are satisfied by the product, in which case he is not in the market; or a few wants that are satisfied, in which case he is in the potential market; or many wants that are satisfied, in which case he is in the actual market. The relative size of the actual, potential, and nonmarket varies with the given product and how attractively the offer is defined.

Market segmentation is the act of dividing a market into meaningful parts or segments. Members of any segment are more alike than are members of different segments. The segmentation might be based on geographical, demographic, or psychographic variables. Some organizations ignore segments and pursue undifferentiated marketing; others pursue concentrated marketing by working in only one segment; still others pursue differentiated marketing in that they serve two or more segments with differentiated offerings or marketing programs.

Market positioning is the act of defining a desired position in the market structure revealed by market segmentation. This position is chosen by analyzing the density of demand and the density of supply in different parts of the market structure. Market positioning calls for seeking a position in the market which is relatively underserved by existing competitors.

Market orchestration is the act of choosing a combination and mix of target segments that can be served effectively by the organization. It calls for defining the target market range—that is, those market segments that will receive marketing attention. It also calls for defining desired segment representation ratios—that is, the percentages of the segments that the company will try to serve or orchestrate.

NOTES

1. See John C. Narver and Ronald Savitt, *The Marketing Economy* (New York: Holt, Rinehart and Winston, Inc., 1971), pp. 56–57, 64–67.

2. See the teaching case "Marketing and Police Recruitment," ICH 14M1 (Cambridge, Mass.: Intercollegiate Case Clearing House, 1971).

3. For a good discussion of this type of marketing, see Mack Hanan, *Life-Styled Marketing* (New York: American Management Association, Inc., 1972).

4. Eric Hoffer, *The True Believer* (New York: Harper and Brothers, 1951).

5. See Maurice J. Gottlieb, "Segmentation by Personality Types," in *Advancing Marketing Efficiency*, Lynn H. Stockman, ed. (Chicago: American Marketing Association, 1959), p. 154.

6. Russell J. Haley, "Benefit Segmentation: A Decision-Oriented Research Tool," *Journal of Marketing* (July 1968), pp. 30–35.

7. See Paul E. Green, Yoram Wind, and Arun K. Jain, "Benefit Bundle

Analysis," *Journal of Advertising Research* (April 1972), pp. 31–36.

8. See Dik Warren Twedt, "How Important to Marketing Strategy is the 'Heavy User'?" *Journal of Marketing* (January 1964), p. 72.

9. There are various techniques for mapping similarity and preference spaces. See Paul E. Green and Vithala R. Rao, *Applied Multidimensional Scaling* (New York: Holt, Rinehart and Winston, 1972).

10. These political dimensions are illustrated for the 1968 election in Richard M. Johnson's "Market Segmentation: A Strategic Management Tool," *Journal of Marketing Research* (February 1971), pp. 13–18, esp. p. 15.

QUESTIONS

1. The American Cancer Society is about to launch a new anti-smoking campaign. How would you advise it to segment the smoking market? Would you recommend that it use an *undifferentiated, differentiated,* or *concentrated* marketing approach?

2. Beaver College is a small (800 students), private, all-female, liberal arts college located in Glenside, Pennsylvania, a wealthy Philadelphia suburb. For years Beaver has had no trouble at all attracting highly qualified, upper-class students to its elegant, secluded campus which contains, among other things, a genuine medieval castle. However, in the late 1960s and early 1970s, Beaver experienced a drastic decline in applications as many upper class, Eastern girls began to attend co-educational schools. What can Beaver do to restore the number of applications it receives to previous levels?

3. Do a benefit segmentation analysis of the market for the services of a YMCA/YWCA.

4. How might the president of the Midwestern college (see discussion in chapter) choose the competitor colleges to include in his market space diagram?

5. An art museum is interested in putting together an exhibit of art from The School of Fontainebleu. The committee in charge of exhibitions is split down the middle between two points of view. One group wants the show to feature a great number of paintings. The other group wants a smaller exhibit highlighting just a few major works. What do you think they should do if they were market-oriented?

6. Discuss the market orchestration problems of a blood bank.

7. Consider a state forestry department. Does it have a market orchestration problem as it makes decisions on the use of state-owned forests? What are its main markets? What are the conflicts in satisfying them? What marketing advice can you give them?

7   Consumer Analysis

It is not very difficult to persuade people to do what they are all longing to do.

ALDOUS HUXLEY

After an organization has determined its target markets, it will need to build up its understanding of the people who make up these markets. To do this, it must have a method of learning and monitoring consumers' needs. Even organizations that simply want to have effective transactions with others must understand the determinants of consumer behavior.

In spite of this, a great many organizations are satisfied with simple-minded pictures of their consumers' needs and wants. Many business organizations still launch products that fail miserably in the marketplace because somehow they misread the consumers' mind. Churches make all-too-simple assumptions about their members' feelings and interests. Legislators often misjudge their constituents' desires. Too many managers assume that they can simply observe and intuit what the target consumer is like, what he wants, how he sees, and how he reacts.

In contrast, the market-oriented organization considers *consumer research and analysis* to be an item of highest priority. The organization sees the target consumer as the starting point for its thinking and planning. It knows how to probe its consumers' needs, perceptions, preferences, and satisfaction. It does this on a systematic and periodic basis.

Fortunately, the field of consumer research is rapidly developing a useful set of concepts, theory, and methodologies. Originally, consumer researchers focused on particular variables, such as motivations, attitudes, or perceptions. In the last ten years, a serious attempt has been made to tie together in a logical fashion the most important variables that operate in the buying situation.[1] Current consumer behavior models view the consumer as a *problem solver* and *information processor*. The consumer starts with strong needs in his system, and certain ones are aroused by cues and become directed toward offerings. He may then search for additional information, which is selectively perceived and distorted. The consumer buys, and then experiences postpurchase feelings. The various models develop some version of this "buying decision process" to help the marketer correctly interpret consumers' wants and influence their choices.

An unsettled question in the field of buyer behavior models is whether one consumer behavior model will work for all situations or each major type of situation requires its own modeling. Many of the consumer behavior models in the profit sector are designed to explain brand choice among frequently purchased items. Many nonprofit organizations, on the other hand, are interested in explaining how consumers choose medical services, educational services, religious services, political candidates, public issues, and so on. Researchers are now formulating specialized consumer behavior models oriented toward specific areas of exchange. It is too early to outline any general model for all these situations.

Instead, this chapter discusses four key psychological variables found in all consumer behavior and of interest to all organizations. An organization will first want to know how to determine the *needs* of its target market; these needs become the orienting point for preparing meaningful offerings. Second, the organization will need to understand how the consumers *perceive* the offering and the organization: consumer perceptions and images greatly influence their disposition toward the organization's offering. Third, the organization will want to study how consumers form their *preferences* among a set of alternative offerings. Knowing how to identify consumer decision criteria helps the organization build in the attributes that will maximize the offering's attractiveness to the potential consumer. Finally, the organization will want to periodically measure its consumers' *satisfaction* with its offering. Evidence of dissatisfaction suggests that the organization is not doing its job and that there are strong and possibly urgent reasons to reexamine its relation to its markets.

NEEDS

Responsive organizations are highly concerned with the needs and wants of their consumers. They want to know the need differences that characterize different groups of their consumers. They want to know the intensity of different needs that are unsatisfied. They want to monitor need changes over time so that they do not suddenly find their products and services obsolete.

Conceptual Problems

Need measurement, however, is not an easy task. There are three major problems.

First, the concept of *need* is not well-defined. In popular parlance, it is used interchangeably with such terms as "want," "desire," and "demand."

A patient in a hospital may want a doctor to visit her five times a day, the nurse to sit continuously at her beside, the meals to be great, and the room to be large, single-occupied, attractive, and quiet. These represent an admixture of needs, wants, and desires. The hospital is not able to respond to all of her needs. It will try to distinguish between her "real" needs and her "trivial" needs.

Second, people are not always able to express clearly their needs or wants. They may have given them little thought; or they may find them hard to describe; or they may be reticent to mention them.

A public housing commission recently decided to build new low-cost housing according to the ideas and wishes of the eventual users rather than the ideas of architects. After all, urban planners have been terribly wrong in the past about the type of housing that would meet the needs of the urban poor; many buildings have subsequently had to be torn down. The commission interviewed low-income families to learn their needs and desires with respect to how high the building should be, how many rooms each apartment should have, how big the kitchen should be, how the halls should look, and so on. To their surprise, they found that many of the families could not describe their ideal apartment or fell back on describing the housing in their past experience, which if taken literally, means rebuilding the same high-rise jungles they had before.

The same inarticulateness is found in many other contexts. Political candidates that want to be responsive find many voters unable to express their needs in a meaningful fashion. High school educators find that unhappy students cannot verbalize what they want from their schools.

Third, it is difficult to assess the intensity of different needs that people mention having. The Committee on National Priorities wanted to determine the relative importance to Americans of such values as clean air, safe streets, stable prices, and so on. They found that respondents had great difficulty rating the relative importance of these needs.

Need Measurement

There are three methods for learning the needs of an individual. The individual might be asked to describe his needs directly (the direct method); he might be asked to respond to vague material on which he will end up projecting his needs (the projective method); or he might be given an experience with a real or prototyped gratification object to help him clarify his needs (the simulation method). These methods are described in the following paragraphs.

The Direct Method. Most marketing researchers use direct questioning to assess consumer needs. They may conduct an interview with a single individual or lead a focused group discussion. They may use open-end questions, such as "What courses would you like to see added to the present high school curriculum?" or "What recreational facilities would you like to see added in the park?" These questions will elicit opinions and clues as to the individual's needs and desires. Closed-end questions may also be included, such as "Rank the following activities of our church in order of interest," or "Rate each of the following city services on a scale of how much improvement is needed." Open-end questions have the advantage of providing more insight and surprises than closed-end questions; on the other hand, they are more difficult to code and summarize into representative findings.

The value of the "needs" information depends a great deal on the specific wording of the questions; whether they are asked over a telephone, on the street, in the home, or through the mails; the motivation of the respondent; his articulateness; the effect of the interviewer; the way the sample is drawn; and many other factors. Survey work is a sophisticated art and the user is well-advised to review the main procedures, pitfalls, and problems in a standard textbook before proceeding.[2]

Recently, Coffing proposed a rigorous and innovative client-need analysis methodology that goes considerably beyond other methods based on direct questioning.[3] The methodology consists of the researcher going through several steps. He first identifies the *decision maker* who needs the client demand data (he may be a politician, health-care provider, educational administrator, etc.). Then he identifies the *clients* (they may be users of services, employees, members, taxpayers, students, etc.). He then identifies the *domains* of interest to the decision maker. At this point he is ready to question a carefully chosen sample of clients about their needs. He seeks to determine and state their needs in the form of unambiguous statements of states or behavior the client would like to see. The client is asked to state his desires, to assign priorities, and to indicate what evidence would convince him that they are being met by the decision maker. A prepared statement of the client's needs is shown subsequently to the client who is asked to verify that the statement accurately reflects his desires. Coffing and his associates have applied this methodology to assessing the academic desires of high school students at Newton South High School in Newton, Massachusetts, and also the desires of clients of the Veterans Administration Preparatory Program at Westover Air Force Base, Massachusetts.

The Projective Method. The direct questioning method assumes that clients are aware of their own needs and motivations and willing to share the information with interviewers. But there are many issues on which they may not know or want to share their true feelings. For example, high school students may ask for more study periods when what they really want is less work. Or they may want younger teachers and what they may really believe is that younger teachers will be less demanding.

Thus the needs that are verbalized may mask the real needs operating in the individual. If the organization responds to the verbalized needs, it might find that this still does not satisfy the clients. Obviously it must probe into the underlying motivational dynamics so that it can offer products and services that will meet the real needs of the clients.

Freud taught that human behavior is never simple, that man is full of powerful drives that demand gratification but are held in check or are transformed. His basic drives may be repressed, sublimated, rationalized. Indirect techniques of probing are necessary to uncover his deeper needs and motives.

The influence of Freud led in the 1950s to a whole new fashion of consumer research called *motivational research* led by men like Ernest Dichter[4] and Pierre Martineau.[5] They challenged the value of large-scale surveys that asked scores of superficial questions and proposed instead that real knowledge of motivation would be better gained by interviewing a smaller sample of consumers in depth. The trained interviewer (usually a psychologist) would involve the person in any one of a number of exercises that would produce data that would be carefully analyzed to reveal the deeper needs and motives shaping consumers' attitudes toward the product. The four main projective techniques are described below.

1. *Word association.* Here the subject is asked to name the word that first comes to his mind when each of a set of words is mentioned. The interviewer might start out by saying "tall" and the subject might respond "short." After a while, the interviewer might say "charity" and the subject might respond "guilt." By slipping in key words related to "the act of giving," the interviewer hopes to infer the associations that people make with giving to charity.

2. *Sentence completion.* The subject is given a set of incomplete sentences and asked to finish them. One sentence might start: "The basic reason most people give to charity is _____." Another might start: "The main complaint people have about charity drives is _____." These sentence completion tests are very helpful in revealing people's attitudes and motivations. When the sentence is worded around other people's behavior than that of the subject, he more freely expresses his own feeling because he is attributing them to others.

3. *Picture completion.* The subject is shown a vague picture and asked to make up a story about what he sees (called the Thematic Apperception Test or TAT). Or he may be shown a cartoon involving two people talking to each other, with one of their remarks deleted. A cartoon might show a volunteer fund raiser ringing a doorbell and stating, "We hope you can contribute $5 or more to Skin Disease research." The subject is asked to fill in the words of the homeowner. If she says, for example, "I don't think you should tell me how much to give!" this suggests something about the attitudes of the subject toward being told how much to give.

4. *Role playing.* Here one or more subjects are asked to act out a given role in a situation that is described in the briefest terms. For example, one subject may be asked to play the role of a successful businessman alumnus of a major university and the other the university president asking for a larger contribution. Through role playing, the subjects project much of their needs and personality into the amorphous situation which provides useful clues on fund raising.

The advocates of projective techniques hold that they are highly effective in uncovering the basic needs that motivate specific behavior. Their indirectness allows persons to project their real feelings toward the product, service, organization, person, place, or idea being tested. Through this method one airline learned that people who were afraid to fly were not concerned with being killed so much as with the "posthumous guilt" they would bear for having abandoned their families by deciding to fly instead of drive. Another study revealed that men smoked cigars not only for enjoyment but also to prove they are masculine—the more odoriferous the cigar was, the more masculine they felt. Another study indicated that women did not like fully prepared cake mixes because they need to have a womanly participation in the act of "giving birth" to the cake.

There are admitted difficulties in proving these assertions because of the highly interpretative nature of the analysis and the usually small sample sizes. It takes skilled psychotherapists weeks and months of working with patients to uncover their basic motivations; it is therefore held suspect that marketing researchers with very superficial training in psychology can draw valid conclusions from brief encounters with consumers. In spite of these alleged shortcomings, however, projective tests generate many insights that are worth following up with further research.

The Simulation Method. A third method of probing consumer needs is to present a prototype of a possible product or solution to a need and let the subject experience and respond to it. It was mentioned earlier that many low-income families find it hard to articulate their wants with respect to new housing that might be designed for them. As a possible stimulus, they might be shown pictures of different room sizes and arrangements and asked to comment on what they like and dislike. As an alternative, they might be taken to model apartments. The simulation method puts clients through an experience with the real or hypothetical product and collects and analyzes their reactions.

PERCEPTIONS

Responsive organizations have a strong interest in how their publics see the organization and its products and services. For it is the organization's image, not necessarily its reality, that people respond to. The organization's leaders, needless to say, have their image of the organization but often this is at variance with the images held by significant publics dealing with the organization. The leadership of the American Red Cross, for example, might see their organization as progressive, dynamic and highly respected; yet image studies might show quite the contrary, that many people see the American Red Cross as old-fashioned, exploitative, and inefficient. Many police departments think that they are fair-minded, effective, and accessible. But many image studies of police forces show the community thinking of them as arbitrary, inefficient, and inaccessible.[6]

When this variance between self-image and other-image is discovered, some organizations will undertake to communicate their reality more effectively, others to change their reality. There are also new organizations that start with no image and seek to find one that will help them to accomplish their goals. An unknown political candidate, for example, will try to fashion an image that will be appealing to the voters. His job is to determine what the public finds appealing and to cultivate that image.

The hidden trap in this logic is that an organization or candidate is not a chameleon capable of acquiring any desired image. The organization's history, personality, and resources act as a constraint. One does not acquire an image simply through public relations planning. The image is largely a function of the actual deeds of the organization. Achieving a desired image may call for drastic changes in an organization's policies and practices. If the image is to have credibility, it must be rooted in the actual behavior of the organization and not just words about the organization.

The responsive organization has an interest in its image for three reasons:

1. It would like to know how it is seen in relation to how competitive organizations are seen.
2. It would like to know how it is seen by different market segments and publics.
3. It would like to monitor changes in its image over time.

Administrators who are interested in images tend to ask the following questions:

1. What is an image?
2. How can it be measured?
3. What determines the image?
4. How can an image be changed?
5. What is the relation between image and a person's behavior toward the object?

We shall discuss these questions in the following paragraphs.[7]

Definition of Image

The term "image" came into popular use in the 1950s. It is currently used in a variety of contexts: organization or corporate image, national image, brand image, public image, self-image, and so on. Its wide use has tended to blur its meanings. Before saying what it is, it would be more helpful to say what it is not.

If one thinks of a hierarchy of behavioral concepts going from *beliefs* to *attitudes* to *behavior,* image must be positioned somewhere between beliefs and attitudes. An image is more than a simple belief. Thus the belief that the American Medical Association is more interested in serving doctors than serving society would be only one element in a larger image that might be held about the American Medical Association. An image is a whole set of beliefs about an object.

On the other hand, the person's image of an object does not necessarily reveal his attitudes toward the object. A person's image of the American Medical Association will influence his attitudes toward the group but is not the *same* as his attitudes. Two persons may hold the same image of the A.M.A. and yet have different attitudes toward it. An attitude is a disposition toward an object that includes cognitive, affective, and behavioral components. Images, on the other hand, are primarily perceptual and cognitive; they lack affective and behavioral aspects.

How does an image differ from a stereotype, which is also a cognitive orientation toward an objective? A stereotype suggests (1) a widely held image (2) that is highly distorted and simplistic (3) and that carries a favorable or unfavorable attitude toward the object. An image, on the other hand, is a more personal perception of an object that can vary greatly from person to person.

We are now ready to define an image.

An image is the sum of beliefs, ideas, and impressions that a person has of an object.

This definition suggests two important things. First, images about an object vary from person to person. This is because a person's beliefs, ideas, and impressions result from his background, needs, and past experiences with the object. The differences in these aspects produce many different images of the same object.

Second, images differ in their clarity and their complexity. Some people may have very few or very fuzzy impressions about an object and others very detailed impressions. The images of two or more persons can be compared by noting the number, fineness, and complexity of their image dimensions.

Image Measurement

The concept of image is so rich and elusive that a number of different techniques for its measurement have been developed. The major techniques fall into two classes. *Response methods* of image measurement do not prespecify any image attributes to the respondents. Rather the respondent is asked to describe his image verbally or perform a task from which the image attributes will be inferred. Three methods in this response tradition are (1) unstructured interviews, (2) object sorting, and (3) multidimensional scaling. In contrast, *judgment methods* of image measurement specify image attributes in advance and ask the respondents to rank, rate, or react to them. The two best-known examples of the judgment approach are (4) item lists and (5) semantic differential. We shall describe each method in the following paragraphs.

Unstructured Interviews. The earliest method used by image researchers were unstructured interviews. The interviewers essentially asked the subjects to describe how they saw the object. This method has the advantage of being completely response-determined and may lead to new and surprising perceptions of the object. It is a good method to use as a prelude to developing a judgmental measurement instrument to use later on a larger sample of people. But standing alone, it has several drawbacks. First, some subjects are not able or willing to verbalize their images of an object. They could respond to specific items that might be presented but cannot articulate much on their own. Second, data analysis is lengthy, complex, and highly subjective. Two interpreters can come up with quite different pictures of the respondent's image toward the object. Third, the method is costlier per analyzed interview than formal questionnaire methods which can be administered to large groups.

Object Sorting. This method was proposed by Scott as a low-cost, easy-to-administer method that does not prespecify the image attributes to the respondents.[8] In this method, the respondents are provided with a set of stimuli and asked to group them in whatever way they wish. No requirement is made concerning the number, size, or nature of these groups.

For example, respondents may be given the following set of seven graduate business schools: Chicago, Harvard, Indiana, Michigan, Northwestern, Stanford, and Wharton.[9] They are told to sort these schools into as many groups as they wish, in which the members of each group have something in common. A school can be included in more than one group and it can also stand alone. Suppose a particular respondent forms the following groups:

Harvard	Wharton		Michigan
Stanford	Northwestern	Chicago	Indiana

This imples that in his mind Harvard and Stanford are seen as possessing some common attribute (prestige, for example), that Wharton and Northwestern possess another common attribute (excellent business schools, for example), Chicago possesses some quality the other schools do not have, and Michigan and Indiana possess still another attribute in common (they are large state schools). These attributes would only be guesses on the researcher's part unless he later asks the respondent what he sees in common in each group. If the same groups appeared in a large sample of respondents' data, they would suggest the existence of strong image attributes.

Multidimensional Scaling. This method is an image measurement technique of growing popularity in recent years.[10] In one of the versions, respondents are given triads of objects and asked to state which two are most similar and which two are most different. A typical question might be: [11]

In your opinion, which two of the following graduate business schools are most similar and least similar?

Stanford—Harvard—Indiana

Answer: _____ and _____ are most similar
_____ and _____ are least similar

This question is repeated with all possible triads of seven schools (35 in number).[12] This similarity data is then analyzed using one of a number of alternative statistical programs. The result is that each school can be plotted in a prespecified n-dimensional space showing its position relative to other schools. Figure 7-1 shows a hypothetical multi-dimensional mapping of the seven schools in a two-dimensional space. The technique does not indicate the names of the two dimensions but they usually can be inferred simply from the ordering of objects along each dimension. The horizontal dimension shows the ordering (from right to left): Harvard, Stanford, Chicago, Wharton, Northwestern, Michigan, Indiana. The researcher would probably conclude that this shows a "prestige" dimension that must have been in the minds of the respondents when they indicated which schools they saw as most similar. The vertical dimension shows the ordering (from top to bottom): Chicago, Northwestern, Wharton, Stanford, Michigan, Indiana, Harvard. This ordering suggests a "theoretical-practical" dimension with the University of Chicago at the extreme of theory and Harvard at the extreme of practice.

Thus multidimensional scaling produces a map showing the image distances of various objects from each other. The image dimensions are

FIGURE 7-1

An Example of Multidimensional Scaling: Images of
Graduate Business Schools (Hypothetical)

inferred rather than prespecified. The administrator of any one of these
organizations can learn the position of the organization and the positions
of its major competitors. The data can be remapped by significant publics
(such as faculty, students, business executives) to discern whether their
images agree or disagree. Finally, the organization can undertake new
programs designed to shift its image to another position and use mapping
at a later period to evaluate whether it has, in fact, succeeded.

Item Lists. Image researchers who regularly canvass large samples of
the public for their images of organizations prefer a method that is easy
and inexpensive to administer and definite in its results. They usually
ask subjects to rate organizations on a list of prespecified attributes. The
list may be formed through a preliminary round of unstructured interviews, or may reflect a standard list of attributes relevant to all organizations.

A good example of this methodology is the Reputation Profile used
by Opinion Research Corporation.[13] The respondent receives fifty state-

ments and is asked to choose the ones that fit his ideas or impressions of the organization in question. Some of the statements are:

You can depend on their products
Tries to understand customer needs
Has imaginative and forward-looking management
Good on training and advancing employees
One of the most progressive companies

The statements relate to basic dimensions of an organization's image. The researcher examines the statements that are most frequently assigned to a particular organization and forms an organizational profile. This profile is compared to the profiles of the organization's major competitors to determine the strengths and weaknesses in the organization's current image. Thus a particular graduate business school might find that it is rarely rated as having imaginative and forward-looking management compared to its competitors.

Two other useful steps are also taken. The respondents are asked to sort the various organizations into five *familiarity classes:*

Never heard of	Heard of	Know just a little bit	Know a fair amount	Know very well

The results indicate the public's awareness of the organization. If most of the respondents place the organization in the first two or three categories, then the organization has an awareness problem.

Another step is to ask the respondents to sort the various organizations into five *favorability classes* according to their opinion of each organization:

Very un-favorable	Mostly un-favorable	About half and half	Mostly favorable	Very favorable

If most of the respondents classify the organization into the first two or three classes, then the organization is in trouble and must look at the reputation profile to see what it lacks.

Semantic Differential. One of the most popular tools in image measurement is the semantic differential.[14] The technique calls for presenting the respondent with a set of bipolar adjective scales assumed to be the most relevant dimensions for the object under consideration.[15] For example, the following bipolar scales may be chosen to measure the image of a graduate business school: [16]

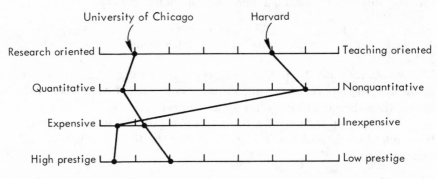

For each school, the respondents check all the scales. After the data are in, the researcher prepares a profile of each school showing its average rating on each scale. For example, Figure 7-2 illustrates the hypothetical

FIGURE 7-2

An Example of the Semantic Differential:
Images of Two Business Schools (Hypothetical)

profiles for two schools on four scales. The two schools are far apart in their teaching orientation and quantitative emphasis; they are close in their expensiveness and prestige. If still more schools are profiled, the administrator of any school can get a good picture of where his institution stands in relation to other institutions.

Although the semantic differential is easy to design in principle, some cautions should be observed to make it as reliable as possible. Because it is a judgment method, the image researcher should first conduct a number of unstructured interviews to find the major bipolar dimensions for rating school images. After he gathers a set of possible scales, he should keep the number small and avoid redundancy. Otherwise the respondent will feel fatigued in trying to rate n organizations on m scales. Osgood and his co-workers feel that there are essentially three types of scales:

Evaluation scales (good–bad qualities)
Potency scales (strong–weak qualities)
Activity scales (active–passive qualities)

Using these three scales as a guide, or performing a factor analysis, the researcher can keep the number of bipolar scales to a minimum. The final caution has to do with the choice of bipolar adjectives. Is the opposite of "expensive" the term "inexpensive" or "cheap"? Is the opposite of "innovative" the term "noninnovative" or "old-fashioned"? The particular word choices have connotations that will affect the responses.

Image Causation

The question still has not been answered: What determines the image that a person holds of an object? A theory of image determinants would help the organization (1) understand the factors that have caused its present image, and (2) understand how to produce a change.

There are two extreme theories of image formation. One holds that image is largely *object-determined*—that is, persons are simply perceiving the reality of the object. If a university campus is located next to a lake and surrounded by beautiful trees, then it is going to strike people as a beautiful campus. A few individuals might describe it as ugly but this would be dismissed as the peculiarity of certain individuals or their lack of real experience with the object. The object-determined view of images assumes that (1) people tend to have first-hand experience with objects; (2) people get reliable sensory data from the object; and (3) people tend to process the sensory data in a similar way in spite of having different backgrounds and personalities. These assumptions in turn imply that organizations cannot easily create false images of themselves.

The other extreme school holds that images are largely *person-determined*. Those holding this view argue that (1) people have different degrees of contact with the object; (2) people placed in front of the object will selectively perceive different aspects of the object; (3) people have individual ways of processing sensory data leading to selective distortion. For these reasons, it is held that people are likely to hold quite different images of the object. That is, there is a weak relation beween the image and the actual object.

Both schools of thought are extreme. The truth lies somewhere in between—that is, an image is influenced both by the objective character-istics of the object and the subjective characteristics of the perceiver. We might expect people to hold rather similar images of a given object mainly under the following conditions: when the object is simple rather than complex; when it is frequently and directly experienced; and when it is fairly stable in its real characteristics over time. Conversely, people may hold quite different images of an object if it is complex, infre-quently experienced, and changing through time. People have quite different images of political candidates because the candidates are com-plex, are infrequently experienced in direct contact, and change for different audiences and through time.

Image Modification

The determinants of image play an immediate role in the next question: How can images be modified? Organizations that have image problems, such as police departments, military services, some copora-tions, certain government agencies, and others are eager to know how to improve their public image.

The object-determined theory of image implies that an organization cannot do very much to create an image of itself different from what it really is. People will form their image on the basis of the actual be-havior of the organization. If the police are rough, then they will be seen as rough. If the organization wants to change its image, it will have to mend its ways.

The person-determined theory of image also implies that an organi-zation has little control over the image that people hold. A great deal of image variance will always exist because people have different ex-periences with the organization and because they will process the sen-sory data differently.

In spite of these theories suggesting that images are hard to manip-ulate, organizations spend millions of dollars a year in trying to build or improve their image. Are these expenditures foolish? Not necessarily. These image programs largely bring information to people about attrib-utes that they are not aware of or of which they have a distorted view. To the extent that the public lacks awareness of certain attributes of an organization, and are not likely to experience them directly, they will add them to their image as long as they are not contradicted by other beliefs. If the public believes one thing about an organization and is told another, it may disbelieve the new message, surrender the old be-lief, or hold the old belief more tentatively waiting for additional evidence. To the extent that the same new message comes repeatedly and from credible sources, the public will begin to accept the new message.

In an advanced society, people have mediated rather than direct experiences with a great number of objects. Before they ever meet a political candidate in person, or travel to a remote part of the world, or step into the headquarters of a major organization, they have an image of these objects that has come through mediated channels. They have read newspaper accounts, seen television coverage, and heard from friends about these remote objects. This information rather than direct experience constitutes their sensory data about the object. Organizations are thus able to "create" images to the extent that they can control all the sources of mediated information that comes to people. In a free society where there are competitive news sources, it is hard for an organization to put across a false image and maintain it for very long.

Students of images have noted that images tend to have a great deal of stability over time even in the face of dramatic changes in the object. Thus the quality of education might have deteriorated at a major university and yet it continues to be highly regarded in the public mind. How can the persistence of image be explained? There are two factors that play a key role in this phenomenon. First, once people have a certain image of an object, they tend to be selective perceivers of further data. If a person has developed a highly favorable image of a university, he tends to see other favorable signs more readily than unfavorable signs. That is, his perceptions are oriented toward dissonance reduction. It will take a highly disconfirming piece of evidence, almost a sensational one, to shake him out of his old beliefs. And highly disconfirming pieces of evidence are usually rare. Second, because most people may initially hold the same favorable attitude, the person will more frequently hear good things about the object than bad things. This leads to continuous reinforcement of the initial image. Thus an image can enjoy a life of its own for a while, especially when people are not likely to have new first-hand experiences with the changed object.

Thus an organization seeking to change its image must have great patience. The change will not be achieved overnight. The organization will first have to study its image and its competitors' images. It will have to decide where it wants to shift its image. It must research the attributes of this class of organizations that may be image-determining. It must decide what real changes to make in its policies. After changing its real behavior, it must disseminate information to its publics who may not experience first-hand the organizational changes. This information must be disseminated to the uninformed and arrive with some regularity. The fact that there is a new organizational reality, and that the organization disseminates frequent and convincing news, will eventually bring about the desired image change.

The Relation between Image and Behavior

The reasons so many organizations are interested in image measurement and image modification is because of the great influence they feel an image has on the behavior of people. They assume that there is a close relationship between the person's image of the organization and his behavior toward it. The organization feels that it can obtain maximum response from its public by acquiring the right image. This explains the strong interest in image formation.

Unfortunately, the connection between image and behavior is not as close as many organizations believe. From a social psychology point of view, images are only one component of attitudes. A Democrat and a Republican may both see Senator George McGovern as very honest and liberal and yet have completely opposite attitudes toward him. Furthermore, the connection between attitudes and behavior is also fragile. One might have a very favorable image and attitude toward McGovern, but on election day, the voter may not go to vote because of laziness or because something came up. Even if he does vote, he might decide to vote straight Republican because it is easier to pull one lever. There are intervening variables between attitude and behavior as well as between image and attitude, and therefore the link between image and behavior is at best tenuous. There is still a great deal of research that needs to be done to arrive at a convincing theory of the determinants of behavior.

There is still another way to indicate the tenuous connection. It used to be widely believed that one's behavior toward an object is determined by the degree of correspondence between his self-image and the object's image. If a person saw himself as active and outgoing and was choosing between two automobiles, a Chevrolet and a Ford, it was assumed that he would choose the make that had an active and outgoing image. This proposition was tested in a well-known study by Evans.[17] He measured the personalities of a sample of Ford and Chevrolet owners and tried to predict which car each man owned on the basis of his personality. At that time, Ford was viewed as a car for the active outgoing man and Chevrolet as a car for the more sedate, conservative person. Evans failed to find a relationship between the measured personalities of these men and the cars they bought. Critics of the study suggested that Evans failed to measure the self-images accurately, or that the two cars lacked a clear image difference in the marketplace, or that other factors influenced the car purchased such as the price or nearness to a dealer. The explanation for the failure may be more complex, however, and point to a flaw in the theory. It lies in the notion of self-image. A person has at least three selves:

> Public self—the self he thinks others see in him
> Real self—the self he really believes he is
> Ideal self—the self he wants to be

When a person is about to buy an automobile, he will consider the car image in relation to his self-image. But in relation to which self-image? It is no longer clear that the object's image will be a good predictor of choice behavior because of the multiple self-images a person has.

Nevertheless, one should not dismiss image measurement and image planning simply because images are hard to change and their effects on behavior are unclear. Quite the contrary. Measuring an object's image is a very useful step in understanding what is happening to the object and to point to some possible desirable changes in its image. Furthermore, though the connection between image and behavior is not strong, it does exist. The connection should neither be overrated nor underrated. The organization should attempt to make an investment in developing the best image it can for the advantages this might bring.

PREFERENCES

Organizations are keenly interested in understanding people's preferences among a set of objects. There are three reasons for this:

1. People fall into different preference groups. It is not easy for an organization or product to satisfy everybody. Preference measurement helps the organization distinguish the different preference groups. The organization can then choose its target market and design the products and services that meet the distinct preferences of the target group.
2. At times the organization meets market resistance for its product. It would like to know the determinants of this aversion (i.e., negative preference) for the clues they suggest about means of altering these feelings.
3. People's preferences change through time. The responsive organization wants to track these preferences in order to adjust its products and services to them.

Three important questions arise in connection with the subject of preferences:

1. What is a preference and how is it related to choice?
2. How can preference be measured?
3. What determines preferences?

The Concept of Preference

Preference can be defined as follows:

Preference shows the relative valuation that a person places over a set of comparable objects when contemplating their value to him.

We can imagine a continuum of psychological states going from *awareness* to *belief, attitude, intention, and purchase.* Preference is more than belief and more than attitude. It does not quite have the quality, however, of intention, which is a verbal expression of a plan to do something, such as buy a particular brand.

There is a large and growing literature in marketing questioning how well preferences predict purchase behavior.[18] In the area of brand preferences and brand purchase, there are several studies that have shown a fairly high correlation between the two, and some other studies that have not found a high correlation. Where the correlation is low, it might reflect many things, such as that people's preferences are not very strong or differentiated among the objects, or that their purchase behavior is influenced by other factors in addition to preference, such as prices, accessibility, and group influence factors. Generally speaking, studying preferences is highly worthwhile in itself—to learn what the market says it wants—and as a possible predictor of what the market actually buys or responds to.

Preference Measurement

How can preferences be measured? Suppose a specific individual is asked to consider a set of three objects—A, B, and C. They might be three political candidates for an office, three alternative advertisements for a charity drive, or three different medical plans offered by a health maintenance organization. Here we shall consider three methods—simple rank ordering, paired comparison, and monadic rating—for deriving an individual's preference map.

Simple Rank Ordering. In this method, the individual is asked to rank three objects in order of his preference. Thus he might order them

A > B > C. This seems simple enough but at least four problems arise with this method.

1. The respondent might be indifferent about some of the objects. He might prefer A to both B and C but be indifferent as between B and C. This can be expressed A > (B = C). The researcher has to decide whether respondents should be allowed to express indifference or whether their choice should be forced.

2. The respondent will find it hard to produce a preference ordering when the number of objects is large. Suppose he is asked to rank fifty American cities according to his preference for living in each one. This task assumes he knows the cities well and has clear feelings toward each. In fact, he is likely to have a lot of trouble deciding where to put many of them on the list. To partially help him perform an ordering of many objects, he might be asked first to sort the objects (listed on cards) into five piles marked most preferred, preferred, in the middle, less preferred, and least preferred. He can then take each of the five piles and rank order further. In this way, the task of rank ordering a large number of objects becomes manageable.

3. The method reveals the individual's relative preferences among a set of objects but not their absolute utility. A respondent may rank three political candidates in the order A > B > C and yet not like any one of them very much. The ranking itself does not say anything about the strength or intensity of preference. Along the same lines, the preference distance between objects is not revealed. The ranking A > B > C could cover the case in which A is much preferred to B and C, or the case in which A is only slightly preferred to B and B is greatly preferred to C, and other cases. Other methods of measuring preference are desirable if strength of preference is required.

4. There is sometimes a problem in aggregating the rank preferences of individuals into a meaningful group preference ordering. This was pointed out by Kenneth Arrow and has since been known as Arrow's Paradox.[19] For example, imagine three voters who submit the following preference orders:

Voter 1	A > B > C
Voter 2	B > C > A
Voter 3	C > A > B

In aggregating this data, we find that two of the three voters prefer A to B (voters 1 and 3). Because they are a majority of the voters, we should conclude that A is the preferred candidate under majority rule. Checking further, however, we note that two of the three voters prefer B to C (voters 1 and 2), and also that two of the three voters prefer C to A (voters 2 and 3). This means that there are three majority choices and they contradict each other, in that a simple transitivity order does not exist. This means that majority preference is not always a clear guide. This paradox has been widely discussed in the literature and may be avoided through other types of preference ordering systems than simple rank ordering.

Paired Comparisons. A second method of obtaining a preference ordering among a set of objects is to present them to the subject, two at a time, asking which he prefers of each pair. In our example, the subject will be presented with the pairs AB, AC, and BC.[20] Suppose he prefers A to B, A to C, and B to C. Then we could conclude that to him $A > B > C$ and there is no ambiguity. If, however, he prefers A to B, B to C, and C to A, he has committed a contradiction that violates normal transitivity relations. No conclusion can be drawn in this case as to his preference ordering for the three objects.

Many organizations resort to the use of the paired comparison method because of two major advantages. First, it may be easier for a person to state his preference between two objects at a time than his preference ordering of a whole set of n objects considered simultaneously. In the case of evaluating ten objects, the simple rank-order method calls for the individual to rank all ten objects simultaneously; the paired comparison method asks him to review forty-five pairs of the ten objects and state his simple preference in each case.

The second advantage is that the paired comparison method allows the individual to concentrate intensely on the two objects, noting their differences and similarities. This quality of concentrated consumer comparison is lost in the simple rank-order method when n is large.

The fact that this method magnifies the differences between two objects is not always an advantage, however.

Suppose a church is trying to decide between offering an expensive Oldsmobile or an inexpensive Ford as a raffle prize in a fund-raising drive. By taking a sample of preferences, they will probably find that most potential raffle buyers would be more interested in the Oldsmobile. The church may conclude that they should therefore feature the Oldsmobile. The real question, however, is if this preference would make a difference to the decision of people about whether or not to buy a raffle when approached. The difference between winning and not winning a car is much more important than the type of car being featured.

Monadic Ratings. The third method of obtaining preference data is to ask the respondent to rate his valuation of each product on a uniform scale. Suppose the following seven-point scale is used:

1	2	3	4	5	6	7
Dislike intensely	Dislike	Dislike slightly	Indifferent	Like slightly	Like	Like intensely

Suppose the respondent returns the following ratings: $A = 6$, $B = 5$, and $C = 3$. This yields more information than the previous preference rating methods. First, we can readily derive the respondent's preference order (i.e., $A > B > C$) and even know the qualitative levels of his preference for each and the rough distance between preferences. Second, we can easily average the ratings of a large number of respondents and derive an unambiguous mapping of group preference. Thus we might get the results:

Object	Mean Overall Rating
A	6.15
B	4.50
C	2.90

This says that the average respondent likes product A, is midway between being indifferent and slightly liking product B, and dislikes slightly product C.

This method is also easier for respondents to use than the previous methods, especially when there is a large set of objects to evaluate. He simply puts down a rating number for each object without having to make comparisons to other objects.

Sometimes the respondent is asked to rate his liking of various product attributes as well as the overall product. For example, the respondent might assign 5 to A's styling and 7 to its drivability. These attribute ratings can then be correlated with overall preference ratings for the whole sample of respondents to discover the main determinants of the preferences.

The Determinants of Preference

This brings us to the important question of the determinants of individual preferences among a set of objects. A theory of preference determination would help the marketer improve his product design, message strategy, and various other marketing decisions.

As was true for image theory, there are two extreme viewpoints as to the source of preferences. The *object-determined school* holds that preferences are based on the true differences in object attributes. Most New Yorkers during the winter prefer a vacation in Jamaica to one in Iceland because Jamaica is objectively warmer and most people seek warmth. Here preference is not the result of idiosyncratic personality and background factors but largely object-determined. On the other hand, the *person-determined school* holds that preferences are largely derived by individual differences in background, motivation, values, perceptions, and tastes. The strong brand preferences of beer drinkers cannot be related too much to real taste differences in these products because they are minimal. They must trace back to individual perceptual and evaluative factors.

Most analysts believe that preferences are formed out of the interaction of both object attributes and personal factors, although their relative importance can vary with the object. For example, the more differentiated the object attributes, the more determinant they are of preference. Analysts argue for an "information-processing" view of preference formation; that is, the individual receives information, real and fancied, about the attributes of the object, and processes some or all of it according to a fairly personal style of information processing. The interest centers on determining the major alternative styles people have in processing information to form preferences.

There are three major theoretical models of the information-processing, preference-formation process: the expectancy-value model, the ideal-point model, and the lexicographic model.[21]

Expectancy-Value Model. This model assumes that people form their preferences through a process of weighing their beliefs about a selected set of attributes of the object with the relative affect they attach to each attribute. The two best-known expectancy-value models are those of Rosenberg and Fishbein.[22] They utilize the same mathematical framework but have somewhat different ways of describing the major variables.

According to Rosenberg, a person's attitude toward an object is a function of the extent to which the object is seen to be potent in furthering his values or goals. Suppose a voter is considering two political candidates for the presidential election. There will be certain values which are important to the voter—suppose they are peace, a steady income, and law and order. These values, however, will not all have the same importance or saliency to him. To find the *value importance,* we might ask the voter to rank each value on an eleven-point scale from "gives me maximum satisfaction" (+5) to "gives me maximum dissatisfaction" (−5). Next we ask the voter to what extent he feels each candidate will deliver each value; i.e., the *perceived instrumentality* of the candidate enhancing or blocking each value. We might use an eleven-point scale from "the condition is completely attained by that candidate" to "the condition is completely blocked by that candidate."

Suppose the results are those shown in Table 7-2A. There are two candidates, X and Y, and three values. The voter rates the value importance of peace as +3, a steady income as +5, and law and order as +4. He sees candidate X as neither advancing nor blocking peace, facilitating

TABLE 7-2

Two Expectancy-Value Models

A. Rosenberg Model

Value	Value Importance	Perceived Instrumentality of Candidates	
		X	Y
Peace	+3	0	+4
Steady income	+5	+3	+2
Law and order	+4	+5	+2
Total weighted evaluation		+35	+30

B. Fishbein Model

Attribute	Affective Evaluation of Attribute	Belief that Candidate Possesses Attribute	
		X	Y
Intelligence	+5	+3	+3
Honesty	+3	+1	+5
Initiative	+1	+4	+2
Total weighted evaluation		+22	+32

a steady income, and maximally facilitating law and order. He sees candidate Y as highly facilitating peace and modestly facilitating a steady income and law and order. Now according to Rosenberg, these values and numbers are sufficient to predict the voter's preference or vote (all other things being equal). The value importances must be weighed by the perceived instrumentalities of the competing candidates. The following formula is used:

$$A_j = \sum_{i=1}^{N} (VI_i)(PI_{ij})$$

where:

A_j = the overall attractiveness of alternative j.

VI_i = the value importance of the ith value.

PI_{ij} = the perceived instrumentality of alternative j for enhancing or blocking value i.

N = the number of salient values.

Applying the Rosenberg formula we get:

Attractiveness of candidate X = 3(0) + 5(3) + 4(5) = 35
Attractiveness of candidate Y = 3(4) + 5(2) + 4(2) = 30

Thus we would predict that this voter would prefer candidate X to candidate Y.

Fishbein uses a model with the same mathematical structure but with the two central terms defined differently. According to Fishbein, a person's attitude toward an object is a function of the beliefs he has about the object and the affective levels of these beliefs. Suppose that the same voter is asked to rate the two candidates with respect to his beliefs about their intelligence, honesty, and initiative. He is to rate his belief about the candidate possessing the attribute on an eleven-point scale from likely (+5) to unlikely (−5). Furthermore, he is to rate his affective feeling about each attribute on an eleven-point scale from good (+5) to bad (−5).

Suppose the results are those shown in Table 7-2B. The voter places the most affective weight on intelligence, then on honesty, and last on initiative in a political candidate. He believes that both candidates are equally intelligent. He believes candidate Y is stronger in honesty than candidate X but weaker in initiative. To predict who the person will vote for, we apply the following formula:

$$A_o = \sum_{i=1}^{N} B_i a_i$$

where:

A_o = the attitude toward the object.
B_i = the ith belief about the object.
a_i = the individual's affective evaluation of the ith belief.
N = the total number of beliefs.

Applying the Fishbein formula we get:

Attitude toward candidate X = 5(3) + 3(1) + 1(4) = 22
Attitude toward candidate Y = 5(3) + 3(5) + 1(2) = 32

We would predict that the voter will vote for candidate Y.

These expectancy-value models have been applied to a number of products and brands with fairly good results in explaining choice or stated preference.[23] Some question has been raised in the literature about whether or not the importance weights (the measure of affect) really influence preference because they did not improve prediction in some of the reported studies. This issue remains to be settled.

Ideal-Point Model. The expectancy-value model assumes that a person's preference rises linearly with the amount of a favored attribute. Thus, the more honest a political candidate, the more he will be preferred. But what if a voter conceives of an ideal level of honesty in a candidate that is less than maximum honesty. He may feel that a maximally effective administrator would score a four on a five-point honesty scale. He might conceive of ideal levels for the other attributes which are not necessarily at the maximums. His preference for an actual candidate would then depend on the "distance" of the candidate's actual standings on the attributes and the voter's ideal standings. Table 7-3 applies the ideal-point

TABLE 7-3

An Ideal-Point Model (Based on Table 7-2B)

	(1)	(2)	(3)	(4)	(5)	(6)
			Belief that Candidate		Weighted Absolute Distance from Ideal Point	
Attribute	Affective Evaluation of Attribute	Ideal Level of Each Attribute	Possesses Attribute X	Y	X	Y
Intelligence	+5	+4	+3	+3	+5	+5
Honesty	+3	+4	+1	+5	+15	+3
Initiative	+1	+5	+4	+2	+1	+3
Total weighted distance from ideal point:					+21	+11

model to the data originally featured in Table 7-2. The voter's ideal levels are shown in column 2. To find the weighted absolute distance of candidate X from the ideal candidate, we subtract column 3 from column 2 and multiply the difference by column 1. This yields the numbers in column 5. The weighted distance of candidate Y from the ideal candidate is found in a similar manner. Because candidate Y is at a smaller distance from the ideal candidate than candidate X, we would predict that the voter would prefer candidate Y.

In using an ideal-point model to explain or predict preference, there are four qualifications to keep in mind.

1. Many individuals may not be able to conceive of an ideal in thinking about certain objects. For example, a music lover's ranking of various symphonies may not be based on a conception of an ideal symphony.

The person can state his relative preference for different symphonies but not in relation to a clear ideal.

2. The rate of decline in preference for objects at a distance from the ideal point might vary for different objects and different individuals. Suppose a person had a very clear and precise picture of his ideal political candidate. Suppose he is rating an actual candidate who is not at the ideal. We can distinguish between three situations. The first is where his preference falls off very swiftly at first and then more slowly as candidates achieve further distances from the ideal. This means that the voter has a low regard for candidates who are not extremely close to his ideal. The second situation is where his preference initially falls very slowly and then more rapidly as candidates achieve further distances from his ideal candidate. In this case, the voter has a high regard for many candidates who are not too far from his ideal. The third situation is where the voter's preference declines linearly with the distance of actual candidates from his ideal. This is the most common assumption made by researchers.

3. The model assumes that surpluses of some attributes will compensate for deficits of other attributes. Suppose one candidate has an excess of honesty and a deficit of intelligence and other candidate has the reverse. If these attributes are equally weighted, the two candidates would be equally well-regarded. It remains to be seen whether or not preference formation is a compensatory process.

4. It is conceivable that a person might have two or more ideal points with respect to a class of objects. The voter, for example, might consider both Abe Lincoln and Lyndon Johnson as his ideals, although for different reasons. That is, if he cannot find a candidate who is close to Abe Lincoln, he would vote for a candidate who is close to Lyndon Johnson. This means that his preference rankings of a set of actual candidates would not be clearly predictable from knowing his ideal points.

If these qualifications are not major, the ideal point approach has a lot to recommend it. The organization can interview a sample of people in the market and ask each person for his ideal point. Three possible configurations of ideal points might result. They might all cluster in one point in the preference space. This means that the market is in high agreement about the ideal object. The marketer will want to design his offering in terms of this market ideal. The second possible configuration is that the ideal points of individuals cluster in a few, say three, distinct areas of the preference space. This means that the market is divided into three preference segments. The marketer can examine where his existing product stands in relation to each preference group and whether he would like to adjust it closer to the ideal of any one of the preference groups. The third possible configuration is that the ideal points of individuals scatter pretty evenly throughout the space. This suggests that people's tastes vary a great deal and no one or few product alternatives will satisfy everyone. The marketer may want to consider introducing several versions of the product matched to the different parts of the preference space.

Lexicographic Model. This model says that preferences are formed on a more simple basis than suggested by either the expectancy-value model or the ideal-point model. It holds that a person normally does not consider all the attributes in arriving at his preferences. In fact, it holds that one attribute may dominate the others and the person compares the objects on this attribute. If one of the objects is higher on this attribute than are all the other objects, the person makes it his first preference. If two objects are equally valued on the first attribute, the person then considers the two objects' standings on the second most important attribute. This method continues until the person finds the most preferred object. This sequential elimination model of preference formation is called the lexicographic model.

We can illustrate this method with the data in Table 7-2B. The person regards intelligence as the most important attribute of a candidate. But neither candidate stands higher on intelligence so the voter has no preference between them. He considers honesty as the next most important attribute. Here candidate Y strikes him as considerably more honest than candidate X. He stops at this point, preferring candidate Y to candidate X.

The lexicographic model, although simple, has been supported by some empirical studies of consumer decision making [24] and has recently been turned into more sophisticated versions that are being researched.[25]

SATISFACTION

The marketing concept holds that the goal of the organization is to satisfy its customers and publics. Although many organizations have adopted this concept, it is amazing how many fail to take the next logical step of periodically and systematically measuring the level of satisfaction of its various publics to see if it is accomplishing this goal. Instead of directly measuring consumer satisfaction, organizations seem content to use sales, enrollment, attendance, or other variables as indicators of consumer satisfaction.

But these measures are not reliable. A museum may have high and growing attendance not because it is creating great satisfaction, but because it is the only museum in town. A hospital may continue to fill its beds with patients but because the doctors make the patients' choice of a hospital, this may not mean that the patients are very satisfied with the hospital. A church may continue to hold its members, but this might be because they feel duty-bound to attend, not because they are happy with the church. In all these cases, patronage data have only a tenuous connection with the real question of how much satisfaction the consumers are feeling.

An organization should attempt to measure consumer satisfaction directly. There are three possible configurations that it might find, each with quite different policy implications. The organization might find everyone highly satisfied, in which case it should continue to do the things it is doing. On the other hand, the organization might find everyone pretty dissatisfied, in which case it should find out the particular areas and causes of dissatisfaction and hasten to remedy them. Or the organization might find some customers very satisfied, some weakly satisfied, and the rest dissatisfied, in which case it might lose certain customers unless it finds out what factors are causing the dissatisfaction and tries to remedy them.

The reason that satisfaction should be measured periodically and not on a one-shot basis is that dramatic changes in satisfaction can occur long before they show up in market behavior and it is best to take action before it is too late. Recent years have witnessed many flare-ups—the consumer movement, urban riots, university disturbances, and prison riots—resulting from growing discontent in various groups that nobody measured or did anything about.

The subject of satisfaction raises several questions of interest to the administrator. They are:

1. What is satisfaction, anyway?
2. How can it be measured?
3. What is the relation between the level of consumer satisfaction and the achievement of other goals of the organization?

The Concept of Satisfaction

Satisfaction is a very difficult concept to define and operationalize. It is related to "happiness," "euphoria," "joy," "ambiance," and yet is not identical with any of these. Webster's Third International Dictionary defines satisfaction as "the complete fulfillment of a need or want." Because complete fulfillment is rarely achieved, this definition may be a bit strong.

Satisfaction does not seem to be reliably revealed by the physical appearance or behavior of a person. Normally a person who emerges from a theater with a smile can be thought to be satisfied. If he does not smile, is he not satisfied? Not necessarily. He may have seen great tragic drama; to come out smiling is rather inappropriate. Or he might have enjoyed the performance but is tired from two hours of sitting. Is he satisfied?

Because of these ambiguities, some researchers have suggested that organizations would find it easier to measure dissatisfaction than satisfaction. Dissatisfaction is more concrete, visible, and traceable to particular causes. But at the same time, the absence of measured dissatisfaction does not mean that there is strong satisfaction.

Two other aspects of satisfaction make it an elusive concept. There is a question of its relative stability as a state over time, even for short periods. A student interviewed in the morning might say he is very satisfied with university life. After sitting in class all day while the sun is shining brightly outside, his same response to this question might be that he is not very satisfied with university life. His satisfaction appears to have two components: the average level of satisfaction he might feel (which is fairly stable) and the transient level of satisfaction, which might affect his response at any single point in time when he is interviewed.

The other problem is that the satisfaction a person feels is related closely to his expectations. The higher his expectations, the higher his dissatisfaction with the current offering. Thus it is possible for a person to grow dissatisfied with a product or service even though it has not changed. The poor, for example, have become more dissatisfied with their housing because their expectations have been increased in recent years.

Satisfaction Measurement

A study by McNeal attempted to determine how leading business firms measure the satisfaction of their customers.[26] His sample included 53 firms operating in a wide range of industries. He found the following methods in use:

Method	Percentage of Firms in Sample Using the Method
Consumer research studies	65.2
Unsolicited consumer responses	65.2
Sales volume/trends	56.0
Share of market	42.0
Opinions of middlemen and salesmen	40.0
Market test results	13.0
Profit	2.0

Over two-thirds of the firms measure consumer satisfaction directly through consumer research studies and unsolicited consumer responses. At the same time, over one-third of the firms do not utilize these direct measures. They rely on indirect measures of satisfaction such as sales volume, market share, and the opinions of middlemen and salesmen. We have commented earlier on the weaknesses of indirect measures.

As for direct approaches to measuring consumer satisfaction, there are four techniques, each a little more rigorous than the preceding one.

Unsolicited Consumer Response. The least rigorous method of measuring consumer satisfaction is to set up systems that make it easy for dissatisfied customers (or satisfied customers) to express their feelings to the organization. Several devices can be used in this connection. For example, a university could place *suggestion boxes* around the campus. It could leave *comment cards* near these boxes which can be easily checked off. It can establish a *student grievance committee* or *ombudsman* available to anyone who wants to vent a complaint.

All these devices leave it to the consumers to initiate a comment or complaint, which can be classified into categories and investigated. On the other hand, there is no reason to believe that the types of complaints are necessarily representative of their real frequency in the population. Furthermore, if there are very few complaints, the administrators may fall into the trap of thinking that there is a high level of consumer satisfaction whereas it might really mean that consumers are apathetic or believe that complaining would not do any good.

Observational Method. This method supplements the results of the previous method by undertaking some direct observation of consumers to determine their level of satisfaction. Thus a dean at a university might mix with students, listen to their conversation, observe their attitude, and infer the level of satisfaction. This method, however, is subject to biases of various kinds, including the observer's selective perception, his affect on other people, his being in only a limited number of situations, and so forth. He might try to check these impressions by examining indirect records of various kinds that are analogous to sales measures, such as the percentage of students who drop out, the average class attendance, the number of students attending student functions, and so forth. Putting together several of these observations can be of some value in indicating the pattern and level of consumer satisfaction.

Directly Reported Satisfaction. A more rigorous method of satisfaction measurement is to distribute a questionnaire to a representative sample of consumers asking them to state their felt satisfaction with the organization as a whole and with specific components. The questionnaire would be distributed on a periodic basis either in person, in the mail, or through a telephone survey.

The questionnaire would contain questions of the following form:

Indicate how satisfied you are on the following scale:

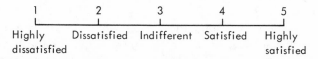

Here five intervals are used, although some scales use only three intervals and some as many as eleven. The numbers assigned to the intervals are arbitrary, except that each succeeding number is higher than the previous one. There is no implication that these are unit distances. When the results are in, a histogram can be prepared showing the percentage of students who fall into each group. Of course, students within any group—such as the highly dissatisfied group—may have really quite different intensities of dissatisfaction ranging from mild feelings of disappointment with the university to intense feelings of anger. Unfortunately, there is no way to make interpersonal comparisons of utility and we can only rely on the self-reported feelings of the respondents.

If the histogram is highly skewed to the left, then the university is in deep trouble. If the histogram is bell-shaped, then it has the usual number of dissatisfied, indifferent, and satisfied students.[27] If the histogram is highly skewed to the right, the university can be very satisfied that it is a responsive organization meeting its goal of delivering high satisfaction to the majority of its consumers. It is necessary to repeat this survey at regular intervals to spot any significant changes in the distribution. Furthermore, the respondents should check similar scales for the significant components of the university, such as its academic program, extracurricular program, housing, and the like. It will help to know how the various components of satisfaction relate to overall satisfaction.

Derived Dissatisfaction. The final method of satisfaction measurement is based on the premise that a person's satisfaction is influenced by his expectation as well as the perceived state of the object. He is asked two questions about each component of the university; for example:

The quality of the academic program:
a. How much is there now?
(min) 1   2   3   4   5   6   7 (max)
b. How much should there be?
(min) 1   2   3   4   5   6   7 (max)

Suppose he circles 2 for part a and 5 for part b. We can then derive a "need deficiency" score by subtracting the answer for part a from part b, here 3. The greater the need deficiency score, the greater his degree of dissatisfaction (or the smaller his degree of satisfaction).

This method provides more useful information than the previous method. By averaging the scores of all the respondents to part a, the researcher learns the average perceived level of that attribute of the object. The dispersion around the average shows how much agreement there is. If all students see the academic program of the university at approximately 2 on a 7-point scale, this means the program is pretty bad. If students hold widely differing perceptions of the program's actual quality, this will require further analysis of why the perceptions differ so much and what individual or group factors it might be related to.

It is also useful to average the scores of all the respondents to part b. This will reveal the average student's view of how much quality he expects in the academic program. The measure of dispersion will show how much spread there is in student opinion about the desirable level of quality.

By finding the need deficiency score for each component of the university's product, the administration will have a good diagnostic tool to understand current student moods and to make necessary changes. By repeating this survey at regular intervals, the university can detect new need deficiencies as they arise and take timely steps to remedy them.

Relation between Consumer Satisfaction and Other Goals of the Organization

Many people believe that the marketing concept calls upon an organization to *maximize* the satisfaction of its consumers. This, however, is not realistic and it would be better to interpret the marketing concept as saying that the organization should strive to create a high level of satisfaction in its consumers, though not necessarily the maximum level. The reasons for this are explained below.

First, consumer satisfaction can always be increased by accepting additional cost. Thus a university might hire better faculty and build better facilities and charge lower tuition to increase the satisfaction of its students. But obviously a university faces a cost constraint in trying to maximize the satisfaction of a particular public.

Second, the organization has to satisfy many publics. Increasing the satisfaction of one public might reduce the satisfaction available to another public. The organization owes each of its publics some specific level of satisfaction. Ultimately, the organization must operate on the philosophy that it is trying to satisfy the needs of different groups at levels that are acceptable to these groups within the constraint of its total resources. This is why the organization must systematically measure the levels of satisfaction expected by its different constituent publics and the current amounts they are, in fact, receiving.

The organization hopes to derive a number of benefits as a result of creating high satisfaction in its publics. First, the members of the organization will work with a better sense of purpose and pride. Second, the organization creates loyal publics and this reduces the costs of market turnover. Third, the loyal publics say good things to others about the organization and this attracts new consumers without requiring as much direct effort on the part of the organization.

SUMMARY

The responsive organization needs to know how to measure four attributes of the target markets it chooses to serve: their needs, perceptions, preferences, and satisfaction.

The starting point for the organization's research are the needs of its clients. Unfortunately, they are not always easy to measure. The three common measurement techniques are direct questioning, projective tests, and simulation exercises.

An organization also wants to understand how the market sees it and its products. A key concept here is image, defined as the sum of beliefs, ideas, and impressions that a person has of an object. Organizations try to measure consumer images in any of five ways: by unstructured interviews, object sorting, multidimensional scaling, item lists, and semantic differentials. They are interested in what has caused the image, how the image can be modified, and the relation between the person's image of the object and his behavior toward the object.

Consumers' preferences are also important to the organization. Preferences can be measured through either simple rank ordering, paired comparisons, or monadic ratings. The determinants of preferences are of great interest to management and three different models claim to explain them: the expectancy-value model, the ideal-point model, and the lexicographic model.

The ultimate intention of organizations is to satisfy their customers, subject to the various constraints that exist. But they do not always take the time to measure whether or not they are succeeding. Customer satisfaction can be measured in any of four ways: by unsolicited consumer response, the observational method, directly reported satisfaction, or derived dissatisfaction.

NOTES

1. The most notable models are John A. Howard and Jagdish N. Sheth, *The Theory of Buyer Behavior* (New York: John Wiley & Sons, Inc., 1969); Francesco M. Nicosia, *Consumer Decision Processes* (Englewood Cliffs, N.J.:

Prentice-Hall, Inc., 1966); and James F. Engel, David T. Kollat, and Roger D. Blackwell, *Consumer Behavior* (New York: Holt, Rinehart and Winston, Inc., 1968), Chap. 3.

2. See, for example, Harper W. Boyd and Ralph Westfall, *Marketing Research: Text and Cases*, 3d. ed. (Homewood, Ill.: Richard D. Irwin, 1972), Part II.

3. Richard T. Coffing, "Identifying Non-Market Client Demands for Services: Methodology at a Point in Time," paper delivered at the 1973 Annual Meeting of the American Educational Research Association, New Orleans, Louisiana, February 25, 1973.

4. Ernest Dichter, *Handbook of Consumer Motivations* (New York: McGraw-Hill Book Co., 1964).

5. Pierre Martineau, *Motivation in Advertising* (New York: McGraw-Hill Book Co., 1957).

6. See the case *The Police and the Community (Image of the Police)*, ICH 12G80 (Boston: Intercollegiate Case Clearing House, 1967).

7. Some of the following discussion is indebted to joint work done with Bernard Dubois and to his *A Comparative Analysis of Brand Image and Brand Preference Models and Measurement Methods*, an unpublished doctoral dissertation, Graduate School of Management, Northwestern University, 1973.

8. W. A. Scott, "A Structure of Natural Cognitions," *Journal of Personality and Social Psychology*, Vol. 12, No. 4 (1969), 261–78.

9. See Dubois, *Comparative Analysis of Brand Image*, for a study of the images of these seven schools.

10. See Paul E. Green and Vithala R. Rao, *Applied Multidimensional Scaling* (New York: Holt, Rinehart and Winston, Inc., 1972).

11. See Dubois, *Comparative Analysis of Brand Image*.

12. The number of distinct groups of r objects that can be formed out of n objects is given by the combinatorial formula $n!/r!\ (n-r)!$ In the case of 7 schools, there are $7!/3!\ (7-3)!$ possible triads—that is, 35

13. John W. Riley, Jr., ed., *The Corporation and Its Public* (New York: John Wiley & Sons, Inc., 1963), pp. 51–62.

14. C. E. Osgood, G. J. Suci, and P. H. Tannenbaum, *The Measurement of Meaning* (Urbana, Ill.: University of Illinois Press, 1957).

15. Note that in the item list method, the statements were not bipolar and therefore respondents could not rate degrees of having the attribute but only whether the attribute was present or absent.

16. See Dubois, *Comparative Analysis of Brand Images*.

17. Franklin B. Evans, "Psychological and Objective Factors in the Prediction of Brand Choice: Ford versus Chevrolet," *Journal of Business* (October 1959), p. 340–69.

18. For a contribution and review of the recent literature, see Frank M. Bass and William L. Wilkie, "A Comparative Analysis of Attitudinal Prediction of Brand Choice," *Journal of Marketing Research* (August 1973), pp. 267–69.

19. Kenneth Arrow, *Social Choice and Individual Value*, 2nd ed. (New York: John Wiley & Sons, Inc., 1951).

20. See footnote 12 for the number of pairs that can be formed out of n objects.

21. For a good overall review of these and other models, see Paul E. Green and Yoram Wind, *Multiattribute Decisions in Marketing: A Measure-*

ment Approach (New York: Holt, Rinehart and Winston, Inc., 1973), Chap. 2.

22. Milton J. Rosenberg, "Cognitive Structure and Attitudinal Affect," *Journal of Abnormal and Social Psychology* (November 1956), pp. 367–72; and Martin Fishbein, "An Investigation of the Relationships Between Beliefs About an Object and the Attitude Toward That Object," *Human Relations* (August 1963), pp. 233–40.

23. See for example Frank M. Bass and W. Wayne Talarzyk, "An Attitude Model for the Study of Brand Preference," *Journal of Marketing Research* (February 1972), pp. 93–96; and Jagdish N. Sheth and W. Wayne Talarzyk, "Perceived Instrumentality and Value Importance as Determinants of Attitudes," *Journal of Marketing Research* (February 1972), pp. 6–9.

24. M. Alexis, G. H. Haines, Jr., and L. Simon, "Consumer Information Processing: The Case of Women's Clothing," in R. L. King, ed., *Marketing and the New Science of Planning* (Chicago: American Marketing Association, 1968), pp. 191–205.

25. For various versions of the lexicographic model, see R. A. Russ, "Evaluation Process Models and the Prediction of Preference," in D. M. Gardner, ed., *Proceedings of the Second Annual Conference of the Association for Consumer Research*, 1971, pp. 256–61.

26. James U. McNeal, "Consumer Satisfaction: The Measure of Marketing Effectiveness," *MSU Business Topics* (Summer 1969), pp. 31–36.

27. The existence of only a small percentage of highly dissatisfied students is no occasion for complacency. In the first place, they may stand high on opinion leadership and therefore exercise a disproportionate influence on other students. Second, a small percentage figure may represent a large absolute number of students if the student body is large.

QUESTIONS

1. How else can one view a consumer other than as a problem solver or information processor?

2. The library in a small, suburban city wants to upgrade its service to the community. Design a study that it could perform to learn more about the library needs of the city's residents.

3. What are the problems with using multidimensional scaling as an image-measurement technique?

4. What are your *beliefs* about the Salvation Army? What sort of *image* does this organization have in your mind? What are your *attitudes* toward the Salvation Army?

5. Discuss how Richard Nixon managed to change his image during his 1968 presidential campaign. Did his success lend support to the object-determined theory or the person-determined theory of image formation?

6. A family planning agency wants to reach the poor. What should it understand about the cultural characteristics of the poor before it develops its marketing program?

Determining the Marketing Program

8   Product Decisions

Two stonecutters were working on the reconstruction of St. Paul's in London when Sir Christopher Wren asked each what he was doing. The first replied, "I am cutting stone." The second answered, "I am building a cathedral."

Once an organization has chosen its basic markets, analyzed their needs and preferences, and considered the values it would exchange, it is ready to enter into a more tactical analysis of the problems of achieving the desired market response. There are a great many marketing instruments that an organization can use to facilitate the relationship it is seeking with its target markets. These instruments make up the *marketing mix.* Various classifications of the instruments in the marketing mix have been proposed. The most popular classification is called the "four Ps": product, price, place, and promotion.[1] Each "P" is in reality a collection of instruments and each is sufficiently complex to warrant a lifetime of specialization. Thus there are specialists in product design, in pricing, in distribution, and in promotion. The general marketer knows the basics of all these instruments and blends them in preparing a marketing plan.

The order in which the instruments are set in formulating a marketing plan is arbitrary because they must all be brought into simultaneous adjustment for effective marketing.

In this chapter, we shall examine the marketing instrument known as product. Product is the first and most important of the four Ps. It is the foundation on which the other elements of the marketing mix are built. We shall address this discussion to the following questions:

1. What is a product?
2. What are the most important product decisions?

THE CONCEPT OF PRODUCT

Here we shall examine the concept of a product, a product line, and a product life cycle.

A Single Product

The idea of a product seems intuitive. One thinks normally of physical objects such as automobiles, toothpaste, aspirin, and other objects designed to meet a want or need. We shall use the term "product" broadly to cover anything that can be offered to a market for attention, acquisition, or consumption: physical objects, services, persons, places, organizations, or ideas.

The character of the product may be seen differently by the buyer and the seller. It is useful to distinguish three concepts of a product: the tangible product, core product, and augmented product.

The *tangible product* is the physical entity or service that is offered to the target market. It is what is readily recognized as the offer. If it is a physical object, such as a camera, it may be recognized by the market as having up to five characteristics: a *quality level, features, styling,* a *brand name,* and *packaging.* If the tangible product is a service, it may have some or all of these facets in an analogous manner. Suppose the tangible product is the government's income tax advisory service. We might say that it exhibits a certain quality level—that is, government tax advisors have a certain degree of competence. The service may have certain features such as being free to the taxpayer but at the same time requiring some waiting time. This service may be presented to taxpayers with a certain styling, such as being brief, cursory, and impersonal. The service is given a certain formal name, that of "federal income tax advisory service." Finally, the service may be packaged within branch offices located in various parts of a city. Not all of these attributes are always present in the case of every product. For example, in the case of a political candidate, it is hard to distinguish between his features, styling, and packaging. We can talk about packaging him for public consumption but this tends to mean the same as featuring and styling him.

At the next level, we can talk about the *core product*—that is, the essential utility or benefit that is being offered to, or sought by, the buyer. The housewife purchasing lipstick is not buying a set of chemical and physical attributes for their own sake; she is buying beauty. The person buying a camera is not buying a mechanical box for its own sake; he is buying pleasure, nostalgia, a form of immortality. The person undergoing a vasectomy is not buying an operation for its own sake; he is buying freedom from parenting. The tangible product is a packaging of that benefit.

Finally, the *augmented product* is the totality of benefits and costs that the person receives or experiences in obtaining the product. The concept directs our attention at everything that happens to the consumer in his effort to obtain the tangible product. The male who contracts for a vasectomy has to get into a car, drive, park, sit in a waiting room, face a doctor, receive instructions, experience pain, and reduce his activities for the rest of the week. All these features constitute the augmented product to the consumer, and affect his likelihood of purchase.

Besides thinking through a product in terms of its tangible, core, and augmented features, it is also possible to describe a product in terms of various dimensions that might cut across many products. Five major dimensions stand out:

1. *Durability*—how long the product lasts
2. *Complexity*—how complicated the product is
3. *Visibility*—how conspicuous the product is
4. *Risk*—how risky the product is
5. *Familiarity*—how familiar the product is

For example, consider three "products" that are offered by family planning agencies: birth control pills, interuterine devices (IUD), and vasectomies (male sterilization). The pill is the least durable product and the vasectomy the most durable. The pill is the least complex to administer, the IUD is of medium complexity, and the vasectomy is the most complex. The pill is the most visible in use, the IUD and vasectomy are of no visibility in use. The pill has a little more risk than the IUD because the user must remember to take it, and a vasectomy has virtually no risk. Finally, the pill has the greatest familiarity, the IUD has medium familiarity, and the vasectomy has the least familiarity. Thus we can describe products in comparative terms. We would summarize our description of vasectomy as a product by saying that it is relatively durable, complex, invisible, riskless, and unfamiliar.

In attempting to develop appropriate new products, it is useful to determine the attributes that the market would ideally like to see combined in the product. Thus Berelson has proposed that the ideal contraceptive is one that would be "logically easy, effective, simple, one-time, reversible, trouble-free, culture-free, doctor-free, coitus-free, and inexpensive." [2] This is a tall order but at least the attributes suggest directions for the search for an improved product concept.

Product Line

Most organizations offer more than one product to their markets. The set of products constitutes the organization's product line. The product line can be described in terms of three dimensions: its width, depth, and diversity. The *width* refers to how many different products are offered by the organization. A family planning agency which offers clients a choice between condoms, pills, IUDs, and vasectomies has a wider product line than one which offers clients only condoms. The *depth* of the product line refers to the average number of items or variations offered within the average product class. A family planning agency that offers many types of condoms and pills has a deeper product line than one that offers only one version of each product. Finally, the *diversity* of the product line refers to how different the various products are in end use, production method, distribution channels, or in some other way. A family planning agency that offers only tangible birth control devices has a less diverse product line than one which also offers counseling services, care for unwed mothers, legal services, and so on.

The width, depth, and diversity of the product line reflects the particular *product-market growth strategy* of the organization. H. Igor Ansoff proposed a useful classification of product-market growth strategies based on cross-classifying product-market extension possibilities. [3] The strategies are shown in Figure 8-1. They are defined as follows:

1. *Market penetration.* The organization seeks growth through increasing its market share in its present markets for its present products.
2. *Market development.* The organization seeks growth through taking its present products into new markets.
3. *Product development.* The organization seeks growth through developing improved and new products for its present markets.
4. *Diversification.* The organization seeks growth by entering new markets with new products.

Figure 8-1

Product–Market Growth Strategies

	Present products	New products
Present markets	1. Market Penetration	3. Product Development
New markets	2 Market Development	4. Diversification

These four strategies are available to various nonprofit and public organizations. For example, consider a public transit company running a city's bus lines. A strategy of market penetration would lead the public transit company to increase the number of its buses to provide greater frequency of service to commuters, thus hoping to increase its penetration in the commuting market. A strategy of market development would lead the public transit company to reach out to new markets, such as offering to rent bus services to special groups, schools, and organizations. A strategy of product development would lead the bus company to improve its buses and possibly add subways and trains to its system of serving the public's commuting needs. Finally, a strategy of diversification would lead the public transit company to enter new businesses, such as offering citywide mail delivery service to compete with the U.S. Post Office. The organization's decision on its product-market growth strategy will determine the width, depth, and diversity of its product line.

Product Life Cycle

Product lines rarely remain static. New products are added; existing products are modified; other products are dropped. The various products in the line are likely to be in different stages of their product life cycles. The concept of product life cycle holds that there are distinct stages in the history of a product's acceptance. By identifying the stage that a product is in or is headed toward, better marketing plans can be formulated.

Product life cycle theory holds that product histories pass through four successive stages, known as *introduction, growth, maturity,* and

FIGURE 8-2

Stages in the Product Life Cycle

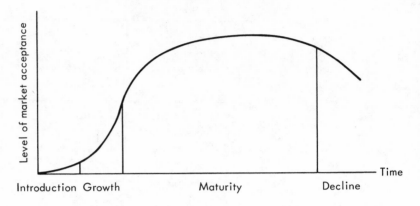

decline. These stages are illustrated for a hypothetical product in Figure 8-2. During introduction, the market is largely unaware of the product. This is followed by a period of rapid growth when the product "catches on." Growth is followed in turn by a longer stage of maturity in which the market is very familiar with the product and transacts with it on a fairly constant basis. Finally, there is a stage of prolonged or rapid decline of market interest in the product.

The product life cycle has characterized the history of many products, services, persons, places, organizations, and ideas. One has only to think of buggy whips, slavery, Hubert Humphrey, the World Federalists, and the Single Tax. These "products" each achieved market acceptance and then entered a period of decline.

The main interest of decision makers in the product life-cycle concept is whether it is predictable and whether it can be altered by management action. As for predictability, the answer is generally no. The probable length of time each stage will last is not knowable in advance for most products. In fact, even the postulated successive stages do not always rigidly occur. A product can have rapid growth from the very beginning, thus skipping the slow market start implied by the introductory stage; or a product, instead of going through a rapid-growth stage, may go directly from introduction to maturity; or a mature or declining product may enjoy a temporary revival of market interest. Some major social causes, such as conservation, consumerism, or women's rights, have exhibited multiple life cycles in American history. For example, consumerism as a social movement appeared and subsided in the early 1900s, reappeared and subsided in the mid-1930s, and reappeared again in the mid-1960s.

As for modifiability, the main point of product life-cycle theory is to try to identify the stage the product is currently in in order to determine the most effective steps to take. Different marketing tactics are effective in prolonging the growth period, or reversing the product's decline.[4] Price, new product features, advertising, and distribution play different roles at each stage.

Consider for example the U.S. Peace Corps. Today the Peace Corps is in a relatively mature stage of its life cycle. When it started in the early sixties, it was backed by great publicity including the support and eloquence of President Kennedy. The appeal was directed at the idealism of young Americans rather than any self-interest. The Peace Corps did not offer a large allowance nor did it minimize the hardships that the recruits would face. In spite of this, and perhaps because of this and the times, the Peace Corps enjoyed a strong and growing demand in the first few years of its existence. In the years that followed, interest began to wane and idealistic young people turned their attention to other problems, such as urban, racial, and military problems at home. The Peace Corps found that its original marketing mix was no longer sound for the new conditions in the marketplace and undertook to find a strategy more appropriate to a mature product. The new conditions of waning interest called for a revision in the target market, incentives, advertising appeals, and branch office strategy. Recruits in the Peace Corps were actively sought and they were offered higher allowances, more comfort, and so on. All of these steps were required if the Peace Corps was to sustain demand for its product in the face of a changing environment.[5]

THE MAJOR PRODUCT DECISIONS

Administrators face three major decisions with respect to products in their line. The *product-addition decision* relates primarily to the introduction stage of the product life cycle and concerns which products should be developed and how they should be introduced. The *product-modification decision* relates primarily to products in the mature stage of the life cycle that need rejuvenation through product and marketing changes. The *product-elimination decision* relates primarily to products in the decline stage of the life cycle that must be seriously considered for phasing out of the product line.

Product-Addition Decision

Product addition is the act of adding new products to the product line. The new product-development process is an essential activity for the adaptation of the organization to a changing environment; at the same time, new product development is very risky. Managers in the public sector in particular are often extremely naive about what it takes to successfully launch a new product or service. Too often the sponsor is so enthralled with the idea that he assumes the market will automatically and irresistibly beat a path to his door. There is insufficient research of actual interest level of potential users and their preferences with respect to product features, price, and other attributes. Even when research is done, it is often crude and inadequate. As a result, the new product failure rate is high. Many new services launched in the nonprofit sector, such as new academic programs and new health services, fail because market size and response have been overestimated or the product's configuration and marketing poorly designed and handled.

The development and launching of successful new products involves six steps.[5] *Idea generation and screening,* the first step, calls for the organized generating and screening of new product ideas of possible value to the organization. These ideas may come from employees, supporters, suppliers, consumers, agents, or the media; and they may be stimulated through brainstorming, morphological analysis, forced relationships, and other creative exercises. Of the many ideas that are generated, only a handful will pass an initial screening test. The purpose of screening is to eliminate from further consideration those new product ideas that are discrepant with either organizational objectives or resources. Ideas are costly to evaluate with any thoroughness. The purpose of screening is to eliminate the weaker ideas as soon as possible.

The surviving good ideas are taken to the second stage, that of *concept development.* A great deal of work has to take place to turn a rough product idea into a finished product concept. *A product concept is a well-thought-out fusion of benefits and features that will have meaning and appeal to a target market.*

> Consider the development of a new academic program by DePaul University.[7] In the early seventies, administrators at DePaul were seeking new ways to extend their educational services in the greater Chicago area. They conceived the idea of offering a new education program for adults only. This constituted the basic idea but much work had to be done to turn it into an appealing product concept. A product idea can be turned into several alternative product concepts, not all of them equally attractive. DePaul could have fashioned the adult education program idea into the concept of a liberal arts program for senior citizens, a vocational program for nonacademically oriented adults, a professional preparation program for married women who wanted to resume their schooling, and so on. It was important to distinguish possible concepts and then limit attention to those concepts that appeared to have the greatest marketability. The sponsors visited many other campuses that had launched new adult education programs and emerged finally with a fairly specific concept for their own program. Their program

would be open to persons over 24 years of age, it would lead to a bachelor's degree, it would give credit for previous experiences and skills that the individual had acquired, it would grade on a pass-fail basis, it would be based on a "learning contract" between the individual and the school, and the program would be named the School for New Learning. These attributes represented the final conversion of the idea into a full product concept; that is, a meaningful and appealing fusion of benefits and attributes as viewed from the target market's vantage point.

The concept development stage must be followed by the *concept-testing stage* to gauge the level of market interest and its reaction to specific concept attributes. Concept testing often reveals some unintended meanings, some confusion, and some omitted features. It calls for selecting a sample of potential target buyers and collecting their reactions to the concept. They may be interviewed individually or several persons can be brought together for focused group discussions. A whole variety of questions can be asked, with the following elements being the most essential ones to probe.

1. Is the concept clear and easy to understand?
2. Do the respondents grasp how the concept is positioned in relation to competing offerings and what its distinct benefits are?
3. Do the respondents show a preference for this concept over competing offerings?
4. Do enough respondents indicate an intention to buy the concept?
5. Do enough respondents say the concept meets a real need of theirs?
6. How do respondents feel about each of the key attributes of the concept: its form, price, quality, accessibility, and so on?

Following the development and testing of the concept is the stage of *economic analysis*. The purpose of economic analysis is to determine whether or not there is a sufficient market potential for the product concept to justify its further development and launching. Economic analysis involves estimating market size and production and marketing costs to see whether the product concept is worth introducing. Will Medicare create enough benefits in relation to the cost or is there a more efficient program? Will a black studies program attract enough students to cover the cost of teacher hiring and training?

If the answer is affirmative, the product concept can be moved into the *product-development* stage. In the case of a physical product, product development will require some laboratory research, engineering, capital equipment, raw material, and packaging. Problems arising during product development may require modification of the original product concept and new concept testing. In the case of a new service, product development will require staffing, training, and preparing various materials.

When the product is ready, marketers may try to take it through a *test-marketing* stage if the product is of the type that can be introduced on a small scale. Test marketing is an attempt to examine the product's performance under real selling conditions. The new product is put into some miniature but real part of the market system and observed in terms of how many persons, and what persons, take to it. The test market results can indicate how big the market is, what potential product or marketing problems exist, and which marketing practices are most effective. It offers a form of risk control to the marketer before he launches the product into wide distribution.

Products that pass the test-marketing stage are ready for product *introduction* on a large scale. Even here, the product cannot be put out everywhere and at once. It is rolled out in stages. The potential agents must be contacted about the new product, trained in its handling and selling, and the final target market must be informed and aroused through promotion. Many questions arise at this stage: Which agencies should handle the product? How much incentive should be given to the agents? How much training should they receive? and so on.

Looking back at the whole process of new product development, it is one that must proceed in logical stages and be based on research, testing, and screening concepts.

Product-Modification Decision

Product modification is undertaken to revitalize a product by developing new features or placing it in new markets. The modification can take place on the tangible, core, or augmented level of the product.

Most often, the modification is of a tangible kind: a change in the product's *quality, features, styling, brand name,* or *packaging.* Consider a well-established health maintenance organization that is facing strong competition from a new HMO. The original HMO may have to modify and improve some of its attributes depending on what would appeal most to potential members. It should survey its current members to make sure they are satisfied with the quality of its services. If it wanted to move into feature competition, it might add free dental coverage to its services or free eyeglasses. It should reconsider its styling and packaging as an organization—i.e., whether users think the premises are attractive or unattractive. If it wanted to move into style competition, it might paint the offices a new color and add more comfortable and attractive furniture. The best steps to take depend on the HMO undertaking a fundamental review of its target markets and marketing mix and determining whether or not it should seek a new position in the market and what concrete steps would help it attain that position.

It is harder to change the core concept of the product, although this can be done with sufficient time. For example, the original population control movement was built on the concept of birth control—that is, methods of preventing birth. This ran into much criticism from religious groups who opposed artificial means of preventing births. To overcome this opposition, the population control movement worked toward a broader core concept, that of family planning. The emphasis is on planning when and how many children to have, not on means of birth control. Thus, an organization can work toward changing the core concept of its product. Finally, the organization can also attempt to modify various aspects of the augmented product that would change the tangible product's attractiveness.

Product-Elimination Decision

An organization's product line is altered by decisions to drop current products that no longer contribute to the company's objective. Organizations tend to neglect the subject of product elimination in comparison with the attention they give to product addition and product modification. Each product builds up vested interests ready to defend it on some grounds. There is often sentiment against eliminating a weak product, especially if it occupies a hallowed place in the organization's history. The elimination step is painful and some people are hurt.

At the same time, maintaining a weak product in the product line is costly, both in tying up current resources and in delaying the aggressive search for replacement products that would improve the organization's future performance. No organization can afford to have most of its products in a declining stage of their life cycles.

The marketer insists on a periodic review of each product in the product line to determine its health and contribution to the organization's objectives.[8] In the case of a commercial company, sales and cost figures are examined for each product to detect any signs of insufficient profit performance. In the case of a nonbusiness organization, other criteria would be used.

Consider the steps recently taken by New York University in the face of a $5 million annual deficit. The deficit forced the university administration to examine each of its major programs to see which ones were too expensive to operate in relation to the university's resources and other requirements. Its School of Social Work, for example, had experienced several years of declining enrollment. This was associated with an oversupply of trained social workers in relation to job opportunities. The program was expensive to operate because it required a high teacher-to-student ratio. As a result, the administration recommended discontinuing the School of Social Work from its academic offerings. This decision fell hard on many teachers and alumni but seemed necessitated by the market outlook and costs of running this program. The administration felt that it had to reduce its overall costs as well as shift its resources to its stronger programs.

Once a product or service has been singled out for elimination, the organization faces three further decisions. First, it has the option of selling or transferring the product or service to someone else or dropping it completely. It will usually prefer the former because this will cause the least disruption to customers and employees. Second, the organization has to decide when the product should be terminated. It could be dropped quickly and decisively, so there is no chance for resistance to build up and reverse the decision. Or it may be discontinued gradually with a timetable to allow resources to transfer out in an orderly and less painful way and allow clients to make other arrangements. Finally, the organization will have to develop plans for interim marketing while the product is being phased out. It might maintain the current level of promotion or reduce or eliminate it; it may raise or lower the price; it may drop certain warranties. The organization needs a clear plan of action for the interim marketing of the soon-to-be-eliminated product.

SUMMARY

Product is the first of the four Ps of marketing and the most fundamental one. Product is used in the broad sense of any complex of tangible and intangible attributes that might be offered to a market to satisfy a want or need; it can cover goods, services, organizations, persons, places, and ideas. It is useful to distinguish between the tangible product, which takes a physical view of the actual product and its attributes, the core product, which represents the essential utility behind the tangible product, and the augmented product, which represents the tangible product and all the benefits and costs associated with obtaining and consuming it.

An organization's product line can be described as having a certain width, depth, and diversity. The various products in the product line are at different stages of the product life cycle, some in the introductory stage, others in the growth stage, still others in the mature stage, and some in the declining stage. The stage of a product has important implications for the appropriate marketing program.

Administrators face three main decisions with respect to their product line. Product addition is the challenge of finding and adding viable new products to the line, and this calls for six carefully handled stages: idea generation and screening, concept development and testing, economic analysis, product development, test marketing, and product introduction. Product modification is the challenge of developing or modifying product attributes—quality, features, style, brand name, packaging—to refresh the market's interest. Finally, product elimination is the task of deciding when a product should be dropped from the line because of faltering performance and how it should be phased out.

NOTES

1. E. Jerome McCarthy, *Basic Marketing: A Managerial Approach*, rev. ed. (Homewood, Ill.: Richard D. Irwin, Inc., 1964), pp. 38–49.
2. Bernard Berelson, "The Present State of Family Planning Programs," *Studies in Family Planning*, 57 (September 1970), p. 8.
3. H. Igor Ansoff, "Strategies for Diversification," *Harvard Business Review* (September–October 1957), pp. 113–27.
4. See, for example, Theodore Levitt, "Exploit the Product Life Cycle," *Harvard Business Review* (November–December 1965), pp. 81–94.
5. See the teaching case called *The Peace Corps* (Boston, Mass.: Harvard Business School, 1970).
6. For additional reading, see David B. Uman, *New Product Program: Their Planning and Control* (New York: American Management Association, Inc., 1969); Eberhard E. Scheuing, *New Product Management* (Hinsdale, Ill.: The Dryden Press, 1974).
7. "DePaul's New Study Plan," *Chicago Tribune*, January 6, 1974.
8. A periodic review system is described in the author's "Phasing Out Weak Products," *Harvard Business Review* (March–April 1965), pp. 107–18.

QUESTIONS

1. Identify the tangible product, core product, and augmented product of a zoo. Discuss the characteristics of a zoo's product line.

2. The marketer faces different demand situations at different stages of the product life cycle. What are his marketing tasks at each stage?

3. Generate some ideas for new products that could be offered by a school's student union. Screen out those ideas that are weak. Develop a finished product concept for one of the remaining ideas.

4. How could a university test market a day-care center for the children of its faculty and students?

5. Several years ago the National Foundation of the March of Dimes was forced to modify its product. What did it do?

6. What are the different ways new product ideas can be screened?

9   Price Decisions

The real price of everything, what everything really costs to the man who wants to acquire it, is the toil and trouble of acquiring it.

ADAM SMITH

Administrators of nonprofit organizations usually have a strong interest in the price question. The U.S. Postal System is constantly reviewing its postage rates with an eye toward whether they should be increased further to cover the postal losses. Universities and hospitals have an interest in whether they can raise tuition or charges, respectively, without a consumer backlash. Charity organizations put prices on different types of membership to potential donors.

Prices are placed on a great range of goods and services and go by various names:

Price is all around us. You pay RENT for your apartment, TUITION for your education, and a FEE to your physician or dentist. The airline, railway, taxi, and bus companies charge you a FARE, the local utilities call their price a RATE, and the local bank charges you INTEREST for the money in loans. The price for driving your car on Florida's Sunshine Parkway is a TOLL, and the company that insures your car charges you a PREMIUM. The guest lecturer charges an HONORARIUM to tell you about a government official who took a BRIBE to help a shady character steal DUES collected by a trade association. Clubs or societies to which you belong may make a special ASSESSMENT to pay unusual expenses. A lawyer you use regularly may ask for a RETAINER to cover his services. The "price" of an executive is a SALARY, the price of a salesman may be a COMMISSION, and the price of a worker is a WAGE. Finally, although economists would disagree, many of us feel that INCOME TAX is the price we pay for the privilege of making money! [1]

In addition, price includes subsidiary decision elements. *List price* refers to the stated long-term price of the product or service. *Actual price* may be greater or smaller depending upon the presence of a *premium* or *discount*. If the buyer finances the purchase he will be interested in the *credit* terms—that is, the monthly cost and time period of payments. Finally, the actual price might include additional charges representing *delivery, taxes,* and so on. All these elements may be varied as part of pricing strategy in an actual pricing decision.

Nonprofit organizations may face several alternatives in pricing a service. Consider the pricing alternatives facing museums:

In the past, most public museums abstained from charging an admission price to the public. They were chartered by the city or state to contribute to public enlightenment. An admission price was seen as a deterrent to attendance, particularly by the poor, who perhaps needed the exposure the most. The rising costs of operating these institutions, however, soon forced their hand. Philanthropic and municipal sources did not provide enough funds. Nor did occasional public fund-raising campaigns. The idea of charging admission finally had to be taken up seriously by museums. Museums faced a choice among at least three alternative pricing approaches.

1. The museum might charge admission on all but one day of the week. The concept of a free day allows the poor or young to visit the museum. The admission charge may also be varied for different visitors, being lower (or waived) for students, people over 65, handicapped people, and veterans.

2. The museum might not set a fixed admission price but instead encourage donations from visitors. At the Metropolitan Museum in New York, there are donation booths to which people are encouraged to contribute. At the same time, the voluntary nature of the donation allows the poor and young to enter without cost.

3. The museum might sponsor a membership plan which provides members with special benefits such as a monthly magazine, an annual report, invitation to exhibit openings, a discount at the gift shop, and

a waiver of admission charges, if any. Furthermore, it might establish different levels of membership and membership privilege, with dues going from $15 (regular membership), to $100 (special membership), to $500 (life membership).

The major difference between the price objectives of profit and nonprofit organizations is that the profit organization tries to find the price that maximizes profit while the nonprofit organization tries to set a "fair" price. However, even nonprofit organizations often seek the profit-maximizing price. The first section of this chapter will therefore examine different objectives that might guide the setting of price. We shall then examine price-setting methods used in practice that tend to be oriented toward cost, demand, or competition. Finally we shall examine the issues facing an organization that is planning to change its price.

PRICE OBJECTIVES

The first thing an organization must decide in attempting to develop a price or pricing policy is the objective that it is trying to achieve. Four different pricing objectives can be distinguished: profit maximization, cost recovery, market incentivization, and market disincentivization.

Profit Maximization

One would think that nonprofit organizations never use the principle of profit maximization. This is not so. There are many situations in which a nonprofit organization will want to set its price to yield the largest possible revenue. Thus a charity organization will set its price for attending a major benefit dinner on the principle of maximizing the net revenue. A university whose faculty developed patented inventions will price these inventions to yield the maximum return to the university. A hospital may set up a dental clinic to maximize the profits on that service.

Profit-maximizing pricing requires the organization to estimate two functions—namely, the demand function and the cost function. These two functions are sufficient for deriving the theoretically best price. The demand function describes the expected quantity demanded per period (Q) at various prices (P) that might be charged. Suppose the firm is able to determine through demand analysis that its *demand equation* is

$$Q = 1,000 - 4P \qquad (9\text{-}1)$$

The cost function describes the expected total cost (C) for various quantities per period (Q) that might be produced. It is customary to distinguish between total fixed costs (those that do not vary with output) and total variable costs (those that do vary with output). In the simplest case, the total cost function can be described by the general linear equation $C = d + eQ$ where d is total fixed cost and e is unit variable cost. Suppose the company derived the following *cost equation* for its product:

$$C = 6,000 + 50Q \qquad (9\text{-}2)$$

With the preceding demand and cost equations, the pricing executive is almost in a position to determine the best price. He only needs two more equations, both definitional in nature. First, *total revenue* (R) is defined as equal to price times quantity sold:

$$R = PQ \qquad (9\text{-}3)$$

Second, *total profits* (Z) are defined as the difference between total revenue and total cost.

$$Z = R - C \qquad (9\text{-}4)$$

With these four equations, the pricing executive is in a position to find the profit-maximizing price. He should start with the profit equation (9-4) because this is what he seeks to maximize. Through substitution, the profit equation can be turned into a pure function of the price charged:

$$
\begin{aligned}
Z &= R - C \\
Z &= PQ - C \\
Z &= PQ - (6,000 + 50Q) \\
Z &= P(1,000 - 4P) - 6,000 - 50\,(1,000 - 4P) \\
Z &= 1,000P - 4P^2 - 6,000 - 50,000 + 200P \\
Z &= -56,000 + 1,200P - 4P^2 \qquad (9\text{-}5)
\end{aligned}
$$

Equation (9-5) shows total profits expressed as a function of the price that will be charged. The profit-maximizing price can be found in one of two ways. The researcher could use trial and error, trying out different prices to determine the shape of the profit response and the location of the maximum price. The profit function turns out to be a parabola or hatlike figure and profits reach their highest point ($34,000) at a price of $150. The same price could have been determined by utilizing the method of calculus.

This model for finding the profit-maximizing price, in spite of its theoretical elegance, is subject to four practical limitations.

1. The model shows how to find the price that will maximize the short-run profits rather than long-run profits. There may be a trade-off between short-run and long-run profit maximization, as when clients get angry at the high price and eventually switch to other sellers.

2. There are other parties to consider in setting a price. The theoretical model only considers the ultimate consumers' response to alternative prices. Other groups that may respond are competitors, suppliers, middlemen, government, and the general public. A high price might lead competitors to raise their price, in which case the demand would be different than suggested by the demand function if it assumed no competitive reaction. Various suppliers—employees, banks, raw material producers—take the price to reflect the organization's ability to pay and they may raise their prices accordingly, in which case the cost function would be different than assumed with no supplier reaction. Middlemen who handle the product may have some strong feelings about the proper price. The government, acting in the interests of the public, might establish a price ceiling, and this may exclude the profit-maximizing price. Finally, the general public might fault the organization if its price appears to be too high.

3. The theoretical pricing model assumes that price can be set independently of the other elements in the marketing mix. But the other elements of the marketing mix will affect demand and must be part of the demand function in searching for the optimal price.

4. The theoretical pricing model assumes that the demand and cost function can be accurately estimated. In the case of a new service, there is no experience upon which to base these estimates. Unless data are available on a similar service, estimates are likely to be highly subjective. Because the demand and cost equations are estimated with an unknown degree of error, the criterion of maximizing profits may have to be replaced with the criterion of maximizing *expected* profits. In any situation of risk and uncertainty, the pricing decision maker will want to see how sensitive the theoretically calculated price is to alternative estimates of the demand and cost functions.

Cost Recovery

Many organizations in the nonprofit sector cannot expect to find a price that would cover their costs. Many nonprofit organizations adopt the objective of pricing to recover a "reasonable" amount of their total cost. This is the idea behind the pricing of toll roads, postal services, and public mass transit services. Although the organizations could conceivably charge higher prices and increase their revenue (because of their monopolistic position), they do not want to precipitate public or legislative reaction.

How much cost should the organization try to recover through its pricing? Some organizations—such as some universities and public mass transit organizations—aim to recoup operating costs only. This would not provide money for expansion but for this they would rely on gifts or debt issues to raise the needed capital. It is quite arbitrary to aim for recovery of operating costs only. The actual prices charged by these organizations are largely determined by tradition, public opinion, and actual or potential competition rather than any scientific standard.

Market Incentivization

On some occasions, an organization will seek to attract the greatest number of customers in the shortest possible time. Business firms call this a rapid market penetration objective. They will set a relatively low price in order to stimulate the growth of the market or capture a large share of it. Any of several conditions might favor setting a low price: [2] (1) The market appears to be highly price-sensitive; that is, many additional buyers would come into the market if the product is priced low. (2) The unit costs of production and distribution fall with increased output. (3) A low price would discourage actual and potential competition.

Nonprofit organizations often set a low price to stimulate adoption of their product. A family planning organization will make contraceptive supplies available at a very low price (sometimes zero) to encourage adoption of birth control methods by as many people as possible. The governments of developing nations will subsidize the price of superior fertilizers to encourage their rapid adoption by farmers. Recently the University of Chicago offered a tuition discount of 50 percent to "returning scholars," persons who are at least 35 and wish to resume academic work without a commitment to a degree program. The use of "markdowns" from a high list price is a very common way to stimulate market interest and growth.

Market Disincentivization

Pricing might be undertaken for the objective of discouraging as many people as possible from purchasing a particular product or service. There are many reasons an organization may want to do this. They may consider the product to be bad for people; or they may want to discourage people from overtaxing a facility; or they may be trying to solve a temporary shortage; or they may want to discourage the patronage of certain classes of buyers. So they resort to setting a high price that will discourage potential buyers.

The theory behind the high government tax on cigarettes and liquor is to discourage people from the use of these products. But the price is never made high enough because the government has come to rely on the substantial revenue produced by these taxes. A tax that is truly disincentivizing would yield the government a revenue of zero. Unfortunately, a prohibitively high tax would also create a large black market and illegal activity.

The Golden Gate Authority of San Francisco sought to introduce disincentive pricing when it learned that the famous bridge structure was overtaxed with traffic. They decided to charge the motorist according to how many passengers he had in the car, with the highest charge made for the car with a single passenger down to a very small charge for the car with four or more passengers. This disincentive pricing scheme led to the formation of more driving pools but not as many as the authority had hoped.

Public mass transit companies have considered using disincentive pricing to discourage travel at rush time. These companies are in a bad financial situation because they have to finance the purchase of enough equipment to cover needs during the rush periods, while the equipment sits idle the rest of the time. The pricing possibilities include raising the fare during rush hours or at least offering a lower fare than the existing one at off-hours. This pricing has not been put into effect, however, because it penalizes those who have no choice but to travel during rush hours and because the fare differential cannot be made large enough to produce the needed shift to off-hour usage.[3]

The emergence of shortages of gasoline, natural gas, electrical energy, and other products will increase the interest of more organizations in the use of disincentive pricing. The theoretical pricing model described earlier can be used in principle to find the price that would achieve a specified reduction in usage.

PRICE SETTING IN PRACTICE

Many pricing models used in practice tend to be less clear about objectives and take a limited view of the pricing problem and opportunities. They tend to base price on one factor such as cost, demand, or competition, to the neglect of the other factors. Although not elegant, they meet some of the more practical requirements for price determination in the presence of imperfect information and multiple publics.

Cost-Oriented Pricing

Cost-oriented pricing refers to price set largely on the basis of costs. The most elementary examples of this are markup pricing and cost-plus pricing. They are similar in that the price is determined by adding some fixed percentage to the unit cost. Markup pricing is commonly found in the retail trades where the retailer adds predetermined but different markups to various goods he carries. It is used by museum shops in pricing their various gift items. Cost-plus pricing is used to describe the pricing of jobs that are nonroutine and difficult to "cost" in advance, such as construction and military weapon development.

Cost-oriented pricing remains popular for a number of reasons. First, there is generally less uncertainty about costs than about demand. By pinning the price to unit costs, the seller simplifies his own pricing task considerably; he does not have to make frequent adjustments as demand conditions change. Second, when all organizations in the industry use this pricing approach, their prices are likely to be similar if their costs and markups are similar. Price competition is therefore minimized, which would not be the case if they paid attention to demand variations when they priced. Third, there is the feeling that cost-markup pricing is socially fairer to both the buyer and the seller. The seller does not take advantage of the buyer when his demand becomes acute; yet the seller earns a fair return on his investment. Thus the popularity of a cost-oriented approach to pricing rests on considerations of administrative simplicity, competitive harmony, and social fairness.

Demand-Oriented Pricing

Demand-oriented pricing looks at the intensity of demand rather than the level of cost to set a price. A high price is charged when or where demand is intense, and a low price is charged when or where demand is weak, even though unit costs may be the same in both cases.

A common form of demand-oriented pricing is price discrimination, in which a particular product is sold at two or more prices. Price discrimination takes various forms.

Pricing that discriminates on a *customer basis* is illustrated when a museum charges a lower price to students than to the general public. Pricing that discriminates on a *product-version basis* occurs when the U.S. Postal System charges more for registered mail than for unregistered mail. Pricing that discriminates on a *place basis* occurs when a symphony charges more for front-row seats than back-row seats. Pricing that discriminates on a *time basis* occurs when a telephone company charges less for long-distance calls placed after business hours.

For price discrimination to work, certain conditions must exist.[4] First, the market must be segmentable, and the segments must show different intensities of demand. Second, there should be no chance that the members of the segment paying the lower price could turn around and resell the product to the segment paying the higher price. Third, there should be little chance that competitors will undersell the firm in the segment being charged the higher price. Finally, the cost of segmenting and policing the market should not exceed the extra revenue derived from price discrimination.

Competition-Oriented Pricing

When a company sets its prices chiefly on the basis of what its competitors are charging, its pricing policy can be described as competition-oriented. It is not necessary to charge the same price as competition, although this is a major example of this policy. The firm that uses competition-oriented pricing may seek to keep its prices lower or higher than competition by a certain percentage. The distinguishing characteristic is that it does *not* seek to maintain a rigid relation between its price and its own costs or demand. Its own costs or demand may change, but the firm maintains its price because competitors maintain their prices. Conversely, the same firm will change its prices when competitors change theirs, even if its own costs or demand have not altered.

The most popular type of competition-oriented pricing is where a firm tries to keep its price at the average level charged by the industry. Called *going-rate* or *imitative pricing*, it is popular for several reasons. Where costs are difficult to measure, it is felt that the going price represents the collective wisdom of the industry concerning the price that would yield a fair return. It is also felt that conforming to a going price would be least disruptive of industry harmony. The difficulty of knowing how buyers and competitors would react to price differentials is still another reason for this pricing.

Going-rate pricing primarily characterizes pricing practice in homogeneous product or service markets. The firm selling a homogeneous product has little choice about the setting of its price. The firm daring to charge more than the going rate would attract virtually no customers. The firm thinking about charging less finds this unnecessary either because it can sell its current output at the going price or because it fears that competitors will cut their prices too.

In markets characterized by *product differentiation*, organizations have more latitude in their price decision. Product differences serve to desensitize the buyer to existing price differentials. Organizations such as private universities try to establish themselves in a pricing zone with respect to their competitors, assuming the role of either a high-tuition university, a medium-tuition university, or a low-tuition university. Their product and marketing programs are made compatible with this chosen pricing zone or vice versa. They respond to competitive changes in price to maintain their pricing zone.

INITIATING A PRICE CHANGE

Pricing is a challenging decision when the organization is thinking about initiating a price change. The organization may be considering a *price reduction* in order to stimulate demand, to take advantage of lower costs, or to gain on weaker competitors. Or it may be considering a *price increase* in order to take advantage of strong demand or to pass on higher costs. Whether the price is to be moved up or down, the action is sure to affect buyers, competitors, distributors, and suppliers, and may interest government as well. The success of the move depends critically on how the parties respond. Yet their responses are among the most difficult things to predict. Hence, any contemplated price change carries great risks. Here we shall examine methods of estimating customer reactions to price changes.

Price Elasticity of Demand

The traditional analysis of buyers' reactions to price change is based on the assumption that all buyers learn of the price change and take it at face value. The magnitude of their response to the price change is described by the concept of *price elasticity of demand.* This term refers to the ratio of the percentage change in demand (quantity sold per period) caused by a percentage change in price.[5] A price elasticity of −1 means that sales rise (fall) by the same percentage as price falls (rises). In this case, total revenue is left unaffected. A price elasticity greater than −1 means that sales rise (fall) by more than price falls (rises) in percentage terms; in this case, total revenue rises. A price elasticity less than −1 means that sales rise (fall) by less than price falls (rises) in percentage terms; in this case, total revenue falls.

Price elasticity of demand gives more precision to the question of whether the organization's price is too high or too low. For example, suppose the price elasticity for the Massachusetts Turnpike is −½. This means that the Massachusetts Turnpike could raise the present toll and increase its total revenue. If on the other hand, the price elasticity of the Massachusetts Turnpike is −2, it could increase its total revenue by lowering the toll. This is why it is critical to measure price elasticity.

In practice, price elasticity is extremely difficult to measure. There are definitional as well as statistical hurdles. Definitionally, price elasticity is not an absolute characteristic of the demand facing a seller but rather a conditional one. Price elasticity depends on the magnitude of the contemplated price change. It may be negligible with a small price change (one below the threshold level) and substantial with a large price change. Price elasticity also varies with the original price level. A 5 percent increase over current prices of $1 and $1.20, respectively, may exhibit a quite different elasticity. Finally, long-run price elasticity is apt to be different from short-run elasticity. Buyers may have to continue with the present seller immediately after his price increase because choosing a new seller takes time, but they may eventually stop purchasing from him. In this case, demand is more elastic in the long run than in the short run. Or the reverse may happen; buyers drop a seller in anger after he increased prices but return to him later. The significance of this distinction between short-run and long-run elasticity is that the seller will not know for a while how wise his price change is.

In addition to the need for a careful definition of elasticity in each situation, major statistical hurdles face the organization wishing to evaluate it. In fact, different techniques have evolved, none completely appropriate or satisfactory in all circumstances. We shall describe four techniques and illustrate them with the situation in which a public mass transit company is thinking about lowering its fare from 50 cents to 25 cents to attract more riders.

Direct Attitude Survey. The transit company can interview a sample of potential riders as to whether they would begin to use mass transit (instead of their automobile) if the fare were lowered from 50 cents to 25 cents. The percentage who said yes could then be applied against the known total number of potential riders to find the number of extra passengers this would mean.

Statistical Analysis of Relationship between Price and Quantity. This can take the form of either a historical or cross-sectional analysis. A historical analysis consists in observing how ridership has been affected in the past by rate reductions. A cross-sectional analysis consists in observing how ridership varies with the rates charged by transit companies in different cities.

Market Test. The company can reduce its fare for one month to see how many new riders are attracted.

Analytic Inference. The company can conjecture how many car riders are likely to find the lower fare to mean a significant saving to them without too much added inconvenience. Persons with lower incomes and longer distances to drive might be more amenable than persons with higher incomes and shorter distances to drive. The estimate would be built up by segments.

These are the major approaches to estimating demand elasticity.[6] They work with different degrees of success in different circumstances, and sometimes two or more of them may be undertaken simultaneously for additional confirmation.

Perceptual Factors in Buyers' Response

In discussing elasticity, we assumed that price changes would be interpreted in a straightforward manner. This is not necessarily true. A *fare reduction* by a transit company may symbolize any number of things:

The quality of the service will go down.
The service has some fault.
The transit company is in financial trouble and may not survive very long.
The price will come down even further and it pays to wait.

A *fare increase* may also be given unorthodox interpretations:

The service is going to be improved.
The service was given away at a cost below its true value.

Thus perceptual factors may lead consumers to react to a price change in a way opposite to the one expected. If riders thought that a lower fare was going to mean poorer service, more crowding, and less safety, then it would not attract more riders. If a university felt that a higher tuition suggested more quality and services, then a high tuition might actually increase the number of applicants. To the extent price is associated with prestige, a higher price may stimulate demand.[7]

Furthermore, price is not the only factor in affecting the buyer's response to a price or price change. The price itself represents what he has to give up of other things in order to obtain the service in question. Even if the organization did not charge a price, the market will still perceive a cost attached to obtaining the "free good." The clients have to expend a certain amount of energy and time studying the offer and competing offers and physically obtaining the desired service. They might undergo some psychological cost as well in order to obtain the offering. Thus energy, time, and psychological costs are part of the total price of the service as viewed from the client's vantage point. The pricing problem is challenging for the organization that is contemplating a price change because of the difficulty of estimating price elasticity. On the psychological level, price changes may have meanings for consumers that vary from those intended.

SUMMARY

Price is an important element of the marketing mix. Nonprofit organizations such as the U.S. Postal System, public mass transit companies, universities, hospitals, museums, charity organizations, and others must make difficult pricing decisions that will affect substantially the amount of money they raise.

An organization can be guided by any of four different objectives in setting its price: profit maximization, cost recovery, market incentivization, and market disincentivization. There is an elegant theoretical model for profit-maximizing pricing that utilizes demand and cost functions, but it may be too simple for practical pricing problems because of long-run considerations, other parties than the buyers, other marketing mix elements, and data estimation problems.

Price setting in practice is normally oriented to cost, demand, or competitive considerations.

NOTES

1. David J. Schwartz, *Marketing Today: A Basic Approach* (New York: Harcourt Brace Jovanovich, Inc., 1973), p. 468.

2. See Joel Dean, *Managerial Economics* (Englewood Cliffs, N.J.: Prentice-Hall, Inc., 1951), pp. 420 ff.

3. See William S. Vickrey, "A Proposal for Revising New York's Subway Fare Structure," *Operations Research* (February 1955), pp. 38–68.

4. George Stigler, *The Theory of Price*, rev. ed. (New York: The Macmillan Co., 1952), pp. 215 ff.

5. In symbols,

$$E_{qp} = \frac{\dfrac{Q_1 - Q_0}{Q_0}}{\dfrac{P_1 - P_0}{P_0}} = \frac{\text{relative change in quantity}}{\text{relative change in price}}$$

where:

E_{qp} = elasticity of quantity sold with respect to a change in price
Q_1 = quantity sold per period after price change
Q_0 = quantity sold per period before price change
P_1 = new price
P_0 = old price

6. Still other approaches are outlined in Edgar A. Pessemier, "A New Way to Determine Buying Decisions," *Journal of Marketing* (October 1959), pp. 41–46; and Wayne A. Lee, "Techniques for Pretesting Price Decisions," in *Pricing: The Critical Decision*, Marketing Division Report No. 66 (New York: American Management Association, 1961).

7. The psychology of pricing has spawned a large literature. See Kent B. Monroe, "Buyers' Subjective Perceptions of Price," *Journal of Marketing Research* (February 1973), pp. 70–80.

QUESTIONS

1. A major university with an excellent football team is thinking about discontinuing its policy of giving free tickets to students for home games. The school never has any empty seats in its stadium on Saturday afternoons. Do you think this would be a wise move? If so, what kinds of pricing alternatives are available to the school?

2. A community organization in a black, urban area has convinced several famous black entertainers to donate performances at a fund-raising concert in a city park. Should the organization charge a profit-maximizing admission price for this concert?

3. How high do you think city governments should set the fine for normal parking violations?

4. Can an organization that has enough funds to eliminate the need to charge a price for its products or services charge a price that is too low? Give some examples of organizations that should avoid under-charging.

5. The New York City subway system experienced a large increase in number of riders as a result of the "Energy Crisis." The subway service in New York is notoriously poor and improvements are needed badly. Should the system take advantage of its increased popularity and charge higher fares to accumulate more funds to pay for improvements?

6. The Zoological Society of Houston is planning a marketing campaign to double its membership. It plans to take full page ads in newspapers using the theme JOIN THE ZOO. The copy will show the full face of a chimpanzee and be headlined "Be a Monkey's Uncle." The Zoological Society is looking for a pricing structure for four classes of membership: family membership, sustaining membership, patron membership, and life membership. Develop a coupon for the ad that might suggest these options and also the benefits of joining the society.

10 Distribution Decisions

"How do you make love to a porcupine?"
"Very carefully."

The third major variable in the organization's marketing mix is called *place* or *distribution,* and it concerns how the organization plans to make its products and services available and accessible to customers.

In applying the distribution concept to nonprofit organizations, alternative names exist to describe the problem. Persons in the field of education, in discussing steps that might be taken to speed up the adoption of educational innovations, describe this as a problem in *dissemination.* They talk about searching for better means to disseminate an educational product, service, or idea. In the field of health care, the problem of providing better services is usually described as one of finding better *health delivery systems.* Others think about the problem as one of locating a set of facilities to serve optimally a given spatially dis-

FIGURE 10-1

**Assigning a Set of Facilities
to Serve a Given Population**

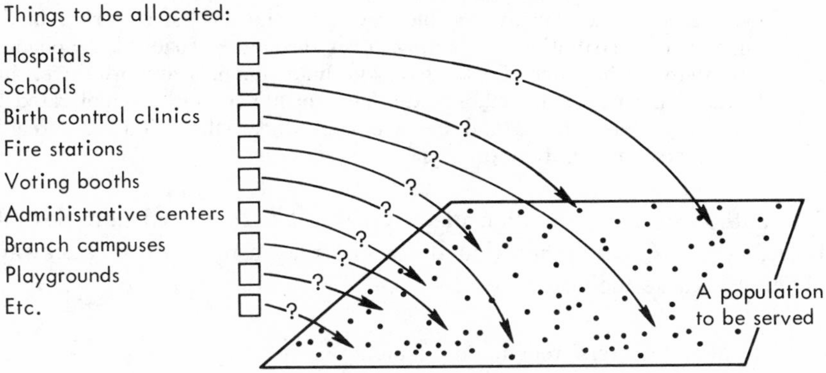

Things to be allocated:

Hospitals
Schools
Birth control clinics
Fire stations
Voting booths
Administrative centers
Branch campuses
Playgrounds
Etc.

A population
to be served

Source: Ronald Abler, John S. Adams, and Peter Gould, *Spatial Organization* (Englewood Cliffs, N.J.: Prentice-Hall, Inc., 1971), p. 532.

tributed population. This is illustrated in Figure 10-1 and characterized in the following terms:

> Hospitals must be located in geographic space to serve the people with complete medical care, and we must build schools close to the children who have to learn. Fire stations must be located to give rapid access to potential conflagrations, and voting booths must be placed so that people can cast their ballots without expending unreasonable amounts of time, effort or money to reach the polling stations. Many of our states face the problem of locating branch campuses to serve a burgeoning and increasingly well educated population. In the cities we must create and locate playgrounds for the children. Many overpopulated countries must assign birth control clinics to reach the people with contraceptive and family planning information.[1]

Channels of distribution must be chosen for persons as well as for goods and services. For example, a professional comedian seeking an audience before 1940 had available seven different channels: vaudeville outlets, special events, nightclubs, radio, movies, carnivals and circuses, and theaters. Then in the 1950s television became extremely popular and vaudeville disappeared as a distribution channel. Politicians also must make a choice among various channels available to them for reaching the voters.

Channels normally are thought to describe routes for the forward movement of product. Recently, there has been more talk about the development of *backward channels*.

> The recycling of solid wastes is a major ecological goal. Although recycling is technologically feasible, reversing the flow of materials in the channel of distribution—marketing trash through a "backward" channel—presents a challenge. Existing background channels are primitive, and financial incentives are inadequate. The consumer must be motivated to undergo a role change and become a producer—the initiating force in the reverse distribution process.[2]

The authors of this quotation identify several current and new possible future types of middlemen that do or can play a role in the "backward channel." These include:

1. Manufacturers' redemption centers
2. "Clean-up Days" community groups
3. Traditional middlemen; e.g., soft-drink middlemen
4. Trash-collection specialists
5. Recycling centers
6. Modernized "rag and junk men"
7. Trash recycling brokers
8. Central processing warehousing

An illustration of distribution channel thinking to a nonprofit organization problem is shown in Figure 10-2. The National Institute of Education (NIE) is responsible for speeding up the dissemination and adoption of worthwhile educational innovations in a nation consisting of 18,000 school districts under local control. Figure 10-2 shows four different distribution models that might be used for this task. The first model calls for direct distribution of innovations from NIE to each of the 18,000 school districts. This is clearly an inefficient system of distribution, involving too many first-hand contacts and the absence of an appreciation of local conditions. The second model calls for NIE to present the innovations to *regional dissemination centers* (RDCs—perhaps major universities) which in turn would disseminate them to all the local schools in their area. The regional dissemination centers would have the advantage of local market credibility and yet possess the skills of a change agent organization. The third model is similar to the second, with the modification that the regional distribution centers would not deal with all the school districts in their region but mainly with those schools designated as innovator schools which are looked up to by other schools in the region. These innovator schools will "retail" the innovations and pre-

FIGURE 10-2
Four Models for Disseminating Educational Innovations

1. Direct Marketing Model
   (Zero-level marketing channel)

   0. NIE —► all school districts

2. Regional Dissemination Center Model
   (One-level marketing channel)

   0. NIE —► RDC
   1. RDC —► school districts

3. RDC and Innovator School Model
   (Two-level marketing channel)

   0. NIE —► RDC
   1. RDC —► innovator schools
   2. Innovator schools —► other schools

4. RDC, Innovator School, and Local
   Change Agent Model

   (Three-level marketing channel)

   0. NIE —► RDC
   1. RDC —► innovator schools
   2. Innovator schools —► school district
      change agents
   3. Change agents —► other schools

Symbols:
   ● NIE–National Institute of Education
   o RDC–regional dissemination center
   ■ Innovator school
   □ School district change agents
   · School district

sumably be more effective because of the high esteem in which they are held by the other schools. Finally, a fourth model adds still one more channel link to the market, in the form of designated school district change agents. Each school district would designate one person to be the school district's change agent. This person would be responsible to the school district for (1) searching for new ideas and solutions to local school district problems by going to the local RDC, the NIE, or elsewhere, and (2) bringing innovations to the right parties within their school district. The establishment of this formal position within all school districts would make it easier for NIE and RDC to determine who to contact for information and communication. Establishing this type of job position requires a number of further questions to be answered, such as what should the change agent's functions be, how much authority and status should he have, and what kinds of people would be most effective in this role.

DECISION PROBLEMS IN DISTRIBUTION

We are now ready to examine the major decision problems that arise in designing and operating an efficient distribution system.

The Level and Quality of Customer Service

The first decision the marketer has to make is to determine the level and quality of service to offer to the target market. Each organization can visualize a maximum level of service that could conceivably be offered. Here are some examples:

> A public welfare department must distribute thousands of checks a year to people on public relief. The maximum level of service would be to mail a check daily to their homes or even to deliver the checks personally to avoid mail theft.

> A public library would render the maximum amount of service if it stood ready to receive calls for books and to deliver them within a few hours to the person's home.

> A city health department could dispatch doctors to the homes of sick patients upon call.

> A university could send a lecturer to any home or site upon the request for an educational service.

These solutions are oriented toward maximum consumer convenience. They are not practical because consumers would probably not pay for the extra convenience and the supplying organization could not afford the cost. Organizations have to find solutions that offer less consumer convenience in order to achieve more economies of distribution. Libraries and health departments, for example, can bring down their costs by offering their services in one or a few locations and leaving the cost of travel to the consumers. They can cut down their costs still further by running a spare organization in which waiting time is borne mainly by customers instead of becoming idle time borne by the staff. If a health clinic had five doctors instead of ten, the doctors would be continuously busy while patients would absorb the cost of waiting. This is a solution which reduces the organization's cost (doctor time) although it increases the consumer's cost. Thus we see that organizations must begin their distribution planning with a concept of the level and quality of service they will offer.

The Number and Location of Branches

The organization that determines that it will retail its service rather than deliver it direct has the further decision of how many retail outlets to operate. It is usually most economical for the organization to have only one branch. By having one large library in a major city, duplication of books, staff, and building costs can be avoided. The citizen will gain to the extent that he will find an extensive collection of books. He pays the price, however, of having to travel a longer distance. A system consisting of many small branches may attract more users for this reason. Most major cities compromise by building one major library in a central location and several branch libraries for the convenience of consumers. Some even go further and operate bookmobiles, which are mobile libraries that park in different neighborhoods on different days and make popular books available to consumers.

The cost of running a state university is normally minimized by operating only one campus. Years ago, the University of California was located in Berkeley, California, the University of Wisconsin was located in Madison, Wisconsin, and the University of Illinois was located in Champaign, Illinois. Gradually these universities opened additional branches, partly out of the concept of offering more convenience to residents in other parts of the state and partly to keep a single campus from becoming overly large and impersonal. Once these universities decided to distribute their product—education—more evenly through the state, they began to face all the classic distribution problems faced by business firms: how many branch locations to establish, how large should they be, where should each be located, and what specialization should take place at each branch.

The Use and Motivation of Middlemen

After deciding on a level of service and method of distribution, the organization can operate its own branches ("company branches") or contract for the services of middlemen. A middleman is defined as "a business concern that specializes in performing operations or rendering services directly involved in the purchase and/or sale of goods in the process of their flow from producer to consumer." [3] Familiar types of middlemen include wholesalers, retailers, and brokers, among others. But why should an organization relinquish any of the selling or supplying activities to middlemen? The delegation usually means relinquishing some control over how and to whom the products are sold. Because the use of middlemen is very common, there must be certain major advantages. Some of them are described below.

Many organizations lack the financial resources to carry out a full program of direct marketing.

> The government of India adopted family planning as an official cause and set up a department to disseminate birth control information and contraceptives. The department's goal was to make contraceptives available to the smallest, remotest villages of a vast nation.[4] The solution took the form of engaging the distribution services of some of the largest packaged-goods companies in India because of their reach into the remotest corners of India. For example, the government used the intricate distribution system of Lever Brothers of India and saved itself the tremendous cost of building its own pipeline to the final markets. In choosing final types of retailers, their objective was to make contraceptives maximally available and accessible to target users. They eventually elected to work with the following retailers: (a) health clinics, (b) barbers, (c) field workers, (d) retail stores, and (e) vending machines. By placing contraceptives in these channels, the Indian government felt that potential users would have no difficulty finding the product.

Even if an organization has the funds to build its own distribution channel to the final markets, it might not be able to do it as cheaply as could an existing distribution system. The cost of distributing contraceptives through India is low because the middlemen carry many other products which share in the cost of the distribution network. In a one-product distribution system, all the cost would be borne by that product.

A further reason for not building its own distribution system exists if the organization can put its funds to better use. Thus the number of births averted may be higher if the Indian government spends its funds to advertise family planning nationwide rather than using all its money to set up efficient distribution.

The use of middlemen largely boils down to their superior efficiency in the performance of basic marketing tasks and functions. Marketing intermediaries, through their experience, specialization, contacts, and scale offer the producing organization more than it can usually achieve on its own.

The decision to use middlemen involves the organization in a number of further decisions. The first is the problem of choosing the best middlemen from the large number who are available. The Indian government had to decide which of several large packaged-goods companies could do the best job. It might decide to use only one of them (*exclusive distribution*), a few of them (*selective distribution*), or many of them (*intensive distribution*). But it might find that a desired distributor is not willing to accept the assignment. Or the distributor might handle the product only if given exclusive distribution. Or the distributor might handle the product only if it receives better financial terms than are being offered. Thus the first problem is to select and interest good distributors.

The organization must follow this up by carefully establishing the terms and responsibilities of the distributors. This is called the *trade-relations mix* and consists of the price policies, conditions of sale, territorial rights, and specific services to be performed by each party. For example, an increasing number of public welfare agencies have decided not to mail checks directly to welfare recipients (because of mailbox theft) but to deposit these checks in bank accounts set up for the welfare recipients. This distribution solution requires clarifying how much the banks as middlemen will charge for checking services, what other services they will offer, and what rights the welfare recipients have.

The next requirement is that the organization provide continuous motivation of its middlemen to do their best job. This may require frequent contact, sales training, joint setting of quotas, and bonuses. Without a plan to provide motivation to the middlemen, they may have a tendency to neglect the organization's product in favor of the many other products they handle.

The final need is to evaluate middlemen performance periodically. Those middlemen who do not perform according to their market potential can be singled out for training in an effort to help them improve their performance; otherwise they may have to be dropped. For example, the U.S. Treasury Department uses commercial banks to retail its bonds. If it wished, it could also invite the U.S. Postal System to become an agent for selling U.S. bonds. Periodically the U.S. Treasury Department may want to evaluate alternative systems and specific middlemen within each system to see how efficient they are at selling U.S. bonds.

The Use of Facilitating Marketing Intermediaries

The last step in designing a distribution system is for the organization to engage the services of *facilitating intermediaries* where they are required. Facilitating intermediaries differ from middlemen in that they are not involved in direct selling or negotiation but rather provide ancillary marketing services, such as shipping, warehousing, financing, advertising, marketing research, and so on. In the case of each of these functions, the organization must decide whether to hire or provide its own service internally. The organization may deliver its own product or contract a professional shipper. It may design its own advertisements or hire an advertising agency. Unless it needs any of these services on a large and continuing basis, the organization usually gains in the long run by contracting for professional distribution and marketing services.

Nonprofit organizations should be alert to new ways to use facilitating intermediaries to get their product to the final buyers.

A few universities have been particularly imaginative in this respect. There is no reason to confine the delivery system for education to the classroom. Some universities offer correspondence courses which enable a student to do his study on his own time at home. Other universities have placed their product on educational television channels, allowing it to flow into the homes or into special classrooms throughout the city or state, thus amplifying the size of the audience for any one lecturer. Occasionally a college conceives of a very novel distribution possibility, such as the commuter railroad classroom. A railroad car is contracted by a university and outfitted as a classroom. As it speeds toward the downtown area each morning, 30 or so executives on their way to work spend 50 minutes in class working their way toward a degree from that university.

SUMMARY

Distribution, the third major variable in the marketing mix, is as relevant to nonprofit organizations as it is to profit organizations. An organization's product or service is typically removed in space from the location of the consumer; and it may be removed in time according to when the consumer would like to use it. This creates a storage and/or distribution problem, the costs of which might be borne entirely by the organization, or by the consumers, or shared by both.

To design an efficient distribution, delivery, or dissemination system, an organization must first decide on the level and quality of service to offer to its target market. Usually it cannot afford to maximize the customer's convenience by direct delivery so it resorts to the less expensive solution of creating one or more retail branches. Its second problem is to decide on the number and location of these branches given the locational pattern of the final consumers. Its third problem is to decide on how much of the sales work of distribution should be subcontracted to established middlemen who, instead of actually raising the costs, can often bring them down because they operate at an efficient scale of distribution. The final problem is to decide how much of the services of facilitating intermediaries to contract for and how much to do internally. The occasional work of advertising, financing, shipping, and so on often can be performed more efficiently and effectively through professional facilitating intermediaries.

NOTES

1. Ronald Abler, John S. Adams, and Peter Gould, *Spatial Organization* (Englewood Cliffs, N.J.: Prentice-Hall, Inc., 1971), pp. 531–32.

2. William G. Zikmund and William J. Stanton, "Recycling Solid Wastes: A Channels-of-Distribution Problem," *Journal of Marketing* (July 1971), p. 34.

3. *Marketing Definitions: A Glossary of Marketing Terms*, compiled by the Committee on Definitions of the American Marketing Association, Ralph S. Alexander, Chairman (Chicago: American Marketing Association, 1960).

4. Nicholas J. Demerath, "Organization and Management Needs of a National Family Planning Program: The Case of India," *Journal of Social Issues*, 23, No. 4 (1967), pp. 179–93.

QUESTIONS

1. Does the marketer of an idea (such as equal employment opportunity) have any distribution problems, or are his distribution problems really promotion problems?

2. Discuss the relative merits of utilizing the eight different types of middlemen listed in the chapter for helping to recycle solid wastes.

3. Compare the advantages and disadvantages of exclusive distribution, selective distribution, and intensive distribution.

4. Governor Dan Walker of Illinois set up several "branch offices" around the state in order to bring government "closer to the people." The offices were to be placed where citizens could go with complaints and problems. Was this the best distribution strategy the governor could have used? What other distribution schemes were possible?

5. Was the government of India taking any risks in using Lever Brothers to distribute contraceptives? What can an organization lose by using other organizations to distribute its products?

6. Describe the distribution system of the Campus Crusade for Christ.

11   Communication and Promotion Decisions

All women, of whatever age, rank, profession or degree, whether virgins, maids or widows, that shall impose upon, seduce or betray into matrimony any of His Majesty's subjects, by scents, paints, cosmetics, washes, artificial teeth, false hair, iron stave hoops, high-heeled shoes, bolstered hips, or padded bosoms shall incur the penalty of the law enforced against witchcraft and like misdemeanors and, upon conviction, that marriage stand null and void.

LAW PASSED BY THE BRITISH PARLIAMENT IN 1770

All organizations find it necessary to direct communications and promotion to their markets and publics. This chapter examines the decision issues in the effective use of five major persuasive communication instruments—advertising, publicity, personal contact, incentives, and atmospherics. These are key elements of the promotion mix which in turn must be skillfully blended with the other major elements of the marketing mix.

200

AN OVERVIEW

Promotion is a special form of communication.

Promotion encompasses all the tools in the marketing mix whose major role is persuasive communication.

Other elements in the marketing mix—product, price, and place—also can be used to make some contribution to persuasive communication. But these tools have other functions to perform as well. Promotion, on the other hand, is primarily dedicated to the task of persuasive communication—that is, presenting messages to the target audience which create interest or desire for the product.

In a modern economy, a great number of promotional tools can be found. Examples include:

Space and time advertising	Point-of-sale displays
Loudspeaker advertising	Sales literature
Mailings	Catalogs
Speeches	Films
Sales presentations	Trade exhibits
Demonstrations	Sales conference
Trading stamps	Packaging
Contests	House-organ publications
Premiums	Product publicity
Free samples	Corporate publicity
Price specials	Corporate identification programs
Coupons	Endorsements
Posters and show cards	Atmospheres

In specific institutional settings, distinct promotional tools may evolve to serve the needs of that institution. Fund-raising organizations, for example, make heavy use of benefit dinners and dances, auctions, bazaars, concerts, telethons, walkathons, door-to-door campaigns, plate passing, and direct mail to raise money. Each of these promotion tools have unique effects and unique complexities and marketing specialties have grown around them.

A classification of the various promotional tools is desirable to facilitate analysis and planning. These tools fall into five groups.[1]

Advertising: any paid form of nonpersonal presentation and promotion of ideas, goods, or services by an identified sponsor.

Publicity: nonpersonal stimulation of demand for a product, service, or business unit by planting commercially significant news about it in a published medium or obtaining favorable presentation of it upon radio, television, or stage that is not paid for by the sponsor.

Personal contact: oral presentation in a conversation with one or more prospective purchasers for the purpose of making sales or building good-will.

Incentives: items of financial value added to an offer to encourage some overt behavioral response.

Atmospherics: efforts to design the place of purchase or consumption in a way calculated to create specific cognitive and/or emotional effects in buyers or consumers.

These promotional tools are discussed on the following pages.

ADVERTISING

Advertising is an extremely salient and pervasive element in modern society. It involves such varied media as magazine and newspaper space; radio and television; outdoor (such as posters, signs, skywriting): novelties (matchboxes, calendars); cards (car, bus); catalogs; directories and references; programs and menus; circulars; and direct mail. It can be carried out for such diverse purposes as long-term buildup of the organization's name (institutional advertising), long-term buildup of a particular product (product advertising) or brand (brand advertising), information dissemination about a sale, service, or event (classified advertising), announcement of a special sale (sales advertising), and so on.

Advertising is coming into increasing use by nonprofit organizations, perhaps amounting to as much as $2 billion annually or 10 percent of total advertising. The following categories of nonprofit organization advertising can be distinguished:

Political Advertising. Political advertising has skyrocketed in recent elections. The 1972 presidential candidates alone spent $80 million in political advertising. Various state and local candidates spent another $320 million.[2]

Social Cause Organization Advertising. For many years, the Advertising Council, Inc., a nonprofit organization financed by American industry, has used advertising to promote social causes such as brotherhood, safe driving, aid to education, religious faith, forest fire prevention, and so on. It accepts a number of causes each year and arranges for the donated services of advertising agencies and media to prepare and broadcast this advertising (estimated value of these services in 1970: $451 million). It tends to avoid more controversial causes. Social cause organizations such as peace groups, ecology groups, family planners, and women's liberation organizations have also stepped up their advertising budgets to get their messages out to the public. They use regular advertising agencies for the most part although they have also turned to a few advertising agencies that are specializing in social issue advertising.[3]

Philanthropic Organization Advertising. Philanthropic advertising is distinguished from social cause advertising in being specifically directed to raising donations, on a regular or emergency basis, where the money will be used to help the needy or unfortunate, or to support education or research into worthwhile areas. Whereas the intent of social cause advertising is primarily propagandistic, the intent of philanthropic advertising is mainly fund raising. Philanthropic organizations are spending increasing amounts of money each year on advertising (including direct mail) to get their messages across.

Government Organization Advertising. Various governmental units are frequent advertisers. Municipalities and states spend considerable sums to attract new residents, tourists, and industrial developers. Park and recreation departments advertise outdoor recreational facilities and police departments issue messages to the general public on safety issues. The military services—Army, Navy, and Air Force—are currently trying to use the full power of advertising to attract a sufficient number of recruits. In 1973, the Pentagon requested $83.4 million in ad funds for the four services, an amount that exceeds the advertising budgets of such major companies as Coca-Cola, Quaker Oats, and Lever Brothers.

Private Nonprofit Organization Advertising. Universities, museums, symphonies, hospitals, and religious organizations all have strong communication responsibilities and are involved in preparing annual reports, direct mailings, classified ads, broadcast messages, and other forms of advertising.

In deciding to use advertising, the organization must develop its advertising objectives, advertising budget, message, media, and advertising evaluation. These steps are described in the following paragraphs.

Advertising Objectives

The first step is to clarify the advertising objectives.[4] This step consists of three decisions. The first decision is who is the *target consumer*. Consider this in terms of a family planning campaign. Should the campaign aim at high reproducing families such as the urban poor (who also happen to be the greatest resistors to family planning) or the low reproducing families such as the well-educated (who are normally more amenable to family planning)? Beyond this, should the specific target in the family be the husband or the wife? Who indeed is the initiator, influencer, and decider in husband-wife interactions over family planning? Thus the first decision is to determine the right target consumer for the communications.

The second decision calls for specifying the *target effect* to be sought. The target consumer can be conceived as being in some stage of readiness in relation to the product, such as *unawareness, awareness, comprehension, interest, desire, action.*[5] If the target consumer is unaware of the product, then the objective is to create awareness. If the target consumer is aware but not knowledgeable, the objective is to create comprehension of the product and its benefits. If the target consumer is knowledgeable, the purpose of the advertising is to create real interest, or even desire. Ultimately, of course, advertising essays to stimulate action toward the object, but this is usually a function of several factors.

We have been talking as if the product is something to be purchased. If the product is a person to be voted on, or an idea to be adopted, or an attitude to be favored, the task is to define possible stages toward these objects and the stage in which most of the audience is in. Sometimes, the audience is distributed over several stages and different tasks must be set for the advertising to create different target effects in different parts of the audience.

The third decision is to determine the optimal *target reach and frequency* of the advertising. Funds for advertising are rarely so abundant that everyone in the target audience can be reached, and reached with sufficient frequency. The marketer must decide what percentage of the audience he hopes to reach with what exposure frequency per period. An anti-smoking campaign may aim to reach mainly the heavy smokers and to reach them frequently as a reminder about the ill effects of smoking. A family planning campaign may aim to reach married couples between the ages of 18 and 30 with a low-frequency reminder per period.

Advertising Budget

After the target effect and audience reach and frequency are specified, the next step is to move toward the overall *advertising budget* needed to do the job. One rough way to estimate the advertising budget is to multiply the desired reach by the desired frequency to determine the total number of exposures that will be needed; and then to multiply the total number of exposures by the average cost of an advertising exposure in the type of media contemplated. For example, suppose the marketer is constructing a campaign to reach 30 million people approximately 4 times during the campaign period. This is a total exposure level of 120 million. Suppose the average mass media cost is approximately $4 per thousand people. Then the rough advertising expenditure level will be $480,000.[6]

In addition to estimating the total size of the required advertising budget, a determination must be made of how the budget should be allocated over different market segments, geographical areas, and time periods. In practice, advertising budgets are allocated to segments of demand according to their respective populations, sales levels, or some other indicator of market potential. It is common to spend twice as much advertising money in segment B over segment A if segment B has twice as much of some indicator of market potential. In fact, however, the budget should be allocated to different segments according to their expected marginal response to advertising. A budget is well-allocated when it is not possible to shift dollars from one segment to another and increase total market response.[7]

Copy Development

Copy development is another step in the advertising planning process, although it does not necessarily come after the budget has been decided. It is conceivable that if extraordinary good copy is developed, the advertiser may want to alter the budget.

The message development process has three components. The first is *theme selection*.[8] Every advertisement or advertising campaign should be built on a central theme (also called motif, idea, appeal, or selling proposition) that brings about the desired effect on the market. This poses two tasks to the advertiser. The first is to generate a sufficient number of good themes. The second is to screen the themes to find the best one.

Theme generation can be handled in a number of ways. One approach is to talk to members of the target market to determine the way they see the service, talk about it, and express their desires about it. This will provide the advertiser with many ideas. A second approach is to brainstorm with key personnel in the organization. A third approach is to examine the product's actual and desired position in the product space and look for the themes that would shift the market's view of the product in the desired direction. The advertisement may try to change the belief about the product's level on some attribute, the perceived relative importance of different attributes, or introduce new attributes not generally considered by the market. A fourth approach is to use some deductive classificatory scheme to generate a set of possible themes. An initial classification of possible themes is that they may involve rational, emotional, or moral appeals.

Consider the search for a theme by the March of Dimes on birth defects. A *rational theme* attempts to present authentic information, such as "700 children are born each day with a birth defect." An *emotional theme* attempts to stimulate some emotion such as fear, guilt, status-seeking, ego, or greed; consider "Your next baby could be born with a birth defect." A *moral theme* suggests that a person should want to support the product out of a sense of rightness or duty; consider "God made you whole. Give to help those He didn't." [9]

Other theme-generating schemes have also been proposed. John Maloney suggested that consumers may be expecting any of four types of reward from an offering: rational, sensory, social, or ego-satisfaction.[10] And the consumer may visualize these rewards from results-of-use experience, product-in-use experience, or incidental-to-use experience. Crossing the four types of rewards with the three types of experience gives twelve modes of possible consumer orientation toward the offering currently found in the marketplace. The advertiser can generate a theme for each of the twelve cells as possible message bases of his campaign.

The task of selecting the best theme out of a large number of possible themes calls for the development of some criteria for judging the market potency of different themes. Twedt suggested that competing themes should be rated on three scales: *desirability, exclusiveness,* and *believability.*[11] A theme must say something desirable or interesting about the offering; it must suggest its distinctiveness from other offerings; and it must be stated in a believable manner. Twedt proposed that each potential theme be rated by members of the target audience from zero to one hundred on each scale. A theme's market potency would be a function of a multiplicative relation among the three scores because if any of the scores is particularly low, the theme's market potency would be greatly reduced.

In ads that make a claim or argument, theme selection must be followed by decisions on *message structure*—that is, the way in which the major arguments will be phrased and sequenced to achieve the maximum impact. Three issues must be faced in message structure. The first is the question of *conclusion drawing,* the extent to which the ad should draw a definite conclusion for the audience or leave it to them. Experimental research seems to indicate that explicit conclusion drawing is more persuasive than leaving it to the audience to draw their own conclusions. There are exceptions, however, such as when the communicator is seen as untrustworthy or the audience is highly intelligent and annoyed at the attempt to influence them. The second is the question of *one- vs. two-sided arguments*—that is, whether the message will be more effective if one or both sides of the argument are presented. Research seems to indicate that two-sided arguments enhance the communicator's credibility, work better with better-educated audiences, and work better with audiences initially opposed to the communicator's position. The third is the question of *order of presentation*—that is, whether the communication should present the strongest arguments first or last. Here the research evidence is mixed. Presenting the strongest argument first has the advantage of establishing attention and interest but this will dwindle as the communicator moves toward weaker and more anticlimactic arguments. About the only finding that stands up is that the strongest arguments do not belong in the middle of the message.[12]

The final step in message development is *copy layout and production*. If the ad is visual, decisions must be made on illustration, typography, the use of space, ad size, and color. One researcher has shown that format factors can be even more important than content factors in determining ad readership.[13] The packaging of the ad may be as important as the message in arousing attention, interest, and conviction.

Media Selection

Media selection is another major step in advertising planning. Some media thinking should take place before the message development stage and even before the advertising budget stage. For it is essential to determine which media are used by the target audience and which are most efficient costwise in reaching them. This information affects the advertising budget size and even the type of copy to be featured.

There are two basic steps in the media selection process. The first is to determine how the advertising budget will be allocated to the major *media categories*. The major media categories are newspapers, magazines, radio, television, and outdoor advertising. Thus a marketer may decide, given the target effect, reach, and frequency objectives, that he will spend 60 percent in television, 30 percent in magazines, and the rest in the other categories. The second step is to select the specific *media vehicles* within each category. Consider a family planning agency trying to reach educated young people: in the magazine category, it must choose among *Time, Newsweek, Atlantic, Harper*, and many other magazines. The media planner has statistics available on the circulation and characteristics of the audiences of different magazines and the costs of different size and color and insertions. Today he can utilize modern computer programs to select an efficient media mix for reaching his target audience.[14]

Not only must media choices be made, but also the specific times and issues. This is the problem known as *advertising timing*. It breaks down into a macroproblem and a microproblem. The macroproblem is that of *seasonal timing*. For most products, there is a natural variation in the intensity of interest at different times of the year. There is not much interest in Senator X until his reelection; or much interest in university affairs during the summer. Most marketers do not attempt to time their advertising when there is little or no natural interest. This would take much more money and its effects would be dubious. Most marketers prefer to spend the bulk of the advertising budget just as natural interest is beginning to ripen in the product class and during the height of interest. Counterseasonal advertising is still rare in practice.

The other problem is more of a microproblem, that of *short-run timing* of advertising. How should advertising be spaced during a short period, say a week? Consider three possible patterns. The first is called *burst advertising,* and consists of concentrating all the exposures in a very short space of time, say all in one day. Presumably this will attract maximum attention and interest and if recall is good, the effect will last for a while. The second pattern is *continuous advertising,* in which the exposures appear evenly throughout the period. This may be most effective when the audience buys or uses the product frequently and needs to be continuously reminded. The third pattern is *intermittent advertising,* in which intermittent small bursts of advertising appear in succession with no advertising in between. This pattern presumably is able to create a little more attention than continuous advertising and yet has some of the reminder advantages of continuous advertising.

Advertising Evaluation

The final step in the effective use of advertising is that of *advertising evaluation.* The most important components are copy testing, media testing, and expenditure level testing.

Copy testing can occur both before an ad is put into actual media (copy pre-testing) and after it has been printed or broadcast (copy post-testing). The purpose of *ad pre-testing* is to make improvements in the advertising copy to the fullest extent prior to its release. There are three major methods of ad pre-testing:

1. *Direct ratings.* Here a panel of target consumers or of advertising experts examine alternative ads and fill out rating questionnaires. Sometimes a single question is raised, such as "Which of these ads do you think would influence you most to buy the service?" Or a more elaborate form consisting of several rating scales may be used, such as the one shown in Figure 11-1. Here the person evaluates the ad's attention strength, read-through strength, cognitive strength, affective strength, and behavioral strength, assigning a number of points (up to

a maximum) in each case. The underlying theory is that an effective ad must score high on all these properties if it is ultimately to stimulate buying action. Too often ads are evaluated only on their attention- or comprehension-creating abilities. At the same time, it must be appreciated that direct rating methods are judgmental and less reliable than harder evidence of an ad's actual impact on a target consumer. Direct rating scales help primarily to screen out poor ads rather than identify great ads.

2. *Portfolio tests*. Here respondents are given a dummy portfolio of ads and asked to take as much time as they want to read them. After putting them down, the respondents are asked to recall the ads they saw—unaided or aided by the interviewer—and to play back as much as they can about each ad. The results are taken to indicate an ad's ability to stand out and its intended message to be understood.

3. *Laboratory tests*. Some researchers assess the potential effect of an ad by measuring physiological reactions—heart beat, blood pressure, pupil dilation, perspiration—using such equipment as galvanometers, tachistoscopes, size-distance tunnels, and pupil dilation measuring equipment. These physiological tests at best measure the attention-getting and arousing power of an ad rather than any higher state of consciousness that the ad might produce.

There are two popular *ad post-testing methods,* the purpose of which is to assess whether the desired impact is being achieved or what the possible ad weaknesses are.

1. *Recall tests*. These involve finding persons who are regular users of the media vehicle and asking them to recall advertisers and products contained in the issue under study. They are asked to recall or play back everything they can remember. The administrator may or may not aid them in their recall. Recall scores are prepared on the basis of their responses and used to indicate the power of the ad to be noticed and retained.

2. *Recognition tests*. Recognition tests call for sampling the readers of a given issue of the vehicle, say a magazine, asking them to point out what they recognize as having seen and/or read. For each ad, three different Starch readership scores (named after Daniel Starch, who provides the leading service) are prepared from the recognition data:

> *Noted.* The percent of readers of the magazine who say they had previously seen the advertisement in the particular magazine.
>
> *Seen/associated.* The percent of readers who say they have seen or read any part of the ad that clearly indicates the names of the product (or service) of the advertiser.
>
> *Read most.* The percent of readers who not only looked at the advertisement, but who say that they read more than half of the total written material in the ad.

FIGURE 11-1
Rating Sheet for Ads

		Maximum points
Attention strength		
How well does the ad catch the reader's attention? (Consider the picture, headline, typography, and layout).	_____	(15)
How well does the ad catch the <u>right</u> reader's attention?	_____	(5)
Read-through strength		
How well does the ad lead the reader to read further?	_____	(20)
Cognitive strength		
How clear is the central message or benefit?	_____	(20)
Affective strength		
How well-chosen is the particular appeal among the variety of possible appeals?	_____	(10)
How effectively is this appeal presented in terms of arousing the desired emotions?	_____	(10)
Behavioral strength		
How well does the ad suggest follow-through action?	_____	(10)
How likely is the aroused reader to follow through?	_____	(10)
	_____	Total

0-20	20-40	40-60	60-80	80-100
A very poor ad	A mediocre ad	An average ad	A pretty good ad	A very effective ad

The Starch organization also furnishes Adnorms—that is, average scores for each product class for the year, and separately for men and women for each magazine, to enable advertisers to evaluate their ads in relation to competitors' ads.

It must be stressed that all these efforts rate the communication effectiveness of the ad and not necessarily its impact on attitude or behavior. The latter are much harder to measure. Most advertisers appear satisfied in knowing that their ad has been seen and comprehended and appear unwilling to spend additional funds to determine the ad's sales effectiveness.

Another advertising element that is normally tested is media. *Media testing* seeks to determine whether a given media vehicle is cost-effective in reaching and influencing the target audience. A common way to test a media vehicle is to place a coupon ad and see how many coupons are returned. Another media testing device is to compare the ad readership scores in different media vehicles as a sign of media effectiveness.

Finally, the advertising expenditure level itself can be tested. *Expenditure-level testing* involves arranging experiments in which advertising expenditure levels are varied over similar markets to see the variation in response.[15] A "high spending" test would consist of spending twice as much money in a similar territory as another to see how much more sales response (orders, inquiries, etc.) this produces. If the sales response is only slightly greater in the high spending territory, it may be concluded, other things being equal, that the lower budget is adequate.[16]

PUBLICITY

Publicity is a second major promotional tool, one in frequent use by nonprofit organizations. In fact, the limited financial resources of many nonprofit organizations lead them to rely substantially on publicity. Publicity is the achievement of news coverage in the press. In contrast to advertising, it is not paid for by the organization. Nor does it appear sponsored by the organization, as an ad does (although much publicity starts with a carefully written publicity release by the organization). On the negative side, the sponsoring organization has less control over the content of the final publicity in contrast with its total control over the content of a paid-for advertising message. Another difference is that those who prepare advertising work with the advertising departments of media and those who prepare publicity work with the reporters and feature writers of the news media. The media are not averse to printing "publicity," for it provides much in the way of interesting news.

A publicity campaign attempts to develop news around a product, service, organization, person, place, or idea. A consumer organization may call a press conference to announce a planned boycott of beef because of the high prices. An aspiring starlet might agree to pose for the centerfold of *Playboy* magazine. A museum might invite the public to tour its new wing. A new resort might seek a feature article in the travel section of the Sunday paper. School teachers might organize a march to dramatize their grievances.

The appeal of publicity to many organizations is that it is "free advertising"—that is, it represents coverage at no cost. However, publicity is far from free because special skills are required to write good publicity and to "reach" the press. Good publicists cost money.

Publicity has three qualities that make it a worthwhile investment. First it may have *higher veracity* than advertising because it appears to be normal news and not sponsored information. Second, it tends to catch people *off guard* who might otherwise actively avoid salesmen and advertisements. Third, it has high potential for *dramatization* in that it arouses attention coming in the guise of a noteworthy event.

In deciding to use publicity as a promotional tool, the organization must perform three tasks. The first is to define the *objectives* of the publicity effort. This calls for specifying the target market or markets at whom the publicity is to be aimed. Then it calls for defining the specific target variable in the target market which the publicity is intended to influence: this might be awareness, knowledge, interest, or desire. Finally, the time frame for the publicity effort must be specified —i.e., whether its aim is to create a single news item, a short campaign, or a long-term educational effort.

The second task is to search for *publicity ideas* that will achieve the desired effects. The number of ideas are limited only by the imagination of the planners. For example, the American Cancer Society distributes a brochure to local units in which they outline the following ideas for special events:

> Dramatic special events attract attention to the American Cancer Society. They bring color, excitement, and glamor to the program. Well planned, they will get excellent coverage in newspapers, on radio and TV, and in newsreels. . . . A Lights-On-Drive, a one-afternoon or one-night House-to-House program have such dramatic appeal that they stir excitement and enthusiasm . . . keep in mind the value of burst of sound such as fire sirens sounding, loud-speaker trucks, fife and drum corps. . . . A most useful special event is the ringing of church bells to add a solemn, dedicated note to the launching of a drive or education project. This should be organized on a division or community basis, and the church bell ringing may be the signal to begin a House-to-House canvass. Rehearsals of bell ringing, community leaders tugging at ropes, offer good picture possibilities.[17]

Following the selection of ideas, the last task is to plan for these events in terms of *specific media involvement*. The face-to-face events must be arranged along with their leveraged treatment in newspapers, magazines, radio, and television. All this takes careful planning in order, ironically, to achieve the effect of apparent spontaneity.

PERSONAL CONTACT

A third major element in an organization's promotion and communication mix is personal contact by the organization's field representatives with the target markets. Nonprofit organizations usually specialize some of their personnel to deal specifically with clients. This is the role of social workers in social welfare agencies; museum guards and admission people in museums; police officers in police departments; and volunteer workers in charity organizations. Some of these personnel —such as volunteer workers—are primarily engaged in *selling;* others— such as social workers and police guards—are primarily engaged in providing *client service.* All of these field personnel create distinct impressions upon clients in the way they dress, speak, and treat people.

Generally speaking, nonprofit organizations do not carefully train their field employees in the nuances of client relations. Government organizations are particularly lax in getting their staffs to treat citizen-users sensitively and amiably. Even public administrators with good intentions often find it difficult to train their field employees in proper concepts of customer service because there are few incentives they can offer and recalcitrant employees are protected by civil service. The most positive development is the increased assertiveness of citizens who are no longer willing to accept shallow treatment from those who are supposed to be serving them.

Our purpose here is to describe the logical steps in organizing an effective personal contact function in an organization.

Personal Contact Objectives

The first task is to define carefully the different roles that are to be played by the personal contact function and to set objectives for them. Personal contact can play three roles in the client relationship, those of selling, servicing, and monitoring.

Personal contact serves a *selling* function to the extent that the organization's representatives are attempting to find and develop new clients or increase sales to existing clients. In such industries as retailing, insurance, heavy machinery, computers, and pharmaceuticals, the company sales force is the major communication and promotion tool. Companies in these industries spend millions to staff, train, and develop effective salesmen. Personal selling is seen as a vastly more effective tool than advertising in many situations. Whereas advertising is very public, indiscriminate, preformulated, and impersonal, personal selling is capable of being adjusted closely to the target customers' needs, interests, and dispositions. Personal selling adds a human element to the relationship between the company and the customer and allows a two-way dialogue and adjustment of interests to be worked out. For these benefits, companies pay a high price. An hour of a salesman's contact time with a customer might cost the organization anywhere from $30 to $60 because the cost must cover not only the contact time but the planning, traveling, and waiting time that makes this contact possible.

Nonprofit organizations on many occasions use sales personnel. Political parties must attract volunteers who will get on the phone or do house-to-house canvassing to sell citizens either on voting for a candidate or making personal contributions to the party. Evangelical religious organizations, such as the Seventh Day Adventists, send out believers and witnesses who stand on street corners or canvass homes attempting to stir up religious "sales." Most nonprofit organizations run fund-raising campaigns that use a sales organization in the true sense of the word. Family planning agencies use workers who attempt to sell families on the idea of carefully planning the number of children they want. In India, some of the workers earn commissions for every person who agrees to adopt a birth control device. To the extent that these organizations employ sales personnel, the principles for running an effective sales force in the commercial area apply to the nonprofit area.

The second function of personal contact is to provide *service* to clients. The service can take the form of consulting, informing, or assisting clients. In the nonprofit area, this role is performed by policemen, social workers, librarians, tax officials, and so on. Although they perform these services typically without a view toward selling, the quality of their service has a direct influence on future patronage and satisfaction of the organization's customers.

The third function of personal contact is to *monitor* developments among clients and competitors. The organization's personnel who deal with clients are in a good position to sense new needs and developments in the marketplace that are not reflected in any statistics or published reports. Commercial organizations encourage their sales and service representatives to listen keenly to those in the marketplace and report back important developments.

It is possible to assign the three personal contact functions—selling, servicing, and monitoring—to three different employee groups in an organization. It is also possible to assign all three functions to one group. The organization has to take a position on this matter. If one group is assigned all three responsibilities, the organization must define how much time is to be spent on each function. Objectives also can be set within each functional category. For example, organizations often specify how much selling time should be spent with current clients versus time spent searching for new clients.

Field Organization Design

After establishing the personal contact objectives, the organization can proceed to develop a blueprint of the *field organization.* Here three issues must be faced. The first is *size* of the field organization. Size will be set as a function of the actual or intended levels of sales and service that the organization wants to or can afford to provide. If we are talking about a pure service organization, the task is one of estimating the actual number of clients to be served annually, and the average amount of service per client per year that will be required. Suppose the organization has 1,000 clients and the average client requires twelve hours of service time a year. This makes a total of 12,000 hours of service to be supplied by the field personnel. If each field worker can provide 1,200 hours of client service a year, then the organization will need approximately 100 field workers. This method of calculation is called the workload approach to estimating field workforce size.[18]

If we are talking about a pure selling operation, the task is one of estimating how much business will be achieved with different numbers of field workers. Additional field representatives tend to add fewer net sales to an organization because the prime accounts and prospects are cultivated by the first field workers. The task is to estimate sales as a function of alternative levels of the field workforce size and then choose the number of field workers that maximize the organization's objectives.

The second issue is that of *organizational design.* Field personnel can deal with all clients or they can be specialized. Large commercial companies often specialize their sales and service personnel by product, type of customer, or territory. If this example were followed by a social welfare agency, field personnel might be specialized by home visits versus office services (different products); by indigent clients versus financially able clients (different customer types); or by North side versus South side clients (different territories). Specialization usually improves the quality of a particular service but leads to problems of coordination when customers require overlapping services.

The third question concerns *territorial design*. When field workers cover a large area, a critical problem is to design territories that are fairly equal in sales potential or workload. Consider the following examples:

> An evangelical organization assigns workers to different parts of a major city in relation to the perceived "sales potential." It may assign several people to canvass a crowded urban neighborhood where many persons are ripe for religious conversion and few or no workers to canvass affluent neighborhoods where the residents are less hospitable to missionary activity.
>
> Large national charity organizations attempt to assign workers to territories characterized by equal workload or geographical coverage. Thus the American Cancer Society wants to have a volunteer representative in each block of each major city. A set of block representatives reports to a district representative; and district representatives report to the city representative; and so on. This territorial structure allows the American Cancer Society to mobilize hundreds of thousands of people for one of its fund drives.

Field Personnel Administration

The final task in managing the personal contact function is to *staff and administer* the blueprinted organization. This breaks down into a logical progression of activities. The first step is to *recruit and select* persons who have the qualifications specified for the personal contact function. After such people are found and hired, they must be *trained* in the philosophy of the organization and its particular methods of relating to the clients. Following training, they must be *assigned* to available jobs in the organization. *Compensation levels* must be set which are sufficiently motivating and rewarding. Often *quotas* must be set to specify desired sales or service levels. Steps must be taken to *supervise and motivate* the personnel because of the many frustrations they experience in client work and problems they confront. Finally, their performance must be *evaluated* on a periodic basis with a view toward helping them improve themselves in the performance of their functions.

Each of the steps in sales and service administration involve sensitive issues and important distinctions that cannot be gone into here.[19] The organization is dealing with one of its most important and sensitive publics—namely, its own employees. Their feelings about the organization will tell in the service they render to clients.

INCENTIVES

A fourth method of promoting an object to a market is through the offering of incentives. *Incentives* are defined as *something of financial value added to an offer to encourage some overt behavioral response.*[20] Incentives are offered to persons or groups who are normally insufficiently motivated, indifferent, or antipathetic to a proposed behavior. They alter the perceived price of an offer in an effort to overcome the market's resistance or indifference.

Incentives play a very large role in commercial marketing. They normally go under the name of *sales promotion,* and include price deals, premiums, contests, free samples, and a host of other "add-ons" to encourage the market to try a product or object. Sales promotion may account for as much as half of the promotion budget behind a brand new product or a very mature product. In nonprofit marketing, various types of incentives also appear. For example, cash, cookware, transistor radios, and other objects of value have been offered in India to persons agreeing to appear for vaccinations, birth control devices, and other social objects. In the United States, many communities offer cash payments or other incentives to stimulate persons to make blood donations. Various charitable organizations sponsor contests and award prizes to those members who raise the largest amount of funds during the annual drive. In general, the incentive is an important promotional tool in the nonprofit area.

The decision by an organization to use incentives as part of its promotional plan calls for seven distinct steps.

The first step is to specify *the objective* for which it is deemed necessary or desirable to undertake the use of incentives. Three objectives can be distinguished. Sometimes incentives are offered to create an immediate behavioral response because the organization has excess capacity or inventory. For example, inventories tend to build up for mature products and companies resort to "cents-off" deals or trade allowances to stimulate early purchase. Incentives may also be offered to promote trial of a product or service by groups which normally would not venture to try the product. Finally, incentives may be offered to win goodwill toward the organization, as when an organization offers to match its employees' contributions to a particular charity.

The second step is to determine the *inclusiveness of the incentive—* that is, whether it will be offered to individuals or to the groups to which the target individuals belong. Most incentives are offered to individuals for their direct benefit. A case of an incentive that is offered to a group is exemplified in communities which offer to provide free blood to all persons in the community if four percent or more of the community's residents make blood donations.

The third step is to specify the *recipient* of the incentive—that is, whether incentives should go to consumers, suppliers, or sales agents. In the commercial field, one finds consumer promotions (e.g., free samples, coupons, price-offs, premiums, trading stamps), trade promotions (e.g., buying allowances, free goods, advertising allowances, push money, and contests), and sales force promotions (e.g., bonuses, contests). The same options occur in the nonprofit area. For example, incentives to promote vasectomies may be offered to the consumer, to the doctor, or to the canvasser who recruits prospects. At one time, canvassers in India were so incentivized to find prospects that they brought in men who were too young to know better and men who were too old for it to matter, in both cases a misdirection of effort.

The fourth step is to determine the *direction of the incentives*—that is, whether they should be positive (rewarding) or negative (punishing). Commercial organizations normally work with incentives rather than disincentives in promoting their offer. Governments work with both with equal facility: they offer subsidies and special advantages to encourage certain types of behavior and impose taxes or costs on other types of behavior. In any particular problem area, either option may be available. Nations wishing to expand the birth rate offer family allowances as an incentive. Nations wishing to contract the birth rate reduce family allowances or disproportionately tax large families.

The fifth step is to determine the *form of the incentive*—that is, whether it should consist of monetary or nonmonetary value. Monetary incentives include price-off, cash, bonds, and savings accounts. Nonmonetary incentives include a whole variety of things such as food, free education, health care, lottery tickets, or old age security. The form of the incentive must be carefully researched because its nuances may offend the target group. For example, although cash is a very tangible incentive, it may be viewed as a corrupt consideration if it is used to influence the decision on how many children to have. An offer of better housing may be received more favorably.

The sixth step is to determine the *amount of incentive*. An overly small incentive is ineffective and an overly large one is wasteful. If the incentive is nongraduated, the amount may seem too small for those in higher income brackets and too much for those in lower income brackets. This has led to interest in graduated incentives whereby the amount offered varies with the consumer's economic circumstances.

The seventh step is the *time of payment of the incentive*. Most incentives are paid immediately upon the adoption of the target behavior. Thus in the family planning area, the adoption of sterilization is usually immediately followed by payment. But the agreement to use birth controls pills may not be rewarded except on the basis of results each year.

In summary, incentives are an important means of promotion but they require, as we have seen, several steps of analysis and research. Commercial companies tend to learn over time what incentives work best and their optimal amounts and timing. In the area of family planning, several propositions are emerging about incentives and their effective use.[21] Similar knowledge is accumulating on the use of incentives in other health-related areas, such as nutrition, immunization, and self-medication practices. The outlook is one of increasing use of incentives in social and organizational marketing.

ATMOSPHERICS

The fifth major element in an organization's promotion and communication mix is that known as *atmospherics*. Atmospherics may be defined as *the designing of buying and consuming environments in a manner calculated to produce specific cognitive and/or emotional effects on the target market*. Atmospherics arise as a consideration when buyers and consumers come into contact with the organization's personnel and physical setting. The dress of the personnel and the physical setting emit, whether by intention or default, visual and other cues that are very telling about the organization. These cues lead to inferences about the organization's efficiency, stability, and concern for the client. The client considers this information and it affects his interest and patronage of the organization. Therefore, organizations should give thought to how the atmosphere of their establishment can promote the desired relationship with the clients.

Commercial marketers are increasingly recognizing the role played by atmospherics in attracting and maintaining customers. Long ago, restaurants recognized that persons selected restaurants as much for their atmosphere as for their food, and new restaurants are investing heavily to achieve surroundings that will attract and excite customers. Furniture stores are moving away from overcrowded and indiscriminate collections of furniture toward spaciously displayed groupings of furniture suites, enhanced by the smell of fine leather and the piping in of tasteful music. Airports and airlines invest heavily in creating atmospheres designed to soothe nerves and provide pleasure to flyers. Advertising agencies are careful to design their offices to suggest in some cases wild creativity and in other cases businesslike attention to detail. Psychiatrists, physicians, and hospitals are increasingly thinking through the design problems of facilitating the comfort of patients.

Atmospheric considerations are often neglected in many nonprofit and public organizations. Functional considerations prevail. There is little that is distinctive about most branch post offices, license bureaus, and clinics. This may reflect a desire to save money or an indifference to the feelings of the users. Atmospherics is not always a matter of extra cost; often it is simply a matter of thoughtfully designing the space for the group that will use it.

Steps in Atmospheric Planning

The first step is to define the target market and the target effect being sought. In designing a neighborhood health clinic, the comfort and convenience of different groups—patients, doctors, nurses—must be planned. With respect to each of these groups, the organization must think through the specific effects that the atmosphere should achieve.

The second step is to specify the elements of the physical setting that are to carry the intended cognitions and affects to target audiences. The elements of the setting include the exterior structure, the interior space, special displays, and the dress of the organization's personnel. Such skills as architecture, interior decoration, windowdressing, and wardrobe design are involved. For example, a new hospital has to think through such things as how it should look from the outside, feel on the inside, and what uniforms its personnel should wear.

The third step is to consider and select among specific sensory elements that convey the desired effects. Visual elements in designing atmosphere include color, brightness, size, and shapes. Aural elements include volume and pitch. Olfactory elements include scent and freshness. Tactile elements include softness, smoothness, and temperature. A fifth sensory element, taste, does not apply directly to atmosphere. An atmosphere is seen, heard, smelled, and felt, but not tasted. At the same time, certain artifacts in an atmosphere can activate remembered tastes.

Certain general propositions can be advanced about where atmospherics assume the greatest importance as a promotional or communication tool. First, atmospherics apply where many purchasers come into physical contact with the organization's physical plant and personnel. Second, atmospherics may be most useful as a device for establishing a distinctive character to an organization where most organizations are hard to differentiate. Third, atmospherics may be quite relevant where it is desirable to attune an organization to a distinctive social class. For example, an illegal abortion service serving middle-class patients made a point of establishing a middle-class look to the office and personnel to insure the comfort and confidence of the target population.[22]

SUMMARY

All organizations engage in communication and promotion activity. This activity can be considered as the fourth major component in the marketing mix. Promotion is defined as the development of persuasive communications. The main tools of promotion fall into five categories: advertising, publicity, personal contact, incentives, and atmospheres.

Advertising is an extremely important tool in the commercial world and is coming into increased use in the nonprofit sector. It is used to promote political candidates, social causes, philanthropic causes, military recruitment, and the services of hospitals, universities, churches, and other nonprofit organizations. It is a sophisticated and expensive tool that calls for skill in setting advertising objectives and budgets, in developing effective messages, media, and timing, and in evaluating advertising results.

Publicity is a familiar tool to nonprofit organizations in their effort to achieve news coverage at a minimum of cost. It has the attractive advantages of high veracity, an off-guard quality, and dramatization. Publicity effort requires definining organizational objectives in terms of target markets and target variables, generating publicity ideas, and attracting specific media coverage.

Personal contact is a major way to reach and communicate with target markets. It can serve the needs of selling, servicing, and monitoring markets. Although everyone in the organization comes into contact with different publics, certain members of the organization may specialize in client relations. Developing an effective field organization calls for two major steps. First, the organization must be properly designed in terms of required size, functional specialization, and territory coverage. Second, field personnel must be effectively recruited, selected, trained, assigned, compensated, motivated, and evaluated.

Incentives, another promotional tool, are used by an organization to achieve early product trial or win customer goodwill. The organization has to decide on such issues as the incentive's inclusiveness (individual or group), the recipient (dealer or final consumer), the direction (negative or positive), the form (monetary or nonmonetary), the amount (large or small), and the timing of payment (immediate or deferred).

Atmospherics are defined as the designing of buying and consuming environments in a manner calculated to produce specific cognitive and/or emotional effects on the target market. Many commercial organizations have discovered that effectively designed atmospheres can be powerful motivators of purchase or consumption. Nonprofit organizations should understand that their atmospheres communicate a great deal to their clients. Effective atmosphere planning calls for defining the target market and target effect sought, determining the key atmospheric variables, and selecting the most effective sensory combinations.

NOTES

1. The first three definitions are essentially found in *Marketing Definitions: A Glossary of Marketing Terms*, compiled by the Committee on Definitions of the American Marketing Association, Ralph S. Alexander, Chairman (Chicago: American Marketing Association, 1960). The term "personal selling" has been changed to "personal contact" and the last four words added.
2. See E. B. Weiss, "Political Advertising Blackens the Other Eye of the Ad Business," *Advertising Age*, February 12, 1973, pp. 35–40.
3. See John A. Zeigler, "Social Change Through Issue Advertising," *Sociological Inquiry* (Winter 1970), pp. 159–65.
4. For a good general discussion of advertising objectives, see Russell H. Colley, ed., *Defining Advertising Goals* (New York: Association of National Advertisers, 1961).
5. This is an example of a "hierarchy-of-effects" model. Different models describe the stages slightly differently, such as *attention, interest, desire, action* (E. K. Strong, *The Psychology of Selling*, 1st ed., New York: McGraw-Hill Book Co., 1925, p. 9); or *awareness, interest, evaluation, trial adoption* (Everett M. Rogers, *Diffusion of Innovations*, New York: The Free Press, 1962, pp. 79–86). All of these models assume that each succeeding stage implies a higher probability that the person will purchase the product. Some researchers, however, have pointed out that the stages are not necessarily unidirectional (Kristian S. Palda, "The Hypothesis of a Hierarchy of Effects: A Partial Evaluation," *Journal of Marketing Research*, February 1966, pp. 13–24).
6. There are more sophisticated ways to estimate the budget level which take into account advertising decay, competitive advertising, sales potential, and other factors. See the author's *Marketing Decision Making: A Model Building Approach* (Holt, Rinehart and Winston, 1971).
7. For a full discussion of marketing budget allocation rules, see Kotler, *Marketing Decision Making*, Chap. 6.
8. One of the best monographs on theme research and selection is found in Eduardo L. Roberto, *An Investigation of the Problem of Advertising Theme Research with Specific Application to the Social Marketing of Vasectomy Services* (unpublished doctoral dissertation, Northwestern University, 1973).
9. William A. Mindak and H. Malcolm Bybee, "Marketing's Application to Fund Raising," *Journal of Marketing* (July 1971), pp. 13–18.
10. John C. Maloney, "Marketing Decisions and Attitude Research," in George L. Baker, Jr., ed., *Effective Marketing Coordination* (Chicago: American Marketing Association, 1961), pp. 595–618.
11. Dik Warren Twedt, "How to Plan New Products, Improve Old Ones,

and Create Better Advertising," *Journal of Marketing* (January 1969), pp. 53–57.

12. For a review of these studies, see James F. Engel, David T. Kollat, and Roger D. Blackwell, *Consumer Behavior*, 2nd ed. (New York: Holt, Rinehart and Winston, 1973), pp. 332–38.

13. Daniel S. Diamond, "A Quantitative Approach to Magazine Advertising Format Selection," *Journal of Marketing Research* (November 1968), pp. 376–87.

14. See John D. C. Little and Leonard M. Lodish, "A Media Planning Calculus," *Operations Research* (January–February 1969), pp. 1–35.

15. See "E. I. duPont de Nemours & Co. (Inc.): Measurement of Effects of Advertising," in Robert D. Buzzell, *Mathematical Models and Marketing Management* (Boston: Division of Research, Graduate School of Business Administration, Harvard University, 1964), pp. 157–79.

16. For an excellent overall discussion of advertising evaluation methods, see Darrell B. Lucas and Steuart H. Britt, *Measuring Advertising Effectiveness* (New York: McGraw-Hill Book Co., 1963).

17. *Public Information Guide* (New York: American Cancer Society, Inc., 1965), p. 19.

18. See Walter J. Talley, "How to Design Sales Territories," *Journal of Marketing* (January 1961), pp. 7–13.

19. See Charles S. Goodman, *Management of the Personal Selling Function* (New York: Holt, Rinehart and Winston, 1970).

20. This definition, and the following discussion, relies largely on two sources: Edward Pohlman, *Incentives and Compensations in Birth Planning* (University of North Carolina: Carolina Population Center, 1971); and Everett M. Rogers, "Effects of Incentives on the Discussion of Innovations: The Case of Family Planning in Asia," a chapter in *Processes and Phenomena of Social Change*, Gerald Zaltman, ed. (New York: John Wiley & Sons, 1973).

21. Ibid.

22. See Donald W. Ball, "An Abortion Clinic Ethnography," in William J. Filstead, ed., *Qualitative Methodology* (Chicago, Ill.: Markham Publishing, 1970).

QUESTIONS

1. The New York Metropolitan Museum of Art is seeking to increase its membership, which begins at $15 a year. It believes that persons would respond more to selfish reasons for joining the museum than to broad social appeals. In this connection, the Met is trying to develop at least five tangible benefits that would go with museum membership. Can you suggest five benefits and prepare an ad that displays them?

2. If you have the money, can you place an advertisement in any media?

3. Ralph Nader has been quite successful at getting government agencies and legislatures to pass pro-consumer laws and regulations. He

has also aroused the public's interest in consumer issues. To what do you attribute Mr. Nader's success?

4. According to psychology professor Robert Sommer: "The cold, bare waiting areas of the typical airport are more discouraging of human contact than a penitentiary." Do you think Dr. Sommer is correct? Do most airports serve their municipalities as well as they possibly could?

5. In Great Britain, it has been found that seat belt usage increases sharply during nationwide advertising campaigns that encourage people to wear their belts at all times. However, usage declines rapidly after the campaigns end. Can you explain this phenomenon?

6. What kinds of incentives could the army use to get more college students to sign up for ROTC?

Administering the Marketing Program

12 Marketing Organization

Nothing ever succeeds which exuberant spirits have not helped to produce.

FRIEDRICH NIETZSCHE

The previous four chapters described the four major components of the marketing mix—product, price, place, and promotion—and their tactical use to accomplish the marketing objectives of the organization.

In this and the following two chapters, we turn to issues in the effective administration of marketing effort. Do organizations such as universities, hospitals, museums, and so on require a formal marketing department and marketing director in order to be effective at marketing (Chapter 12)? What are the most effective procedures for carrying out annual marketing planning and control (Chapter 13)? What is the role and design requirements of an effective marketing information system to aid in marketing planning and control (Chapter 14)?

In this chapter, we shall focus on questions of marketing organization. Most commercial companies have marketing departments or marketing job positions. This leads to the following questions:

1. Do nonprofit organizations require formal marketing personnel and positions in order to make sound marketing decisions?
2. How might marketing services be introduced into an organization for the first time?
3. What does a full-size marketing department look like?

DO NONPROFIT ORGANIZATIONS NEED FORMAL MARKETING PERSONNEL?

In this book, we have sought to establish that every organization faces markets and publics for which it is necessary to prepare plans and carry on relations. Every organization carries on marketing activities whether or not anyone in the organization is officially designated as a marketing manager. Now the question arises: Is it necessary to establish formal marketing positions in order for an organization to carry on its marketing activities effectively?

There are three possible stands to take on this issue. The first is that no special positions need to be created because the organization's various managers will possess enough sensitivity to the marketing issues and requirements to handle them effectively. Thus in a university, it might be argued that the deans of admission, students, faculty, and alumni can carry out planning for their constituencies without needing special marketing training. Furthermore, it can be argued that the organization's managers can buy outside marketing services from marketing research agencies, advertising agencies, public relations firms, and so on, as needed. The organization does not have to create its own job positions in the marketing area.

The second view is that the organization would benefit from establishing an internal marketing services department from which various managers could draw assistance to meet special needs that arise. The marketing services department might consist of a marketing director, a skilled marketing researcher, an advertising manager, and a customer service manager. Thus a university dean of admissions who wanted to know more about the knowledge and attitudes of high school students in different parts of the country toward this university would request a study by the marketing research director. The requesting dean would be billed at a rate to cover the actual costs of the research and overhead. The dean would have the option of buying outside marketing research, however, if he was not satisfied with the inside service.

The third view is that the organization would benefit from establishing a high-level marketing officer in addition to marketing services of various kinds. The high-level marketing officer would have four responsibilities. First, he would supply the other top administrators with the latest facts about the environment, market size, composition, and trends. Second, he would participate in the setting of annual objectives and be responsible for establishing plans and the needed resources required to achieve these objectives. Third, he would serve as the marketing conscience of the organization to overcome the tendency of other administrators to become so engrossed in their operations as to lose sight of fundamental market forces and relationships. Fourth, he would be responsible for managing and coordinating the various marketing services needed by others in the organization.

Given these three models for formal marketing in a nonprofit organization, where do most organizations stand? Most nonprofit organizations operate without any marketing personnel as such, with the possible exception of a public relations officer. The public relations officer in an organization is responsible for managing the organization's routine communications with its regular publics, developing campaign strategies for special projects, supplying information to requesting parties, and generally trying to put the organization in a favorable light. These activities cover some, but not all of the marketing activities normally occurring in an organization. Public relations normally does not carry out marketing research into consumer needs, perceptions, and preferences. It does not take responsibility for developing and introducing new products or services. It does not determine the characteristics of the basic products being offered to the market. It does not solve problems related to making services highly accessible and available. Public relations is an important function that is limited largely to the public communication needs of the organization and thus provides only one part of the total marketing services required by an organization.

Small organizations generally cannot afford the cost of establishing full-time marketing positions because their marketing needs are simple and less frequent, and their budgets are tighter. Their best recourse is to buy marketing services from outside suppliers when they need them. Religious and charity organizations are often in a good position to obtain "free" marketing counsel by requesting it from members or supporters who have these skills.

Large organizations that deal with several publics and sponsor many campaigns have a more continuous need for marketing services. The establishment of some internal marketing services is more justified. For example, a family planning organization may need a regular group of workers who go out into the community to find and educate new families to family planning concepts and methods. This group is essentially a sales force and might be headed by a manager who runs it according to the best concepts in sales force management, including careful recruiting, training, motivation, and incentivization of the field force. Similarly, a large university that uses advertising throughout the year might benefit from having its own full-time advertising director who grows up with the problems of educational institution advertising.

Large nonprofit organizations that provide a major service to the public—such as the U.S. Postal System, Amtrak, or specific mass transit companies—can benefit greatly from setting up a formal marketing department with a chief marketing officer. Today the U.S. Postal Service has a marketing department with specialists in marketing research, promotion, and selling to improve the postal system's understanding of the needs of different markets and to create viable new services. Lewis Schneider has argued that mass transit companies have not been too successful in reviving public interest in mass transit because they have failed to assign authority and responsibility for marketing functions in the same way as is done for operations and personnel functions.[1] We can expect to see the establishment of more marketing departments in nonprofit organizations where their size and problems call for continuous study, planning, and implementation of market-related concerns.

INTRODUCING MARKETING POSITIONS INTO AN ORGANIZATION

The establishment of formal marketing positions in an organization can occur in a number of ways. Sometimes it occurs in connection with a particular marketing activity that is carried out in different parts of an organization on a fairly continuous basis without the benefit of skilled and focused management. There may be a lot of buying of outside services and a general uneven quality of performance. This activity is a good candidate for the establishment of a formal marketing position. For example, the U.S. Postal System used to satisfy its marketing research needs by letting its various managers go out and buy these services as needed. Marketing research activity was sufficiently continuous to lead the system to establish for the first time a marketing research position at the headquarters level. The person hired for this position had several mandates, including identifying the major research needs of the U.S. Postal System, establishing project standards and procedures, developing subcontractor relations with various private marketing research suppliers, and educating post office management to the benefits and uses of marketing research. In general, this person is assigned to bring order, focus, and efficiency to this function. The marketing research position was established in the U.S. Postal System without much thought being given at the time to other marketing positions that might be created.

Sometimes an organization decides to establish a high-level marketing position rather than a particular staff service. The head of the organization might feel that the organization lacks marketing thinking and strategy and that someone skilled in marketing concepts must be added at the highest level. Thus a group seeking to establish a new Health Maintenance Organization might simply feel that it faces so many marketing problems that nothing less than a full-time, high-positioned marketing director must be added to the top group to guide strategy making and tactical marketing.

At other times an organization is of such a size and scope that it already carries on many separate activities of a marketing nature, such as advertising, marketing research, personal selling, and so on. The main problem may be that these activities are scattered in different parts of the organization and reporting to different officers. Furthermore, they may be working at times at cross-purposes; for example, an advertising manager in a university might develop an ad to interest students in coming for interviews for an evening education program not knowing that the school is short of admissions counselors to handle the expected number of inquiries. In this situation, the head of the organization might recognize the benefit of grouping various marketing activities under one head who can give them unified direction and leadership.

Thus, establishing new marketing positions in an organization is largely a matter of organizational size, resources, opportunities for improving efficiency, and the need for some central source of marketing leadership.

FULL-SIZE MARKETING DEPARTMENTS

If a nonprofit organization wanted to establish a full-size marketing department on the model of those found in commercial organizations, what would it look like? Even here, great variations are found within commercial organizations. The basic model, however, calls for a head of the marketing department, normally called the marketing vice-president, marketing director, or marketing manager. Several managers report to him. Some of them are responsible for *marketing functions,* such as sales force, advertising, marketing research, marketing planning, and customer service. Others are responsible for specific products and they are called *product managers.* For example, a university has someone responsible for the day degree program, someone else responsible for the evening degree program, and still another person responsible for the extension program. Still others are responsible for specific markets and

FIGURE 12-1
Generic Marketing Organization

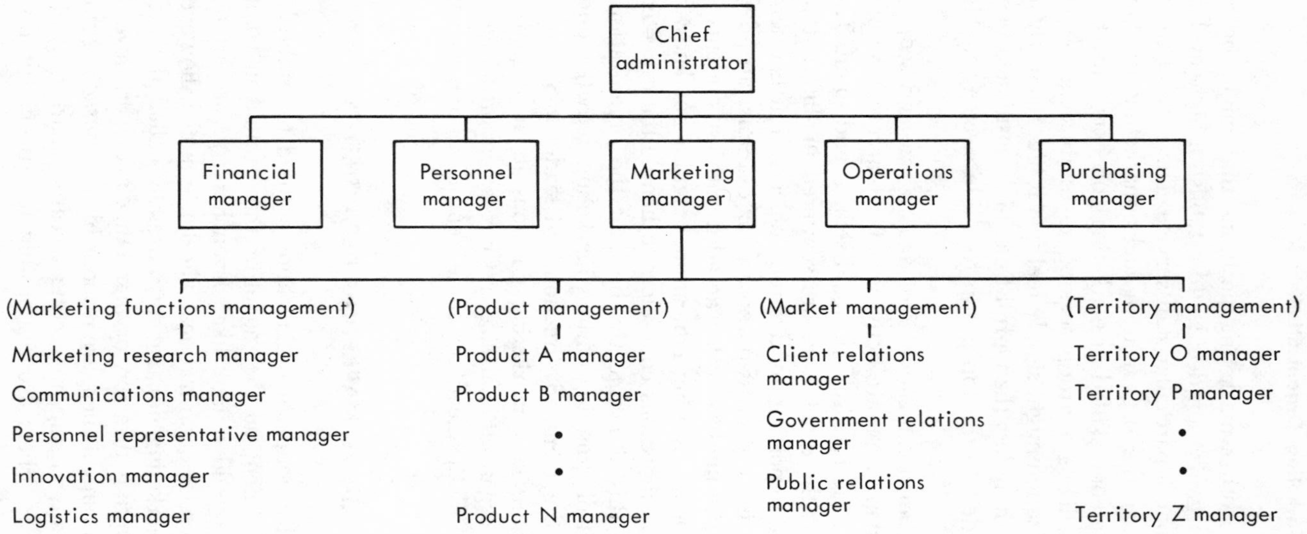

Chief administrator

Financial manager

Personnel manager

Marketing manager

Operations manager

Purchasing manager

(Marketing functions management)

Marketing research manager

Communications manager

Personnel representative manager

Innovation manager

Logistics manager

(Product management)

Product A manager

Product B manager

Product N manager

(Market management)

Client relations manager

Government relations manager

Public relations manager

(Territory management)

Territory O manager

Territory P manager

Territory Z manager

are called *market managers.* Thus a university has someone responsible for the current students, someone responsible for the faculty, and someone responsible for alumni. Finally, there may also be *territorial managers* reporting to the marketing manager who are responsible for the organization's activities in different regions. Figure 12-1 shows a generic marketing organization reflecting all four dimensions of marketing organization: functions, products, markets, and territories. A detailed description of these job positions is presented in Table 12-1.

TABLE 12-1

Generic Marketing Positions

Marketing manager
1. Other names: vice-president of marketing, marketing director, chief marketing officer, marketing administrator.
2. The marketing manager is a member of the top administration. His tasks include providing a marketing point of view to the top administration; helping to formulate marketing plans of the organization; staffing, directing, and coordinating marketing activities; and proposing new products and services to meet evolving market needs.

Product manager
1. Other names: program manager, brand manager.
2. A product manager is responsible for managing a particular product or program of the organization. His job is to propose product objectives and goals, create product strategies and plans, see that they are implemented, monitor the results, and take corrective actions.

Marketing research manager
1. Other names: marketing research director.
2. The marketing research manager has responsibility for developing and supervising research on the organization's markets and publics, and on the effectiveness of various marketing tools.

Communications managers
1. Other names: advertising manager, advertising and sales promotion director.
2. The communications manager provides expertise in the area of mass and selective communication and promotion. He is knowledgeable about the design of commercial messages, media, and publicity.

Personal representatives manager
1. Other names: sales manager.
2. The personal representatives manager has responsibility for recruiting, training, assigning, directing, motivating, compensating, and evaluating personal representatives and agents of the organization. He is responsible for coordinating the work of the personal representatives with the other marketing activities designed to accomplish the organization's objectives.

TABLE 12-1

Continued

Innovation manager

1. Other names: new-product manager; new-product director.
2. The innovation manager has responsibility for conceiving new products and services; screening and evaluating new product ideas; developing prototypes and testing them; and advising and helping to carry out the innovation's introduction in the marketplace.

Logistics manager

1. Other names: channel manager; physical distribution manager.
2. The logistics manager has responsibility for planning and managing the systems that make the organization's products and services accessible to the potential users.

Client relations manager

1. Other names: customer service manager, account executive.
2. The client relations manager has responsibility for managing client services and handling client complaints.

Government relations manager

1. Other names: legislative representative; lobbyist.
2. The government relations manager provides the organization with intelligence on relevant developments in government and manages the organization's program of representation and presentation to government.

Public relations manager

1. Other names: public affairs officer.
2. The public relations manager has responsibility for communicating and dealing with various publics in matters involving the organization's image and activities.

Territory manager

1. Other names: regional manager, district manager.
2. The territory manager has responsbiility for managing the organization's products, services, and programs in a specific territory.

An organization should establish only those marketing positions that make sense in terms of its objectives, resources, and opportunities. A marketing orientation is a new concept for nonprofit organizations and the existence of a formal marketing department is even more novel. Each organization has to develop its own solution to implementing the marketing concept organizationally. On the one hand, establishing formal marketing positions promises to yield greater service to the various markets and publics and more efficient use of certain resources. On the other hand, it can mean higher costs because each job position is an additional cost.

As in all such matters, a benefit-cost analysis is desirable for determining which marketing positions to establish in an organization.

SUMMARY

Most nonprofit organizations carry on marketing activities without the benefit of formal marketing positions. They assume that the key managers are sufficiently sensitive to market forces and can buy whatever specialized marketing services they need from outside suppliers. Some nonprofit organizations have established one or more formal marketing positions to provide special services that might be in great demand, such as marketing research or advertising. A few nonprofit organizations have established a top-level marketing position filled by a person who is responsible for bringing in the marketing point of view to top management, counseling on strategy, developing marketing plans, and providing marketing services. A full-size marketing department resembling those found in commercial organizations would be headed by a marketing director with persons reporting to him who are responsible for particular marketing functions, products, markets, and territories.

NOTE

1. Lewis M. Schneider, *Marketing Urban Mass Transit—A Comparative Study of Management Strategies* (Boston, Mass.: Division of Research, Harvard Graduate School of Business Administration, 1965).

QUESTIONS

1. The marketing director of a large family planning agency has been doing an excellent job of getting people to use the agency's services. In fact, he has been doing such a good job that the agency is having trouble supplying people with all the contraceptives and other services that they want. The marketing director is quite disturbed about the periodic stock-outs in contraceptives and the long waiting lines in the agency's offices. He is pressuring the purchasing director (who controls the inventory) to stock more contraceptives and the medical director (who controls the hiring of professional personnel) to hire more doctors, nurses, and other professionals. However, the purchasing director and the medical director do not think the agency can afford what the marketing director wants. What should be done in this situation?

2. The central administration of a suburban school district has juris-

diction over eight very large high schools (over 2,000 students each). It also runs a large adult education program. At the present time, the administration has no marketing specialist, although it does have two people who take care of public relations and advertising. What type of marketing organization would be best for this school district?

3. If the U.S. Postal System were to adopt a product management system, how might its products be divided up among managers?

4. Over the years, how do you think the marketing departments of most business corporations evolved? Should the marketing departments of most nonprofit organizations be forced to go through the same evolutionary process?

5. What makes a good product manager?

6. Many people are unclear about the relation between a public relations department and a marketing department. In a nonprofit organization, are they (1) unrelated, (2) related but separate, (3) overlapping somewhat, (4) identical, (5) public relations is the larger idea and subsumes marketing, or (6) marketing is the larger idea and subsumes public relations?

7. The Boy Scouts of America is having trouble recruiting new scouts, volunteers, and funds, particularly in urban areas. What type of marketing organization should it have to help it overcome these problems?

13   Marketing Planning and Control

*Some problems are so difficult they can't be solved in a million
years unless someone thinks about them for five minutes.*

H. L. MENCKEN

Nonprofit organizations need to increase their understanding and use of formal methods of marketing planning and control
to guide their activities. The environment is changing too fast for any
organization to just coast along each year hoping to do better without
engaging in concrete analysis and planning. Consider major universities.
Normally, a university develops a budget for the coming year based on
extrapolating current levels of student enrollment, operating costs, and
endowment income. There is little in the way of forecasting the long-
run environment, future student population, level of tuition and cost, and
in general, new threats and new opportunities. There is little in the way
of establishing a long-range set of market missions and plans for achieving
them. The university does not ask each academic department to lay out
long-run objectives and plans within the university's large plan. Each

part of the university coasts along on a day-to-day basis meeting problems as they arise.

Because objectives are not set with any precision, the task of control is also up in the air. Control calls for a periodic checking into the results being achieved and the taking of corrective actions when there are deviations between plan objectives and actual results. Organizations that do not put themselves on a management-by-objectives basis are destined to be weak in their planning and control.

Management by objectives is sorely lacking in the planning framework of universities, hospitals, museums, churches, unions, and many other nonprofit organizations. This chapter attempts to spell out some of the basic principles and practices of modern planning and control.

MARKETING PLANNING

Marketing planning is one of the most important activities that the management of an organization engages in. It comprises the determination of a set of market missions and the steps necessary to achieve these missions. *It is the act of specifying in detail what will be done by whom to whom with what, and when, to achieve the organization's objectives.* It is the means by which an organization reconciles its resources, objectives, and opportunities.

Planning Procedures

Although all organizations plan, they vary considerably in how extensively, thoroughly, and formally they do it. Organizations face a number of issues in establishing their planning system.

What Kind of Planning Should Be Done?   The typical organization starts out with no formal planning, only occasional management meetings to review accomplishments and agree on the next steps. After a time, most management recognizes that ad hoc irregular planning leads to problems it is unprepared to handle. It then decides to adopt some procedure for annual planning. Eventually the organization realizes that meaningful annual planning requires a broader framework of long-range planning to be effective. Still later, the organization recognizes the desirability of product-by-product and market-by-market planning. Ultimately, it will install procedures to carry out organization planning—that is, the long-run development of people, positions, and an effective organizational structure.

Who Should Do the Planning?   There are three different views on who should perform the planning in an organization. *Top-down planning* holds that plans should be developed by top management and carried out by everyone else. This is essentially the model used by military organizations and many business firms. The men at the top review the economic outlook and the organization's resources and opportunities. They determine an attainable set of objectives and refine them into a set of sales quotas for various product and territory managers. They allocate to each manager what they believe to be a reasonable budget to attain his quota.

Bottom-up planning takes a different view of effective planning. Bottom-up planners believe that top-down planning is too authoritarian and not likely to generate the commitment, enthusiasm, and realism needed. They prefer to see the objectives set from the bottom up. That is, each operating manager prepares a tentative set of objectives and plans showing what he feels capable of achieving. These move up to higher management levels and as long as they seem to spell improvements in accomplishment over the previous year, they are approved. Because they are developed by the managers who must carry out the plans, it is felt these managers will be more enthusiastic and effective.

Participative planning, the third method, is a happy compromise between the two planning methods just elaborated. Top-down planning has the fault of being too removed and authoritarian; bottom-up planning lacks the assurance that managers will set their goals high enough. Participative planning starts with a review by top management of the organization's situation and opportunities, and the development by top management of a broad set of planning parameters and objectives to be filled in by lower levels of management. Thus top management might indicate that the organization should try to achieve an overall 10 percent increase in sales. However, not every product or territory can achieve this increase; some can achieve more, some less. Each manager does his planning in the light of the broad parameters and objectives set by management. Their plans are submitted to higher management, and in some cases are approved and in other cases require revision. Though there is central direction, each manager takes a reasonable share of responsibility in developing his own objectives. Most companies are finding participative planning to be the most effective in the long run.

An issue that usually arises concerns the need for and role of a professional planning department, or at least a director of planning to aid in the planning process. Some people feel that a planning director is not needed, that the best plans are produced by the men who are responsible for carrying them out. But a planning director can help managers in a number of ways to make the planning more professional.

He can train management in techniques of planning. He can provide the basic environmental and competitive information that is needed. He can construct a company plan for planning. He can oversee the flow of planning during the planning period.

What Should a Plan Contain? A full written marketing plan should contain six major parts. Part I should contain a statement of the overall *objectives* and market missions of the organization. Part II should describe the organization's *current and forecasted situation.* Part III should pose the major *alternative strategies* available to the organization and indicate the choice and reasons for the selection of one of these. Part IV should list the *specific actions* to be taken during the period by various departments and personnel. Part V should contain the *budget* for carrying out the various activities. Finally, Part VI should cite the *target variables that should be reviewed* each month or quarter to be certain that the overall objectives are being achieved.[1]

Optimum Planning through Market Response Functions

One of the most difficult decisions facing an organization is how much it should budget for marketing effort. A public mass transit company knows that it could increase ridership by offering more service. A medical charity knows that it can increase donations by increasing its solicitation mailings. A political candidate knows that he can increase his votes by advertising more heavily. They all know that increases in marketing effort will produce increases in market response.

The relation between marketing expenditures and market response (in the form of sales, preference, or awareness) is known as the *market response function.* There are at least three competing conceptions of the likely shape of the market response function. The first holds that it is fairly linear so that equal-amount increases in marketing expenditure will produce equal-amount increases in market response. The second holds that it is concave and shows diminishing returns throughout. The rationale is that the first marketing dollar will be spent in the best possible way and successive marketing dollars will be spent in successively less effective ways, thus producing increases in market response at a diminishing rate. The third conception holds that the market response function is S-shaped, with market response initially increasing at an increasing rate and then increasing eventually at a decreasing rate. The rationale is that small amounts of marketing effort are not very effective in the marketplace. They may create some awareness and interest, but are insufficient to motivate action. They are below the threshold level. But higher levels of marketing effort produce both the awareness and the action.

The actual shape of the market response function in each particular situation requires estimation. One method of estimation is to statistically fit past levels of marketing expenditure and market response. This requires sufficient past data and the expectation of continuity between the circumstances of the past and the future. Another possible method is to spend high, medium, and low levels of marketing expenditures in matched territories and observe the difference this makes in market response. This experimental method is ideal in principle but fraught with many difficulties in practice. The third estimation method is judgmental, in that experienced executives are asked to supply their best guesses as to the market responses that would accompany alternative levels of marketing expenditure.

Now suppose an organization has managed to determine the approximate shape of its market response function and it turns out to be S-shaped, as in Figure 13-1 (here called the *revenue curve*). This func-

FIGURE 13-1

Relationship among Sales, Marketing Expenditures, and Profits

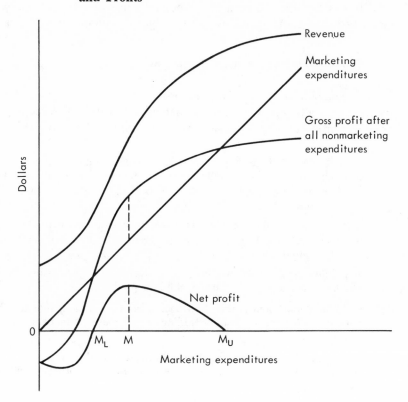

tion indicates the marketing expenditures it would take for an organization to achieve any particular level of market response. Suppose the organization is a medical charity and it wants to maximize its net profits—i.e., its revenue less its total costs of raising money. Some additional curves would have to be derived to find the point of optimum marketing effort. First, all nonmarketing costs must be subtracted from the revenue curve to derive the *gross profit curve*. Next a 45° line is drawn representing the *marketing expenditures curve* so that a dollar on the horizontal axis can be projected into a dollar on the vertical axis. The marketing expenditures curve is subtracted from the gross profit curve to derive the *net profit curve*. The net profit curve shows positive net profits with marketing expenditures between M_L and M_U, which could be defined as the rational range of marketing expenditures. The net profit curve reaches a maximum at M; thus M marketing dollars is the optimum marketing budget.

This is the theory underlying the choice of an optimum marketing budget where the objective is to maximize the difference between the organization's revenues and costs. Nonprofit organizations typically pursue additional or other objectives that require special techniques of analysis. It has become increasingly popular to use *benefit-cost analysis* to make program choices and allocate budgets in nonprofit organizations.

Choosing Programs through Benefit-Cost Analysis

A common problem facing nonprofit organizations is that of choosing between alternative programs that all fall within the scope of the organization's objectives. Consider the following typical situations:

A park district is trying to decide between building a bicycle path through a major park or building several tennis courts. Both are desired by different members of the community. It does not have enough funds to do both.

The American Cancer Society is trying to decide between sponsoring a national cervical cancer detection program or a national breast cancer detection program.

A public school system is trying to decide between establishing a gifted children program or a retarded children program.

A police department is trying to decide between a campaign to educate people against pickpockets or adding a few more permanent policemen to the force.

An art museum is trying to decide between establishing an arts library within the museum or adding a few more major paintings to its collection.

A university is trying to decide between building some badly needed dormitories or building a badly needed student union.

A public library is trying to decide between adding a bookmobile to bring books into neighborhoods or using the same funds to permit opening the library on Sundays.

These examples feature organizations facing a choice between two programs. They can choose one of the programs or allocate funds to the two programs in which each may be operated at a smaller scale than planned. In principle, the nonprofit organization can make a calculation similar to the profit organization. It should attempt to measure the benefits and the costs expected from each program. The benefits are all the contributions that the particular program will make to the organization's objectives; the costs are all the deductions that the particular program will take from alternative organization objectives. A particular program is considered worthwhile when its benefits exceed its costs.

Benefit-Cost Analysis. Suppose a nonprofit organization is considering a choice between three programs, called X, Y, and Z, respectively. Each of the programs is estimated to cost about the same, say 10 (in thousands of dollars). But, each program is estimated to yield a different level of benefits. The data on the three programs are shown in Table 13-1A.

All three programs show a net benefit (B–C) and a benefit cost

TABLE 13-1
Examples of Benefit-Cost Comparisons

		A. Equal Costs		
Program	*B* *Benefits*	*C* *Costs*	*B-C* *Net Benefit*	*B/C* *Benefit-Cost Ratio*
X	60	10	50	6
Y	30	10	20	3
Z	20	10	10	2

		B. Unequal Costs		
Program	*B* *Benefits*	*C* *Costs*	*B-C* *Net Benefit*	*B/C* *Benefit-Cost Ratio*
X	60	30	30	2
Y	30	10	20	3
Z	20	5	15	4

ratio (B/C) greater than one. On both criteria, the best program is X, the next Y, and the last Z. If the organization has funds of only 10, it should invest in program X. If the organization has funds of 20, it should invest in programs X and Y. If the organization has funds of 30, it should invest in all three programs, because in all programs the benefits exceed the costs.

Now consider the data in Table 13-1B, where the three programs differ in costs as well as benefits. In this case, the net benefits and the benefit-cost ratios do not show the same rank order. Program X stands highest in net benefit but lowest in benefit-cost ratio. Which criteria should dominate? Generally, the benefit-cost ratio is the more rational criteria because it shows the productivity of the funds. If funds of 5 were available, they should be spent on Z because they will yield four times the benefit per dollar of cost. If funds of 15 are available, they should be spent on Y and Z and this will yield benefits of 50 altogether, which is an average benefit-cost ratio of $3\frac{1}{3}$ per dollar of cost. Notice that program X, although yielding net benefits of 30, only shows a benefit-cost ratio of 2. The only time program X would be preferred is if the three programs were mutually exclusive, funds of 30 were available, and the objective was to maximize the net benefit.

Having examined how to use benefit-cost data, let us move a step backward and ask how these benefits and costs are quantified in the first place.

The measurement of certain costs poses a problem. The organization is usually in a position to quantify the dollar costs of the program. If the program leads to some social costs, these are harder to estimate. A city government, for example, typically looks at the cost of building a cross-town expressway in financial terms. But an expressway destroys certain neighborhoods and increases local pollution and noise. These social costs should be included in the total evaluation of costs.

Evaluating benefits poses many tough problems. Benefit-cost analyses requires identifying each type of benefit expected from the program and attempting to express it in terms of a common value, such as dollars. Upon consideration the various benefits tend to fall into three groups in terms of their quantifiability. They are:

1. *Monetarily quantifiable benefits*—benefits whose total value can be expressed in dollars.
2. *Nonmonetary quantifiable benefits*—benefits whose total value can be expressed in some specific nonmonetary measure, such as "lives saved."
3. *Nonquantifiable benefits*—benefits whose total value cannot be expressed quantitatively, such as amount of happiness created or beauty produced.

Now suppose a certain program i is estimated to have m different benefits. Let B_{ij} represent the amount of benefit j expected from program i. If all the benefits can be measured in dollars, then we can find the total amount of benefit expected from the program by summing the individual benefits. Thus,

$$B_i = \sum_{j=1}^{m} B_{ij}$$

where

B_i = total amount of benefit of program i
B_{ij} = amount of benefit j in program i
m = number of different benefits being evaluated.

A second possibility occurs when all the benefits can be measured in terms of a common nonmonetary value, such as "lives saved." In this case, we proceed as before by summing up the lives saved as a result of each benefit of the program.

A third possibility occurs when the various benefits do not all share a common value. Some analysts prefer to make a two-stage analysis, the first stage including only the quantifiable benefits and costs. If the benefit-cost ratio exceeds one, the program is considered good, unless there is a strong feeling that the nonquantifiable costs substantially exceed the nonquantifiable benefits. If the benefit-cost ratio is less than one, the program may nevertheless be good if there is a strong feeling that the nonquantifiable benefits substantially exceed the nonquantifiable costs.

The value of trying to quantify the benefits in dollars or some other common denominator is readily apparent. This has led to a number of ingenious ways to try to capture the dollar value of a benefit. The first approach is to try to find an existing market price for this benefit. If a school dropout prevention program is expected to increase the lifetime earnings of so many persons who are persuaded to stay in school, the discounted values of their increased lifetime earnings can be used as a measure of the value of the program. If a farmer fertilizer education program is expected to increase farm output, the expected market value of the additional crops attributable to the educational program could be used as the monetary value of this benefit. If there is no existing market price for the type of benefit being created by the program, people can be asked how much they would be willing to pay for that benefit. If a tennis court is being considered for a local park, local residents could be asked how much they would be willing to pay per hour to use it, or how much additional taxes they would be willing to accept. If the National Aeronautical Space Agency is contemplating a ten-year program to send a manned flight to Mars, it might ask people how much they would be willing to pay over a ten-year period to achieve a successful mission.

In attempting to quantify benefits, it is desirable to distinguish the different groups in the market that will benefit. Analytically, suppose there are k different groups who will benefit. Let n_g represent the number of persons in group g. Let b_{ig} represent the average amount of benefit that a person in group g will get from program i. Then:

$$B_i = \sum_{g=1}^{k} b_{ig}\, n_g$$

That is, the total amount of benefit generated by program i is the summation of the average benefit to a member of each group multiplied by the number of members in each group.

Problems in Benefit-Cost Analysis.   Some of the problems in putting benefit-cost analysis to practical use should now be apparent. Even if one does manage to achieve dollar values for the various benefits and costs, the technique makes certain assumptions that should be stated clearly.

First, the technique assumes that the program, if adopted, would not yield outputs sufficient to change the market prices that were used to estimate the benefits of the program. For example, if school dropout prevention programs are introduced throughout the country, they will increase the skill level of the population and probably result in a fall in the market price of skilled workers. Therefore the life earnings calculation based on today's earnings of skilled workers overstates the market value of the benefit. Likewise, if a large farmer education program leads to a great increase in farm output, this will depress the price of farm output and therefore the existing prices may overstate the benefit of the program.

Second, the technique makes no allowance for redistributional benefits caused by the program. For example, a vocational education program and a gifted children program may both improve lifetime incomes to the same extent. But the vocational education program may improve mainly the incomes of the poor and a gifted children program may improve mainly the incomes of the well-off. Some analysts believe the technique should give weight to positive redistribution effects. Along the same lines, other measures such as "lives saved per thousand dollars" ignore whose lives are saved. If two programs would save an equal number of lives for the same cost, but one would save the lives of children (say leukemia research programs) and others would save the lives of octogenarians (say geriatric research programs), preference should be given to the former program. This would imply using a measure of the weighted number of lives saved, with agreed-upon weights for age, family size, and possibly income and education.

Third, the technique assumes that economic value should be given the main weight in deciding between programs. Critics resent the notion that everything worthwhile can be measured in dollars or that the growth of GNP is the major goal. They see the value of a school dropout prevention program not so much in increased dollars of earnings but in terms of increased self-esteem and improved social attitudes. They see the value of an environmental protection program not in economic terms but in quality-of-life terms.

Finally, the technique assumes that the rank ordering of projects is insensitive to the particular measure of benefit used, providing each is a highly respected measure. In a study of the net benefit of investing in different disease control programs, the ailment of arthritis did not seem important when the criterion "lives saved" was used because arthritis does not kill people. On the other hand, arthritis rates as a high-priority research problem when the criterion "dollars saved through avoiding medical treatment" was used.[2] Thus various programs may rank differently depending on the benefit criterion used.

These difficulties are not created by the technique but exist because life itself is complex. The technique was never intended to replace judgment but rather to systematize and quantify it where possible. Benefit-cost analysis suggests the important factors that should be considered, and the information that is needed. It inputs relevant data into what otherwise would be a wholly subjective act of decision making. It rests on the premise that organized ignorance is better than disorganized ignorance for making decisions.

Cost-Effectiveness Analysis. In benefit-cost analysis, the task is to compare different programs in terms of the benefits they yield per dollar of cost. Nothing was said about varying the cost of each program to see what effect this had on the amount of benefit produced. For example, as more money is put into a school dropout prevention program, the benefit-cost ratio is likely to diminish as one reaches the more hard-core dropout types. As more money is put into a motivation program to attract women to take Pap tests, the benefit-cost ratio is likely to diminish because it is harder to reach certain types of women. Generally, one would expect the benefit-cost ratio to show diminishing returns after a certain point. On the other hand, it might show increasing returns at low levels of expenditure.

Cost-effectiveness analysis is the general name given to researching the effect of variations in cost on benefit. Let us consider cost-effectiveness analysis in relation to different methods of attempting to attract people to donate blood to a blood bank. The blood bank is contemplating three different promotion methods: the use of newspapers, direct mail, and group sessions. Suppose it wishes to utilize only one of these media. Figure 13-2 shows the hypothetical benefit-cost function (here called cost-

FIGURE 13-2
Cost-Effectiveness Functions

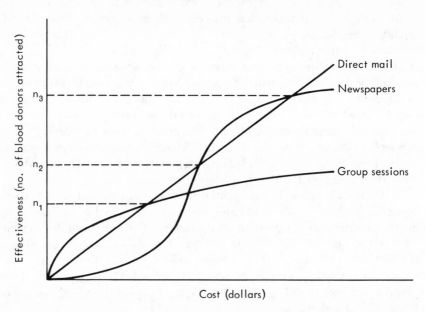

effectiveness function) for each promotional method. The use of direct mail produces a linear cost function—that is, a constant percentage of donors are attracted with different levels of direct-mail usage. The use of newspaper advertising produces a rather low response if used at a low level but increasing returns if used at a medium level and then diminishing returns if used at a high level. The use of group sessions produces a high number of donors if used at a low level (because the most likely groups are contacted first) and diminishing returns throughout.

Given the cost-effectiveness functions shown in Figure 13-2, which method is the most cost-effective to use to attract blood donors? The answer depends on how many donors the blood bank is seeking. If the blood bank is trying to attract fewer than n_1 donors, then group sessions are the most efficient promotional strategy. If the blood bank is trying to attract between n_1 and n_2 donors, then direct mail is the most efficient promotional strategy. If the blood bank is trying to attract between n_2 and n_3 donors, then newspaper advertising is the most efficient method. If the blood bank is trying to attract more than n_3 donors, then direct mail is once again the most efficient method.

If these promotional methods reached entirely different segments of the market, it would be better to use a combination of methods to attract a given number of blood donors. Each method would be used to a level at which all marginal productivities were equal.

In general, cost effectiveness analysis goes beyond benefit-cost analysis in looking at the variation of benefit with variations in cost. The two methods together constitute the only known formal approach to evaluating investment proposals by nonprofit organizations.

MARKETING CONTROL

Marketing control must go hand in hand with marketing planning. It is possible to set marketing objectives, analyze markets, develop marketing plans, and establish a marketing organization and yet fail miserably because of a failure to establish control. Control is the process of designing and implementing procedures to bring actual results in line with desired results.

Organizations differ greatly in the amount of control they exercise over the plan's implementation. Some organizations, after writing their plans, merely file them in desk drawers to gather dust. There is little or no systematic checking against the target objectives. Other organizations go to the opposite extreme of almost continuous checking to see that the planned results are being achieved. Ford Motor Company, for example, checks sales every nine days to see if sales targets are being achieved; if they are not, they make an immediate analysis of the problem and take drastic steps to correct it.

A number of questions usually arise about the subject of marketing control.

What Is the Theory of Control?

An organization or process is said to be under good control when it is performing according to the expectations set for it. This is never assured because the environment is never perfectly predictable. Therefore an agent must set up a control system to make sure that expectations are being met.

All control systems possess four common elements. The first consists of a clear set of quantitative *objectives*. The second consists of the *measurement* of current results against planned results. The third consists of *diagnosing* the cause of any discrepancies. The final step is to take *corrective actions* based on the causal analysis to bring the system back under control.

In an organization that uses management by objectives, each member knows what is expected of him for the coming year. A fund raiser, for example, knows his sales target and expense budget. Control requires that each supervisor periodically review the performances of all people under him to see whether they are achieving their objectives. The regional fund raiser will make a periodic review of each individual fund raiser's performance in his region. He will contact underachievers to find out the cause and to assist them to do a better job. Meanwhile the regional fund raisers are being viewed by the general fund-raising manager, who is being reviewed by the marketing vice-president, who in turn is being reviewed by the top executive. Thus the control system consists of these periodic evaluations of distinct performance variables that each man makes of the men below him.

What Variables Should Be Controlled?

There are many variables that can be reviewed periodically to assess the organization's progress toward a set of objectives. Here are some of the more important ones.

1. *Total market response.* Total market response would be measured by sales or orders in the case of a commercial organization, student applications in the case of a university, candidate voting intentions in the case of a political party, and so on. The marketing manager would want to compare actual response to date with planned response. He would go further and determine specific areas in which market response is lagging and undertake to analyze the causes and prepare corrective steps.

2. *Market share.* Organizations will want to watch how well they are doing relative to those whom they regard as their major competitors. A university may be achieving its objectives with great difficulty and notice one of its competitors growing almost effortlessly. It may notice that students applying to both universities increasingly make their choice in favor of the other university. Thus market share, in addition to total market response, can be an important indicator of organizational performance.

3. *Cost per dollar of market response.* The effectiveness of a marketing program must also take into account the cost of achieving a given level of market response. Two fund raisers may both raise the same amount of money, but one may go way over budgeted expense. He is spend-

ing too much to achieve the desired response. The company will also want to make sure that other normal cost relations are maintained, such as the normal advertising to sales ratio and the normal salaries to sales ratio. A fund-raising organization has to watch its mailing costs, brochure costs, salaries, and other costs in relation to the contribution raised.

4. *Other performance ratios.* Management has to keep an eye on other performance ratios that say something about the efficiency of marketing effort. An experienced fund-raising director, for example, periodically checks the following ratios: revenue per fund raiser, number of prospects contacted per fund raiser per day, number of minutes per contact, revenue per contact hour, percentage of closure per contact, percentage of potential contributors covered, and number of lost contributors.

5. *Market attitudes.* Organizations should go beyond measuring marketing inputs and market response and make periodic checks on market attitudes. For example, General Electric sends a questionnaire every month to a national probability sample of 1,000 persons inquiring about their satisfaction with each appliance available in the respondent's household.[3] Analogously, a university can sample its students each quarter to determine their mood and satisfaction.

What Corrective Steps Should Be Taken?

When the objectives of a marketing plan are not being achieved, there is a need for a deep review of the causes. There are various places the plan could be failing. The first question is whether the implementation is at fault. Perhaps fund raisers are being insufficiently supervised or motivated. If the implementation is not at fault, the next question is whether the plan itself is at fault. Perhaps the wrong marketing strategy is being used. If the plan is sound, inquiry can be directed to whether the original objectives set by management are valid. Perhaps they are no longer realistic because of a drastically changed environment. Thus the problem is held to lie somewhere in either the plan's implementation, the plan itself, or the original objectives.

SUMMARY

Marketing effectiveness requires that an organization design a system of formal planning and control to guide the marketing effort. In designing a planning system, it must address itself to the questions of what should be planned, who should do the planning, and what the plan should contain. A full planning system would develop annual plans, long-range plans, product plans, and organizational development plans. It would probably follow the model of participative planning, which attempts to achieve the advantages, without the disadvantages, of top-down planning and bottom-up planning. It would produce plans that contain sections on objectives, the current and forecasted situation, alternative strategies, specific actions, budgets, and control variables. Nonprofit organizations would rely on the tools of market response functions and/or benefit-cost analysis in determining marketing expenditure levels and program choices.

In designing a control system, the organization must decide which variables should be reviewed, how often, and what corrective steps would be taken under different contingencies. Organizations tend to watch market response, market share, cost per sales, other performance ratios, and market attitudes. In cases of underperformance, they analyze whether the fault lay with the plan's implementation, the plan itself, or the original objectives, and then take the necessary corrective actions.

NOTES

1. An excellent discussion of marketing planning is found in John M. Brion, *Corporate Marketing Planning* (New York: American Management Association, 1967).

2. "Benefit/Cost Analyses in Health Care Systems," *The Annals of the American Academy of Political and Social Science* (January 1972), pp. 90–99, esp. p. 94.

3. Robert W. Pratt, "The Index of Consumer Satisfaction and Corporate Marketing Policy," Comments made at the Third Annual Conference, Association for Consumer Research, November 5, 1972.

QUESTIONS

1. Make a list of the benefits of planning.

2. What are the different types of techniques the U.S. Navy can use to forecast its future number of recruits?

3. A marketing plan must begin with a set of objectives. Consider a museum, for example. There are many alternative objectives that a museum might have regarding the attendance of visitors. For example, it might (a) try to maximize the number of persons who attend the museum at least once during the year, (b) maximize the number of persons who attend five or more times a year, (c) maximize the number of poor people who visit the museum, (d) maximize the satisfaction per visit. Name some additional attendance goals a museum could have, and discuss.

4. Many organizations have become enamored of managing their

organization by objectives. Do you see any potential problems in management by objectives?

5. There are many ways a college can recruit more students. Compare the cost effectiveness of the following strategies: (1) placing ads in newspapers, (2) having admissions personnel visit high schools, (3) upgrading the quality of the football team, (4) improving the national reputation of the faculty, and (5) raising the percentage of students who receive financial aid.

14 Marketing Information System*

A wise man recognizes the convenience of a general statement, but he bows to the authority of a particular fact.

OLIVER WENDELL HOLMES, JR.

The crucial administrative steps of marketing planning and control cannot be carried out effectively unless the organization has developed an adequate and reliable base of marketing information. An urban transit company cannot hope to develop a sound marketing plan to increase ridership unless it has adequate information on the characteristics of riders and nonriders, the perceptions and objections of nonriders to mass transit, and their susceptibility to switching to mass transit. A charity organization cannot develop an effective fund-raising plan without knowing the past contributions of various donors, the characteristics of high-potential new donors, the income and charity attitudes of persons in various geographical areas, and so on. These and other nonprofit organizations need major amounts of information to plan their marketing

* Selected portions of this chapter have been taken from Chapter 10 of my *Marketing Management: Analysis, Planning, and Control,* © 1972. Used by permission of Prentice-Hall, Inc.

activities. They need timely, accurate, and adequate information as a basis for determining target markets and effective marketing mixes.

We shall use the term *marketing information system* to describe the organization's system for gathering, processing, storing, and disseminating relevant marketing information. Figure 14-1 presents a picture of the main components of a total marketing information system. The *marketing information system* stands between the *environment* and the *marketing executive-user*. The organization receives a *marketing data flow* describing developments in the *macroenvironment* (economy, technology, law, and culture) and the *task environment* (buyers, channels, competitors, and suppliers). The data are *gathered, processed,* and *utilized* through one of four marketing information system components: the *internal records system,* the *marketing intelligence system,* the *marketing research system,* and the *marketing management science system.* These turn out a *marketing information flow* which goes to managers for use in *planning, execution,* and *control.* The results of their decision making become a *marketing communication flow* that goes back to the environment.

In the following sections, we will describe the four main components of the marketing information system.

INTERNAL RECORDS SYSTEM

The oldest and most basic system used by managers is the internal records system. It is the system of data on orders, sales, inventory levels, receivables, payables, and so on. Marketing executives need up-to-date sales and cost information broken down by product, territory, salesmen, and type of customer. In small organizations, these data might be manually processed; in large organizations, they are typically entered and stored on magnetic tape and processed through the computer.

Let us consider the internal records information needs of managers of a fund-raising organization. They need a *contributor file* listing every contributor and such data as his past annual contributions, his income and wealth, interests and hobbies, memberships, and so on. They need a *campaign progress file* showing the amount raised to date broken down by major sources of giving. They need a *cost file* showing how much money is being spent on mail solicitation, newspaper advertising, brochures, salaries, consultant fees, and so on.

Various managers may have more specific marketing information needs. In designing an internal records system, a cross-section of manager-users should be queried as to their information needs. Table 14-1 shows the major questions that should be put to them. Once their opinions are

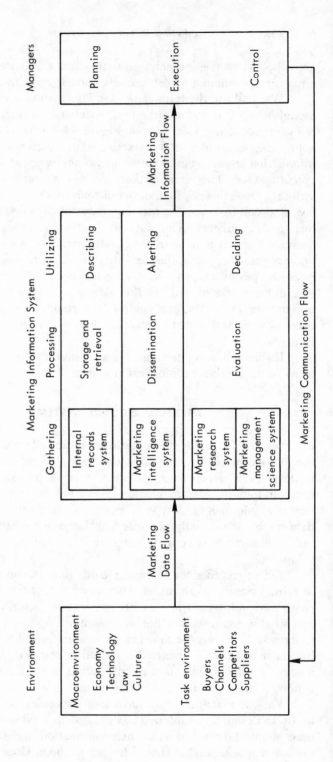

FIGURE 14-1
Components of the Marketing Information System

Table 14-1

Questionnaire for Determining Marketing
Information Needs of Managers

1. What types of decisions are you regularly called upon to make?
2. What types of information do you need to make these decisions?
3. What types of information do you regularly get?
4. What types of special studies do you periodically request?
5. What types of information would you like to get that you are not now getting?
6. What information would you want daily? weekly? monthly? yearly?
7. What magazines and reports would you like to see routed to you on a regular basis?
8. What specific topics would you like to be kept informed of?
9. What types of data-analysis programs would you like to see made available?
10. What do you think would be the four most helpful improvements that could be made in the present marketing information system?

gathered, the information specialists can proceed to design an efficient internal records system that reflects a resolution of (a) what managers think they need, (b) what managers really need, and (c) what is economically feasible.

Highly sophisticated internal records systems are found in large business firms where a premium is placed on speed, comprehensiveness, and accuracy of information. Sophisticated systems are also found in such government agencies as the Pentagon and the U.S. Treasury Department. Several private hospitals have built quite advanced internal records systems containing patient files, cost files, medical treatment files, and so on. A few universities have built extremely sophisticated alumni records systems for fund raising.[1]

An outstanding decision-oriented information system was designed by Glen L. Urban for the Atlanta Area Family Planning System.[2] Its purpose is to help family planning managers understand their market better, make better forecasts, and improve their ability to evaluate alternative plans. The basic thrust of the information system is to help the family planning agency deliver better contraceptive information to indigent families so that they can prevent unwanted births. The information system contains current information on the family planning status of a target group of women in the area who are between ages 15 and 45 and indigent. The record for each woman shows her as either pregnant, not pregnant but using contraception, or not pregnant and not using contraception. Women are further identified by race, age, number and results of previous visits, and type of contraceptive practice. This basic data is manipulated through a process model that traces movement from the target group population through postpartum and non–postpartum family planning program events. The managers can study how the "birth averted" rate of the target group population is affected by investments in advertising, outreach programs, and referral systems.

MARKETING INTELLIGENCE SYSTEM

Whereas the internal records system supplies managers with *results data,* the marketing intelligence system supplies them with *happenings data* which they need to interpret results and to become aware of new problems and opportunities. We shall define the *marketing intelligence system as the way in which the organization's managers are kept current and informed about changing conditions in the macroenvironment and task environment.*

Executive Intelligence-Gathering Styles

Only recently have studies appeared that throw light on the ways in which management gathers information about outside events that might affect its planning and control. According to Aguilar, managers are engaged in four modes of environment scanning:

1. *Undirected viewing:* general exposure to information where the viewer has no specific purpose in mind.
2. *Conditioned viewing:* directed exposure, not involving active search, to a more or less clearly identified area or type of information.
3. *Informal search:* a relatively limited and unstructured effort to obtain specific information or information for a specific purpose.
4. *Formal search:* a deliberate effort—usually following a preestablished plan, procedure, or methodology—to secure specific information or information relating to a specific issue.[3]

All managers engage at different times in all modes of scanning. The mode being used at a given point in time is determined largely by the type of information sought and value and cost considerations, such as the importance of the issue, the existing amount of information, and the cost of generating more information. A high-level marketing manager in the chemical industry, for example, carries on a lot of intelligence the "births averted" rate of the target group population is affected by reading newspapers and trade material, relying on subordinates for search information, and getting some unsolicited information from outside sources. This is the normal mode of marketing intelligence found in companies, and one that is usually not very efficient. To the extent that the intelligence function is highly decentralized, valuable information will often come in too little or too late. Managers may learn of a competitive move or a new customer need too late to make the best response.

Improving Intelligence-Gathering Activity

Three essential steps an organization can take to improve its intelligence-gathering activity are to (1) improve the field force's intelligence activity, (2) utilize additional intelligence resources, and (3) buy information from special marketing research services.

Field Workers As Intelligence Agents. Field workers are in a good position to pick up significant bits of information that would never appear in the usual summary statistics. When these bits and pieces of information are correlated at headquarters, they often spell out a revealing picture of new developments in the marketplace.

The critical task is to get field workers to be alert to important developments and to pass information on to their superiors. Thus a family planning social worker who hears a lot of negative imagery about a certain type of contraception should pass this information on. Unfortunately, many field workers view their main job as providing service to their clients and feel little responsibility for bringing back important information to their superiors. There are so many demands on their time that they neglect their responsibility to behave as intelligence officers. Some of this can be overcome by a program of training to illustrate how the quality of service depends on receiving grassroots information from the field workers. Commercial organizations typically provide their salesmen with blank call reports which must be filled out and sent to the supervisor reporting the results of each call and any important developments.

Additional Means of Gathering Intelligence. Other agents of the organization (employees, dealers, advertising agency, and so on) should also be incentivized to pay more attention to gathering and passing along information. It may also be desirable to hire a full-time specialist in marketing intelligence. His job would be twofold. First, he would set up systems to facilitate the orderly gathering of information and its dissemination to key managers. This would involve carrying on a clipping service, building a small library, abstracting and disseminating reports, and so on. Second, he would place himself in the field frequently to mix with target users and publics in order to maintain an up-to-date picture of their needs, perceptions, and dissatisfactions.

Purchase of Special Marketing Intelligence Services. Many organizations purchase supplementary information or research services to increase their information about the market. Universities subscribe to services which list various foundations and the type of grants they make. Charities buy mailing lists of various kinds to improve their reach into particular population segments.

MARKETING RESEARCH SYSTEM

Besides internal records information and marketing intelligence, the nonprofit organization manager often needs specific studies of problem and opportunity areas. Consider the following two examples:

> Carnegie-Mellon University would like to know how applicants who they have admitted make their final choice of which school to go to. Specifically, how much weight do applicants put on such factors as the cost of the school, its reputation, its distance from their homes, and so on? They would also like to probe deeper and learn the knowledge, attitudes, and perceptions that students in different parts of the country have of Carnegie-Mellon University and its major competitors.

> The Chicago Metropolitan Sanitary District (CMSD) regularly transports sludge to Fulton County where it is added as topsoil over strip-mined land owned by the CMSD. Recently the residents of Fulton County started to voice objections to being a dumping ground for Chicago's waste. The administration of the CMSD would like to undertake research to learn who is doing the objecting, what the objections are, and how acceptable different possible proposals by the CMSD would be to the citizens of Fulton County.

In other cases, a manager may need a market survey, a preference test, a forecast, or an advertising-effectiveness study. These studies require the talents of skilled researchers who can apply principles of sample size, sample design, and questionnaire construction to the task. These researchers usually make up the marketing research department of an organization.

Organizational Characteristics of Marketing Research

Since its humble beginnings sixty years ago, marketing research has steadily expanded. Every five-year period has seen the formation of more new company marketing research departments (consisting of more than one full-time employee) than in the immediately preceding five-year period.[4] Over half of all business firms have formal marketing research departments.

There has also been a rapid expansion in the number of companies selling marketing research services. *Bradford's Directory of Marketing Research Agencies* lists over 350 marketing research firms.[5] These marketing research and consulting firms fall into three categories.

1. *Full-line marketing research firms.* These firms offer general marketing research services. Their clients range from organizations that are too small to support their own marketing research departments to large organizations that subcontract a portion of their work to relieve backlog or to obtain an independent point of view.

2. *Specialty-line marketing research firms.* These firms specialize in particular marketing research services, such as market analysis and forecasting, survey research work, product research, or brand-name testing. They may also specialize in consumer, industrial, international, or nonprofit organization research.

3. *Information-selling firms.* These firms specialize in gathering continuous trade or consumer data, which they sell to clients on a fee-subscription basis. Well-known examples include A. C. Nielsen Company, Market Research Corporation of America, Brand Rating Index Corporation, Daniel Starch, and Gallup-Robinson.

Marketing research departments have been steadily expanding their activities and techniques. Table 14-2 lists thirty-four different marketing research activities along with the percentage of firms carrying on each. The eight most common activities, in order of importance, are determination of market characteristics, development of market potentials, market-share analysis, sales analysis, competitive-product studies, new-product acceptance and potential, short-range forecasting, and studies of business trends. Less than half of the firms do their own advertising research or carry out any marketing operations research.

These studies have benefited over the years from increasingly sophisticated techniques. Many techniques were developed outside of marketing by researchers in economics, statistics, sociology, social psychology, and psychology. They were drawn in and amended by marketing researchers who recognized opportunities for their use. Table 14-3 shows the approximate decade when various techniques began to be substantially considered or used in marketing research. Many of them—such as questionnaire construction and area sampling—came along naturally and were quickly and widely accepted as belonging in the corpus of marketing research practice. Others—such as motivation research and mathematical methods—came in uneasily, with prolonged and heated debates among practitioners over their practical usefulness. But they, too, settled in the

TABLE 14-2

Research Activities of 1,703 Companies

Type of Research	Percent Doing
Advertising research:	
Motivation research	32
Copy research	38
Media research	47
Studies of ad effectiveness	49
Other	13
Business economics and corporate research:	
Short-range forecasting (up to 1 year)	61
Long-range forecasting (over 1 year)	59
Studies of business trends	60
Profit and/or value analysis	53
Plant and warehouse location studies	46
Diversification studies	49
Purchase of companies, sales of divisions	45
Export and international studies	41
Linear programming	33
Operations research	36
PERT studies	29
Employee morale studies	36
Other	7
Product research:	
New-product acceptance and potential	63
Competitive-product studies	64
Product testing	53
Packaging research—design or physical characteristics	45
Other	6
Sales and market research:	
Development of market potentials	67
Market-share analysis	66
Determination of market characteristics	69
Sales analysis	65
Establishment of sales quotas, territories	56
Distribution channels and cost studies	50
Test markets, store audits	37
Consumer-panel operations	41
Sales compensation studies	43
Studies of premiums, coupons, sampling, deals	32
Other	5

Source: Dik Warren Twedt, ed., *1968 Survey of Marketing Research: Organization Functions, Budget, Compensation* (Chicago: American Marketing Association, 1968), p. 41.

TABLE 14-3

Evolving Techniques in Marketing Research

Decade	Technique
Prior to 1910	First-hand observation Elementary surveys
1910–20	Sales analysis Operating-cost analysis
1920–30	Questionnaire construction Survey technique
1930–40	Quota sampling Simple correlation analysis Distribution-cost analysis Store auditing techniques
1940–50	Probability sampling Regression methods Advanced statistical inference Consumer and store panels
1950–60	Motivation research Operations research Multiple regression and correlation Experimental design Attitude-measuring instruments
1960–70	Factor analysis and discriminant analysis Mathematical models Bayesian statistical analysis and decision theory Scaling theory Computer data processing and analysis Marketing simulation Information storage and retrieval
1970–	Nonmetric multidimensional scaling Econometric models Comprehensive marketing planning models Test marketing laboratories

corpus of marketing research methodology—or at least the parts that stood the test of time.

Marketing Research Procedure

Marketing research is undertaken in the effort to learn something reliable about a marketing problem facing management. The value of the results depends upon the skill with which the marketing research project is designed and implemented. The investment of money and time can all be wasted or even be positively misleading if the marketing research project is ill-designed.

Effective marketing research involves the following five steps: *problem definition, research design, field work, data analysis, and report preparation.*

Problem Definition. The first step in the conduct of research calls for a careful definition of the problem. If the problem is stated vaguely, if the wrong problem is defined, or if the uses of the research are not made clear, then the research results may prove useless to the manager.

The poor definition of the problem is often the fault of the manager requesting the study. Thus a top administrator in the U.S. Postal System might ask the marketing research director to find out everything he can about public attitudes toward the postal system. The marketing research director has a right to feel uneasy about the assignment. It is too general. It is not clear how much interviewing should be done of nonusers, light users, and heavy users of the postal system. It is not clear what aspects of the postal system they should comment on: personnel, postage cost, delivery reliability, speed, and so on. Although all this information would be interesting, none may help management come any closer to making good policy decisions. There is something sterile about facts that are not made part of a larger model of decision-making alternatives that themselves come out of a definition of the real problem.

The kind of research assignment just mentioned is called exploratory research and this is mostly warranted in situations in which the organization's ignorance of the marketplace is substantial, and it may uncover much that is interesting. Yet the research effort is generally more efficient when the problem and alternatives are well-defined. This is because the cost of research is generally related to the total amount of information gathered, while the value of research is associated only with the proportion of information that is useful.

There is no magic formula for knowing how to define a research problem carefully enough, or to know whether it is the real problem. All that can be said is that too often organizations take the least time with problem definition and get into research design and field work prematurely.

Research Design. The problem definition stage should lead to the development of a clear set of research objectives stated in writing, if possible. The marketing research director faces a choice among many alternative ways to collect the information that will satisfy the research objectives.

He must decide on the *data collection method, research instrument,* and *sampling plan.*

DATA COLLECTION METHODS. The first decision of the marketing researcher is how to gather the data he needs. In simple cases, the data already exists in an accessible form and he has simply to find it. This is called *secondary data.* It might be present in the organization's internal records; in advertising agencies, or professional associations; in government, commercial, or trade publications; [6] or purchasable from marketing research firms. If the data are found in existing sources, the researcher has saved time and expense. However, he must be careful to evaluate secondary data, because they have been collected for a variety of purposes and under a variety of conditions that may limit their usefulness. Marketing researchers should check these data for impartiality, validity, and reliability.

When satisfactory secondary data are not available, the researcher must collect *primary data.* The data can be gathered from customers, middlemen, salesmen, competitors, or other information sources. There are three basic primary data collection methods.

The first is *observation,* in which case the researcher attempts to learn about the problem through observing the relevant actors. For example, a museum could use the observational method to study the movement of visitors through the museum, the behavior of museum personnel toward the visitors, the popularity of different exhibits, and so on. In the last case, some museums judge the popularity of different exhibits by observing the amount of carpet wear-out next to each exhibit.[7]

At the other extreme of observation is *experimentation* as a method of gathering primary data. The experimental method consists of introducing selected stimuli into a controlled environment and systematically varying them. To the extent that extraneous factors are eliminated or controlled, the observed effects can be related to the variations in the stimuli. The purpose of control is to eliminate competing hypotheses that might also explain the observed phenomena. Marketers have applied this data collection method to such marketing problems as finding the best sales training method, the best incentive scheme, the best price level, the best ad campaign, and so on.[8]

A third method of generating primary data, and the most common, is through *surveys.* Compared with either direct observation or experimentation, surveys yield a broader range of information and are effective for a greater number of research problems. Surveys can produce information on socioeconomic characteristics, attitudes, opinions, motives, and overt behavior. Surveys are an effective way of gathering information for planning product features, advertising copy, advertising media, sales promotions, channels of distribution, and other marketing variables.

If the survey method is chosen, the researcher has three alternative methods available for reaching the group he wants to sample: telephone interviews, mail questionnaires, and personal interviews. *Telephone interviewing* stands out as the best method of the three for gathering quickly needed information. It has the advantage over a mail questionnaire of permitting the interviewer to talk to one or more persons and to clarify his questions if they are not understood. The response rate for telephone interviewing seems to be a little better than for mail questionnaires. The two main drawbacks of telephone interviewing are that only people with telephones can be interviewed (this used to be a more serious disadvantage) and only short, not too personal, interviews can be carried out.

The *mail questionnaire* may be the best way to reach persons who would not give personal interviews or who might be biased by interviewers. It is typically the least expensive of the three methods. On the other hand, mail questionnaires require simple and clearly worded questions and are usually slow in returning to survey headquarters. The response rate to mailed questionnaires is typically low.

Personal interviewing is the most versatile of the three methods. The personal interviewer can ask more questions and can supplement the interview with personal observations. These advantages come at a high cost, however. Personal interviewing is the most expensive method and requires much more technical and administrative planning and supervision. In a real sense, companies turn to telephone interviewing or mail questionnaires as a second choice for reasons of cost.

RESEARCH INSTRUMENT.   The researcher has to use or design a reliable research instrument to gather the information he is seeking. The observational methods make use of such instruments as tape recorders, cameras, tally sheets, and so forth. The experimental method might involve similar instruments if the subjects are put through a task. The survey method, and to some extent the experimental method, commonly rely on questionnaires.

The construction of good questionnaires calls for considerable skill. Every questionnaire should be pretested on a pilot sample of persons before being used on a large scale. A professional marketing researcher can usually spot several errors in a casually prepared questionnaire, and these errors can invalidate some of the information. The more common errors arise in connection with the *types of questions asked,* the *form and wording of the questions,* and the *sequencing of the questions.*

The most common errors in regard to the *types of questions asked* are the inclusion of questions that cannot be answered, or would not be answered, or need not be answered, and the omission of other questions which should be answered. Each question should be checked to determine whether or not it is necessary in terms of the research objectives. The form should avoid questions that are just interesting (except for one or two to start the interview on a good basis) because they lengthen the session and try the respondent's patience.

The *form and wording of questions* can make a substantial difference to the response. An open-end question is one to which the respondent is free to answer in his own words. A closed-end question is one in which the possible answers are prescribed. The respondent may be asked to respond in one or two ways (dichotomous questions), to check one of several answers (multiple-choice questions), to place marks along a scale (scaling questions), and so forth. The choice between open-end and closed-end questions affects the thoughtfulness of responses, the costs of interviewing, and the quality of the subsequent analysis.

The *choice of words* calls for considerable care. The designer should strive for simple, direct, unambiguous, and unbiased wording. A good rule is always to pre-test the questions on a sample of respondents before they are used on a wide scale.

Other "dos" and "don'ts" arise in connection with the *sequencing of questions* in the questionnaire. The lead questions should create interest, if possible. Open questions are usually better here. Difficult questions or personal questions should be used toward the end of the interview, in order not to create an emotional reaction that may affect subsequent answers or cause the respondent to break off the interview. The body of questions should be asked in as logical an order as possible in order to avoid confusing the respondent. Classificatory data on the respondent are usually asked for last, because they tend to be less interesting and are on the personal side.

SAMPLING PLAN.   The third element of research design is a sampling plan. The sampling plan answers three questions: who is to be surveyed (sampling unit); how many are to be surveyed (sample size); and how they are to be selected (sampling procedure).

Perhaps the basic issue concerns who is to be surveyed. The proper *sampling unit* is not always obvious from the nature of the information sought. In a survey designed to uncover attitudes toward the legalization of marijuana, should the primary sampling unit be the housewife, the husband, the children, or some combination of the three? Where the roles of instigators, influencers, deciders, users, and/or purchasers are not combined in the same person, the researcher must determine not only what information is needed but also who is most likely to have it.

The next issue is *sample size*. Larger samples give more reliable results than smaller samples. However, it is not necessary to sample the whole universe or even a substantial part of it to achieve satisfactory precision. Samples amounting to less than 1 percent of the whole population can often give good reliability, given a creditable sample procedure. In exploratory research, very small samples suffice. Much insight about marketing processes and attitudes can be gained from a sample of fewer than 100 persons. In motivation-research studies, fewer than thirty depth interviews usually suffice to uncover significant attitudes.

Sampling procedure also depends upon the research objective. For exploratory research, nonprobability sampling procedure may be adequate. However, to make an accurate estimate of population characteristics, a random (probability) sample of the population should be drawn. Everyone in the universe should have an equal (or known) chance of being selected for the sample. Different types of persons tend to appear in the sample in rough proportion to their frequency in the population.

Random sampling allows the calculation of confidence limits for sampling errors. It is possible to place a specified degree of confidence in the precision of the sample estimates. One could say "the chances are ninety-five in a hundred that the interval '20 to 25 percent' contains the true percentage of people who attend a museum annually."

Unfortunately, random sampling is almost always more costly than non-random sampling. Some marketing researchers feel that the extra expenditure for probability sampling could be put to better use. Specifically, more of the money of a fixed research budget could be spent in designing better questionnaires and hiring better interviewers to reduce response and non-sampling errors, which can be just as fatal as sampling errors. This is a real issue, one that the marketing researcher and marketing executives must carefully weigh.

Field Work.   After the research design has been formulated, the research department must supervise, or subcontract, the task of collecting the data. This phase is generally the most expensive and the most liable to error. Four major problems arise:

1. *Not-at-homes.* When an interviewer does not find anyone at home, he can either call back later or substitute the household next door. The latter is the less expensive alternative, because the interviewer will not have to travel back to the same block. The only problem is that there is no easy way to learn whether the adjacent household resembles the original one precisely, because no data were collected on the original. The substitution may be biasing.

2. *Refusal to cooperate.* After finding the designated individual at home,

the interviewer must interest the person in cooperating. If the time is inconvenient or if the survey appears phony, the designated person may not cooperate.

3. *Respondent bias.* The interviewer must encourage accurate and thoughtful answers. Some respondents may give inaccurate or biased answers in order to finish quickly or for other reasons.

4. *Interviewer bias.* Interviewers are capable of introducing a variety of unconscious biases into the interviewing process, through the mere fact of their age, sex, manner, or intonation. In addition, there is the problem of conscious interviewer bias or dishonesty. Interviewers face a great temptation to fill their quota of interviews as quickly or as cheaply as possible. This can be done by not making the required number of call-backs or claiming refusals to cooperate, or, in extreme cases, actually falsifying an interview.

Data Analysis. The fourth step in marketing research procedure is to attempt to extract meaningful information from the data. Anyone who has had the experience of amassing data knows that further work has to be done to reveal underlying magnitudes and patterns of association or causality. The first step is to calculate relevant averages and measures of dispersion. The second step is to cross-tabulate the data to produce useful tables. The third step is to measure correlation coefficients and perform goodness-of-fit tests. The fourth step is to attempt multivariate analysis of the data using such statistical techniques as multiple regression analysis, discriminant analysis, factor analysis, and cluster analysis.[9]

Report Preparation. The last step is the preparation of a managerially oriented report presenting the major findings and recommendations coming from the study. The report should begin with a short statement of the problem and the major findings. This should be followed by an elaboration of the findings. A brief description of the research method should follow, with the more technical details being saved for an appendix. Much of the data should also be appendixed. The last section should discuss the major reservations and qualifications. In general, the report should be written to facilitate the understanding and interest of the executives and their ability to derive actionable information.

MARKETING MANAGEMENT SCIENCE SYSTEM

An increasing number of organizations have been adding a fourth information service to help their administrators—management science (also called operations research). A management scientist applies scientific methodology to organizational problems in the search for improved understanding, prediction, and control. Management scientists are often called model builders, and quite appropriately, because "model" is one of the central defining concepts in their field. A model is the specification of a set of variables and their interrelationships designed to represent some real system or process, in whole or in part.

Although management science is a relative latecomer in marketing, it has already yielded useful insights and decision models in such areas as new-product development, competitive pricing, advertising budgeting and media selection, sales-call time allocation, and marketing mix planning. Beginning in the late 1950s, marketing management scientists have produced a rich harvest of models on almost every conceivable quantifiable marketing problem or process. Unfortunately, usage has lagged substantially behind model development, in some cases owing to the inappropriateness of the models, in other cases to the lack of empirical data, and in a large number of cases owing to marketing management's widespread lack of understanding and sympathy for quantitative approaches to marketing. Today some models are fully established and running in some larger companies but they constitute the exception rather than the rule. The vast majority of marketing decisions are still made intuitively in spite of the availability of more rigorous decision procedures born out of years of patient management science work.

Complex Factors in the Marketing Process

Although organizations spend large sums of money collecting information about their customers, competitors, and the general environment, administrators still feel substantial uncertainty surrounding their marketing decisions. At least nine types of complexity can be identified.

Shape of Response Function. The shape of the market's response to additional marketing expenditure is typically unknown. If an organization doubles the level of its marketing expenditures, will its sales double, more than double, or less than double? Adequate data to learn the answer are difficult to collect and analyze in any real situation.

Marketing Mix Interaction. Marketing effort is a composite of many different types of activities undertaken by the firm to improve market response. The organization's task is to develop a sound mix of marketing activities in the face of great uncertainty as to their separate and joint effects. The market's response to variations in the level of any one marketing input is conditional on the level of the other activities. Furthermore, variation of two or more marketing activities at the same time can have joint effects that are greater or less than the sum of the separate effects. To model and estimate these interactive effects is an extremely challenging task.

Competitive Effects. Market response is a function of the relative marketing efforts by the organization and its competitors, and the organization has no control over competitors' moves. At best, the organization imperfectly forecasts the behavior and reactions of competitors. The notion of optimal decision making means choosing the best decision that could be made in the light of forecasted competitors' behavior or response.

Delayed Response. The market's response to current marketing expenditures is not immediate, but in many instances stretches out over several time periods beyond the occurrence of the expenditures. A well-known organization can stop all its advertising and continue to enjoy high market response for a while because of the advertising carryover effect. The carryover effect of marketing expenditures makes the optimal timing of marketing expenditures particularly challenging.

Multiple Territories. The market's response to different levels of marketing expenditure will vary by territory, making it difficult for the firm to determine the best way to allocate its marketing funds. Should a major university concentrate its recruiting effort in the areas in which it is already doing well or in the areas in which it is doing poorly? In one form or another this question plagues most organizations, and their present methods of resolving it leave much to be desired.

Multiple Products. Most organizations produce more than one product or service and face a difficult problem of allocating marketing effort among them. Marketing strategies cannot be determined for each product separately if there are strong demand and cost interactions among the different products of the organization.

Marketing-Finance-Operations Interactions. Marketing decisions cannot be optimized without simultaneous decision making in the operations and financial areas. Whether or not a new advertising campaign is sound depends not only on the market response it produces but also on whether the organization can handle this response. Unfortunately, most departments are guided by departmental instead of organization-wide utility criteria when they plan their respective actions.

Multiple Objectives. An organization tends to pursue multiple objectives. It must somehow state its goals in such a way that a clear objective function emerges to guide the choice of a marketing strategy from a potentially large number of strategies.

Uncertainty Effects. Marketing processes are full of uncertainties beyond those just isolated. Relations between marketing efforts and market response are subject to systematic and random disturbances through time and space which must be taken into account in the marketing planning process.

Specific Applications

The most viable marketing management science models have been developed in the areas of (1) new products, (2) pricing, (3) advertising, (4) sales-force management, and (5) marketing mix planning.[10]

New-Product Models. New-product development has become a major management function in recent years in commercial companies and to a lesser extent in nonprofit organizations. New-product development is absolutely necessary for survival; on the other hand, it is fraught with great risk and expense. The facts show that (1) most new-product ideas that go into product development never reach the market; (2) many of the new products that do reach the market are not successful; and (3) successful products tend to have a shorter life span than new products once had.[11]

Therefore it is not surprising that many companies have sought new-product models to aid in their new-product decision making. Several well-known new-product models have been developed and published in the literature bearing such names as SPRINTER, DEMON, NEWS, and STEAM.[12] They fall into three classes.

The first type of model aids management in attempting to identify new-product opportunities. One of the best methodologies in this connection is described by Stefflre and is called *market structure studies*.[13] Essentially this methodology maps current consumers' perceptions of a product space to reveal the location of existing brands and to indicate possible new brands. Any interesting new-product possibility can be turned into a product concept that is then tested on a sample of consumers. At an early stage, the company will want to evaluate the new-product idea's fit with the company's resources and objectives, using some version of a weighted factor score device.[14]

The second type of new-product model consists of models for estimating the potential sales and profits for new-product concepts before they are launched. Even if the company finds it can justify the new-product idea in terms of the firm's resources and objectives, it must be convinced that it would yield a good return in the long run. The typical model calls for projecting expected revenues and costs over the product's planning horizon. The expected revenue stream calls for estimating total market volume and growth, future prices, and company share of market. Total market volume itself is a function of target market size, per capita consumption, effective purchasing power, and the availability of sub-stitutes. Market share is a function of the relative attractiveness and force of the company's marketing mix in relation to competitors' marketing mixes. The future cost stream is estimated on the basis of the opportunity value of the funds invested in the product and required to meet the ex-pected demand levels. The company must choose some decision criteria —early payout, present value, or return on investment—to make the final decision.

The third type of new-product model forecasts the future demand for recently launched products on the basis of their initial market results. It turns out that early sales alone are an insufficient basis for making a confident forecast of future sales. Initial sales do not reveal how satisfied the market is with the product and what users are saying to nonusers. High initial sales may reflect an effective promotion campaign designed to get high trial; if the product fails to meet expectations, sales may shortly turn down. For this reason, total sales must be broken down into sales to first-time purchasers, second-time purchasers, third-time pur-chasers, etc., to learn something about the rate of repurchase and satis-faction.[15]

Pricing Models.   Management scientists have lent their talents to helping management determine optimal prices for their products. The basic theoretical model for optimal pricing [16] serves as a frequent starting point for specific elaboration to meet the problem at hand. For example, the same model can help in pricing two or more interrelated products in the company line if the product cross-elasticities are known. Pricing models also have been developed to help the executive determine a price in the face of competitive and environmental uncertainty. These models use *decision tree analysis,* which calls for distinguishing the pricing-level alternatives and the probabilities and payoffs of different possible events. This analysis yields an estimate of the expected values of different pricing alternatives to the firm.[17] For firms that do competitive bidding, management scientists have developed elegant bidding models which identify the optimal price under different assumptions about com-petitors' bidding behavior.[18]

Advertising Models.   Companies feel that they are very much in the dark when they spend money on advertising. Management scientists have looked at two particular problems to introduce some efficiency into the advertising decision process. The first is the spending-level problem and the second is the media-selection problem.

There have been several interesting models to aid in the determina-tion of an optimal advertising expenditure level. One of the earliest and still most interesting models was developed by Vidale and Wolfe.[19] The model expresses the sales effect of advertising as a function of four variables: the advertising budget level; the sales response constant; the saturation level of sales; and the sales decay constant. Given the last three quantities, the model can be manipulated to determine the optimal advertising budget. Subsequent advertising budget models introduced the desirability of estimating sales/advertising response functions by experimenting with different levels of advertising.[20] The analytical use of planned advertising experiments allowed one major brewery to achieve substantial increases in sales and market share while bringing down the per-case expenditures on advertising.[21] Most recently, management scientists have been turning to *evolutionary model-building techniques.* Instead of coming to a manager with a predetermined model, they work with the manager to build a model of how he thinks advertising works. This model goes through subsequent refinements as the manager shows a readiness and wish to add further variables. The great advantage is that the manager feels involved and he understands what the model is doing.[22]

The other major area of advertising model building is in media selection. The media planner's job is to select a set of media that will maximize the number of effective exposures in the face of a given advertising budget, minimum and maximum usage constraints for each media vehicle, and minimum exposure rates desired for different market segments. Given the great number of media and their cost variations for different types of ad purchases, it is strongly felt that a computerized media model would facilitate advertising planning and improve advertising results. Over a dozen alternative models have been designed using such different procedures as linear programming, dynamic programming, simulation, heuristic techniques, and so on.[23] A few are being used on a regular basis by some advertising agencies but by and large, the adoption rate has been slower than expected.

Sales-Force Models. The great cost of sales-force operation and the interesting problems posed in efficient management have attracted the attention of management scientists. They have worked in at least three problem areas.

The first is the problem of creating optimal sales territories. A sales territory must have enough sales potential to keep the salesman busy but not so busy that he only skims the surface. Furthermore, sales territory boundaries must be periodically revised because of population and income shifts over time. Hess has formulated a computer program that creates geographical sales territories that are equal in either sales potential or workload and as compact as possible to minimize traveling time.[24]

The second area of model building is in the problem facing the individual salesman of how much call time to allocate to different customers each period. If he allocates too little time to a customer, he may lose him; if he allocates too much time, he is wasting it. Lodish designed a model called CALLPLAN, which allows a salesman to sit at a computer terminal and input his best estimates of expected sales in response to several alternative call levels on each account and prospect. The computer takes this data and computes a customer call-time plan that maximizes expected profits for the company.[25] Another model called DETAILER was recently designed for use in the pharmaceutical industry to help salesmen (detailmen) know which pharmaceutical products to promote to which accounts on each trip.[26]

The third is the problem facing a salesman of optimally routing himself through his territory to reach a specified set of customers. Several traveling salesman algorithms are available to find the optimal routing for the salesman.[27]

Marketing Mix Models. A final area of management science in marketing is the development of computer-based models to help marketing managers, particularly product managers, develop short-run and long-run marketing plans. Increasingly, companies are requiring their product managers to submit a detailed marketing plan that is quantified in terms of expected sales, costs, and profits. To help them in this task, several companies have developed their own version of a conversational computer program for marketing planning. A model used by a large consumer packaged-goods company provides a good example.[28] The product manager seats himself at a computer terminal, activates the program, and types in the product's name. The computer prints out historical data for the last five years on the product's total market volume, company sales, company market share, price, gross margin, overhead, advertising, promotion, and net operating profits. The computer also proceeds to print out a projection for each of these variables over the next five years, using the most plausible extrapolation rule in each case. The manager scans the extrapolated values of these variables and modifies any that appear unreasonable in the light of new developments. The computer then summarizes the revised extrapolation (called the planning base). In the next phase, the manager tries out other marketing mixes that might produce an improved picture of future profits.

SUMMARY

Organizations need great quantities of marketing information that is timely, accurate, and easily retrievable if they are to make intelligent marketing decisions. The way the organization gathers, processes, stores, and disseminates relevant marketing information can be called its marketing information system. These systems range from very primitive to very sophisticated ones. They all have up to four major components.

The first component of an organization's marketing information system is its internal records system, which is the system that contains the data on past orders, sales, costs, and so on by product, territory, salesman, and customer type. Large business firms have highly sophisticated internal records systems and some government agencies, universities, hospitals, and fund-raising organizations also have built quite advanced systems.

The second component is the organization's marketing intelligence system, which describes the informal ways in which managers keep abreast of new developments in markets, customers, competitors, and the macroenvironment. Each executive gathers market intelligence in his own way but the organization can take several concrete steps to formalize and improve the marketing intelligence flow.

The third component is the organization's marketing research system, which describes the formal way in which an organization gathers specific information needed to solve a marketing problem. Marketing research procedure consists of five steps: problem definition, research design, field work, data analysis, and report preparation. Marketing researchers are skilled in defining how to collect information (secondary sources, observation, experimentation, or survey) and in designing research instruments and sampling plans to assure that the information is impartial, reliable, and valid.

The last component is the organization's marketing management science system, which describes the use of formal mathematical techniques to develop optimal solutions to recurrent marketing problems. Management scientists have developed many useful models in the areas of new products, pricing, advertising, sales-force management, and marketing mix planning. Some of these are in active use in large companies and a few are beginning to be looked at by nonprofit organizations.

NOTES

1. J. D. Casher, D. S. Diamond, and T. I. Nelson, *Prototype On-Line Information Processing System for the M.I.T. Alumni Association*, a paper presented to the M.I.T. Alumni Association, January 23, 1967.

2. Glen L. Urban, *A Model for the Management of a Family Planning System* (Working paper, 613-72, Alfred P. Sloan School of Management, M.I.T., September 1972).

3. Francis Joseph Aguilar, *Scanning the Business Environment* (New York: The Macmillan Co., 1967).

4. For the status of marketing research in the United States, see Dik

Warren Twedt, ed., *1968 Survey of Marketing Research: Organization, Functions, Budget, Compensation* (Chicago: American Marketing Association, 1968).

5. Ernest S. Bradford, *Bradford's Directory of Marketing Research Agencies and Management Consultants in the United States and the World,* 15th ed., 1973–74 (Middlebury, Vt.: Bradford Co.).

6. For a comprehensive description of these publications, see Harper W. Boyd, Jr., and Ralph Westfall, *Marketing Research: Text and Cases,* 3rd ed. (Homewood, Ill.: Richard D. Irwin, Inc., 1972), Chap. 6.

7. An excellent discussion of observation methods with many examples germane to nonprofit organizations is found in Eugene J. Webb, Donald T. Campbell, Richard D. Schwartz, and Lee Sechrest, *Unobtrusive Measures: Nonreactive Research in the Social Sciences* (Chicago, Ill.: Rand McNally & Co., 1966).

8. For an excellent exposition and evaluation of the experimental method in marketing, see Seymour Banks, *Experimentation in Marketing* (New York: McGraw-Hill Book Co., 1965).

9. See David A. Aaker, ed., *Multivariate Analysis in Marketing: Theory and Applications* (Belmont, Calif.: Wadsworth Publishing Co., 1971).

10. For a detailed discussion of various models, see the author's *Marketing Decision Making: A Model-Building Approach* (New York: Holt, Rinehart and Winston, 1971).

11. See *Management of New Products,* 4th ed. (New York: Booz, Allen & Hamilton, Inc., 1965).

12. See Kotler, *Marketing Decision Making.*

13. Volney Stefflre, "Market Structure Studies: New Products for Old Markets and New Markets (Foreign) for Old Products," in F. M. Bass, C. W. King, and E. A. Pessemier, eds., *Applications of the Sciences in Marketing Management* (New York: John Wiley & Sons, Inc., 1968).

14. Barry Richman, "A Rating Scale for Product Innovation," *Business Horizons* (Summer 1962), pp. 37–44.

15. Glen L. Urban, "SPRINTER MOD III: A Model for the Analysis of New Frequently Purchased Consumer Products," *Operations Research* (September–October 1970), pp. 805–54.

16. See Chapter 9, pp. 178–80.

17. Paul E. Green, "Bayesian Decision Theory in Pricing Strategy," *Journal of Marketing* (January 1963), pp. 5–14.

18. See C. W. Churchman, R. L. Ackoff, and E. L. Arnoff, *Introduction to Operations Research* (New York: John Wiley & Sons, Inc., 1957), Chap. 19.

19. M. L. Vidale and H. B. Wolfe, "An Operations-Research Study of Sales Responses to Advertising," *Operations Research* (June 1957), pp. 370–81.

20. John D. C. Little, "A Model of Adaptive Control of Promotional Spending," *Operations Research* (November 1966), pp. 1075–97.

21. A. G. Rao, *Quantitative Theories in Advertising* (New York: John Wiley & Sons, Inc., 1970).

22. John D. C. Little, "Models and Managers: The Concept of a Decision Calculus," *Management Science* (April 1970), pp. 466–85.

23. Dennis Gensch, *Advertising Planning: Mathematical Models in Advertising Media Planning* (Amsterdam, N.Y.: Elsevier Scientific Publishing Co., 1973).

24. S. W. Hess and S. A. Samuels, "Experiences with a Sales Districting

Model: Criteria and Implementation," *Management Science* (December 1971), pp. 41–54.

25. Leonard M. Lodish, "CALLPLAN: An Interactive Salesman's Call Planning System," *Management Science* (December 1971), Part II, pp. 25–40.

26. D. B. Montgomery, A. J. Silk, and C. E. Zaragoza, "A Multiple-Product Sales Force Allocation Model," *Management Science* (December 1971), Part II, pp. 3–24.

27. R. L. Karg and G. L. Thompson, "A Heuristic Approach to Solving Traveling Salesman Problems," *Management Science* (January 1964), pp. 225–48.

28. "Concorn Kitchens," in H. W. Boyd and R. T. Davis, *Marketing Management Casebook* (Homewood, Ill.: Richard D. Irwin, Inc., 1971), pp. 125–36.

QUESTIONS

1. The coach of a university college basketball team needs a good marketing intelligence system to help him recruit high-quality players. Design a marketing intelligence system for this coach.

2. Mr. X has just been elected to the U.S. Congress. During his campaign, Mr. X promised that if he were elected he would keep a close watch on what was bothering the people in his district. As part of an overall effort to create an information system for himself, Mr. X would like to conduct periodic surveys of his constituency. Recommend a survey method for him to use.

3. The local U.S. Navy recruiter has hired you to conduct a marketing research study that will give him information he can use to recruit more college graduates for officers' training school. Design a marketing research study for him.

4. Briefly describe what is done in (1) multiple regression analysis, (2) discriminant analysis, and (3) factor analysis.

5. Some marketing men view the emergence of mathematical model building in marketing with hostility. They will make the following statements: (a) "We don't use models"; (b) "Models are typically unrealistic"; (c) "Anyone can build a model"; (d) "A model is of no help unless you can get the data." How would you answer these objections?

6. The marketing manager of a state lottery system would like to build a model to help him predict how the public will respond to a large advertising campaign he would like to run. He needs an accurate prediction of how much ticket buying will increase as a result of the campaign to help him convince the state legislature to appropriate the necessary funds. What kinds of things should the manager consider in building his model?

PART

V Applications

15   Social Marketing

Man does not live by GNP alone.

PAUL SAMUELSON

We are now ready to apply marketing logic in a number of specific areas. Although marketing logic has a unity that transcends particular organizations and products, there is a creative challenge to selecting those concepts and tools that are particularly appropriate in each context. Each area of management endeavor has its own goal structure, publics, marketing problems, and general outlook. The concepts that would work best for hospitals, museums, universities, political parties, churches, and public agencies will vary. In this part of the book we will consider a few situations in detail. In particular, we will examine the role of marketing in the area of social causes, health services, public services, educational services, and political campaigning.

This chapter focuses on a generic problem facing many nonprofit organizations—that of marketing a social cause or idea. Examples abound of organizations striving to motivate some public to adopt a new idea or practice.

> The National Safety Council wants people to wear their safety belts when driving. The American Cancer Society wants people to stop smoking. The American Medical Association wants people to take an annual physical checkup. The Federal Energy Office wants people to conserve on fuel and energy. The New York Police Department wants people to keep their car doors locked. The World Federalists wants people to get together in a one-world government. The National Organization of Women wants men to view women as their equals. The National Federation of Churches wants people to give greater support to religion in American life.

These efforts to alter the beliefs, attitudes, values, or behavior of target publics go under different names. They are called propaganda efforts by their critics and educational efforts by their supporters. They are perfectly normal activities and are found in all societies. Every group has its cause and actively attempts, if allowed, to propagate its viewpoint to others. In a totalitarian society, only one group is allowed to propagate openly for official causes. In a free society, all groups propagate their viewpoints in "the marketplace of ideas."

The technicians who carry on this activity are called propagandists, publicists, journalists, lobbyists, and many other names. Very often they see their task in very narrow terms, as that of manipulating persuasive symbols and messages. We shall argue, however, that effective communication is only one part of the total task required to successfully market an idea. The adoption of an idea, like the adoption of any product, requires a deep understanding of the needs, perceptions, preferences, reference groups, and behavioral patterns of the target audience, and the tailoring of messages, media, "costs," and facilities to maximize the ease of adopting the idea. We use the term *social marketing* to cover these tasks. We believe that social marketing provides a rich conceptual system for thinking through the problems of bringing about changes in the ideas or practices of a target public. This chapter will examine the concept of social marketing, conditions requisite for its effectiveness, its applicability to different types of social causes, and the administrative system necessary to plan and control social marketing efforts.

Before proceeding however, it is desirable to allay the reader's suspicion that this chapter provides Machiavellian guidance on how to get people to do what they do not want to do—that is, a means of social manipulation and control. In the first place, it is a very difficult task to change people for good or bad.[1] Those who work in a face-to-face relation to other persons and who have their trust, such as psychiatrists, social workers, physicians, or relatives, know how difficult it is to change another person. It is even more difficult to change a whole group of people when the means are mass media that appear infrequently and not from a necessarily disinterested source. Although social marketing attempts to harness the insights of behavioral science and exchange theory to the task of social persuasion, its power to bring about actual change, or bring it about in a reasonable amount of time, is highly limited. The greater the target group's investment in a value or behavioral pattern, the more resistant it is to change. Social marketing works best where the type of change counts for least.

Second, social marketing goes on in society whether or not its methods are discussed in any book. Some groups will be better at it than others. Rather than keep social marketing methodology a deep secret and thus leave certain groups with an advantage, this methodology should be openly discussed and examined. This visibility will allow both sides of an issue to formulate sophisticated plans as well as alert the public to how groups market a social cause. Hopefully this will cancel the advantage of any single side and lead more often to the resolution of public issues on their merits.

CONCEPT OF SOCIAL MARKETING

We define social marketing as follows:[2]

Social marketing is the design, implementation, and control of programs seeking to increase the acceptability of a social idea or practice in a target group(s). It utilizes concepts of market segmentation, consumer research, idea configuration, communication, facilitation, incentives, and exchange theory to maximize target group response.

There are three major differences between social marketing and business marketing:

1. Business marketers typically try to meet the identified needs and wants of target markets; social marketers typically try to change the attitudes or behavior of target markets.
2. Business marketers typically feel that their major aim is to make a profit through serving the interests of the target market or society; social marketers typically aim to serve the interests of the target market or society without personal profit.
3. Business marketers typically market products and services through the medium of ideas; social marketers typically market the ideas themselves rather than products or services.

As an illustration, consider a campaign to motivate people to brush their teeth more regularly. Without knowing the sponsor, we would conjecture that this is a social marketing campaign. It appears to be the use of marketing to serve the public interest rather than a private interest. There is little question that this is social marketing if the sponsor is either the U.S. Department of Health or the American Dental Association. In fact, this campaign would cut the income of dentists if successful. However, if the sponsor is a large toothpaste manufacturer such as Procter & Gamble, the extent to which this is a social marketing campaign is a little more ambiguous. It is more like a business marketing proposition, an attempt by the manufacturer to expand the market's use of his product. At the same time, the campaign itself may be indistinguishable whether its sponsor is the U.S. Department of Health, the American Dental Association, or Procter & Gamble.

Social marketing usually implies that the social marketer is primarily acting in the interest of the target group or "society." Many social causes would be accepted unambiguously as falling under social marketing—for example, civil rights, better nutrition, better health care, and environmental protection. There are other causes that are more ambiguous. The marketing of family planning is an example of social marketing but so would be the antimarketing of family planning by religious groups who think it is not in society's interest. The protagonists and antagonists of abortion both regard their position to be in the interest of society and can plan the marketing of their idea in a social marketing framework. Any social cause, in fact, can be marketed; we cannot assume that everyone will agree that it is in the public interest.

The social marketer differs from the straight social propagandist in a number of ways. The propagandist usually comes into the social planning after the objectives, policies, and "products" have been determined. He has no influence on product design, pricing, or distribution. His job as propagandist, publicist, or public relations man is to promote the organization's objectives and products, using communication media. The social marketer, on the other hand, participates actively in the organization's planning. He advises what products will be acceptable to the target publics; what incentives will work best; what distribution structures will be optimal; and what communication program will be effective. He thinks in exchange terms rather than in one-way influence terms. He has as much an interest in improving the offer of the organization as in modifying the target market's acceptance of the offer. Whereas the propagandist takes the product, price, and channels as given, the social marketer treats these as variables.

THE REQUISITE CONDITIONS FOR
EFFECTIVE SOCIAL MARKETING [3]

Some clues concerning the difference between social propaganda and social marketing are contained in papers by Lazarsfeld and Merton [4] and by Wiebe [5] which attempt to explain the limitations of social propaganda.

Lazarsfeld and Merton's Analysis

Lazarsfeld and Merton have taken exception with the view of many people that mass media can easily be used to control people's minds: "It is our tentative judgment that the social role played by the very existence of the mass media has been commonly overestimated." [6] They believe that the effectiveness of mass media for propaganda purposes depended on three conditions, one or more of which is lacking in most propaganda situations. The first condition is real or psychological *monopolization* by the media; that is, a condition marked by the absence of counterpropaganda. This characterizes the totalitarian state and accounts for the greater effectiveness of these regimes in molding public opinion through mass media. It is found occasionally in free societies under special circumstances, such as a wartime effort. For example, Kate Smith's effectiveness in selling war bonds over the radio during World War II was partially due to the marathon nature of the event and the fact that everyone believed in the cause; i.e., there was no counterpropaganda. However, most campaigns in a free society in peacetime compete with so many other causes and everyday distractions that the monopoly condition is lacking, and this condition reduces the effectiveness of such campaigns.

The second condition required for effective mass propaganda is *canalization*, the presence of an existing attitudinal base for the feelings that the social communicators are striving to shape. Typical commercial advertising is effective because the task is not one of instilling basic new attitudes or creating significantly new behavior patterns, but rather canalizing existing attitudes and behavior in one direction or another. Thus, the seller of toothpaste does not have to socialize persons into new dental care habits, but rather into which brand of a familiar and desired product to purchase. If the preexisting attitudes are present, then promotional campaigns are more effective, because canalization is always an easier task than social reconditioning.

The third condition is *supplementation*—e.g., the effort to follow up mass communication campaigns with programs of face-to-face contacts. In trying to explain the success of the rightist Father Coughlin movement in the thirties, Lazarsfeld and Merton observe:

> This combination of a central supply of propaganda [Coughlin's addresses on a nationwide network], the coordinated distribution of newspapers and pamphlets and locally organized face-to-face discussions among relatively small groups—this complex of reciprocal reinforcement by mass media and personal relations proved spectacularly successful.[7]

This approach is standard in many closed societies and organizations and suggests a key difference between social advertising and social marketing. Whereas a social advertising approach contrives only the event of mass media communication and leaves the response to natural social processes, social marketing arranges for a stepdown communication process. The message is passed on and discussed in more familiar surroundings to increase its memorability, penetration, and action consequences. Thus supplementation, monopolization, and canalization are critical factors influencing the effectiveness of any social marketing effort.

Wiebe's Analyses

In 1952, G. D. Wiebe raised the question, "Why can't you sell brotherhood like you sell soap?" This statement implies that sellers of commodities such as soap are generally effective, while "sellers" of social causes are generally ineffective. Wiebe examined four social campaigns to determine what conditions or characteristics accounted for their relative success or lack of success. He found that the more the conditions of the social campaign resembled those of a product campaign, the more successful the social campaign. However, because many social campaigns are conducted under quite unmarketlike circumstances, Wiebe also noted clear limitations in the practice of social marketing.

Wiebe explained the relative effectiveness of these campaigns in terms of the audience member's experience with regard to five factors:

1. *The Force.* The intensity of the person's motivation toward the goal as a combination of his predisposition prior to the message and the stimulation of the message.
2. *The Direction.* Knowledge of how or where the person might go to consummate his motivation.
3. *The Mechanism.* The existence of an agency that enables the person to translate his motivation into action.

4. *Adequacy and Compatibility.* The ability and effectiveness of the agency in performing its task.
5. *Distance.* The audience member's estimate of the energy and cost required to consummate the motivation in relation to the reward.

To show how these factors operate, Wiebe first analyzed the Kate Smith campaign to sell bonds during World War II. This campaign was eminently successful, according to Wiebe, because of the presence of force (patriotism), direction (buy bonds), mechanism (banks, post offices, telephone orders), adequacy and compatibility (so many centers to purchase the bonds), and distance (ease of purchase). In fact, extra telephone lines were installed on the night of the campaign at 134 CBS stations to take orders during her appeal. The effort to buy bonds

> was literally reduced to the distance between the listener and his telephone. Psychological distance was also minimized. The listener remained in his own home. There were no new people to meet, no unfamiliar procedures, no forms to fill out, no explanation, no waiting. . . .[8]

In the case of a campaign to recruit Civil Defense volunteers, many of the same factors were present except that the social mechanism was not prepared to handle the large volume of response, and this reduced the campaign's success. Teachers, manuals, equipment, and registration and administration procedures were *inadequate,* and many responding citizens were turned away and disappointed after they were led to believe that their services were urgently needed.

The third campaign, a documentary on juvenile delinquency, did not meet with maximum success because of the *absence of a mechanism.* Instead of being directed to an existing agency, people were urged to form neighborhood councils themselves. This certainly takes far more effort than simply picking up the phone to buy a war bond, or "stopping in" to register at the nearest Civil Defense unit.

The fourth campaign revolved around the goal of the Kefauver committee hearings to arouse citizens to "set their house in order." This campaign met with a notable lack of success, however, because citizens were not *directed* to an appropriate mechanism despite the fact that one existed in principle in the political party organizations. Political party organizations apparently left much to be desired in terms of availability and compatibility. The skepticism prevalent at the time concerning the chances of anything beneficial happening as a result of the hearings was ample evidence that considerable psychological distance existed between the audience and the mechanisms for action.

DISTINCTIONS AMONG TYPES OF SOCIAL CAUSES

Social marketing aims to produce an optimal plan for bringing about a desired social change. The fact that the plan is optimal, however, does not guarantee that the target change will be achieved. It depends on how easy or difficult the targeted social change is. Without social marketing thinking, it may be that the desired social change has only a 10 percent chance of being achieved; the best social marketing plan may only increase this probability to 15 percent. In other words, some social changes are relatively easy to bring about, even without social marketing; others are supremely difficult to bring about, even with social marketing.

We will distinguish among four types of social changes of varying difficulty to bring about. They are, respectively, cognitive change, action change, behavioral change, and value change. A social cause at any time may be attempting to produce one or more of these changes.

Cognitive Change

There are many social causes which have the limited objective of creating a cognitive change in the target audience. They are called public information or public education campaigns. Many examples can be cited:

Campaigns to explain the nutritional value of different foods.
Campaigns to explain the work of the United Nations.
Campaigns to expand awareness of Medicare and Medicaid benefits.
Campaigns to bring attention to pressing social problems, such as poverty, bigotry, or pollution.

Cognitive change causes would seem to be fairly easy to market effectively in that they do not seek to change any deep-rooted attitudes or behavior. Their aim is primarily to pass on information. The optimal marketing approach would seem to be straightforward. Marketing research would be used to identify the groups that need the information the most. Their media habits are identified to serve as a guide for distributing and timing effective messages. The messages themselves are formulated on the basis of behavioral analysis of the target audiences. They are carried to the audiences through mass advertising, publicity, personnel, displays, exhibitions, and other vehicles. The effectiveness of the campaign can be measured by post-sampling members of the target groups to see how much increase in comprehension has taken place.

Although it would seem that information campaigns should easily succeed, the evidence is quite mixed. A massive campaign in Cincinnati to inform citizens about the United Nations produced no measured increase in the level of citizen knowledge.[9] A two-year campaign during World War II to inform people that war bonds were intended primarily to curb inflation rather than raise money produced no measurable increase in understanding whatever.[10] Other campaigns that failed to produce cognitive change are documented by Hyman and Sheatsley.[11] These authors give several reasons why information campaigns may fail:

1. There exists a hard core of "chronic know-nothings" who cannot be reached by information campaigns. In fact, "there is something about the uninformed that makes them harder to reach, no matter what the level or nature of the information."
2. The likelihood of being exposed to the information increases with interest in the issue. If few people are initially interested, few will be exposed.
3. The likelihood of being exposed to the information increases with the information's compatibility with prior attitudes. People will tend to avoid disagreeable information.
4. People will read different things into the information that they are exposed to, depending on their beliefs and values. The bigot, for example, often does not perceive antiprejudice literature as such. People emerge with a range of different reactions to the same material.

Thus, much thought has to be given to planning the simplest of campaigns—those designed to produce cognitive change. The material must be interesting, clear, and consonant with the intended audience values.[12]

Action Change

Another class of causes are those attempting to induce a maximum number of persons to take a specific action during a given period. Many examples can be cited:

Campaigns to attract people to show up for a mass immunization campaign.

Campaigns to attract eligible people to sign up for Medicaid.

Campaigns to influence the greatest number of voters to approve a school bond issue.

Campaigns to attract women over forty to take a cancer detection test.

Campaigns to influence senators to vote for a particular environmental protection bill.

Campaigns to attract student dropouts back to school.
Campaigns to raise a large amount of money for charity.
Campaigns to attract blood donors.

Action causes are somewhat harder to market than cognitive change causes. The target market has to comprehend something *and* take a specific action based on it. Action involves a cost to the actor. Even if his attitude toward the action is favorable, his carrying it out may be impeded by such factors as distance, time, expense, or plain inertia. For this reason, the marketer has to arrange factors that make it easy for target persons to carry out the action. The Kate Smith campaign cited earlier is a good example of arranging conditions to make it extremely easy for people to take the desired action (in this case, buying bonds). Two other examples will be cited.

In 1965, Medicare was enacted into law to provide medical benefits for the *elderly*. The following year, Medicaid was enacted into law to provide medical benefits for the *indigent and handicapped*. In the state of New York, persons and families earning under $6,000 were eligible for Medicaid. One year after Medicaid was enacted, only one million of the three million eligible persons in New York City were enrolled. A survey revealed three factors behind the low enrollment rate:

1. A widespread lack of knowledge of Medicaid and its benefits.
2. Confusion of Medicaid with Medicare by elderly indigents who failed to realize the additional benefits available from Medicaid.
3. A mistaken belief that one had to be literally on the welfare rolls to be eligible.

The city of New York decided to launch a one-month campaign in June 1967 to increase the number of eligible persons who signed up for Medicaid. The plan for social marketing Medicaid included the following elements:

1. The mayor declared the month of June as Medicaid Month.
2. Health educators in thirty health districts went into the community to organize public support. They enlisted the support of professional leaders, active lay leaders, informal leaders, volunteers from the police auxiliary, and persons from antipoverty programs.
3. Personnel and sound trucks appeared at busy locations on different days to answer questions.
4. Information tables were placed in three department stores in Brooklyn to reach shoppers who might be eligible for Medicaid.

5. Literature was distributed in the streets and through department stores, banks, post offices, supermarkets, and schools.
6. Publicity was placed in newspapers, radio, and television.
7. Car cards were placed in the city subway system.
8. Posters were distributed at hospital out-patient clinics, health centers, and antipoverty offices.

This campaign was so successful that it was extended into the month of July and for the two months, a total of 450,000 additional persons were enrolled in Medicaid.[13]

Another illustration of action marketing are efforts to get local populations to show up for mass immunization campaigns. Medical teams in Africa make one-day scheduled visits to different villages to inoculate the local populations. Their hope is to inoculate everyone in each village. This is difficult in the face of a lack of understanding of germ theory, a fear of the needle, superstitions, and many other circumstances that interfere with showing up. Over the years, medical teams have evolved a procedure to increase the number of villagers they attract. A marketing team is sent to each village a few weeks before the appearance of the medical team. The marketers meet the village leaders to describe the importance and benefits of the program so that the leaders in turn will ask their people to cooperate. The marketers offer monetary or other incentives to the village leaders. They drive a sound truck around the village announcing the date and occasion. They promise rewards to those who show up. Posters are placed in various locations. The medical team arrives when scheduled and uses inoculation equipment that is relatively fast and painless. The whole effect is an orchestration of product, price, place, and promotion factors calculated to achieve the maximum possible turnout.

Behavioral Change

Another class of social causes aims to induce or help people change some aspect of their behavior for the sake of their well-being. The person's current behavior is viewed as injurious to his health. He may recognize this but be unable or unwilling to take the necessary steps to change his behavior. Behavioral change causes include:

Efforts to discourage cigarette smoking.
Efforts to discourage excessive consumption of alcohol.
Efforts to discourage the use of hard drugs.
Efforts to help overweight people change their food habits.

Behavioral change is harder to achieve than cognitive or one-shot action changes. Often the person is aware of the bad effects of his consumption habits. There is not one action that he can take to end forever the temptations he is subject to. The challenge is to assist him to change an entire behavioral routine that has become well established in his makeup.

Social marketing suggests some of the possible strategies that might be used to help people give up or alter self-destructive habits. Let us apply the framework to the problem of reducing cigarette consumption. The weight of scientific evidence demonstrates a link between cigarette smoking and such medical ailments as lung cancer, heart disease, and emphysema. Most cigarette smokers are aware of the bad effects of cigarette smoking. The problem is one of formulating and distributing solutions that will give them the means or will to reduce their cigarette dependence. The four Ps suggest several possible types of solutions:

1. *Product*
   a. Require manufacturers to add a tart or bitter ingredient to the tobacco.
   b. Find a way to cut down further the tar and nicotine in cigarettes (for example, develop better filters).
   c. Find a new type of tobacco for cigarettes that tastes as good but does not have harmful ingredients (for example, lettuce leaf).
   d. Find or promote other products that will help people relieve their tensions such as gum chewing or other oral pacifiers.
2. *Promotion*
   a. Increase fear of early death among smokers.
   b. Create guilt among cigarette users.
   c. Create shame among smokers.
   d. Strengthen some other goal of the smoker that supercedes his satisfaction from smoking.
   e. Urge smokers to cut down the number of cigarettes they smoke or to smoke only the first half of the cigarette.
3. *Place*
   a. Make cigarettes harder to obtain conveniently.
   b. Make cigarettes unavailable.
   c. Make it easier for cigarette smokers to find places offering help, like anti-smoking clinics.
   d. Make it harder to find public places which allow cigarette smoking.
4. *Price*
   a. Raise substantially the price of a pack of cigarettes.
   b. Raise the cost of life and health insurance to smokers.
   c. Offer a monetary or nonmonetary reward to the smoker each period he forgoes smoking.

These ideas are prompted by the four Ps framework of marketing. They would have to undergo further screening in terms of their feasibility and cost effectiveness. The challenge is to find those programs that will bring about the greatest decrease in cigarette consumption per dollar expended.

In addition to campaigns directed to present smokers, anti-smoking planners must determine the best ways to discourage new people from taking up smoking. It should be easier to prevent a new smoker from coming into being than to unsell an existing smoker. An analysis of why young people start smoking reveals such factors as a desire to be accepted, a desire to feel grown up, a desire to reduce tension, and so on. Social marketers must try to show young people how to satisfy these drives without turning to smoking. In general, anti-smoking planning requires careful segmentation of potential and actual smokers and tailored "offers" directed at each separate market segment.

Kindred to anti-smoking campaigns are the anti-drug campaigns being waged through school programs, media advertising, and media publicity. In the late sixties when many young people were experimenting with hard drugs, advertising agencies, social agencies, and legislators became convinced that advertising in particular would be a powerful weapon for combating hard drugs Advertising agencies saw this as an opportunity to prove the power of advertising to serve the public good. Much money was funded privately and by the government, with donations of time by advertising agencies and media organizations. Fear appeals were first tried, followed by more informational advertising. Soon some people began to voice doubts about the good that this was doing, and in fact suggested that anti-drug advertising might actually lead to a net increase in the number of addicts! U.N. Secretary-General Kurt Waldheim, presenting a drug evaluation study to the U.N., cautioned in 1972: "Special care must be exercised in this connection not to arouse undue curiosity and unwittingly encourage experimentation." [14] Anti-drug messages, especially on television, reach a lot of young persons who may never have thought about drugs. These young persons do not necessarily perceive the message negatively and might in fact develop a strong curiosity about the subject. This is accompanied by the feeling that if the older generation is spending that much money to talk them out of something, there must be something good in it. They start discussing drugs with their friends and soon learn where to obtain illegal drugs, how to use them, and that they are not that dangerous if used carefully. Thus mass advertising might provoke initial curiosity more than fear and lead the person into exploration and experimentation.[15] The main point is that nonprofit organizations often resort to advertising with insufficient knowledge of the audience or testing of the probable effects of their message upon the audience.[16]

Value Change

The final class of causes attempts to alter deeply felt beliefs or values that a target group holds toward some object or situation. Examples include:

Efforts to alter people's ideas about abortion.
Efforts to alter people's ideas about the number of children they should have.
Efforts to change the values of bigoted people.
Efforts to socialize peasants into a factory work ethic.

Efforts to change the deeply held values of people are among the most difficult causes to market. A person's sense of identity and well-being are rooted in his basic values. His basic values orient his social, moral, and intellectual perceptions and choices. The intrusion of dissonance into his value set creates heavy strain and stress. He will try to avoid dissonant information; or rationalize it away; or compartmentalize it so that it does not affect his own values. The human psychological system resists information that is disorienting.

Any effort to change people from one basic value orientation to another requires a prolonged and intense program of indoctrination. Even then it is likely to succeed only to the smallest degree. Consider the classic case of the Chinese indoctrination program for American prisoners of war during the Korean War.[17] The circumstances were most propitious for attempting to change the values of a target group. The Chinese had complete control over the informational, physical, and social environment of their captives. Their aim was to alter the beliefs and values of the prisoners toward communism and toward who was to blame for the war. The Chinese suffused their captives with their newspapers and radio so that the prisoners saw and heard only the Chinese point of view. They divided the prisoners into small groups without their friends and without the normal leadership of officers. They planted spies in the midst of each group to create fear and a lack of trust of other Americans. They lectured endlessly on American war crimes and rewarded the prisoners who gave the slightest positive response. They started with trivial demands for intellectual concession and as Americans acceded, they escalated the responses required. They presented photographs, experts, etc. as evidence for their point of view. They tailored their techniques to the intelligence, race, and political views of each man. In the end, they succeeded in persuading only 21 prisoners out of tens of thousands to refuse repatriation after the armistice, although many more underwent some alteration of beliefs.

The major factor in the limited success of the Chinese, in spite of their total control over the environment, was that they were a negatively regarded source. Because they were the enemy, the prisoners discounted their credibility. At the same time this points out how effective a totalitarian state can be if it does have the trust of the people. Having control over all the instruments of information and reward, the totalitarian state can undertake to alter the value orientations of its people. Small-group experiments, conducted by Asch, Lewin, and others confirm the readiness of participants in a group to go along with the group's judgment in spite of their initially resistant opinions.[18]

The values that people hold often are pragmatic as well as ideological, making them even more difficult to change. For example, the preference of rural farmers in India for large families makes economic sense. The farmer sees his old age protection coming in the form of male heirs who will take care of him when he is old. Of six children that his wife might bear, only three or four may reach adulthood. Of these, only one or two may be male. So he thinks in terms of six children to produce a living male heir when he is 65. Furthermore, birth delivery in the rural area costs virtually nothing and he can feed his children with scraps of food. At age 6, his child starts running errands, helping in the field, or taking the mother's place, thus being productive. Consequently, when the rural farmer in India hears arguments that he should have fewer children because of overpopulation, it has no meaning for him in his life situation. Persuasive communication can have very little impact. In such cases, the state must resort to other measures if it is serious about bringing down the birth rate. Offering a positive economic incentive to have few children may not work because the value of the incentive is usually too small in relation to the value of having another child. The state may try negative economic incentives such as a tax on the number of children. Or they might make schooling compulsory at the age of 6, thus reducing the productivity of children in rural areas. Or they might require that all children be born in hospitals, which would increase the cost of children to the family. These are harsh measures, but they may become necessary as it becomes clear that the major target groups for family planning, families in rural areas who have lots of children, are the least likely to change their minds because of persuasive communication.

When values are highly resistant to change, many social planners prefer to use the law to require new behaviors even if they are not accompanied by attitudinal change. The theory is that as people have to comply with the new law, forces will be set into motion which will begin to produce the desired attitude change. Consider the hundred years of persuasive effort to get Southern schools in the United States to voluntarily desegregate. All attempts to change racially prejudiced attitudes failed. These attitudes were not only ideological but practical in supporting the system of white supremacy in the South. Unable to wait any longer for an attitude change, the Supreme Court in 1954 declared that all schools had to be desegregated. In the years that followed, school districts and citizens were forced to comply with a law that they did not like. Some resisted the court orders, so that their behavior would be congruent with their attitudes. Others who complied gradually found their attitudes softening somewhat to come more into line with their behavior. The passage of a widely disliked law sets several forces in motion that may accelerate the adoption of the targeted attitude change:

1. The new law helps the law's supporters gain new strength. They coalesce their forces and work harder for its implementation.
2. The new law stimulates more radical proposals, leading citizens to accept the original change in order to ward off the more radical proposals.
3. The new law creates sustained media attention and word-of-mouth discussion which leads people to examine their ideas and values more carefully.
4. The new law elicits conformity on the part of citizens who believe laws are to be obeyed. Conformity eventually leads from mere compliance to acceptance through processes of dissonance reduction.

Thus, when it comes to changing basic attitudes, the most effective means may be to pass laws requiring behavioral conformity, which set forces into motion that might accelerate the acceptance of new values.[19] In this case, the social marketer's role is to build a climate favorable to the passage and acceptance of the new law.

THE SOCIAL MARKETING PLANNING PROCESS

Whatever type of social cause is involved, some agency or agencies will bear the burden of planning and organizing the social action. The "four Ps" of marketing management are integrated in an administrative process framework in Figure 15-1. Continuous information is collected from the *environment* by the *change agency*. *Plans and messages* are created and sent through *channels* to *audiences,* and the results are monitored by the *change agency.*

The change agency operates a research unit and a planning unit. The research unit collects several types of information. It monitors the environment—economic, political, technological, cultural, and competitive influences—for important developments affecting its social policies and

FIGURE 15-1
Social Marketing Planning System

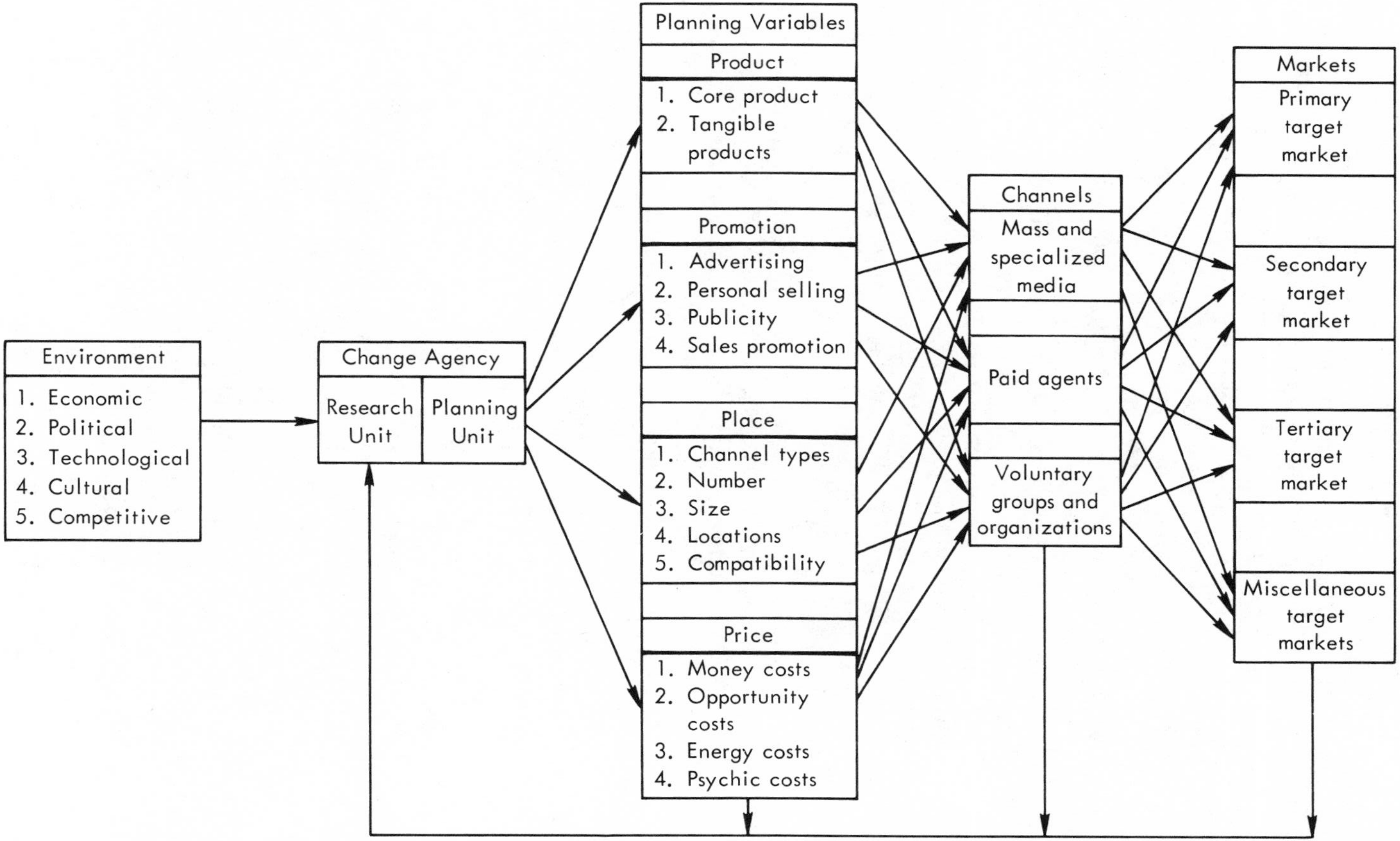

Environment	Change Agency	Planning Variables	Channels	Markets
1. Economic	Research Unit	Product	Mass and specialized media	Primary target market
2. Political	Planning Unit	1. Core product		
3. Technological		2. Tangible products	Paid agents	Secondary target market
4. Cultural		Promotion		
5. Competitive		1. Advertising	Voluntary groups and organizations	Tertiary target market
		2. Personal selling		
		3. Publicity		Miscellaneous target markets
		4. Sales promotion		
		Place		
		1. Channel types		
		2. Number		
		3. Size		
		4. Locations		
		5. Compatibility		
		Price		
		1. Money costs		
		2. Opportunity costs		
		3. Energy costs		
		4. Psychic costs		

objectives. For example, a family planning agency would monitor economic-demographic developments (income and population trends), political developments (liberalization of birth control information), technological developments (new birth control techniques and devices), cultural developments (attitudinal changes toward birth control), and competitive developments (actions of similar and competing groups). The research unit also collects information on the past effectiveness of various programs as well as information on audience attitudes, desires, and behavior.

The change agent's planning unit formulates short- and long-range social marketing plans on the basis of this information. For example, the family planning organization carefully considers the role of different products, promotions, places, and prices. It would identify the major channels of communication and distribution, such as mass or specialized media, paid agents, and volunteer groups. It would differentiate the programs intended for its primary target market (large and low-income families), secondary target market (other childbearing families), tertiary target market (sources of funds and additional volunteer efforts), and miscellaneous target markets (politicians and church groups). Finally, it would continuously gather effectiveness measures on these programs for recycling its planning.

This approach represents an application of business marketing principles to the problem of marketing social change. It is already manifest in some of the larger social change agencies. For example, consider the work of the National Safety Council. Its staff includes an advertising manager, a sales promotion management, an Advertising Council of America coordinator, a research director, and a program director. One of its products is a defensive driving course. Figure 15-2 shows the various channels through which this course is marketed along with the promotional tools it uses. The National Safety Council reaches potential prospects through business firms, service organizations, schools, and the police and court system. For the 1970s, the National Safety Council has adopted

a four point marketing program. . . . One of the first objectives is to increase the sales effectiveness of our existing 150 state and local safety council cooperating agencies. . . . The second part of the program is to create 500 new training agencies in communities not now served by safety councils. . . . A third part of the marketing program will be aimed at selling big industry on adopting DDC as a training course for all employees or selected categories of employees in plant-run training programs. . . . The fourth part of the marketing plan deals with a nationwide promotional effort built around a series of community special-emphasis campaigns running from February 1 through Memorial Day each year of the decade.[20]

FIGURE 15-2

Marketing Channels and Tools: Defensive Driving Course

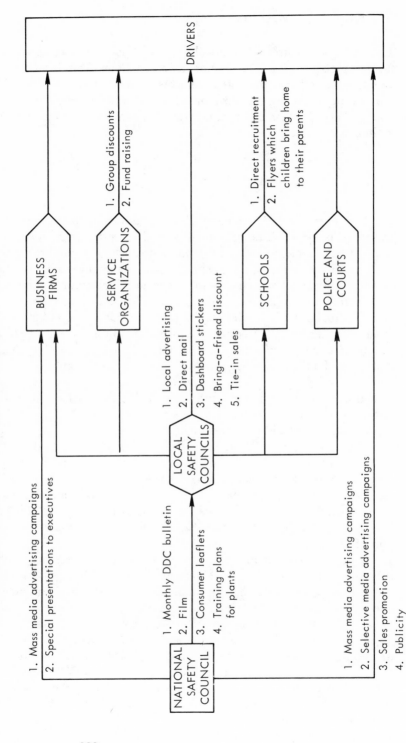

This example illustrates the possibilities of the marketing approach for further social causes. The National Safety Council and several other social agencies have graduated from occasional campaign organizations to full-time marketing organizations which go through cycles of information gathering, planning, product development, measuring and reprogramming.

SUMMARY

Social marketing is the design, implementation, and control of programs seeking to increase the acceptability of a social idea or practice in a target group(s). It utilizes concepts of market segmentation, consumer research, idea configuration, communication, facilitation, incentives, and exchange theory to maximize target group response.

Too often, propaganda rather than social mraketing is practiced by social campaigners. Lazarsfeld and Merton attributed the failure of many social campaigns to the frequent absence of conditions of monopolization, canalization, and supplementation in the social arena. Wiebe, in his examination of four campaigns, concluded that a campaign's effectiveness depended on the presence of adequate force, direction, an adequate and compatible social mechanism, and distance. To the marketer, the success of the campaign depends on the proper use of product, place, and price considerations, in addition to promotion.

The effectiveness of social marketing will vary with the type of social change being sought. Cognitive change is perhaps the most susceptible to social marketing. Social marketing may also be effective in producing action change—that is, a particular act. Behavioral change, such as the modification of food, smoking, or drinking habits, is still harder to achieve. So is value change, that is, efforts to modify the value orientation of a target market.

The social marketing process calls for marketing research and the subsequent development of a well-conceived product and appeals moving through mass and specialized communication media and through paid agents and voluntary groups to reach targeted audiences.

A marketing planning approach does not guarantee that the social objectives will be achieved, or that the costs will be acceptable. Yet social marketing appears to represent a bridging mechanism which links the behavioral scientist's knowledge of human behavior with the socially useful implementation of what that knowledge allows. It offers a useful framework for effective social planning at a time when social issues have become more relevant and critical.

NOTES

1. There is an old story told by a religious leader. As he grew up, he developed a great idealism and made up his mind that he would try to change the world. As he grew older and found how impossible this was, he decided that he would try to change his community. He found this too difficult and so he lowered his sights to trying to change his own congregation. This too failed, but he would not give up. He began to concentrate his efforts on changing his friends. He finally realized that the human problem was in himself and began to focus his idealism on trying to change himself. Now he is an old man and still has not succeeded in even changing himself.

2. See Philip Kotler and Gerald Zaltman, "Social Marketing: An Approach to Planned Social Change," *Journal of Marketing* (July 1971), pp. 3–12.

3. This section is drawn from Kotler and Zaltman, "Social Marketing."

4. Paul F. Lazarsfeld and Robert K. Merton, "Mass Communication, Popular Taste, and Organized Social Action," in *Mass Communications,* William Schramm, ed. (Urbana, Ill.: University of Illinois Press, 1949), pp. 459–80.

5. G. D. Wiebe, "Merchandising Commodities and Citizenship on Television," *Public Opinion Quarterly* (Winter, 1951–52), pp. 679–91, esp. p. 679.

6. Lazarsfeld and Merton, "Mass Communication, Popular Taste, and Organized Social Action."

7. Ibid.

8. Wiebe, "Merchandising Commodities and Citizenship on Television," p. 633.

9. Shirley A. Star and Helen MacGill Hughes, "A Report on an Educational Campaign: The Cincinnati Plan for the United Nations," *American Journal of Sociology,* 55 (1950), 389–400.

10. See Mason Haire, *Psychology in Management* (New York: McGraw-Hill Book Co., 1956).

11. See Herbert H. Hyman and Paul B. Sheatsley, "Some Reasons Why Information Campaigns Fail," *Public Opinion Quarterly,* 11 (1947), 412–23.

12. For an information campaign that succeeded (on mental retardation), see Dorothy F. Douglas, Bruce H. Westley, and Steven H. Chaffee, "An Information Campaign That Changed Community Attitudes," *Journalism Quarterly* (Autumn 1970), pp. 479–92.

13. For a full description, see Raymond S. Alexander and Simon Podair, "Educating New York City Residents to Benefits of Medicaid," *Public Health Reports* (September 1969), pp. 767–72.

14. "Wrong Publicity May Push Drug Use: UN Chief," *Chicago Sun-Times,* May 8, 1972, p. 30.

15. See "Drug Ed a Bummer," *Behavior Today,* November 13, 1972, p. 2.

16. See Michael L. Ray, Scott Ward, and Gerald Lesser, *Experimentation to Improve Pretesting of Drug Abuse Education and Information Campaigns: A Summary* (Cambridge, Mass.: Marketing Science Institute, September 1973).

17. Edgar H. Schein, "The Chinese Indoctrination Program for Prisoners of War," *Psychiatry* (May 1956), pp. 149–72.

18. Solomon E. Asch, "Effects of Group Pressure Upon the Modification and Distortion of Judgment," in *Group Dynamics,* Dorwin Cartwright and

Alvin Zander, eds. (New York: Harper & Row Publishers, 1953), pp. 151–62; and Kurt Lewin, "Group Decision and Social Change," in *Readings in Social Psychology*, Theodore M. Newcomb and Eugene L. Hartley, eds. (New York: Holt, Rinehart and Winston, 1952).

19. For some further readings, see Joel B. Grossman, "The Supreme Court and Social Change," and C. Thomas Dienes, "Judges, Legislators, and Social Change," both in *The American Behavioral Scientist* (March 1970).

20. Chris Imhoff, "DDC's Decisive Decade," *Traffic Safety Magazine* (December 1969), pp. 20 and 36.

QUESTIONS

1. How relevant is the marketing concept to the social marketer?

2. There is a radio advertisement in which the announcer makes a statement similar to the following:

> You're old enough now to know about drugs and what they can do to you, but your kid brother isn't. He's a perfect set-up for a pusher.

What type of social change is this ad designed to bring about?

3. Analyze why it was so difficult to get people to voluntarily wear seat belts?

4. Use Wiebe's five factors to analyze the growing success of the Zero Population Growth movement in the United States.

5. A suburban community wants to get a large-scale recycling program started. The first item they would like to recycle is newsprint, because they feel they have the equipment and people necessary to collect newspaper bundles. Two trucks are available which could be used to make a monthly pick-up and several people have volunteered their services to help in this pick-up. However, the community is unsure about how to get people to leave unsightly newspaper bundles on their front porches at a given time each month. One of the volunteers, a woman with a Ph.D. in psychology, has offered the following suggestion:

> Several weeks before any pick-ups are to be done, conduct a door-to-door campaign in which community residents would be asked to display a small sticker in their front windows. The sticker would state something like: "Save our scarce resources. Support recycling!" Residents would not be asked at this time to participate in the recycling program. After a few weeks, a different person should return to the homes that have stickers and residents should then be asked to participate in the program.

Do you think this strategy will work?

6. Design a social marketing campaign for an organization that supports prison reform.

7. Develop a social marketing campaign to influence people to buy two-way bottles instead of the convenient throwaway bottles. What appeal would you use? What pricing mechanism? How much funding would you need? Do you think the campaign has much of a chance?

16 Health Services Marketing

If I knew a man was coming to my house to help me, I would run for my life.

THOREAU

Health care is one of the nation's largest industries, accounting for over $83 billion or close to 8 percent of the Gross National Product.[1] It is also one of the nation's fastest-growing industries, growing at a compound annual rate of 11 percent. Over 4 million persons work in the health-care industry as physicians, nurses, hospital administrators, public health officials, and in other capacities.

This industry will be examined in this chapter because of its importance, its nonprofit elements, and its relative backwardness with respect to marketing concepts. There are important questions of what people want in the way of health-care services, the best ways to deliver these services, and the best way to motivate people to preventive health-care behavior.

The American health care industry is very complex. The most important elements are shown in Figure 16-1. At the far right stand over

FIGURE 16-1
The Health Care Industry

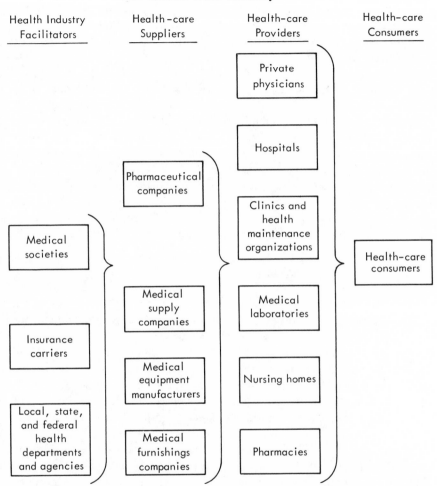

Health Industry
Facilitators

Health-care
Suppliers

Health-care
Providers

Health-care
Consumers

Private
physicians

Hospitals

Pharmaceutical
companies

Clinics and
health
maintenance
organizations

Medical
societies

Health-care
consumers

Medical
supply
companies

Medical
laboratories

Insurance
carriers

Medical
equipment
manufacturers

Nursing homes

Local, state,
and federal
health
departments
and agencies

Medical
furnishings
companies

Pharmacies

200 million consumers of health products and services. Next to them stand the main providers of health care: physicians, hospitals, clinics, health maintenance organizations, medical laboratories, nursing homes, and pharmacies. Next to them are companies that supply health products to providers and consumers, such as pharmaceutical companies, medical supply companies, equipment manufacturers, and medical furnishing companies. At the far left are major organizations that facilitate medical practice and consumption, such as medical societies, insurance carriers, and local, state, and federal health departments and agencies.

The health industry suppliers shown in the second column of Figure 16-1 are organized on a private-for-profit basis and conduct their marketing activities on a sophisticated basis. At the other extreme are physicians, who assiduously avoid any semblance of organized marketing activity. In between are hospitals and other health agencies that are increasingly attempting to learn about marketing as they confront challenging problems with their markets.

Because of the great variety and complexity of health-care institutions, it will not be possible to present more than a few selective applications of marketing thinking in the health field. We have selected three important areas of health care to examine. First we will consider the role of marketing in a *modern hospital.* Then we will examine how a *health maintenance organization* may use marketing to gain acceptance and support in a new community. Finally we shall examine how marketing might aid *public health officials* in appraising the health needs of a community, improving health-care delivery systems, raising money for health causes, and motivating people to more healthful behavior.

HOSPITALS

Today there are approximately 7,000 hospitals in the United States.[2] They fall into two classes of ownership: government and nongovernment hospitals. *Government hospitals* are found on the federal level (Army, Navy, Air Force, Veterans Administration, and Public Health Service hospitals), state level (long-term psychiatric, chronic, and state university medical school hospitals) and local level (county and city hospitals). *Nongovernment hospitals* include two types: voluntary and proprietary hospitals. *Voluntary hospitals* are run on a nonprofit basis and include church-affiliated hospitals (Lutheran, Catholic, Baptist, etc.) and others (community, industrial, Kaiser Plan, Shriners, etc.). *Proprietary hospitals* are run on a profit basis and include hospitals that are individually owned, owned by partners, and owned by corporations (single or chained).

This diversity in the institutional forms of hospitals makes it difficult to make many generalizations about the role of marketing in hospitals. Certain things, however, can be said. Historically, physicians rather than nonphysician administrators have been responsible for setting overall hospital policy. Increasingly, however, nonphysician administrators have been taking over more responsibilities in the hospital's operation, including admission, purchasing, personnel, finance, public relations, education, information systems, and routine services; and many play a vital role in policy making. These administrators are able to introduce more businesslike approaches to managing a modern hospital. At the same time, they have not entirely succeeded because in many cases they lack specific business training, they are not always under great competitive pressure, and there is third-party payment of patient expenses that helps meet rising hospital expenses to some extent.

Hospitals attempt to carry out up to four different services: patient care, education, research, and community service. Most hospitals develop these services without setting up or making use of any formal marketing department. Hospitals typically have a planning and development department and a public relations officer. But they lack a "marketing service department" that could research and influence their products and markets to a substantial degree.

The organization of a typical voluntary hospital is shown in Figure 16-2. At the top stands a board of trustees, which oversees hospital policy

FIGURE 16-2
Internal Organization of a Hospital

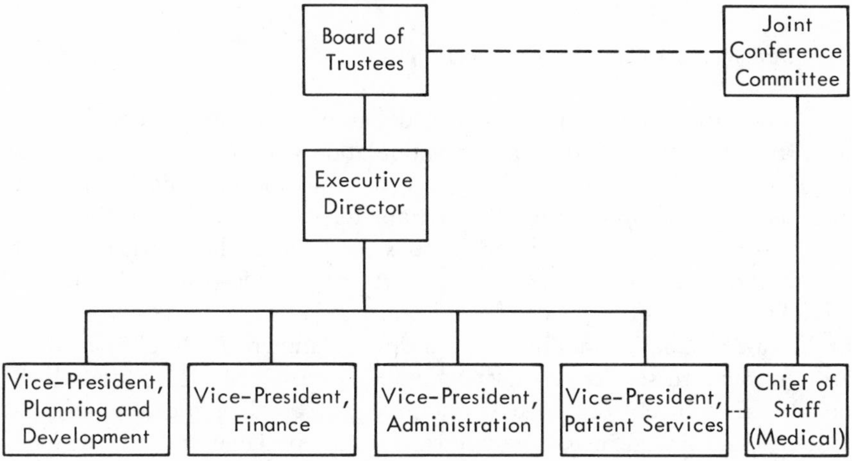

and financing. Under the board are usually found two autonomous organizations. One is the medical staff headed by the chief of staff. He reports to a joint conference committee that is responsible to the board of trustees. The other is the hospital administration, headed by an executive director. The executive director oversees four major departments: planning and development, finance, administration, and patient services. Administration, for example, includes plant operations, medical records, food services, housekeeping, and so on. Patient services include radiology, pathology, anesthesia, and medical education. The vice-president of patient services works closely with the chief of staff.

In looking at this organization chart, it is clear that different administrators deal with the various markets, publics, and marketing activities. The key to organizing any institution is for the top executive to assign a specific person to handle each major *public, market,* and *activity* that would benefit from specialization. Thus a hospital should have persons managing doctors, nurses, government relations, finance, and so on. Each manager should be sensitive to marketing issues although he need not be a trained marketer. The hospital could also establish a *director of marketing services* who can supply advice and various services to the key managers as they need marketing assistance in dealing with their publics. These services would include market measurement and forecasting, consumer research, communication planning, and product development.

Here we will focus on marketing questions that arise in a hospital's dealings with four important publics: patients, doctors, the local community, and donors.

Patient Marketing

The first task of a hospital is to define carefully its patient population. Its definition of a target patient population will influence the services it will offer, new doctors it will add to its staff, the potential sources of financial support, and many other parameters of hospital operation.

Hospitals face three broad options in defining their target patient population. The first option is a *community orientation*—that is, the hospital defines its target population as all persons who have health-care needs in the surrounding community. The hospital stands ready to offer a broad array of medical services to meet the wide spectrum of illnesses to which people are subject. The second option is a *special public orientation*—that is, the hospital meets the needs of some special public not defined by the surrounding community. There are hospitals that serve veterans, certain religious groups, psychiatric patients, terminal patients, and other special publics. Hospitals serving a particular illness group have a narrower product line defined by the needs of that illness group. The third option is a *referral orientation*—that is, the hospital specializes in the skilled treatment of certain special medical problems and is nationally or world-reknowned for these specialties. This is the status of such hospitals as Massachusetts General of Boston and Rush Presbyterian of Chicago. These hospitals have top physicians and equipment to carry out their work.

Some hospitals straddle between two or three of these orientations not quite able to make up their mind as to their target patient population.

The Michael Reese hospital in Chicago started under the sponsorship of the American Jewish Federation. It served the Jewish population on the South side of Chicago. It also achieved eminence in certain specialties that made it a referral hospital for those specialties. Over time, the community surrounding the hospital changed to a largely black population that made demands for equal service from the hospital. The hospital responded generously to the surrounding community. Thus the hospital is now carrying on activities in three different directions. Many of its doctors want the hospital to place its primary emphasis on serving the immediate community. Another group of doctors wants the hospital to continue its eminence in research and referral work. A third group wants the hospital to relocate in the far north suburbs of Chicago where the original Jewish population it served has moved. As long as this issue of target patient population is not settled, the hospital administrators have a difficult time developing forward plans for patient services, doctor staffing, and so on.

The decision of a target patient population facilitates the determination of which medical services to emphasize. For example, a Veterans Administration hospital will develop specialties in orthopedic work and general surgery. A community hospital in a poor neighborhood will develop specialties in maternity, accidents, and dental work. The incidence of different diseases varies over groups and the hospital's target population will suggest the needed specialties.

These specialties in turn suggest the doctor mix needed in the hospital. The doctors not only deliver medical care but also attract the hospital's clientele. Hospitals do not do direct marketing to attract patients; that is, they do not place ads saying that they have first-rate facilities for maternity or any other service. They rely entirely on their affiliated physicians to refer patients to the hospital. The doctors are marketing intermediaries. More about this will be said shortly.

An important marketing issue facing the hospital is the level of care and satisfaction to render to patients. On the one hand, the hospital cannot cater to every wish and whim of the patient. This would be too expensive and too trying on the staff. No organization takes as its responsibility to completely satisfy every wish a customer has, but only those it takes as serious and valid. On the other hand, the hospital cannot ignore patients' wants and expectations. It would be neglecting its responsibilities and risking bad-mouthing from patients. Dissatisfied patients can lead to an exodus of doctors, withdrawal of accreditation and state license, diminished benefactor support, and other undesirable consequences.

On the whole, hospitals have probably not done as much as they could to insure patient satisfaction. There are many reasons for this. Hospitals are more doctor-oriented than patient-oriented. In cases of conflicting interest, hospitals have tended to favor the doctors' interests. Patients are in a relatively helpless situation and must accept the treatment they are getting; they do not have the option of transfer to another hospital. They did not choose the hospital but rather their doctor. They may not return to a hospital for many years. Their dissatisfaction may be forgotten or not matter if they like their doctor. As a result, there are often weak service efforts on the part of hospitals.

What are some of the things that hospitals can do to show more sensitivity and attention to patients' wants and expectations? The key phases of a person's experience in a hospital are three: admission, patient care, and exit. Each is capable of being improved from a consumer point of view.

A patient enters a hospital with anxiety and possibly physical pain. The patient's first contact with the hospital is with an admissions staff member who needs information from the patient. The quality of this experience is important in orienting the patient's feelings and expectations. On the one hand, consider a patient who is kept waiting a long time before being serviced by an admissions staff member, is greeted coolly and perfunctorily, is asked a great number of questions, especially stressing his financial responsibilities, and is kept waiting before being taken to the assigned room. This obviously increases the separation anxiety of the patient. Contrast this to an efficiently run admission service in a bright part of the hospital with a smiling and concerned admissions staff member who asks few questions and takes pains to insure the patient's comfort.

The next phase consists of the patient's bed-care experience. This is made up of several factors: the atmosphere of the corridors and room; the responsiveness and warmth of the nursing staff; the quality of the food; the visiting hours; and the efficiency with which various services are supplied such as diagnostic tests, medications, television, telephone, and so on. Hospitals are increasingly recognizing the contribution that consumer-oriented interior design can make to the comfort of patients. They are trying to get away from a "sickness" look by the choice of brighter colors and a hotel-type atmosphere. Building structures may be designed in a sawtooth shape which allows additional sunlight for each room and improved noise control. Single care units are replacing semi-private rooms because of the strong preference of patients for single units (if priced equally with double occupancy units). Physicians claim that private rooms decrease contagion and patients normally get well faster. Finally, new structures are being developed so that halls radiate out from nurses' stations to permit nurses to be closer to the patients and use up less time of their total workday in walking.

Patient satisfaction is highly related to the attentiveness and warmth of the nursing staff. Nurses may be hired primarily for their medical knowledge and efficiency rather than their bedside manner. Because they are responsible for many patients, some of whom want excessive attention, nurses often become task-oriented rather than patient-oriented. Increasingly, schools of nursing are attempting to train nurses in the whole patient concept and the importance of responding to the patient's real and perceived needs. A hospital that wants responsive nurses must employ this criterion at the time of hiring. It can also run periodic training sessions to remind the nursing staff of the patients' feelings and expectations.

Other factors in bed-care satisfaction—the quality of the food, the visiting hours and rules, and the efficiency of certain services—will have some importance that varies with different patients. The director of patient services must attempt to determine the relative importance patients attach to different factors and the level at which they perceive these factors to be.

The handling of the exit phase of a patient's stay in a hospital can also affect his satisfaction. Many hospitals that create high satisfaction in the patient while he is in the hospital lose much of his goodwill at the cashier's office. The patient may find items on his bill which he did not anticipate and which are high in price. The exit staff member must make a conscientious effort to explain these items and their cost so the patient does not feel the hospital is either exploiting him or the insurance carrier. Some hospitals will not let the patient leave until he has made a cash payment. All of this interferes with the positive mood of the patient usually associated with being released from the hospital.

The purpose of thoughtful steps in patient handling is not to maximize patient satisfaction but to provide enough good service so that the patient feels that he has been fairly and thoughtfully treated. The hospital needs the patient's goodwill because he will be a source not only of future patronage but of influence on others, such as doctors, friends, donors, and government.

Physician Marketing

Although hospitals are concerned with patient satisfaction, many are even more concerned with doctor satisfaction. They rely heavily on their doctor staff for the patients that come to the hospital. Many of their doctors have private practices and when a patient has a serious problem, it is the doctor who recommends the patient to a hospital. Each affiliated doctor can be counted on to recommend a certain number of patients to the hospital.

A hospital has two marketing problems with respect to the physician market. The first is to attract good physicians in the needed specialties. The second is to make sure that these doctors, if they have multiple hospital appointments, favor this hospital with most of their patients.

At any point in time, a hospital may be seeking doctors with certain specialties. If the hospital is well located and/or has good teaching programs, research opportunities, or medical center affiliations, it may have little trouble attracting able physicians; in fact, it will usually have a waiting list of physicians seeking affiliation with the hospital. If the hospital is less well-known or poorly located, it is likely to have considerable trouble attracting qualified physicians. In such cases, the hospital faces the problem of marketing itself to prospective physicians.

The main marketing principle to observe in this connection is that of understanding the prospective physician's requirements and desires. The hospital must correctly assess what the physician is seeking and whether it is capable of offering these benefits. What a physician is seeking varies with his specialty and personal characteristics. Consider the varying motivations of the following types of specialists:

> *Surgeons* are interested in a number of factors. They want to affiliate with a hospital that will admit their patients without delay. They want a good schedule of operating hours. They want a good quality post-operative staff (residents, interns, and nurses) to reduce their own involvement in patient care after the operation.
>
> *Neurologists* are primarily interested in the amount of special equipment the hospital will provide. They also need specialized technicians, nursing staff, and rehabilitation facilities.
>
> *Psychiatrists* are concerned with the type of psychiatric facility run by the hospital. They do not want to work in hospitals in which the psychiatric section resembles a prison. They want to affiliate with a hospital that has a modern facility and progressive treatment philosophies.
>
> *Dermatologists* do not plan to use the hospital's bed-care facilities very much. They want affiliation with a hospital that does not load heavy committee work on them. They would like to see a good potential for patient references from other physicians on the staff.

Each individual physician has further desires with respect to the research orientation of the hospital, the collegial atmosphere, the amount of time he will be expected to give, and so on. The medical staff recruitment committee has to be sensitive to what the physician prospect wants and whether the hospital can provide or should provide these things.

After the hospital attracts a doctor, it must make efforts to fulfill his expectations about equipment, patient care, committee work, and collegial atmosphere. A dissatisfied physician can hurt the hospital in two ways. He can terminate his affiliation and bad-mouth the hospital to patients and other physicians, or he can affiliate with a second hospital and refer most of his patients to that hospital. One hospital in Chicago found many of its physicians referring a large number of their patients to their other hospitals. This strongly suggested that something was amiss in the physicians' satisfaction with the hospital.

Community Marketing

The hospital is a very important and conspicuous institution in a community arousing many types of feelings and expectations. Those in the immediate neighborhood of the hospital will be concerned with its physical appearance, the amount of ambulance noise, the litter and parking problems caused by hospital traffic, and the hospital's impact on real estate values. Those in the larger community will be concerned with whether the hospital is open to the patients in the community on a non-discriminatory basis, whether it provides an efficient and responsive emergency-room service, and whether it has fair hiring practices.

Because of the multiple interfaces of a hospital with the surrounding community, many hospitals have a director of community relations. The director has at least five responsibilities. The first is to develop a close relationship with the main organizations in the community—the bank, the local businessmen and women's clubs, and the local business firms. The second is to gather periodic information on community health needs and on community perceptions of the hospital. The third is to prepare and disseminate news and information about the hospital through annual reports, newspaper publicity, and appearances before groups. The fourth is to offer educational programs to the community that will improve community health and appreciation of the hospital. The fifth is to establish outreach health programs such as drug clinics, alcoholism clinics, and smokers' withdrawal clinics. Through the performance of these community services, the hospital is able to build a positive feeling in the community.

Donor Marketing

Hospitals depend very much on the services and contributions of individual volunteers, donors, and philanthropic organizations. Volunteers include a variety of persons who feel a social responsibility to lend their time to hospitals to help them carry on their important work. These volunteers give their time to running the hospital's coffee shop and gift shop, visiting with patients, and fund raising. There is usually a director of hospital volunteers who recruits, assigns, and supervises volunteers. The director's leadership style greatly affects the volunteer efforts on behalf of the hospital. Volunteers do not expect any payment other than appreciation. Many directors have instituted special programs to honor their volunteers for so many years of service. They treat volunteers to occasional talks by staff physicians and give them a feeling of pride in their work.

Individual donors include a few wealthy people who have given substantial support to the hospital and many other people who make small but thoughtful donations. The hospital's director of development has the task of attracting and maintaining generous and loyal donors. To be effective, the director has to have a good understanding of the motivations of people for supporting a hospital. Among the strongest contributors are past patients who were satisfied with the care they received. Contributors also include persons who expect to use the hospital's services someday and want the hospital to be a strong one. Contributors include people who want to feel pride in their local hospitals. The director of development, in addition to needing empathy with these various groups, must exhibit other skills. He must have a well-organized approach to fund raising. His information system must contain the names of prospects and past donors and their past contributions. He must be able to develop effective communication appeals that inspire people to contribute. He must follow up their contributions with acknowledgments and programs for further involvement. His general aim is to create feelings in donors that they are worthwhile supporters of a worthwhile cause.

The director of development will also attempt to raise funds from government granting agencies and philanthropic organizations. In the past, government funds have been available for capital financing of hospital construction. Various philanthropic organizations and foundations will support certain forms of research and medical education. The alert director of development will identify potential funding sources for the many programs carried on by his hospital and prepare effective plans to market his proposals.

MARKETING A HEALTH MAINTENANCE ORGANIZATION

Whereas a hospital is an institution that is well-understood and accepted by American people, new forms of health-care units are being created in various parts of the country to provide alternative delivery systems for health care. These new organizations have to be carefully planned and marketed to their target populations if they are to achieve acceptance and patronage. One such institution is known as a *health maintenance organization* (HMO). This particular type of organization has received strong governmental backing in recent years as a major answer to the high and unpredictable costs of health care.

> A health maintenance organization is defined as a public or private organization that provides health services, including at least hospital and physician services, on a prepaid, per-capita basis, either directly or through arrangements with others, and that guarantees and is responsible for the quality and availability of all such services that it provides.[3]

It represents an alternative to the dominant system of medical service in the U.S. in which the individual seeks the services of a private physician on the occasion of an illness and is charged for each consultation. A person who enjoys good health during a year escapes with little medical expense and a person who experiences poor health bears large medical bills that must be paid from his own pocket except to the extent that medical costs are incurred in connection with hospitalization and covered by some hospitalization insurance plan he has. Thus in the dominant model of health-care delivery, the family has a variable medical cost from year to year. In the prepaid model of health purchase, the family has a constant and known medical cost from year to year.

Health maintenance organizations go back at least to the late forties when the Kaiser Foundation Health Plan was started in California. This plan represents one of the most successful HMOs to date, with a membership of over two million and several owned hospitals. Many other plans have been formed in other parts of the nation and now cover about 5 percent of the U.S. population. Some are sponsored by communities, others by physician groups, and still others by insurance carriers. The arrangements for sharing risks of various kinds between physicians, hospitals, and carriers vary widely. Most of the plans encounter major difficulties in getting started and covering their costs for the first few years. Several also fail in the first few years.[4]

Starting an HMO in a community is a complex undertaking requiring careful financing, planning, and marketing. It is comparable to the launching of a major new product. Many new HMOs fail because of insufficient marketing analysis and implementation. Here we would like to discuss the marketing requirements for launching an HMO.[5] The following steps must be undertaken:

1. Appraising whether the HMO meets a strong community need.

2. Formulating the HMO's service features based on consumer research and cost evaluation.
3. Developing a strategy and plan for attracting the type of support needed for HMO success.

Market Analysis

The HMO concept is not intended to replace private medical practice but rather to offer an alternative that some people in the community might prefer. There are two types of communities that would not have a high interest in an HMO. Persons residing in poor communities normally could not afford the prepayment charges of an HMO. This will become less of a problem as Medicaid programs tie in with HMOs. Persons residing in affluent communities have a strong preference and ability to pay for the services of private physicians. Thus a key question is whether there are enough people in the given community who could afford and would be interested in joining an HMO. Even in those communities with successful HMOs, not more than 10 percent of the eligible population has joined. This percentage will probably rise because the new HMO legislation requires employers to offer dual choice—either an HMO or an insurance plan—to their employees.

An HMO may need as many as 3,000 subscribing families to be financially viable. Many interested persons may be reluctant to break their ties with their family physicians. They also do not want to terminate their hospitalization insurance, the cost of which is partly borne by their employer. If the employer does not offer an HMO option, these people really are not free to join an HMO without losing certain benefits. Thus the organizers of the HMO must be confident that there are a lot of people with strong interest, ability, and willingness to join.

Several concrete steps can be taken to measure the potential demand level for an HMO in a given community. A demand estimate can be formed on the basis of the demographic characteristics of the persons in the community. Certain characteristics are associated with the likelihood of a high interest in an HMO, based on the experience of successful HMOs in other parts of the country. Thus persons with medium incomes and good educations are good prospects for HMOs. Actually, several demographic groups can be distinguished and graded for their level of probable interest. Then the size of each demographic group in each census tract surrounding the proposed site of the HMO can be measured. An estimate should be made of the number of persons in each demographic group in each census tract who might join, allowing for the fact that the proportion falls off with distance from the HMO.[6] This exercise will provide a rough statistical estimate of the available population for membership.

In addition, the HMO organizers can survey a randomly selected group of residents to learn whether their interest in an HMO (after it is explained to them) would be high, medium, low, or nonexistent. The percentage of respondents who say that they will definitely or probably join is a useful statistic.

Formulating the HMO's Service Features

At an early stage, the HMO must be turned from a simple idea into a full concept. People who are told about an HMO will raise dozens of questions and concerns. These cannot be put off or brushed aside but must be met by a clear statement of planned services and costs. The organizers of the HMO must formulate their concept of the HMO's features as early as possible because (1) they will have to explain it to others, (2) these features will determine the best target population, and (3) the organizers will need to estimate breakeven enrollment based on the concept they are offering.

Here are some of the issues that the sponsors of the HMO will have to resolve before they can begin their marketing program:

1. What services will be included in the plan? Will the plan include eye examinations, dentistry, drugs, and so on?
2. What benefits can a member obtain if he needs medical care while out of the city on a business trip or vacation? Will the plan reimburse him for the fees he pays to out-of-town physicians?
3. What health educational programs will the HMO offer? Will educational programs play a small or large role in its offering?
4. Will the patient be permitted to choose and regularly use a specific doctor on the staff or will he have to accept whichever doctor is available at the time?
5. What will the hours of the HMO be? What about housecalls and night cases?
6. What will be the membership cost? Will it be a flat fee or vary with the number of family members? Will the cost vary with the age of the head of the household? Will there be a small fee per visit? Will the HMO give out a certain number of free memberships to indigent persons in the community?
7. Will members participate in policy determination or will policy be entirely in the hands of a small group?
8. What hospitals will the HMO use for in-patient services?

Developing a Strategy of Market Acceptance

After the HMO's features are defined, the sponsors must prepare a plan and program to communicate the concept to key groups who must lend their support if the program is to come into being. The HMO must achieve the support of the following groups:

1. Subscribers
2. A competent medical staff
3. One or more hospitals
4. An insurance carrier
5. Foundations or government for financing

Although all of these groups must be cultivated, there is a strategic question concerning the order in which this should be accomplished. If the HMO sought enrollees before hiring a medical staff, it might find that many potential enrollees would not join until they knew who the doctors would be. Conversely, physicians are not likely to commit themselves until the HMO has proven that it has enough community support and members. The insurance carrier cannot determine its risk and fees until it has an idea of the number of people covered and the degree of services to be offered. Foundations or government may not support the HMO group unless they first see sufficient evidence of community support.

In order to make progress, the HMO's organizers should each assume responsibility for working with a specific public or market. Each organizer should develop objectives, plans, and a timetable for cultivating his market. Consider, for example, the person responsible for attracting subscribers. His first objective should be to disseminate the HMO concept to as many members of the target population as possible. This can be done through community news announcements, mailings, coffee parties, and club appearances. The purpose of this informational activity is not to get people to sign up immediately but rather to develop their interest and understanding. Another purpose is to learn how the proposed attributes of the HMO strike the various potential subscribers to see if any changes should be made in the final attributes of the HMO. During this period, the organizers might try to ask those who have a strong interest to help fund further development work by contributing a small annual fee, such as $3. This will serve both as a sign of how many people are interested and also as a "foot-in-the-door" technique to increase their involvement in the idea. As community support increases, this can be used as data to present to other groups—such as physicians, hospitals, and fund services—to elicit more of their support.

An alternative or supplementary route to achieving a large enrollment is to target certain large employers in the area to see if they would consider altering their employees' health plan to permit their employees the option to join the HMO. The employers presumably offer hospitalization insurance coverage to their employees. The HMO "salesman" must meet with each employer and attempt to show the benefits to the employees and employer of offering dual choice to the employees. The employer will feel many reservations about the HMO which must be thoughtfully answered. The HMO organizer is essentially doing industrial selling—that is, attempting to identify the decision makers in a complex organization, arranging for the opportunity to make a presentation and hoping for a fruitful exchange that creates confidence and a positive attitude toward the "purchase" of the HMO concept.

The recruitment of an adequate number and mix of physicians to work in the HMO will be difficult. The HMO requires competent internists, pediatricians, obstetricians, neurosurgeons, and so on. It will want some of these physicians to work full-time for the HMO. The HMO should strive to attract at least one locally prominent physician to lend a degree of legitimacy to the HMO as well as to transfer his patient roll to the HMO. He would also serve as an attraction to other possible physicians. The HMO has to determine the best sources of potentially interested physicians who would see the benefits of HMO affiliation as higher than the costs (see Chapter 2, pp. 26-28). High potential candidates are apt to be younger and more idealistic. At the same time, the HMO must avoid taking inexperienced or marginal physicians because the experiences of subscribers in the first few months will make a great difference in the amount of favorable word-of-mouth about the HMO. A special effort should be made to attract warm and personable physicians, because a major subscriber concern is that an HMO may be very impersonal in contrast to a private practice. Every effort must be made to create a team of physicians who give patients the feeling that they are being treated like private patients.

While relationships are being forged between the HMO and potential subscribers and physicians, other organizers of the HMO are engaged in making presentations to hospitals, government agencies, and potential funders. The HMO would like each group to play a role in its development and the organizers must study the needs, perceptions, and expectations of each target group and prepare effective communications. It must also be alert to major agents of resistance such as local physicians who feel threatened by the new institution. The HMO must design a strategy to win them over or at least neutralize their attack. Other members of the HMO in the meantime will have to handle the mechanics of finding a site or building, arranging for general publicity, and other things. In general, the formation of an HMO requires a major organizing effort with various activities that have to be orchestrated and timed carefully.

Robert Heyssel has carefully summarized the major requirements for creating a viable HMO, based on his study of many successful and unsuccessful cases: [7]

1. A mechanism for prepayment must be present in order to remove the barrier of a fee at the time of service.
2. The concept of a group practice must be present. The medical group itself must have a contractual relationship with a prepayment organization, be autonomous and self-governing (not employed by hospitals) and paid by capitation. All members of the medical group must be full-time.
3. A hospital base is vital. There should be a single medical record of both in-patient and out-patient care with unified data of laboratory services, purchasing, accounting, and administration from in-patient and out-patient areas.
4. There must be voluntary enrollment and dual choice. The potential member must have a choice either of the prepayment group practice or an indemnity program which customarily pays on a fee-for-service basis.
5. There must be capitation payments to reverse the conventional economics of medical care. In the usual circumstances, physicians and hospitals are paid for illness, and the more illness or the more beds occupied, the greater is the payment. Under the capitation arrangement, a predictable budgetary allowance is created and the economic advantage operates to keep people out of the hospital.
6. There must be comprehensive coverage or benefits which include the full spectrum of out-patient care, in-patient care, extended care, home health services, drug coverage, and mental health services. Comprehensive coverage in itself directs an appropriate use of the budgeted dollars toward the service that is most effective but least expensive.

He concludes by saying that the major factors in aborted plans have been insurance and marketing considerations, deficient consumer attitudes and understanding, and too high a cost of comprehensive coverage.

PUBLIC HEALTH

Another group that has a vital effect on the nation's health are public health officials and planners. They are found in city, county, and state health departments, local alcohol and addiction centers, comprehensive health planning organizations, and the Department of Health, Welfare and Education. These officials carry on a variety of tasks, including: (1) appraising the health needs of a community, (2) developing comprehensive plans for the improved delivery of health care, (3) planning drives to raise more money for health causes, and (4) stimulating healthful behavior on the part of the public. Here we shall look at the marketing aspects of each of these tasks.

Determining Community Health Needs and Status

One of the most important tasks of public health officials is to determine the health needs and status of people living within specified geographical areas. These data reveal those areas of health care that are in the greatest need of attention and suggest how the community's health resources ought to be allocated.

There are two broad approaches to measuring the health status of a community. The common approach is to measure the incidence of different diseases and infirmities. Thus it may be determined that the venereal disease rate in Community X is 2 per thousand against a national average of 1 per thousand. This suggests that Community X is experiencing a higher-than-normal incidence of venereal disease and that higher-than-normal resources should go into programs designed to combat venereal disease in Community X.

The World Health Organization disputes this conception of health. According to it, "health is a state of complete physical, mental, and social well-being and not merely the absence of disease or infirmity." They feel that more positive measures of well-being should be used to indicate the community's health status. Too many health officials see their job as curative—that is, to treat outbreaks of illness—rather than preventative—to create a climate that produces good health.

These two views lead to different conceptions of community health-care planning. The narrow view of health as sickness care leads to investing public money into more health-care facilities and doctors who can administer to the diseases and medical problems that exist. The broad view of health as a state of well-being takes a look at a larger set of causal factors that affect the health status of a community. The health status of a community is affected by at least three broad forces: *environment, life style,* and *health-care facilities and doctors.* If the environment is unhealthy or dangerous, this will produce a higher rate of disease and accident. Therefore public money might be better spent in improving the quality of the environment than in simply creating more health services to take care of those who get sick. If the life styles of the population are leading to health problems—that is, if people overeat, smoke, or have more children than they can afford—then health suffers; again, public money might be better spent in influencing life-style changes as an alternative to training more doctors to take care of these problems. In general, improving public health is more than a matter of increasing doctors and health facilities.

The Delivery of Health Care

Public health officials and planners are greatly interested in seeing to it that a high standard of health care is accessible and available throughout the country. Yet the sad fact is that the quality and quantity of health care is marked by extreme maldistribution in different parts of the country. For example, there are 220 physicians per 100,000 persons in the state of New York and only 80 physicians per 100,000 in the state of Mississippi (against a national average of 140 physicians per 100,000). There are over 5,000 communities (mostly rural) in the United States without a doctor. There is also maldistribution of health-care services and quality to different racial groups and income classes. For example, a white person visits a physician an average of 4.0 times a year and a nonwhite person visits a physician an average of 2.7 times a year. Persons with incomes of over $10,000 make 7.2 visits per year and those earning between $3,000 and $10,000 make 4.4 visits a year. Perhaps the most limited medical service is received by families who are too poor to afford much private care and too rich for Medicaid.

The maldistribution of health personnel and facilities is not likely to be corrected simply by larger doses of money to train doctors and to build hospitals. Doctors will still tend to locate where financial opportunity is highest, and hospitals will not necessarily appear where they are most needed. The large element of voluntarism in the present system leads medical resources to move to locations that are attractive financially or geographically and not where they are most needed. This suggests the need for comprehensive health planning organizations at the local, state, regional, and national levels to determine geographical areas of deficit services and to fund long-range solutions.

Many solutions have been proposed to improve the delivery of health-care services. One type of proposal is to offer subsidies to attract the resources—doctors and hospitals—that a particular area might need. This solution poses the least threat to the traditional principles underlying the American health-delivery system—that is, one of free enterprise responding to incentives. This can be supplemented by the development of government-owned hospitals and health units as an alternative to subsidization of private facilities.

A second proposal calls for creating new types of health service delivery units that will increase consumer options. The spirit of the health maintenance organization, for example, is to provide a type of health service unit that would allow people to receive unlimited medical care by making regular prepayments. Other types of health delivery units are also being experimented with. Neighborhood health clinics located in poor areas and open continuously have a role to play. Mobile medical vans which would appear in different communities on different days and offer on-the-spot health services are also being looked at.

A third proposal calls for encouraging the hospitals and health service units in an area to merge and/or form a supraorganization as a means of achieving economies in the delivery of health services as well as filling gaps with new health services where needed. Many hospitals in an area attempt to be full-service hospitals having the latest equipment in a variety of specialties. This often duplicates the facilities and costs of hospital care and is one of the factors responsible for the high cost of health care. The hope is that hospitals can complement each other rather than duplicate each other and that this will bring down the cost of providing medical service to the public.

A fourth proposal calls for reforming the basic channels of distribution of health care into a more vertically integrated health-care delivery system. The current system is very atomistic and the individual consumer has to contract separately with a doctor, a hospital, an insurer, and so on. It resembles the individualistic marketing channels found many years ago in retailing. Several observers have called for higher levels of integration of the medical service delivery system so that consumers can deal with one agency and acquire all their medical needs.[8]

The fifth and most extreme proposal calls upon the government to nationalize and rationalize the American health system. The government would be the major or sole supplier of health-care services and seek to provide balanced service to every group and community in the nation. This system is used in England, the Scandinavian countries, and in socialist countries but seems to be of less immediate possibility in the United States.

Marketing can play a meaningful role in the facilitation of these alternative possible systems. To the extent that subsidies are to be used to attract more health services to an area, the marketer can research and advise on their feasibility, on the level of the subsidies that would be needed, and on other appeals that might be communicated to target resources. This comes out of the marketer's ability to understand buying decisions; that is, what resource units—doctors and hospital financers—are seeking and what will motivate exchanges with them. Marketers can also help in the shaping and launching of new types of health service units, the design of vertical health-delivery marketing systems, the location of attractive sites, and the forecasting of demand.

Attracting Contributions to Medical Causes

Another role for marketing in the health sector is to aid public and private administrators of health programs in attracting needed resources to carry on their activities. Health organizations are continuously seeking donations of money, time, or blood. The American Heart Association runs major fund-raising drives each year to raise the millions needed for heart-disease research and health education about heart disease. Various medical charities and hospitals seek to attract donated time from individuals to carry out many activities that otherwise would add considerable cost to their organizations. Local blood banks run recurrent drives to collect enough blood to serve the community's health needs.

All of these efforts seem to involve appeals for a one-way flow of resources—that is, appeals to groups to donate resources without receiving anything in return. But this is a naive view of altruism because the donor is receiving something in return. The donor is receiving a certain set of feelings that are gratifying, such as a good conscience, a feeling of enhanced self-esteem, or a feeling of social involvement. In some cases, the donor receives even more tangible benefits, such as preferred treatment by the receiving source should the donor eventually need help. Those who would seek to attract the free gifts of others must carefully analyze the exchange expectations and flows that surround the transaction.

All the important concepts in marketing play a role in developing a campaign to attract donations to a cause. We will illustrate this with the problem of attracting blood donations, a problem that faces every community in the nation. In the past, many localities relied heavily on paid donors for the needed supply of blood. However, studies show that hepatitis and certain other diseases are transmitted more often by blood collected from paid donors than from volunteer donors, because the former are frequently in poorer health. As a result, most communities have been trying to increase the percentage of blood they collect from voluntary donors, although they find highly seasonal patterns of giving. The worst blood shortages usually occur in January because fewer persons contribute over the holidays and more people are ill, and in August because of vacations. Thus marketing strategists face a problem of increasing the overall volunteer rate of blood donorship and also influencing the timing of giving because blood has a shelf life of only three weeks.

Many voluntary drives in the past simply relied on broadcasting appeals to the whole community to donate blood as a matter of public need. This often works, although it fails to put blood donating on a regular basis or to penetrate the potential donor market very deeply. More current efforts attempt to define the donor market better and to target appeals to the high-potential segments of the market. The potential donor market consists of all persons between the ages of 18 and 65 who weigh more than 110 pounds and who are free of a transmittable disease. Nationwide, this population may be estimated at about 90 million eligible donors. Penetration of this market by the blood-banking system has, however, been slight; rarely do more than 3 percent of the persons in a community supply its blood needs. Thus there is a need for target marketing. Demographic segmentation shows that donors tend to be predominantly male and slightly younger and better educated than the general population. They come more often from the suburbs than the central cities because of higher civic pride in smaller and less anonymous communities. Psychographic segmentation of the motives for giving has been done by Titmuss with the following resulting groups: [9]

1. *Walk-ins*—those who respond at the moment to a cash offer.
2. *Regulars*—those who come regularly for cash.
3. *Paid-induced*—those who accept cash but say it is not their primary motive.
4. *Responsibility fee*—those who give to replace the blood given to a friend or relative.
5. *Family credit*—those who give to gain assurance that they would get free blood in case of need.
6. *Captive voluntary*—those in prisons or the military who give because of pressures put on them.
7. *Fringe benefit*—those who respond to noncash benefits that might be offered such as football tickets, free meals, or time off.
8. *Voluntary community donor*—those who appear to give out of altruistic motives.

In the United States Titmuss estimated that about 47 percent of the donors are motivated by payment, 39 percent by fee avoidance or credit, 7 percent by altruism, and the rest by miscellaneous factors.

The marketing task is to analyze the market response expected from each potential group in relation to the marketing and collecting cost. After determining the best target segments, work must be done to determine their locations, media habits, and responsiveness to alternative appeals.

In designing a strategy, the marketer must take the major barriers to giving into account, such as fear (of pain, or loss of blood, or the medical situation in general), inconvenience (time lost, distance to travel, waiting time in lines), and ignorance (of the need for blood, the rewards of blood donation, and what is involved). The blood bank must attempt to design the product, the place, and the service to be maximally attractive, accessible, and reassuring to the donor. The donor must experience a pleasant staff, little or no waiting, and some recognition to maximize his good feelings about giving. By doing a thorough marketing analysis of the potential donors' characteristics, motives, and expectations, and by arranging for good communication and service, blood banks should be able to increase their effectiveness in attracting the voluntary supplies of needed blood.

Motivating Health-Seeking Behavior

Public and private health officials will find marketing concepts helpful in still another context—that of trying to motivate the general public to adopt more healthful practices. In America, there are 52 million people who smoke, and smoking is closely linked to lung cancer and heart disease. The fact that millions of Americans are hard drinkers is a factor in the prevalence of liver disease and mental illness. The fact that millions of Americans are overweight or undernourished or malnourished accounts for a significant amount of illness in this society. The fact that millions of Americans are not motivated to have regular dental checkups, eye examinations, and cancer and heart tests contributes to much of the high incidence of health problems in these areas.

A large number of researchers are looking at these problems and attempting to understand their causes and possible solutions. Many important studies have been done about cigarette smoking, particularly the major motives for smoking, the effectiveness of different communication appeals, and the durability of dissuasion efforts.[10] Similar studies have been done in the areas of nutrition, alcohol, and hard drugs. As this knowledge accumulates, it must be culled by social marketing strategists and translated into mass and selective campaigns that will motivate healthful behavior on the part of target markets. Social marketers must attempt to understand the benefits that users of these products are seeking and how these benefits can be delivered in less dangerous forms, or how the perceived costs to the users can be increased. Recent consumer buyer-behavior models relating to health showing such factors as perceived susceptibility to a medical problem, the perceived seriousness of the medical problem, and the perceived benefits of a change are promising in their suggestions of potent marketing strategies.[11] The social marketer's task is to motivate the target groups to alter their habits or seek help from those agents who can supply help. For example, smoking withdrawal clinics are present in most communities today and can help smokers reduce their smoking through behavioral conditioning techniques and/or group processes. It is the marketer's job to motivate a sufficient number of persons to seek the help that these health agents can provide. The literature on motivating people to health-seeking behavior is growing and one day a good body of generalizations will be available.[12]

SUMMARY

The concept of marketing is relatively new to the health-care industry and yet there are many fruitful applications. Hospitals have to deal with several markets and publics, including patients, physicians, the general community, and volunteers and donors. A hospital needs to do research on these groups to learn their perceptions, needs, and preferences in order to prepare more effective services and communications. Newer types of health units, such as health maintenance organizations and neighborhood clinics, need to utilize marketing concepts to get established in communities and offer the services that are needed. Public health officials will find marketing analysis and planning of value in connection with appraising the health needs of communities, improving the methods of delivering health-care services, raising money for health causes, and motivating people to more healthful behavior.

NOTES

1. "National Health Expenditures, Fiscal Year 1972," *Research and Statistics Notes*, U.S. Department of Health, Education and Welfare, Note 19 (November 29, 1972).

2. *Hospital Statistics*, 1972 (Chicago: American Hospital Association, 1972), p. 8.

3. This definition is found in Richard T. Burke, *Guidelines for HMO Marketing* (Minneapolis: InterStudy, 1973), p. 1.

4. See Robert Heyssel, "Causes of Retarded Growth in Prepayment Plans," *The Johns Hopkins Medical Journal* (January 1971), pp. 4–8.

5. Several detailed manuals are available on how to market an HMO in a community. See the previous footnote and also *Marketing of Health Maintenance Organization Services* (Washington, D.C.: U.S. Department of Health, Education and Welfare, DHEW Publication HSM 73-13006); and Robert L. Bilbo, *Marketing Pre-Paid Health Care Plans: A Collection of Approaches* (Washington, D.C.: U.S. Department of Health, Education and Welfare, DHEW Publication No. HSM 73-6207).

6. The role of distance in affecting the demand for medical service at any site is examined in Gary W. Shannon et al., "The Concept of Distance as a Factor in Accessibility and Utilization of Health Care," *Medicare Care Review*, 26 (1969).

7. See Robert M. Heyssel, "Causes of Retarded Growth in Prepayment Plans."

8. For a marketing analysis of different models of health-care delivery, see Louis P. Bucklin and James M. Carman, "Vertical Market Structure Theory and the Health Care Delivery System: An Analysis," and the accompanying "Critique" by Louis W. Stern and Frederick D. Sturdivant, papers presented at the National Conference on Social Marketing, University of Illinois (Urbana-Champaign), December 2–5, 1972.

9. R. M. Titmuss, *The Gift Relationship: From Human Blood to Social Policy* (London: Pantheon Press, 1971).

10. See the various papers in Edgar F. Borgatta and Robert R. Evans, eds., *Smoking, Health, and Behavior* (Chicago: Aldine Publishing Co., 1968).

11. See Irwin Rosenstock, "Why People Use Health Services," *Milbank Memorial Fund Quarterly* (July 1966), pp. 94–127; and Gerald Zaltman and Ilan Vertinsky, "Health Services Marketing: A Suggested Model," *Journal of Marketing* (July 1971), pp. 19–27.

12. The following articles are suggestive of studies of marketing efforts to motivate health behavior: Barbara S. Hulka, "Motivation Techniques in a Cancer Detection Program," *Public Health Reports* (November 1966), pp. 1009–14; Raymond Fink et al., "Impact of Efforts to Increase Participation in Repetitive Screenings for Early Breast Cancer Detection," *American Journal of Public Health* (March 1972), pp. 328–36; and Teresa J. Katz and Martin Svigir, "Effects of Souvenir Giveaways on Response to Offers of Free Chest X-Rays," *Public Health Reports* (August 1967), pp. 735–38.

QUESTIONS

1. Many family planning organizations have added vasectomies to their "product line" of birth control methods. Lever and Shaw of the Midwest Population Center say that the intent of a vasectomy marketer is not to encourage or discourage prospective clients but to help them make a "considered and informal decision about obtaining a vasectomy." What are some of the advantages and costs that should be mentioned to prospective clients?

2. Some hospitals give the parents of new-born babies a steak and champagne dinner the night before mother and child are to be released. What do you think of this policy?

3. Should doctors be allowed to advertise their services? How about hospitals and HMOs? How about abortion clinics?

4. How would you go about convincing the executive director of a large hospital that he needs to add a director of marketing services to his staff? Where would this director fit into the organization chart of the hospital?

5. A small hospital in a rural community has to decide whether it is feasible to continue operating an extended-care facility (nursing home) in a separate building. This facility is now located in the building that formerly housed the hospital. This building is over 100 years old and must be replaced with a new structure that will cost thousands of dollars. What should the hospital administrators do before making the decision to either abandon the facility or build a new one?

6. Discuss the advantages and disadvantages to an HMO of allowing its patients to choose and regularly use a specific doctor on its staff.

17 Public Services Marketing

Talking once with a miner, I asked him when the housing shortage first became acute in his district; he answered, "When we were told about it."

GEORGE ORWELL

Public administrators are showing an increasing interest in the subject of marketing. They are facing a variety of problems whose solutions can be made easier by the application of rigorous marketing thinking and planning.

The U.S. Postal System has been losing business to United Parcel Service and other private carriers that offer the mailing public more efficient service. Local school tax districts must periodically convince their voters of the benefits of supporting a school tax increase. The U.S. Atomic Energy Commission must overcome the apprehensions of citizens about the construction of an atomic power plant in their area. Large cities must convince citizens that a new freeway through town is desirable, or that voting for a regional transportation authority would improve urban mass transportation in an area. A specific mass transit system must convince commuters of the benefits of using public transportation over private transportation.

The purpose of this chapter is to probe the nature, role, benefits, and problems of a marketing orientation in government organizations. The question is not whether government agencies should engage in marketing—they can hardly avoid this—but rather what objectives, efficiency, and controls should be used.

The chapter first examines the rationale for a marketing function in four types of government agencies. Then examples are provided to show the use of marketing research, design, innovation, distribution, pricing, communication and promotion, and customer sales and service in government operations. Finally, the major benefits and problems of an explicit marketing orientation in government agencies are presented.

THE RATIONALE FOR A MARKETING ORIENTATION IN GOVERNMENT AGENCIES

Government agencies, like other organizations, are surrounded by several publics with whom they must maintain good relations. Many agencies are established specifically to provide a public service, such as transportation, protection, relief, commercial information, health service, education, and so on. Although they often provide the service as a monopolist, there are usually substitutes that consumers can resort to if the quality of the public service offering is poor. Public agencies that do a poor job of meeting the needs of their clients are subject to criticism from public interest groups and media, as well as the withdrawal of client patronage. One of the agency's most important publics is the legislature, which presumably scrutinizes the quality of service the agency offers in deciding on its funding. Thus there are many publics that an agency must satisfy if it is to function effectively.

The government agency that wishes to operate smoothly, receive adequate funding and powers from the legislature, and avoid bad press relations must pay attention to its level of service to each of its publics. The role of marketing in the agency is to establish the needs of its various publics, develop the appropriate products and services, arrange for their efficient distribution and communication, and audit the degree of satisfaction. In this way, it achieves and fulfills its goals as an agency.

MARKETING VARIES WITH THE TYPE OF GOVERNMENT AGENCY

Although all government agencies can use a marketing perspective, the particular marketing activities that it carries on will vary with the type of government agency. Four types of government agencies are distinguished in Table 17-1 and discussed below.

TABLE 17-1
Four Types of Government Agencies

Type	Function	Examples
Business-type government agency	Produces goods and services for sale	Postal service, toll roads, nationalized industries
Service-type government agency	Produces and disseminates services at no direct charge to the users	Public schools, public libraries, police and fire department, park districts, public hospitals, highway commissions, government tourist bureaus
Transfer-type government agency	Effects unilateral transfers of money	Social Security Administration, city and state welfare departments, Internal Revenue Service
Intervention-type government agency	Exists to regulate the freedom of some group for the sake of promoting the public interest	Penitentiaries, courts, Federal Trade Commission, Federal Food and Drug Commission

Business-Type Government Agencies

A business-type government agency, also called a public enterprise, is one that produces goods and services for sale. In the United States, such agencies as the postal service, toll road commissions, public mass transit, and public hospitals come to mind. Public enterprises are much more prominent in other countries, especially socialist countries and many developing nations. They frequently include the railroads, airlines, telephone company, electric utility, steel industry, and fertilizer industry.

The business-type government agency, for all practical purposes, can use marketing theory and marketing management in the normal way found in private-for-profit business firms. Public enterprises are concerned with identifying their markets, determining customer needs, producing appropriate products and services, setting up distribution channels, utilizing mass communication and personal selling, and carrying on marketing research and sales analysis to keep abreast of their markets. Many are establishing conventional marketing departments to carry out marketing analysis, planning, and control activities.

There are, however, two major differences between the private-for-profit firm and the public enterprise. First, the public enterprise is not guided by the profit motive but rather the responsibility of serving some sector of public need. It is not under the same pressure as the private firm to sell the maximum amount of its output in the period, or face the critical scrutiny of stockholders who have invested money and want a good return. As such, it is less likely to practice hard-sell marketing with its heavy reliance on mass advertising, personal selling, sales promotion, and discount pricing. However, when the public enterprise has over-produced certain goods, it will resort to similar techniques to eliminate high inventories. But in general, the public enterprise operates under less pressure to develop or stimulate demand.

The second difference involves the question of competition. Many public enterprises exist as state monopolies and therefore do not face immediate competition. Consequently, their marketing planning revolves more around meeting the expected growth in total demand rather than in trying to achieve market share. The absence of vigorous competition means that public enterprises pay less attention to the elaboration of product and packaging differences, the creation of brand images, and the adornment of retailing atmospheres.

Service-Type Government Agencies

A service-type government agency is one that produces and disseminates services at no direct charge to the users. The users may pay in their role as citizen-taxpayers but not in their role as users. Such service agencies come to mind as public schools, public libraries, police and fire departments, park districts, public hospitals, and highway road commissions.

Service-type agencies each have a client group for whom their service is intended. Public libraries aim to serve the reading public; public schools aim to provide educational services to children; police and fire departments offer protection services to citizens; and park districts create recreational services for the citizens. These "consumers" represent the agency's most immediate market. The agency has to make decisions on which groups will be served, which of their needs will be served, what level of service will be offered, and how much will be spent to communicate and distribute the available services. That is, these agencies carry on the traditional marketing functions of market analysis, product and service design, distribution, and communication-promotion. The only traditional marketing function that they do not perform is pricing, because the user is not directly charged for the service. Even pricing, however, comes into play when a service organization decides to make a small charge to cover some of its costs, such as when a library decides to charge for overdue books or a city museum decides to charge for admission.

Transfer-Type Government Agencies

A transfer-type government agency is one that exists to effect unilateral transfers of money rather than to produce a basic good or service. Examples of such agencies are the Social Security Administration, city and state welfare departments, the Internal Revenue Service, and the U.S. Customs Service. The Social Security Agency and welfare agencies dispense money to those who are entitled to it because of past contribution or present need. The U.S. Internal Revenue Service and U.S. Customs Service collect money from those who have been designated to pay a tax.

Because transfer-type agencies do not produce a basic good or service, it would seem that they have no marketing functions to perform. But a basic question that establishes the role of marketing in an organization is whether or not the organization has any *clients*. Once a client group is identified, we can begin to ask how their needs are measured; how the organization communicates with them; how the organization distributes its product or service to them; and how the organization treats them. These are the concerns of the marketing practitioner.

In these terms, it is clear that transfer-type government agencies have clients. The public welfare department must distribute money and goods to the needy in a city. The needy constitute its "market." It serves this market with a certain level of service. It engages in market analysis, communication, and distribution. It may even engage in promotion, as in recent years when the Social Security Administration advertised that people should find out their rights and collect their due. On the other hand, these agencies do little or no product development or pricing. The question of product development might arise in the basic sense of whether the agency is producing the right product—here, grants of money—to relieve poverty or whether another product—such as job training—would offer a more long-run solution.

Even those transfer-type agencies known as taxing bodies have increased their marketing orientation in recent years. The Internal Revenue Service is increasingly viewing taxpayers as people to serve rather than people from whom to exact levies in a high-handed fashion. It has been increasing its tax services to the public and attempting to improve overall client-agency relations.

Intervention-Type Government Agencies

An intervention-type government agency is one that exists to regulate the freedom of some group for the sake of promoting the public interest. Examples include penitentiaries, courts, and various regulatory agencies such as the Federal Trade Commission and the Federal Food and Drug Administration.

It might appear that intervention-type government agencies truly have no marketing functions to perform. Consider a penitentiary, for example. Does it have a client group? Our first answer is that the prisoners are the penitentiary's clients. But they are strange clients. They did not choose the organization that is serving them. Their needs are met at a minimal level. There is no concept of the penitentiary trying to create a high level of satisfaction among its customers.

But let us consider this question more carefully. Is the prison trying to sell something to the prisoners? Here we must be more affirmative. A prison tries to sell its clients on the proposition that they would be better off if they became "good citizens." Some penitentiaries try to sell this proposition by making prison life so punishing that the prisoner, if paroled, will want to lead a straight life so as not to return to prison. Other prisons do this by trying to create skills in the prisoner so that he will find it easier to lead the good life. Other approaches are used, all attempting to market this "product" to the prisoners.

But are we right even in designating the prisoners as the main client of the prison authorities? They are really the consumers, not the purchasers. Could we not argue more cogently that the prison's customer is the general public who hires the penitentiary to provide this protective and rehabilitative service? The prison is providing a service to the general public and it is important that the prison satisfy the general public. The prison also has more immediate clients, such as the legislators who decide how much money to budget for the prison system. Prisons are also involved in trying to market ex-convicts to business firms as potentially good employees. Thus the prison authorities face several publics with differing needs. Marketing management has a positive role to play in making sure prison services are satisfying the major clients.

The same goes for other regulatory bodies whose immediate client might appear to be the group that is regulated and whose ultimate clients may be the legislature and the general public. Such tasks as market analysis and market communication, at a minimum, are necessary for regulatory bodies to carry out their mission successfully.

MARKETING ACTIVITIES IN THE PUBLIC SECTOR

Although not all marketing activities are used by every type of government agency, all of them find some use in one or more agencies. This section presents illustrations in a public sector context of such basic marketing activities as marketing research, design, innovation, distribution, pricing, communication and promotion, and customer sales and service.

Marketing Research

Marketing research can play an important role in helping a government agency learn the needs, wants, consumption habits, and attitudes of its markets. Here are some illustrations:

The public library in a large Midwestern city wanted to decide between expanding its central library or opening several neighborhood branches. A large sample of citizens was interviewed on their attitudes and desires regarding library services. The information was helpful in making the decision along lines that would maximize their service to the community.

The U.S. Postal Service periodically considers raising its rates on third class, so-called "junk" mail. Higher mail rates will discourage direct-mail advertisers to some unknown extent. The Postal Service recognizes the desirability of first surveying a sample of advertisers to estimate the probable response to increased mail rates.

Design

Government agencies, like business organizations, are growing increasingly conscious of the value of good design in their public image and offerings. Here are some examples:

Until recently, the only design problem of the Postal Service seemed to be the designing of postage stamps. Today the Postal Service is becoming aware of other design questions. What should post offices look like? What should they feel like? Should they be bright or dull, spacious or small, noisy or quiet? What about the mail boxes, mail trucks, mailmen's uniforms? At present, there are only weak design ideas. A well-thought-out design plan for post offices could boost employee morale, increase customer satisfaction, and reduce customer complaints. It could lead to mass production of postal architecture and materials and bring down building and operations costs.

The police departments in many cities have a poor image. Some police departments have replaced the formidable blue police uniforms with blazer outfits that project a more youthful, friendly police image. It is felt that the police behavior, as well as citizen attitudes, may be modified in a favorable direction as a result of the "new look."

The airlines in many countries are owned and operated by the state. The state managers rely heavily on design principles to build a distinctive image for their airline. An example is El Al, the national airline of Israel. El Al has designed its ticket offices and its planes to suggest a technologically progressive company, yet one that is distinctly Mediterranean. The interior of an El Al office is "gay, warm, and friendly . . . these effects being achieved by colour scheme and lighting." A cactus plant in the office suggests young Israel and the warm climate. The office atmosphere and personnel give the impression of super-efficiency and up-to-dateness with strong technological overtones. All this prepares the traveler for a confident and pleasurable trip.[1]

Innovation

Public agencies could benefit through establishing an innovation function within their organization to research new products, services, and operations. Here are some examples:

Auto license bureaus in many states require drivers to appear once a year to buy their license plates. Some years ago, license bureaus agreed to allow sales of license plates through currency exchanges and banks, thus saving citizens time and travel inconvenience. More recently, some states have begun to dispense with the replacement of license plates each year. In these states, citizens mail in a payment and receive a small metal date showing the new year. This innovation has saved the taxpayers and citizens millions of dollars.

Park districts have many opportunities to innovate new products and services for their citizens. A passive park district simply cuts the grass and patrols the area. More active park districts develop imaginative playgrounds for the children. Some districts sponsor nature tours, lectures, and film programs; others sponsor local theater groups. Some parks have night-lighted their tennis courts and charge a small fee for court use. In these and other ways, parks can serve better the leisure and recreational needs of citizens.

Various government units are seeking fresh solutions to the staggering costs of public welfare. One proposal is the *guaranteed minimum income,* which guarantees families a minimum income plus a large share of any additional earnings. The federal government is testing this program on a sample of families to determine how much incentive it actually provides indigent families to seek employment. On the basis of the test market results, the scheme will be refined and proposed for legislative action.

Distribution

The problem of efficient distribution is found in the public sector as well as the private sector. Here are some examples:

Public welfare departments need to develop an efficient system for distributing welfare checks. Some welfare departments require welfare recipients to pick up their checks at the welfare office and this causes some hardship and ill-will. Other welfare departments use social workers to deliver welfare checks, which amounts to an expensive method of distribution. Welfare departments that mail the checks to welfare recipients find that a substantial number of checks are stolen or lost. Thus there is a distribution problem that calls for innovative marketing thinking. Among the proposed solutions are direct payments to merchants who sell to the poor; or welfare checks sent to bank accounts established for welfare recipients.

Public libraries are in the business of providing information, edification, and entertainment through the medium of books. Their major distribution method has been fixed-site retailing—that is, the books are gathered in one spot called a library and customers come shopping at the library. In recent times, alert libraries have experimented with other distribution channels. One is the bookmobile, or traveling library, which parks in different neighborhoods on different days and makes books available almost on a door-to-door basis. Another solution is the mailing of requested titles, although this is somewhat expensive. In the future, the entire distribution problem may be radically solved by utilizing home television sets and a device that can be used to dial the library card catalog, scan the titles, select books, and display their pages on the home television screen.

The Treasury Department faces the problem of how to make the purchase of its series-E bonds as convenient as possible. Their solution has been to use commercial banks as a retail system for these bonds. Many other possibilities exist. For example, the thousands of branches of the post office could also be used. Or a phone-in service could be established to make bond buying as easy as phoning one's neighbor. A marketing man could develop many systems that would stimulate the purchase of bonds by households.

A police department is in the business of providing security services. Its resources are patrolmen and squad cars. It must decide how to distribute these services throughout the city on a twenty-four-hour basis to minimize crime. Several useful studies have already appeared on optimizing the distribution of police services.[2]

Pricing

In the public sector, all kinds of pricing practices are found. There is a trend today toward greater use of *user charges* for government services. The argument for user charges is that they will lead to better resource allocation. Public agencies that want to apply user charges face many complex issues, as the following two illustrations show.

State universities have traditionally charged low tuitions for in-state students. Because of rising university costs and tighter state budgets, many state universities are finding it necessary to raise their tuitions by several hundred dollars. Their problem is to determine a tuition level that reconciles the conflicting interests of students and taxpayers and still produces enough money to sustain and expand university services. As tuition is raised, the university also has to increase its financial aid. Thus, there must be a joint determination of tuition and financial aid levels. Furthermore, the university can decide to establish or increase user charges for specific services as a partial alternative to a full tuition hike.

Toll road authorities face a classical pricing problem in that the charge will affect the number of drivers using the road. The authorities must carefully estimate the elasticity of demand in their search for the revenue-maximizing price. They must also consider that too high a price will generate unfavorable public reaction and too low a price will lead to faster road wear-out and higher maintenance costs.

Communication and Promotion

Government agencies engage in communication activity to keep their publics informed and to promote various products and services. Here are some examples:

Several police departments have run advertising campaigns on the theme "How to Make a Thief," in which they make the point that people who leave their keys in their cars are helping to tempt young people into crime. The New York Police Department finds that this campaign cuts down auto theft for a few months following its airing. Such public information campaigns save car owners from unnecessary aggravation, young people from criminal sentences, and the state from the high costs of crime prosecution.

The U.S. Postal Service introduced the ZIP code system some years ago to increase the efficiency of mail sorting. Yet many people initially did not use their ZIP codes. The Postal Service intensified its ZIP advertising campaign and the advertising costs were more than covered by the savings in postal handling costs through increased cooperation.

The Bureau of Forestry sponsors the classic "Smokey the Bear" campaign that has made millions of Americans fire-conscious when they picnic in woods, saving millions of dollars of timber from potential destruction.

The National Aeronautical and Space Agency (NASA) has spent large sums of money during the years in advertising and publicizing space explorations. In 1963, NASA had a public relations staff of 173 persons and an annual public relations budget of $14.7 million. Before the moon landing became an accomplished fact, the public was beginning to lose interest in the space program; NASA therefore shifted its communication program to citing new technology and products as the main reason to support continued investments in the space program.

Customer Sales and Service

Employees in many public agencies—postal employees, tax collectors, policemen, welfare workers—come into regular contact with the public. These contacts contribute strongly to the image the public develops of the efficiency and the value of each public agency. The following situations illustrate how some public agencies handle this function.

The image of the police force stems not only from how policemen look in their uniforms but also how they act toward citizens. Policemen in the past often assumed a hard bearing designed to create fear, especially in potential offenders. Today the philosophy is that the police officer is a public servant who should be friendly and helpful to citizens. Many police departments have instituted Officer Friendly programs, in which police officers visit neighborhood schools and describe their jobs to children. Officer Friendly programs have been created not only to change children's and citizens' images of the police but also to change policemen's images of themselves.

In the past, many public librarians wanted to keep as many books in the library as possible; every circulating book was potentially a lost one. Today, libraries have moved toward a greater retailing and service concept. Librarians will ask persons what they would like to read, make suggestions, and put up exhibits to whet readers' appetites. Whereas formerly borrowers could take out one or two books for two weeks, increasingly they can take out up to a dozen books for three weeks to a month.

City hospitals have traditionally treated their indigent patients in a cold, perfunctory way. These patients often spent long hours in dimly lit waiting rooms, were hastily examined by an impersonal medical staff, and made to feel like charity cases. Increasingly, this inhumane face of the city hospital is being replaced by a concept that the patient must receive personal and humane attention.

BENEFITS OF
A MORE EXPLICIT MARKETING ORIENTATION

We have indicated a large number of manifestations of marketing in the public sector. But the essential question is what benefits, and what costs, might more explicit governmental marketing activities entail? What will a government agency gain, and possibly lose, by adopting an explicit marketing orientation? In this section, we will consider the benefits. At least four potential benefits can be identified.

Improved Service

A marketing orientation normally leads to improved *public service*. The chief characteristic of the modern marketing concept is concern with the needs and desires of the groups being served by an organization. The marketer sets up systems to sense, serve, and satisfy the various publics. He is conscious of all the forces impinging on consumer and public satisfaction and his performance is measured by how well he builds favorable attitudes toward the organization.

Improved Efficiency

A marketing orientation also tends to improve *efficiency* in the accomplishment of various organizational goals. The government agency can design its products and services in a better relationship to the purchase and consumption patterns of its markets. The agency can coordinate its marketing activities to achieve goals that might otherwise not be attained if they were pursued in an uncoordinated fashion. For example, a police department is not likely to improve its public image substantially by simply redesigning police uniforms. The problem calls for a set of coordinated actions including police retraining and reassignment and a public information program. If a marketing problem is seen only in design terms, or distribution terms, or communication terms, little will be accomplished. *The agency's major hope lies in integrated and continuous marketing planning.*

Improved Legislative Support

A marketing orientation should also help in the task of securing more *legislative support*. A major public of any agency consists of the legislators. To the extent that a marketing orientation improves the agency's public service and efficiency, it provides a powerful argument for continued and generous support of its activities. Furthermore, the same marketing orientation leads the agency to be more sensitive concerning the legislators as one of their publics, and to this extent, they may be more effective at improving their services and communication to this group.

Improved Accountability

Finally, a marketing orientation could help to improve *public accountability*. If the marketing activities are made explicit instead of being left implicit, and furthermore are placed under centralized responsibility and control, it would be easier to audit these activities and know their expense and content. It would also be much easier for auditors to raise the right questions about marketing activity and address them to the right party.

PROBLEMS RAISED BY GOVERNMENT AGENCY MARKETING

Introducing a marketing orientation into the operations of government agencies is designed to make them more responsive to the needs and desires of their publics. But it is also possible for marketing activity to be overdone, or used in harmful ways. Involved here are three major concerns.

The Problem of Excessive Cost

Public sector marketing could lead to excessive expenditures on marketing research, design, innovation, and communication. Many citizens may not want their tax dollars to be spent on market surveys, more attractive government buildings and facilities, more services, and increased communication. They may feel that other social investments have higher priority. They may not want to support the cost of the additional job positions required by the marketing concept. Marketing expenditures in the private sector are kept down to an economic level by competition and the need to show profits. What mechanism can work in the public sector to insure that marketing expenditures are productive and that genuine public needs are being satisfied? The answer may partially lie in the growing use of *benefit-cost analysis* as an underlying rationale for all public programs.

The Problem of Intrusion

To the extent that the government adopts the marketing concept, it will spend more money in researching citizen desires and reactions to public services. More surveys will be conducted and more citizen-feedback systems will be established. Some citizens feel that marketing research surveys and other devices are intrusions in their privacy. Marketing raises the question of whether taxpayers' money will be used increasingly to pry into citizen affairs, and whether the government will make political use of this knowledge.

The Problem of Manipulation

Although the need for government agencies to communicate with their publics is well-accepted, there is always a danger that this communication could become excessive and indeed manipulative. Where is the line to be drawn between genuine public information activities and propaganda activities? The television documentary on *The Selling of the Pentagon* indicated how easy it is for a government agency to use public funds to build up its influence in ways not clearly required to serve the public better. How are agencies to be prevented from engaging in self-marketing not connected with improved service or efficiency?

It should be noted that these problems existed in government long before there was any talk about a marketing orientation. The public has always been concerned about the costs of government operations, their intrusiveness, and their possible manipulativeness. There is no particular reason to believe that an explicit marketing orientation will *increase* these problems. In fact, it may be argued that an explicit marketing orientation will create greater clarity as to what marketing activity is going on in government, what costs and benefits are expected through various activities, and where responsibility lies for their planning and control. This information might make it easier for public and legislative scrutiny of agency marketing activities than when no specific function called "marketing" exists.

SUMMARY

We have suggested that government agencies need increased inputs of marketing thinking to carry on their work efficiently and beneficially. Marketing is relevant to all four types of government agencies: business-type, service-type, transfer-type, and intervention-type. Different agencies would find value in marketing research, design, innovation, distribution, pricing, communication-promotion, and customer sales and service. These functions go on, in varying degrees, in all public agencies whether or not they are recognized as marketing activities. By giving explicit recognition to marketing as the overarching and coordinative concept for these activities, public agencies may be able to improve their service, efficiency, legislative support, and public accountability. On the other hand, legislators and the public must maintain constant vigilance so that agency activities, whether or not they are called marketing, do not produce excessive cost, intrusiveness, or manipulation. Explicit recognition of the marketing function may, in fact, facilitate better control of these potential problems insofar as a center of marketing responsibility is established in government organization.

NOTES

1. James Pilditch, *Communications by Design: A Study in Corporate Identity* (London: McGraw-Hill Book Co., 1970), pp. 18–21.
2. Ernst Nilsson, *Police Systems Analysis* (unpublished doctoral dissertation, Northwestern University, 1969).

QUESTIONS

1. Design a marketing research study that could be used to help an urban mass transit system find ways to increase ridership on weekends and off-hours.

2. "Without the profit motive to push them, organizations like the postal service, toll roads, and public hospitals will never provide their clients with good service." Discuss.

3. The city of Rolling Meadows, Illinois, owns a fleet of Mercedes-Benz garbage trucks. The city has also had tremendous success in getting its citizens to cooperate with recycling efforts of all kinds. Do you think there is a connection between these two things?

4. New York City has a very serious dog-waste problem. A large number of the grassy spots in Manhattan are consequently hazardous to walk on, and residents find this annoying and distasteful. The city also incurs large expenses trying to clean up after the dogs. What could be done to solve this problem?

5. Several people have suggested that the traffic lights in Chicago's Loop district should be changed to allow pedestrians to cross in all directions from a corner while all automobile traffic would be stopped. How would a good marketing manager evaluate this suggestion?

6. Many public recreational facilities are plagued by chronic over-popularity. Cite some examples. What can be done to remedy these situations?

18 Educational Services Marketing*

I find the three major administrative problems on a campus are sex for the students, athletics for the alumni, and parking for the faculty.

CLARK KERR

The education industry is one of the largest service industries in the United States. It employs 3 million people in over 120,000 establishments serving over 60 million customers at an annual cost of $74 billion, or 7 percent of the Gross National Product.[1]

Historically, this industry has enjoyed overwhelming public support. Parents, government bodies, and philanthropists have been generous in their outlays on the public and private school system and have de-

* This chapter was co-authored with Professor Bernard Dubois and published in *Broadening Marketing's Horizons,* Jagdish N. Sheth and Peter L. Wright, eds. (Urbana, Ill.: University of Illinois, Bureau of Economic and Business Research, 1974).

veloped highly favorable attitudes toward education. Students have accepted the product as something they should consume. Critics have periodically attacked certain educational practices but have rarely questioned, until recently, the need for schools.

This confidence in the education system reached its peak in the mid-sixties in the United States, to be followed by a set of unanticipated shocks and setbacks that are still rocking the educational establishment. It began with college students attacking their teachers for their failure to get involved in significant national problems and their school administrators for their unwillingness to share power with them in the determination of educational policy. It stretched over several years in the form of costly and occasionally tragic campus disorder. Private philanthropists, witnessing the turmoil on the campus, increasingly wondered whether they were subsidizing a generation of radicals, and began to reduce their contributions. Some of the major private colleges, such as Columbia, Yale, and the University of Chicago, faced for the first time substantial and growing deficits.

Some of the college anti-establishment fever filtered down to the high schools and elementary schools. In addition, the downturn of the economy in the late sixties complicated the problem of public school financing. Further troubles came from critics who began to question the whole educational enterprise and talked openly about the need for de-schooling, open classrooms, and other changes in basic educational premises.

One question naturally arises: Is the education industry the innocent victim of social problems and trends beyond its responsibility and control? Or have some of its own practices contributed to and inevitably produced the crisis in the classrooms? The evidence seems to indicate that many practices of the educational field contributed to its own troubles. The industry grew unresponsive to its markets. There were demands in the marketplace that were not being supplied by the industry; and there were suppliers in the industry who were trying to sell products that were not in demand by the market. These conditions generate what Alderson has called "a discrepant market"—that is, a market in disequilibrium.[2] Such a market calls for adjustment in the form of product innovation, demand simulation, or both. The slowness of these adjustments is a major factor in the current crisis in education.

This chapter is divided into four parts. The first part examines the nature of the educational product. The remaining sections examine, from a marketing point of view, the three major educational problems facing this country—insufficient funds, lagging innovation, and unmotivated students.

THE NATURE OF THE EDUCATIONAL PRODUCT

The current crisis in education makes it desirable to examine the basic nature of the educational product and the existence of an industry that is formally organized to supply that product. This kind of examination might provide clues about the real nature of the problems facing education today.

Every society thinks enough of itself to make active provision for its continuance. The societal function of transmitting its culture and technology and developing the intellectual capabilities of its young members is called education. In a simple society, this educational process may take place entirely within the home. The child watches and learns from its mother and father, older brothers and sisters, other relatives, friends, and neighbors. No one is "teacher" in the specialist sense and everyone is a "teacher" in the broad sense.

In most societies, however, family education is eventually partly superseded by formal education. Even in primitive societies, persons emerge who specialize in the product known as education. This occurs for a number of reasons—first, it is the reflection of an effort to achieve *efficiency* in the educational process. A specialist teacher can free the time of many parents who otherwise would have to educate their children on a one-to-one basis. Second, specialist teachers hold out the chance of achieving more *effectiveness* in teaching. By specializing in the task of teaching, they become skilled in effectively communicating that part of the culture for which they are responsible. Third, specialist teachers arise to supply *specialized knowledge* which parents usually cannot give to their children.

The transfer of the educational responsibility from the home to the school is significant in other ways than simply achieving more efficiency, effectiveness, and depth in education. Progressively, the parents relinquish the idea that they are participants in the education of their children and partners with the schools in formulating educational policy. They feel that teachers are more competent than themselves in that area. They want their children to receive "an education," but surrender any pretension to knowing what it should consist of. The result is that an entire industry grows up to supply a service in which the home and the family show less and less interest and capability.

Partly because of parental disengagement from the educational process and partly in spite of it, the teachers preempt the job of defining what the educational product should be. They arrive at definitions of what they think is right for the community and prefer not to have it become a point of open discussion, but to be accepted more as an article of faith. In marketing terms, we would say that the education industry takes on a *product-oriented character* almost by default.

The fate of most industries that are product-oriented rather than market-oriented is to eventually lose customers to other suppliers whose products are better adapted to evolving needs and desires. The education industry, however, can stave off this development in part for many years because of the peculiar monopoly position enjoyed by the public elementary and secondary school system. At this level, *the industry both defines the product and requires people to consume it, at least until they reach the age of 16.* The result is a rather conservative and unresponsive elementary and secondary school system.

Higher education in the United States has shown more market responsiveness, although still far from ideal. Because institutions of higher learning cannot require consumption of their product, they must do a better job of market satisfaction. Because competition is much keener in higher education and funding less secure, there is a closer matching of product to heterogeneous segments of demand. But this responsiveness is only relative to that found in the elementary and secondary school systems.

With this perspective on the origin and nature of formal schooling, we are now ready to examine what we consider to be the three major problems facing the education industry today: *insufficient funds, lagging innovation,* and *unmotivated students.*

THE PROBLEM OF INSUFFICIENT FUNDS

The education industry is a money-poor industry. Education is not produced and sold to consumers at a price covering its costs. Money is raised through public funds and private gifts to supplement the inadequate user charges. In the case of private higher education in the United States, tuition covers only about 26 percent of the total cost.

Traditionally, educational institutions have not paid the kind of attention to the development and management of their financial resources that is found in most business organizations. This relative lack of concern went unpenalized as long as the educational product was in high demand and funds were relatively easy to obtain. Today, the situation is different. Major sources of financial support are moderating their generosity at a time when the cost of educating a student is rapidly increasing at all educational levels and for all types of institutions. Therefore, an educational institution has to make sure that no potential source of funds is overlooked and that all contributing sources are producing at their maximum. This takes certain skills and understandings. Fund raising may be viewed as a separate art, or in wider terms as a marketing problem.

Viewed as a marketing problem, the task is to analyze the level of current money flow from various sources and to consider ways to increase this flow. Ultimately, educational institutions must analyze their markets for funds as carefully as soap and auto companies analyze their markets for detergents and automobiles. This means developing models of fund-giving behavior and determining the best way to increase the perceived benefits to the fund suppliers in return for their support.

If we are to advance beyond this general formulation, we must recognize that although the fund-raising problem is faced by all types of educational institutions, the structure of this problem varies greatly from one type of institution to another: elementary and secondary schools receive most of their funds from local public sources; publicly controlled colleges and universities obtain the major part of their resources from federal and state assistance; and privately owned colleges and universities rely mainly upon their students' tuition fees. Accordingly, we shall analyze the funding problem at these three different levels.

Public Elementary and High School Funding: The Referendum Issue

Although elementary and secondary schools do receive a certain amount of aid from federal and state sources, over half their financial support comes from local funds directly approved by the public through the procedure of funding referendums. This situation is the result of a widely accepted principle that if the citizens of a certain school district want educational resources beyond the minimum level provided by the federal government and by the state, they have to tax themselves in order to provide the extra funds.

In the last several years, the referendum procedure has met considerably less success than in the past. Figures show that the percentage of approval of school funding proposals was down to 46.7 in 1971, from a high of 74.7 in 1964. Many factors have been cited in the weakening of public support, such as a deteriorating economic situation (employment, inflation), the increased criticism of public schools (busing, strikes, frill courses), and alleged poor marketing of the referendums. It is clear that if public schools are to survive the rising cost of educating their pupils, the referendum procedure has to be made more productive.

Marketing logic offers three ideas for the more effective conduct of referendum elections. The first is that of *market segmentation*. Many school funding campaigns fail because the school district assumes a homogeneous voter group to whom a single persuasive message must be addressed to overcome their concern. The fact is that the local citizens are quite heterogeneous in their perceptions, attitudes, and interests in the school system. Voter attitudes toward supporting the school system vary with their age, education, income, presence of school-age children, political views, and occupational classification. For example, families with school-age children typically vote more favorably in referendums than do families without school-age children. Real estate men often oppose new school referendums because they will raise the cost of real estate and make it more difficult to sell property in the community (overlooking the increased community attractiveness offered by a good school). Because of these variations in attitude, it is crucial in a referendum campaign to identify the main attitude segments of the market and prepare different marketing programs.

The second idea is that of "benefitizing." Many school districts operate on the assumption that citizens will see it as their duty to support the public school system, and that therefore no special effort need be undertaken to connect the voter's short-run or long-run interests with the referendum outcome. They overlook the fact that the citizen feels many public obligations (to his religious institution, college, and favorite medical charities), and in a period of tight financial resources, he must make a choice. Whether or not he will make a choice to support public education depends a great deal on whether he has been prodded to think about the benefits of a strong school system. The school system must therefore be benefitized to them.

> For example, the public schools in Oklahoma City were in desperate need of funds to prevent a deterioration of facilities and exodus of teachers. The public and legislators were largely indifferent. The school system scraped up enough funds to dramatize on television the work of the public school system, particularly to fight the high school dropout problem, develop new teaching techniques, and enrich the children. The parents' response and interest were tremendous, once the issues were dramatized.

The third idea is that of the "campaign concept." Passing a referendum is not a matter of developing some favorable newspaper publicity and then hoping that enough sympathetic citizens will show up on election day. It calls for a professionally organized campaign that plans and harmonizes research, concept development, publicity, meetings with different groups, canvassing, election day "get out the votes," and other important forces. At least four important tactical questions should receive consideration in the planning of a referendum campaign:

1. When should the referendum be scheduled?

Certain seasons are better than others, and certain days of the week are to be favored. As a cynical observation, referendums have a better chance of being passed in winter in Northern climates because fewer older people, who often vote against referendums, show up.

2. How much should be asked for?

A school district has a choice between asking for a large amount of money in one major referendum or asking for half as much money in two referendums spaced by several months. Generally, the more they ask for in any one referendum, the greater the chance for defeat. On the other hand, if they come back to the voters too often, the voters may also feel that their pockets are being picked.

3. What appeals should be used?

This ties in closely with the benefits question but goes beyond it. A school district can surround the benefits message with several appeals, such as urgency, duty, fear, or humor. An appeal such as urgency may only work once. A fear appeal could backfire. There is much research that needs to be done in this area.

4. What sources and media should be used?

The campaign concept must also be built upon a good idea of the effectiveness of various media and sources that bring the message to voters. How important is newspaper endorsement? Should the school children be used as a media channel to the parents? What kinds of community leaders have the most credibility for certain messages delivered to certain groups?

The concepts of market segmentation, benefitizing, and the campaign concept can make a contribution to improving the probability of voter support. They can help a good product do well, but it should be pointed out that they cannot compensate in the long run for product deficiencies. If a school district has been doing a poor job of educating the children, or has developed a reputation for extravagance, or for any other reason does not have the confidence of the public, no amount of sophisticated marketing and especially cosmetic marketing will help in the long run. Modern marketers stress the priority of product quality over promotional effort in determining the long-run success of a product.

Public College and University Funding: The Lobbying Issue

Public colleges and universities receive most of their funds from governmental sources. More specifically, their budgets are mainly financed through an annual appropriation from the city or state legislature. In order to ensure that this source of funds is at its optimum level, it is necessary that educational institutions develop a full understanding of the legislative market. One of the most distinctive features of this market is its competitive nature. Educational administrators soon realize that as far as government funding is concerned, their product is in competition with hundreds of other causes and issues.

The mistake made too often by public colleges and universities is to converge on the legislators only near the time of the sale. The annual appropriation meeting is well-known in advance and this usually perks college administrators to start campaigning among the legislators for support. As soon as the appropriations are voted on, school lobbying activity subsides or ceases, only to pick up again when the next appropriation period comes around.

This is based on the mistaken notion that making a sale is more important than building a relationship with the legislators. The legislators represent one of the most important publics of the institutions. As such, they deserve to be regularly informed about the institution's accomplishments and needs. They should receive periodic reports and visits from school officials with the general aim of creating an atmosphere of understanding and interest.

Not all legislators should receive the same amount of attention from school officials. They, too, fall into segments with different priorities of importance to the school. In every legislature, there is a group of key legislators, such as the chairmen of the education committee and finance committee, who deserve special attention. Efforts should be made to bring them to school functions and involve them in school affairs. Then there is a group of legislators who generally support higher education; a group who generally opposes generous support of higher education; and a group of legislators in the middle. The schools have to identify these different entities and determine which relationships are the most fruitful to cultivate, both in terms of the chance of really influencing them and the value of their support.

The search for legislative support must go beyond market segmentation into an understanding of legislator motives and interests. It would be naive to see legislators as only prompted by selfless motives to serve the public. Legislators seek different things from their careers: some seek fame, others fortune, others power. They are also individually in different situations with respect to their constituencies and rival candidates. Some are so constrained that they cannot vote more taxes in; others rest a major part of their candidacy on being a prominent supporter of education. The school officials must research the legislators as part of an informed, intelligent approach to building a strong relationship with them.

At an operational level, school officials must improve their understanding of the comparative effectiveness of various tactical approaches to the legislators. Lobbying tactics include direct personal communication techniques such as personal presentation of arguments or research results and testifying at hearings; indirect communication techniques such as contacting through friends or constituents and letter, telegram, and public relations campaigning; and channel-opening techniques such as entertainment and party planning.[3] People in charge of the educational product should consider and evaluate each of these tactics in order to find out which would most advance their cause.

Finally, school officials must recognize the necessity of working through other groups to make their case known to the legislators. Legislators are always interested in the vote implications of the public stands they take. They will try to perceive how the public stands on higher education, how business feels, how various organizations feel. For this reason, the colleges and universities must not confine their activities to direct cultivation of the legislators. They must cultivate the general public through a steady stream of information about higher education. They must present their case to business and professional groups as well, with the hope that these groups also express their support of education to the legislators. This is an example of what in marketing is called a "pull strategy" in contrast to a "push strategy."

Private College and University Funding: The Pricing and Private Gift Issues

The plight and desperate situation of the nation's private universities is well known. New York University, the nation's largest private university with 44,000 students, faced in 1972 a $10 million deficit which according to its president could have led to the largest financial collapse in the history of higher education. The situation was so desperate that the university had to consider the prospect of eliminating entire schools, such as the Graduate School of Social Work. Nor were they alone. The average institution ran a $161,000 deficit. Over a fourth of the private colleges dipped into endowments to meet operating expenses. A report of the Association of American Colleges, entitled "Redder and Redder," predicts that 48 percent of the nation's private, accredited four-year colleges and universities would exhaust their liquid assets in the next decade.[4]

Two of the most important opportunities for the private university for more support are *student fees* and *private gifts*. A marketing perspective on these two problems will be given here.

To marketing people, the tuition problem is not unfamiliar. It is in essence a pricing problem and its solution would require an analysis of demand response to alternative price levels. At the same time, most countries in the world have adopted the view that consumption of the educational product is desirable in itself and should be made available to anyone who has the capacities, regardless of his financial abilities. In the United States, the application of this principle has led most private colleges and universities to set up a financial aid policy. Many higher education institutions therefore approach the pricing problem as a two-stage decision process. They first decide upon the level at which they can feasibly price their product in the market; then they decide how much they can allocate to financial aid.

The rapidly rising cost of education and the very competitive nature of the college and university market are such that the level of tuition fees has become practically the same for private institutions competing in the same segment. Today, a private university has little choice as far as price setting is concerned but to respect the going rate.

By contrast, financial aid is becoming a major factor of differentiation between educational institutions. Given the fact that financial aid has been found to be the most important factor affecting the decision made by the student to attend a given university,[5] educational administrators have to determine carefully the level of available financial aid and its allocation to applicants. In deciding upon the level of aid, college and university administrators have had to appraise carefully their competitive standing. An institution whose reputation is rated by students as slightly lower than another has to somewhat increase the level of its financial aid in order to get a corresponding quality of incoming students.

To know how their universities are seen by various publics, educational administrators must conduct formal *image studies*. Students, faculty, donors, and foundations all have their own images of universities. They see some universities as great, several as good, many others as average, and still many others as poor. Their image of any educational institution may not be a currently accurate one and may reflect the type of school it was ten or twenty years earlier. Yet on the basis of these images, resources are allocated.

With respect to foundations, the private university's task is to treat them as an important public whose support must be cultivated, not by a sporadic set of visits but by a well-thought-out relationship-building plan. Top university officials should cultivate key relations with foundation officers and keep them regularly informed, through mailings and personal visits, of their needs and accomplishments. These university officials should understand that foundations vary in their missions and motives, and the university's varying financial needs should be matched to each foundation's interests as carefully as possible. A foundation wants to give money not only to help a particular university but because they expect its work will contribute to social betterment.

With respect to wealthy private individuals, both alumni and non-alumni, the university officials must be alert to their existence and to their diverse interests and motives. Too often the administrator takes an overly simple view of the motives for giving to a university. People give to worthwhile causes in expectation of something in return, and it is important to correctly identify the major motives operating in each particular market segment as they might interlace with the university's character. Some individuals give because the university gives them a sense of pride; some give because they feel it increases the chance their children will be accepted; some give because the university lacks a reputation and they want to help it get one to enjoy a sense of pride; some give because the university's program is moving in a direction that appeals to them; some give because they are kept very involved in its activities and enjoy contact with faculty and university administrators; and so on. The university must carefully analyze the various motives operating in each market as a basis for building a long-term relationship and designing and delivering the satisfactions that the various segments of the private-gift market are seeking from the university.

THE PROBLEM OF LAGGING INNOVATIONS

A second major problem facing educational institutions is that of backward teaching methods. Innovation is as desirable for the education industry as it is for any other type of industry. If successfully managed, innovation contributes to making the educational system more *efficient*, more *effective*, and more *responsive*.

At the same time, evidence indicates that the rate of diffusion of new teaching practices and processes is remarkably slow in this industry. In reviewing a large number of diffusion studies of educational innovations, Mort concludes that "fifteen years typically elapse before [an educational innovation] is found in three percent of the school system . . . additional twenty years usually suffices for an almost complete diffusion in an area the size of an average state." [6] Thus, the full adoption of an average educational innovation takes about thirty-five years. A number of reasons can be advanced to explain this phenomenon.

First, the education industry has an inborn conservative tendency stemming from the very nature of its task. The major role of education is the transmission of our cultural heritage from one generation to the next. As a result, the education industry tends to focus upon past and well-established contributions to knowledge rather than present ones still in the process of formation and validation. Schools tend to resist changes in the content of their programs or teaching methods until the advocated changes are proven to be more effective than the ones presently in use. Because it is not easy to measure educational effectiveness, the verification process takes considerable time and slows down the rate of diffusion of educational innovations. In addition to this, the rapid expansion of education in this country has led to the imposition of uniform regulations and impersonal procedures aimed at maintaining standards and insuring common practices throughout most of the industry. These regulations play a critical role in retarding the rate of innovation diffusion.

Second, innovative behavior is weak in the education industry because of a notable lack of competition. A school is not going to be out of business because it fails to adopt the latest teaching innovations and/or instructional methods. Besides, there is no specific reward attached to the adoption of an educational innovation. Furthermore, the adopter has to face the added risk of a possible failure.

Third, strong resistance to the adoption of these innovations often comes from the teachers themselves. In many cases, an educational innovation represents a threat to a teacher's status. Consider the example of the "new math." Although teachers may realize the benefits of the new math, they also may feel insecure in learning and teaching it. Furthermore, no economic incentive is offered to teachers who adopt educational innovations. As noted by Eichholz and Rogers, "teachers are generally paid on the basis of longevity and personal educational attainment. Thus, what is accomplished in the classroom seldom influences the economic level of the teacher." [7]

Fourth, the pupils' parents often actively resist changes in educational method or curriculum. Their idea of what is right goes back to the type of education they received a generation earlier. If they learned by rote methods, they find it hard to see their children being handled more permissively. They also resent certain subject matters, such as sex education, being taught in the school, because it reduces their home control of the subject.

Finally, the ultimate consumers of the educational product, the students, may resist educational innovations they do not consider desirable. This is especially true at the college and university level. The introduction or maintenance of NROTC programs, for example, has elicited much criticism from students. The introduction of black studies programs has also been a matter of much controversy.

In brief, because of the many parties involved in the educational innovation-adoption decision, the diffusion process is lengthy and complex. An educational innovation has to go through a number of stages before it is finally adopted and put into practice.

From the foregoing analysis, it clearly appears that the education industry is faced with a dilemma. The development and successful diffusion of needed innovations is basic to its progress but many factors inherent in the educational system make this diffusion difficult. Does marketing offer at least any partial solutions to this dilemma?

A marketing planner faced with the problem of speeding up the rate of adoption of educational innovations would typically analyze it as a "facilitation" problem; a problem consisting of finding ways of reducing the "distance" existing between the innovation and its potential adopters.

We saw earlier that these adopters do not constitute a homogeneous group but fall into various segments such as administrators, teachers, parents, and pupils, each with his own cognitions and motivations. Reducing the psychological distance between the innovation and these segments calls for three specific steps.

The first step calls for a detailed analysis of the overall decision-making process involved in the adoption or rejection of educational innovations so that the role and responsibility of each participant group is clearly defined. In analyzing the decision structure, attention should be paid to informal channels in addition to authority relationships. In some elementary and secondary schools, it may occur that although the principal is the one who formally makes the final decision, he is in fact under the influence of his teachers to such an extent that the teachers can be considered as the real decision makers. In other cases, the parents can exert such a pressure upon the school that the major part of the promotional effort has to be directed toward them. Information is needed concerning the respective influence and role of each of the major participants in the decision-making process.

The second step calls for an investigation of the beliefs, attitudes, and motivations of each segment with respect to the innovation under consideration. These beliefs, attitudes, and motivations may appear quite different from one segment to another. Teachers, for example, will be sensitive to any aspect of the proposed innovation that affects their economic and social status within the school. Principals and superintendents may be interested in the kind of impact that the adoption of the innovation would have upon the school and the surrounding community. Parents will want to know the extent to which the innovation is really going to increase the quality of their children's education. Pupils, finally, will probably react to those attributes of the innovation which make its consumption dull or exciting.

The third step consists in tailoring promotional programs corresponding to each segment's specific needs. This step involves a number of decisions including the nature of the appeals to use, the specific structure of the messages to convey, and the type of media to select. After the micropromotional programs are developed, the final task consists in integrating them into a coherent and meaningful organizational change strategy.

THE PROBLEM OF UNMOTIVATED STUDENTS

Whereas the problem of insufficient funds has to do with how schools cultivate their outside publics, and the problem of lagging innovation with how schools change their teaching practices, the problem of unmotivated students deals with the issue of student satisfaction. It is safe to say that there always has been a substantial group of students who find formal schooling a painful experience and who cannot wait for the day when they will be freed from forced consumption of the product. No amount of educational innovation, new facilities, or good marketing of the product will ever reduce the number of dissatisfied students to zero.

At the same time, marketing can offer some insights into the problem of student dissatisfaction and suggest some possible remedies. We will concentrate on one aspect of the total problem, that of the unmotivated student. This problem will be examined in two different contexts:

1. The high school dropout problem
2. The unmotivated college student problem

The High School Dropout Problem

It is estimated that between one-third and two-fifths of American children drop out of school before high school graduation.[8] The word "dropout" is somewhat unfortunate because it suggests a difficult self-willed child or a child of low intelligence who is at fault rather than the school system or socioeconomic system. A closer look shows that those who drop out of school withdraw for a number of diverse reasons, such as economic necessity, a feeling that school subject matter is irrelevant, negative self-images created more by the method of teaching rather than the intelligence level of the child. These different factors suggest that remedial action is not simply a matter of convincing recalcitrant young people to stay in school but of making needed and fundamental changes in the school system and possibly society.

A student begins to think about dropping out of school when he perceives the rewards from leaving the school to be greater than the rewards from remaining in it. Three marketing variables—product, incentives, and promotion—suggest ways to alter this ratio.

The first line of attack is to make the product better. Perhaps the most obvious step is to increase the amount of individual attention given to potential dropouts. Teachers can be assigned to work with problem students on a one-to-one basis or a small-group basis, concentrating on improving basic skills which so often constitute the main learning barrier in weaker students. Another hope lies in the development of more effective technologies for teaching basic skills and knowledge to large groups of students. Programmed learning, operational gaming, team projects, and so on promise to make learning easier and more exciting. Still another product improvement is to strengthen athletic and musical programs, which frequently tap a more natural interest in those students who are potential dropouts, thus making it easier for them to accept the chore of school work because of the other pleasures they might enjoy. Finally, the product might be made more attractive by dropping some of the stringent rules that make high schools seem so suffocating and prisonlike to a large number of students: rules about dress, class attendance, and so on. Some schools are experimenting with letting students take short excused leaves of absences upon such claims as being fatigued, needing a change, and so on.

A second line of attack that is being tried in a growing number of school systems is that of supplementary incentives in the form of payments (real or honorific) for progress in learning or good attendance. For example, a student might be paid 25¢ for every acceptable homework assignment he turns in, or he might receive 100 S&H stamps for every week he attends school without an absence. The underlying theory is that of behavioral conditioning, which says that target habits can be built up by associating rewards with desired acts and costs with undesired acts. In principle, a point is presumably reached where the rewards are no longer necessary, the target habit having become functionally autonomous in the person's makeup. This approach is still highly controversial, particularly because of its materialistic flavor, which is offensive to many critics; nevertheless, there is evidence that it works under certain circumstances and this may be the main consideration.

A third line of attack is the use of promotion to either strengthen the positive motives for staying in school or increase the felt fears and risks of dropping out of school. Positive approaches would involve a public service advertising campaign, usually under the auspices of the Advertising Council of America, indicating the set of good feelings that one gets when he receives his high school diploma and the types of rewards that one may expect from the possession of that degree. This positive approach has generally not been put into practice; instead public service advertising has tended to feature fear appeals.[9] Previous campaigns have stressed the lower employment level and the lower earnings of dropouts. The facts are quite clear on the earnings issue. Among men 25 years of age and over in 1968, the median income of college graduates was almost $11,300; for high school graduates, more than $7,000; and for elementary school graduates, almost $5,100.[10] The real problem is therefore to effectively communicate these facts to the potential dropout in the hope that it will alter his perception of the reward/cost ratio in favor of remaining in school.

The question is not which one of the several approaches should be used but rather to what degree and under what circumstances should each of them be used. Each approach may be effective in certain contexts and segments of the potential dropout market. It must, however, be stressed that different costs attach to implementing each solution so that some restraints are necessary. For example, individualized instruction as an attack on the dropout problem involves very high cost.[11] Altogether, much more work has to be done on evaluating different methods of reducing the dropout rate from the point of view of their relative effectiveness and cost.

The Unmotivated College Student

It is no surprise to find so many unmotivated students in elementary and high schools, given the compulsory nature of the educational product until the age of 16. It is more surprising to find unmotivated students in colleges and universities, because these students are free to buy or reject the product. Students graduating from high school can work, travel, or loaf rather than go to college. The decision to give up these alternatives and go to college—which is a major commitment—would normally signify a choice positively and enthusiastically made. Furthermore, the option of dropping out of college anytime if the product stops satisfying should lead us to expect to find few unmotivated students in college.

The facts are otherwise. Although there are no figures available, one suspects that the number of unmotivated students can range from 20 to 80 percent in different colleges. In the best colleges, where student motivation is high and teaching is excellent, some 20 percent of the students may still fall in the unmotivated class. In the poorest colleges, the percentage of unmotivated students may reach as high as 80 percent.

At first sight, it might seem that undermotivation is a personal problem rather than a social problem; that it is unfortunate that these students do not take more from the educational process but it is really mainly their loss. This view is mistaken. Their passive presence on the campus constitutes a major social cost and waste. Unmotivated students emerge from college with less skill than they could have obtained and therefore earn less and contribute less. They could have gone to work instead of college and enjoyed immediate income and possibly more job satisfaction. And they create negative spillover effects in the classroom and on the campus. Their apathy and, sometimes, cynicism spread to other students and create an atmosphere in which it is difficult for educational excitement to be generated.

Marketing analysis suggests four ways in which the number of unmotivated students may be reduced. All of them seek the objective of trying to make the market work better.

First, the true nature and value of higher education must be clarified to the various buyers, users, and supporters. Too many students are attracted by the status symbol or the hope for a good time without work. Some systematic demarketing of a college education to those who would seek the wrong values may be desirable.

Second, the present heterogeneity of institutions should be supplemented by newer types of institutions that meet unsatisfied market needs. Too many students go to a particular type of college because another type that they would really want and get excited about is not available. One such concept would be the vocational college that teaches technical skills to students who want to work with their hands rather than absorb the primarily verbal learning that is offered in the typical college. Another concept is the social action college that gives students training and exposure to social problems both in and out of the classroom that many students consider more relevant to their interests and needs. As new programs emerge that are better matched to the tastes and interests of students, there should be less dissatisfaction.

Third, information flows must be improved to give prospective students a better chance to find the right college for their needs. Not too long ago the information gap was substantial and students were choosing colleges—one of their major lifetime decisions—on no more than the report of a single friend or some image obtained from the sports pages of their newspaper. Much has been done to improve market information in recent years, such as the appearance of several books describing various campuses, both academically and socially; the emergence of better academic counseling in high schools; and the improvement of statements by various colleges in their catalogs as to what kind of places they are and what kind of students they seek. This last point seems very important, in that colleges must move away from a market aggregation philosophy of trying to draw all the students they can get, toward a target marketing philosophy where they go after a planned mixture of potential students to achieve certain aims of education. But much more remains to be done in the way of improving the amount and accuracy of the information available to consumers who are facing this difficult choice.

Fourth, there must be an improvement in the information flows within each college between its students and its administration. Schools range all the way from the many that do no systematic monitoring of student opinion to the few that use fairly elaborate procedures. No school to our knowledge carries out what many large business firms do, a periodic audit of their customers' needs, attitudes, and satisfaction level. Also, the university must determine the extent to which its current students should be allowed to participate in university policy making and the effect of participation on student motivation and satisfaction. The university's stand on the degree of student power becomes part of the product being offered to the prospective and current students. It becomes an expression of the university's basic attitude toward students. Student participation implies that the students are not just "consumers" of the educational product but also "partners" in its elaboration, improvement, and promotion.

SUMMARY

The days when the educational product was unanimously praised and regarded by everyone as needed and desirable are gone. Today, many indicators are available which show that the present educational system is undergoing a major crisis. Financial difficulties, lack of innovativeness, and student passivity are among the most visible.

Marketing concepts can offer useful insights for responding constructively to major educational problems. The problem of insufficient funds for education calls for elementary and high schools to deliver a better educational product to their publics to make it easier to obtain in return their confidence and votes in school tax referendums; for state colleges to do a better job of understanding and cultivating the support of legislators; and for private colleges to develop better principles of tuition pricing and fund raising.

The problem of backwardness in educational practices calls for finding better ways to speed up the diffusion and adoption of worthwhile educational innovations. This means researching the perceptions and attitudes of administrators, teachers, parents, and pupils as a prelude to designing the product and benefits that will motivate the various "buyers" to see value in the innovation.

The problem of unmotivated students calls for identifying the different reasons for undermotivation as they might lie in the product, the teaching methods, the school atmosphere, and so on. By altering the product, offering alternative products, and changing incentives, the institution might succeed in improving student views of the potential excitement or at least value of the educational product.

NOTES

1. U.S. Department of Health, Education and Welfare, Office of Education, National Center for Educational Statistics, *Digest of Educational Statistics,* 1970 edition.

2. Wroe Alderson, *Dynamic Marketing Behavior* (Homewood, Ill.: Richard D. Irwin, 1965), p. 27.

3. Lester W. Milbrath, "Lobbying as a Communication Process," *Public Opinion Quarterly* (Spring 1960), pp. 32–53.

4. Some of this information is found in an article by James C. Crimmers, "Our Friends in Nonprofitland Say a Major Financial Crisis Is on the Way," *Institutional Investor* (August 1972).

5. G. M. Naidu, *Systems Approach to the Marketing Aspects of Higher Education* (unpublished Ph.D. dissertation, Michigan State University, 1969).

6. P. R. Mort, *Educational Adaptability* (New York: Metropolitan School Study Council, 1953).

7. Gerhard Eichholz and Everett M. Rogers, "Resistance to the Adoption of Audiovisual Aids by Elementary School Teachers: Contrast and Similarities to Agricultural Innovation," in Mathew Miles, ed., *Innovation in Education* (New York: Teachers College Press, Columbia University, 1964), pp. 299–316.

8. S. M. Miller, "School Dropouts and American Society," *New Society,* November 7, 1963, p. 2.

9. The *Continue Your Education* campaign of the Advertising Council features the headline "The Odds are 2 to 1 against a Dropout" and goes on

to read: "Twice as many dropouts are out of work as high school graduates. If you're in school, stay there." Another slogan frequently used is "Drop now, you will pay later."

10. U.S. Department of Commerce, Bureau of the Census, *Current Population Reports*, Series P 60, No. 66, 1970.

11. An interesting experiment was evaluated by Weisbrod in which a group of potential dropouts were divided into an experimental and a control group, the former receiving "special counseling services, assistance in getting placed on jobs and remaining on jobs, and special assistance on the job from employer and school personnel." By the end of two years, 44.1 percent of the experimental group and 52.0 percent of the control group had dropped out of school. The 7.9 point difference was statistically significant at better than the 5 percent level, indicating that the special-attention program did reduce the number of dropouts. However, a benefit-cost analysis showed that the adjusted cost per prevented dropout was $6,500. The question arose whether this was too much to pay to keep a student in school. Another calculation revealed that the measured social benefit to society of keeping the student in school was $2,740. Clearly, this particular solution to the dropout problem had a negative benefit-cost ratio and could seriously be questioned. See Burton A. Weisbrod, "Preventing High School Dropouts," in Robert Dorfman, ed., *Measuring Benefits of Government Investments* (Washington, D.C.: The Brookings Institution, 1965), pp. 139–49, esp. p. 140.

QUESTIONS

1. Most major universities in the United States have made it extremely difficult for faculty members to earn tenure. At many schools, young assistant professors are expected to publish enormous quantities of materials before they will be promoted and awarded job security. Does it make sense for these universities to employ a "publish or perish" policy when so many of them are having serious financial difficulties?

2. Cite some dangers in using incentives to get poorer students attending high schools to "buy" the idea of taking education seriously.

3. In the chapter, it is mentioned that New York University faced great financial difficulties in 1972. One of the problems the school was having was that it could not attract enough students who were willing to pay the school's high tuition fees and to live in New York City. Develop a plan that could have helped N.Y.U. to recruit more students.

4. There are a number of private colleges and universities around the country which have "Class Gift" programs. During their senior years, students pledge to give their alma mater, say, $20 during each of the twenty years after they graduate. Over this time period, all the money accumulated from a particular class is put into investments selected by class members. At the end of twenty years, the class votes on how it

would like to see the school use the invested funds (e.g., unrestricted, new construction, scholarships, etc.). Does this sound like a good fund-raising program to you? Why?

5. Develop a course evaluation questionnaire that would be filled in by college students at the end of each term to evaluate the classroom performance of professors.

6. Discuss how the development of adult education programs can help a university. How should these programs be designed?

19 Political Candidate Marketing

My center is giving way, my right is falling back, the situation is excellent. I attack.

MARSHALL FOCH

In this final chapter, we shall examine marketing concepts in the context of marketing a political candidate. Up to now, we have examined the marketing of products and services, organizations, and ideas but not the marketing of persons. Person marketing is a major activity in the areas of politics, celebrities, and everyday job hunting and recruitment. In person marketing, there is a major effort to cultivate the attention, interest, and preference of a target market toward a person. We have chosen political candidate marketing as our major example of person marketing.

Political candidate marketing has become a major industry and area of specialization. Every few years the public is treated to an endless number of campaigns attempting to put various candidates for local, state, and national offices in the best light. In the 1972 presidential election year, the various candidates for all offices managed to spend over $400 million in less than two months on their campaigns.[1] The money was spent on media advertising, direct mail and telephone, and in other ways.

Political campaigns have increasingly been compared to marketing campaigns in which the candidate puts himself in the voter market and uses modern marketing techniques, particularly marketing research and commercial advertising, to maximize voter "purchase." The marketing analogy is more than coincidental. It is argued here that the very essence of a candidate's interface with the voters is a marketing one, not only in recent times but far back into the past. Candidates seeking to win elections cannot avoid marketing themselves. The only question is how to do it effectively. How does a candidate proceed if he wants to treat his candidacy strictly as a marketing problem?

In the analysis that follows, we shall make the assumption that a politician has a dominant goal, to be elected (or reelected) to office, and that all of his plans and actions are chosen with this goal in mind. We will not make any further assumption as to why the politician wants office, whether it is to acquire fame, fortune, or sheer power. We will not get into the particulars of the type of office sought, although it might be helpful to think of the proposed analysis as most relevant to a senatorial or presidential contest. We will not be concerned with the varying political rules, mores, and institutions found in different political units, which the politician must master. They are important but only at a secondary level of analysis. We will confine our attention to the question of how he can best allocate his resources and schedule his activities to achieve the goal of being elected. Before analyzing this problem in detail, we will be on firmer ground by first examining more closely the relationship between business and political marketing.

THE RELATIONSHIP BETWEEN BUSINESS AND POLITICAL MARKETING

Interest in the marketing aspects of elections has been stimulated to a large extent by the spectacular growth in *political advertising*. There has also been a substantial growth of *scientific opinion polling* (i.e., marketing research), *computer analysis of voting patterns* (i.e., sales analysis), and *professional campaign management firms* (i.e., marketing organizations). The subtleties of the marketing approach go beyond the rising expenditure levels and the use of certain information and planning approaches. They are delineated in a series of popular books, such as White's *The Making of the President 1960* [2] and McGinness' *The Selling of the President 1968*.[3] In a quieter way, several scholarly works have also noted the marketing character of political elections.[4]

It would be a gross mistake to think that election campaigns have taken on a marketing character only in recent years. *Campaigning has always had a marketing character*. Prior to the new methodology, candidates sought office through the handshake, baby-kissing, teas, and speechmaking. They still use these methods. *The "new methodology" is not the introduction of marketing methods into politics but rather an increased sophistication and acceleration of their use*. According to Glick:

> The personal handshake, the local fund-raising dinner, the neighborhood tea, the rally, the precinct captain and the car pool to the polls are still very much with us . . . the new campaign has provided a carefully coordinated strategic framework within which the traditional activities are carried out in keeping with a Master Plan. It centers on a shift from the candidate-controlled, loosely knit, often haphazard "play-it-by-ear" approach to that of a precise, centralized "team" strategy for winning or keeping office. Its hallmarks include the formal strategic blueprint, the coordinated use of specialized propaganda skills, and a more subtle approach to opinion measurement and manipulation. And, though there is a world of difference between selling a candidate and merchandising soap or razor blades, some of the attributes of commercial advertising have been grafted onto the political process.[5]

Nimmo takes a cynical view of this development:

> In screening potential candidates the mercenaries have given a new definition to the notion of "availability"; the marketable candidate is selected on the basis of his brand name, his capacity to trigger an emotional response from the electorate, his skill in using mass media, and his ability to "project." Analysis of social· problems and issues yields to parroting of themes; televised debates between contenders produce meaningless confrontations rather than rational discussion. Negotiations with party politicians assume the form of "out-of-town tryouts"; primary elections are approached as "presale" campaigns; and general elections emerge as the "Giant Sweepstakes." In the end one candidate owes his election not to party but to his personal organization of paid and voluntary workers; once elected he responds not to party programs, but to the interests also represented by the professionals.[6]

The major fault with Nimmo's observation is that it takes on a moral, judgmental tone. It implies that something is happening to political contests that is called marketing and it is bad. It fails to recognize that the marketing problem exists no matter what means or style of marketing is used. In fact, marketing styles vary from product to product and time to time; but the marketing problem is always present.

The Anatomy of Political Marketing

Figure 19-1 presents two maps comparing business and political marketing. The *business marketing map* shows a seller dispatching goods,

FIGURE 19-1
Business and Political Marketing Compared

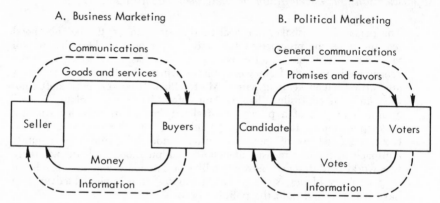

A. Business Marketing   B. Political Marketing

services, and communications to the market; in return he receives dollars and information. The inner loop is an exchange of money for goods; the outer loop is a flow of information. The *political marketing map* shows a political candidate dispatching specific promises and favors to a set of voters in exchange for their votes. He uses general communications to convey these and gathers voter information to plan next period's marketing effort. Schematically, the structural processes of business marketing and political marketing are basically the same. Both can be analyzed in terms of exchange theory.

Figure 19-2 shows the political candidate's marketing problem in greater detail. (1) The environment which defines the salient issues and opportunities for the candidates is shown at the far left. (2) The candidates, their parties, and their interest group alliances are the sellers. (3) Each candidate develops a product concept that he believes is merchandisable to the voters. The concept is built on a mixture of political philosophy, stands on particular issues, personal style, and background qualifications. (4) Each candidate seeks to reach the voters through three major distribution channels: mass and selective media, personal appearances, and volunteer and party workers. These channels interact—e.g., a personal appearance reaches an immediate audience and also a larger

FIGURE 19-2
A Comprehensive Political Marketing Map

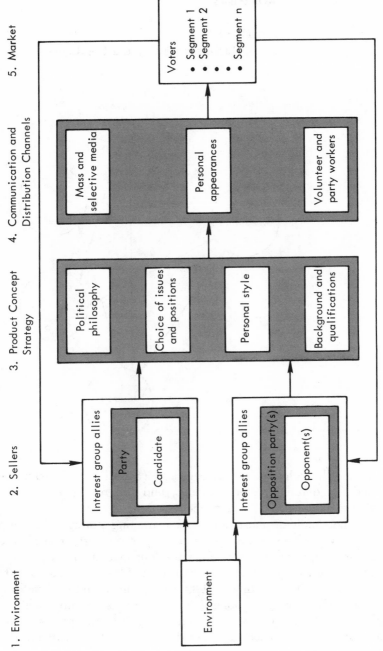

1. Environment   2. Sellers   3. Product Concept Strategy   4. Communication and Distribution Channels   5. Market

FIGURE 19-3
Four Markets Faced by the Candidate

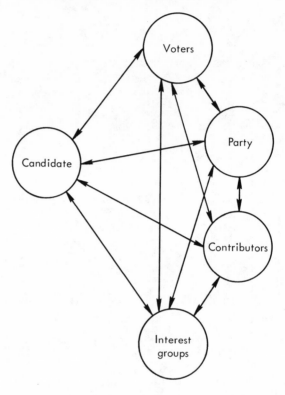

audience through mass media coverage. (5) All of these efforts are adjusted for different voter segments, and the results are continuously reviewed for further campaign modification.

The candidate must develop a marketing strategy not only calculated to win the support of voters but also of the party, contributors, and interest groups. Figure 19-3 shows the four markets he faces. The interactions among these markets are complex and the candidate cannot afford to formulate his marketing strategy simply on the basis of voter market response. For example, taking a strong stand as an anti-machine candidate will gain voters' votes but hurt party support and some contributions. Furthermore, each stand has distributive effects within a particular category. Taking a pro-labor stand increases the contributions from labor and reduces the contributions from business. Thus, political marketing strategy cannot be developed by simply calculating the distributive effects within the voters' market. Similarly, business marketing strategy aiming at building buyer support cannot ignore the impact on dealers, stockholders, government, and competitors. In this chapter, we will concentrate on the candidate's positioning himself in the voter market while recognizing that this is insufficient for comprehensive marketing planning.

Alleged Differences between Political and Business Marketing

Certain differences between political marketing and business marketing are alleged to exist in the public mind. They relate to characteristics of the product, buyers, and sellers.

1. Any specific commercial product, such as a can of beans or a ton of steel, is relatively fixed in its characteristics at a given point in time. The political candidate, on the other hand, is more variable. For one thing, the political candidate can talk back.

Comment. The variable nature of the political product is matched in the commercial world by services. Services are inseparable from the people who render them. The housewife can testify that her hairdresser can talk back, that his hairdos vary in quality, and so on. Physical products, too, can be changed through product reformulation, sizing, or packaging.

2. It is held that the political candidate cannot be as thoroughly formulated for the market's needs as can physical products or services. For example, new foods and soap products can be formulated to meet specific market wants. But a given political candidate cannot be varied freely in the same way. He has a history and fairly set personality. It it not easy or even possible to remake a humorless old candidate into a vigorous young one.

Comment. The freedom of manufacturers to alter the character of some commercial products is also quite limited. Steel is steel and salt is salt. On the other hand, a political image can be changed to some extent. Richard Nixon in successive campaigns has taken on the image of an anticommunist, a statesman, and most recently, a man of action. There are limits, of course, and organizations often choose to launch brand new products rather than to do the job of repairing the old one.

3. Business products are normally available for purchase any time at the discretion of the buyer. Political products, however, are only "put on sale" every few years.

Comment. There are instances of economic products that buyers can only buy at certain times. One can buy a Rembrandt only when it is put up for sale or auction. One can enroll in a college only during certain times of the year. Many government contracts carry announced dates for bidding. Purchase frequency is not a basis for distinguishing between commercial and noncommercial products.

4. The buyer of a commercial product or service usually expects personal benefits enjoyed within a reasonable time period. Many citizen voters do not expect to accrue any personal or early benefits from their act of voting.

Comment. There are various commercial products and services that do not appear to give personal or short-run benefits, that people nevertheless buy. Examples are insurance, wills, and estate plans. People also contribute to various charitable causes from which they do not anticipate personal benefits. On the other hand, many voters get quite involved in some election contests and act as if they anticipate personal benefits. The charismatic candidate is someone who gives a great number of voters the feeling that they will personally benefit through the candidate's election.

5. Buyers of commercial products and services are used to hard-marketing tactics whereas voters do not expect, and somewhat resent, hard-marketing tactics in the political area. A political candidate who offered trading stamps or who overdid hard-sell advertising would be taking great risks.

Comment. Hard-sell marketing tactics are characteristic of certain goods such as automobiles, cigarettes, soap, and cosmetics. The marketing of earth-moving equipment, computers, and airplanes is conducted much more on the rational merits of the product and the company's reputation for service and reliability. There is nothing about *marketing method* that requires hard-sell tactics.

6. The messages reaching the public about a commercial product are largely marketer-controlled, through paid advertising. The media rarely feature or comment on a brand of beans or toothpaste. On the other hand, the messages reaching the public about a political candidate are largely developed by the news media. As a result, the political candidate finds it necessary to market himself as much to the press as to the ultimate public.

Comment. It is true that the press takes an active role in commenting on and interpreting political candidates to the public. This makes the political candidate's marketing task easier in some ways (he gets more free publicity) and harder in other ways (he has less control over what the press says).

7. A business firm succeeds if it obtains any market share that yields a good return on its investment; the political candidate succeeds only if he obtains a plurality of the voters—that is, the largest market share.

Comment. There are business markets, too, where the seller either gets all or none of the business. For example, an airplane manufacturer who bids for a government contract either wins or loses. The criteria of what constitutes a viable market share make little difference to whether marketing planning and strategy are useful.

8. The aims and means of the business seller and the political candidate are different. The business seller is seeking profits. The political candidate is seeking power. The business firm tries to secure more profits through creating satisfied customers. The political candidate does not as clearly try to secure more power by creating satisfied citizens.

Comment. Business firms actually pursue multiple objectives, as do political candidates. There are, in fact, business firms that pursue power and political candidates who seek profits. Furthermore, business firms and political candidates can choose from a range of philosophies on which to base their marketing. There are politicians who aim at producing satisfied citizens; and business firms that aim at quick profits.

THE MARKETING PROBLEMS OF THE POLITICAL ASPIRANT

We are now ready to analyze in marketing terms the office-seeking process of a candidate. We will assume that the candidate has decided to enter politics and his ultimate goal is to achieve an elective office. At the beginning, he is an unknown product. The office seeker must put himself on a market, the voters' market. He has to go through many of the steps that occur in product marketing: develop a personality (brand image), get the approval of an organization (company image), enter a primary election (market test), carry out a vigorous campaign (advertising and distribution), get elected (market share), and stay in office (repeat sales).

Looking ahead, he must solve four successive problems in the achievement of a successful political career.

First, he must join a political organization and become known. He will want to develop a political style that will earn respect and leadership in his party. He knows that this means finding out what the members of the political organization appear to want from the political process and the extent that he can appear to be instrumental in their desires.

Second, he must eventually exhibit an interest in becoming his party's candidate in an upcoming election. He must fraternize with the leaders and attempt to get their backing. He must enter a primary election and win the support of the party's voters.

Third, if he wins the primary, he will have to go before the voters in the general election. He will have to make important decisions on campaign strategy, including issues, advertising, appearances, and funding. He will face a problem in voter analysis, choosing targets, allocating resources, and timing them for maximum impact.

Fourth, if he is elected, he must do the kind of job in office that will get him reelected. This will be a function of the organization he builds, the positions he takes, and the rhetoric he uses.

Thus the new political aspirant faces four practical problems: *getting started, getting nominated, getting elected,* and *getting reelected.* At each stage, he must squarely face the problem of personal marketing.

GETTING STARTED

There are three ways to come into the role of being a political candidate in a forthcoming election. One is to run as an independent by announcing candidacy and building up an organization or even a new political party. A second is to wait for an existing political party to ask him to run for office as their nominee. The third is to join a political party and seek its nomination for a particular office. We shall consider mainly the third method.

The person who sees his political future in joining a party, working hard, and achieving the party's nomination faces a series of decisions from the start. He must make a *party decision,* a *role decision,* and a *timing decision,* in that order.

Party Decision

The political aspirant must decide which political party to join. Just as a product is not much without a company, a politician is not much without a party. The party provides the communication and distribution system and resources for reaching the voters. The party's image will add to or subtract from the stature of the candidate standing by himself. It puts a credibility on his personal image. It defines his concepts more sharply.

Therefore, the candidate must carefully choose the party to join. He may decide purely on the grounds of having strong political convictions that are more consistent with the one party than another. However, the two major parties in the United States are not very different in political philosophy: the right-wingers of the Democratic Party are to the right of the left-wingers of the Republican Party. The candidate who is without strong party preference faces the choice of a party. If he is going to be a *family brand,* which family would add more power to his political career? Which party has more of a future in local or national politics? In which party is the leadership vacuum greater? He must recognize that he will not be standing on his merits alone but on the party's merits when his name goes before the public.

Role Decision

The political aspirant must also determine what role he will assume in the party organization. The major roles in political organizations are *loyal party worker, party gadfly,* and *party statesman.* The *loyal party worker* role means that he attends all the meetings, volunteers for various assignments, carries them out efficiently and uncontentiously, and exhibits all the traits of a dependable party man whose interest in the welfare of the organization is paramount. The *party gadfly* role means that he plays a provocative role at party meetings, challenges various proposals, urges innovations, stimulates discussions and party soul-searching. This role guarantees early attention and under certain conditions can lead to quick leadership of the organization, especially if he conveys the feeling of trying to serve the best interests of the organization, not himself. At the same time, it is a high-risk strategy because it is noisy, boat-rocking, and may make early enemies. The *party statesman* role falls in between the loyal party worker role and the party gadfly role. The aspirant participates in party discussions, makes judicious, well-balanced suggestions, and avoids acting aggressively or exhibiting a personal ambition. He takes on a mediator role, showing that he can smooth over frictions and keep the party moving forward.

There are not enough studies to indicate the frequency and effectiveness of these different roles under different circumstances. The loyal party worker role takes the most patience to play and is likely to be rewarded eventually with an opportunity to run for office if other characteristics are also present in the candidate. The gadfly role is the more risky because it is likely to cause frustration in the organization regarding the candidate or frustration in the candidate regarding the organization, in either case possibly ending his political career or freezing it. The statesman role may be the most appropriate for persons with their ultimate sights on high political office because it involves the development of those skills that create a highly marketable candidate. He is respected within the party and can be promoted to the voters as a candidate with mature political traits.

The aspirant should be sensitive to these alternative roles and consciously assume one with clear consistency. In practice, his personal attributes will limit or dictate his choice. A role can be played convincingly only if the aspirant's temperament and resources permit it.

The Timing Decision

One does not join a political party and announce the next day that he wants the party's nomination for an office. Normally he spends some months or years learning the ropes, building up friendships, getting known, doing work. He must spend time in building up qualifications and a record that speaks for itself. He normally avoids announcing his ultimate aspirations until the time is right. If he makes his ambitions clear too early, he invites possible efforts from actual or potential rivals to block him. In commercial marketing, too, we find rivals not announcing plans for a new product until they are sure of the product, of distributors' support, of sufficient resources, and of ultimate market success.

The aspirant may want to wait for some political opportunity that will add an *accelerative thrust* to his career. This opportunity might come in the form of a rising star within the party whose career he might assist. By working actively for a "comer," he moves at the comer's rate. This carries the risk of misjudging a comer and being over-identified with a loser; but this risk may be worth taking. The opportunity might also come in the form of a new issue in which the aspirant is particularly qualified. The community may be concerned about law and order and he may be an ex-district attorney with a tough reputation. Thus, timing is not simply a matter of the candidate's preference but may also be left to the right opportunities coming along to provide maximum accelerative thrust to his career.

Normally, an aspirant would prefer to be drafted by his party without provoking or manipulating his candidacy. This obviates charges that he is a self-seeker using the party for his own ends. On the other hand, he may be drafted at the wrong time, when the party is bound to lose and he may be the sacrificial lamb. This means he sometimes has to "demarket" his candidacy if he does not think the office or timing is right.

Once he announces his candidacy for an office or is drafted, everything changes. He must now assume a role as leader, get people to believe in him, believe in his motives, and his probability of winning. He cannot afford to lose his first contest because the stigma of loser is a difficult handicap if and when he receives a second chance.

Throughout he must study his party. It is his market at this stage. He must carefully observe its recruitment processes. What kinds of candidates does the organization like? What is the adoption process? How can he create maximum congruence between the normal recruitment processes of the party and his traits as a potential candidate?

GETTING NOMINATED AND ELECTED

Whether the aspirant has announced his own candidacy or has been nominated by a particular clique within the party, he typically has to enter the primary election and run against others seeking the party's nomination. The primary is an election by the members of his political party in which they choose among alternative candidates. It is at this stage he starts undertaking marketing activities designed to introduce him to a wider audience beyond the local actives of his party. It is a *test market,* a trial run. If he wins, he must place himself before the voter market using all the marketing activities at full scale.

The marketing activities that he must engage in to win the primary contest and the subsequent election are virtually the same. For this reason, no difference will be drawn between the two stages. The marketing activities common to both stages are:

1. Marketing research
2. Product concept and strategy
3. Communication and distribution strategy

Marketing Research

The first rule of effective campaigning is that the campaign must be addressed to the interests of the voters. The voters' interests can only be ignored by politicians not seeking to win the election, who are in the contest for reasons of personal vanity, or to educate voters, or to shock them. The typical office seeker must assess the voters' needs, interests, and values and represent himself as the best perceived instrument for the voters to achieve their desires.

Some politicians may feel that they know the voters' opinions and interests so well that they need little if any marketing research. Dollars invested in marketing research are a subtraction from dollars that could be spent in advertising. But the politician is usually mistaken in thinking that he knows what is on the electorate's mind. Even if he could guess at the major issues, he is not likely to know their relative importance in the minds of various groups of voters. He is even less likely to guess how the voters feel about different issue positions he might take.

Manufacturers of mass products no longer develop them and launch them on a hunch. They carefully research the major market segments and their needs, desires, product involvement, and loyalties. Some consumers will never buy the product; some will be loyal to competitive brands; some will buy the new brand because of the company's reputation; and some buyers are independent and capable of switching brands. Politicians are increasingly doing this, too, in the form of elaborate precinct analysis. They research the demographics, past voting patterns, and involvement levels of voters in each precinct. They conduct simple opinion polls to learn the major issues and voters' stands on these issues.

Is there anything in modern marketing research theory or practice not already in use in voter studies? The answer is yes. Most voter research takes the form of *opinion polling* and this is reminiscent of the "nose-counting" phase of marketing research of over twenty years ago. In the 1950s, marketers began to recognize that buying motives went much deeper than "yes-no" answers to superficial questions and this ushered in a wave of motivation research. Marketing researchers began to experiment with depth-interviewing methods such as free association, thematic apperception tests, open-ended questions; they began to run group discussion panels. These methods revealed a deeper dimension to human attitudes and motives toward product categories. In the sixties, marketing researchers began to employ multivariate statistical techniques such as *multiple regression analysis* (to reveal relations between various marketing stimuli and consumer response), *discriminant analysis* (to determine the variables that predicted the probable group affiliation of subjects), *factor analysis* (to determine the basic underlying factors making up an attitude), and *cluster analysis* (to determine optimal grouping of individuals). Today, marketing researchers are increasingly using *multidimensional scaling techniques* to identify the major attributes defining a product's perceptual space, the position of competing products in that space, and the characteristics of ideal products.[7] Extensive interviewing of various political campaign managers and researchers indicates that the state of their research into the voter market nowhere approaches the sophistication found in commercial marketing, thus suggesting future opportunities for the alert political researcher.[8]

The nagging question still remains: How much marketing research expenditure is feasible for the candidate in view of its alternative productivity in direct promotion. Business firms spend money on marketing research to the extent that this will contribute to creating a better product and more effective messages. They recognize that nothing is gained in spending advertising money on the wrong message or the right message reaching the wrong audience. The politician likewise must carry out enough marketing research to feel confident that he is able to formulate the best message and identify the best media for reaching the intended target audiences.

Product Concept and Strategy

Voters rarely know or meet the candidates; they only have an image of them. They vote on the basis of their images.

Candidates attempt to transmit a particular image of themselves to voters. But the transmitted image is not always the perceived image. Voters start with different cognitive maps and predispositions and this causes them to see different things in candidates. Furthermore, they are exposed to stimuli that come from sources other than the candidate himself that modify the candidate-intended image.

The politican who wishes to succeed cannot leave his image-making to chance. His clothes, manner, statements, and actions become news and shape the impression people have of him. The politician who wants to win must treat himself very much like a new product. He must formulate a look and behavior that match the target voters' perceptions and needs.

The term used in marketing to orient the image planning for the product is called the *product concept.* A product concept is the *major orienting theme around which buyer interest will be built.* It is the "unique selling proposition," the "promised benefit" of the product. The political candidate must choose a product concept on which to market his candidacy. Does he want to come across as "the hard-hitting reformer," "the mature statesman," or "the experienced legislator"? It would be wrong to think of the product concept as only a slogan. *The product concept is the basis for planning and organizing the entire campaign.* It shapes the coalitions that are formed, the issue positions that are embraced, the statements that are made, the public appearances, the allocation of effort to voter segments, and many other decisions. Choosing the product concept is the most important single decision made by the candidate.

How does the vote-seeking candidate choose his product concept from the multitude of attributes he could feature? He must first determine the major issues in the election as seen and felt by the voters. At any point in time, the voters are seeking something from the candidates, some promise or answer to the problems they face. This varies from election to election and district to district. It might be "honesty in government" in one place, "law and order" in another, and "progressive legislation" in a third. The politician must listen for this voters' message with a third ear. It provides the major clue as to the type of symbolic reassurances that the voters want. It suggests major themes or product concepts that might guide the campaign.

Given several possible product concepts, the candidate must eschew any that is unnatural or unbelievable as a role for him to play, no matter how much it may match the voters' needs and feelings. The candidate will be placed in too many performance situations that could strain or destroy voter credibility in the candidate's concept. Mayor John Lindsay would not pass easily for a law and order man just as Richard Nixon would not pass easily as a sexy, progressive young candidate. The candidate must choose from a set of alternative concepts that are reasonably congruent with his personality and background. This still leaves a lot of possibilities.

Given a set of feasible alternative concepts, there is a need for pre-campaign *concept testing*. The possible themes are shown to a sample of target voters who are asked to rank or rate them in terms of interest or preference. Voters indicate how strongly they feel about "an honest candidate" versus "an experienced candidate" versus "a conservative candidate." The assumption is that the voters are in need of a certain political character at a given time who will champion their hopes and assuage their fears. The relative appeal strength of different concepts would be reflected in the survey.

The final choice of a product concept is influenced by this research and also by the expected product concepts of the opposition candidates. The voter chooses from a field of possible candidates. Each candidate is presumably carrying out the same research on the best product concept. It is quite possible for them to arrive at the same ideal concept and all build their campaign on it. This happens in many commercial product campaigns and the audience gets the feeling that the brands are all the same. All the detergents promise whiteness and all the razor blades promise a better shave.

Thus the candidate must not adopt the ideally best concept, but rather the one that best *positions* him with respect to the product concepts adopted by the other candidates. This is called *product positioning*.[9] If his opponent is a "law and order man," would he be more effective as a "civil rights candidate" or as a "fiscal watchdog candidate"? He must recognize that the voter market is made up of many segments and each concept will win him a certain market share in each segment, given his opponents' concepts.

Two additional points should be made about the choice and use of the product concept. First, the candidate must decide how much emphasis to place on the chosen product concept. He can, at one extreme, project that product concept in all his talk and action. This is the policy of *concept specificity*. Or he can use it more loosely so as not to become totally bound up with that concept. This is the policy of *concept diffuseness*. This is similar to a product that can be advertised strongly as offering one major benefit or weakly and by implication as offering a variety of benefits including this one. The choice is a difficult one. By pursuing concept diffuseness, the candidate may just fail to come across with any specific identity in the voters' minds. The policy might be appropriate for the majority party candidate who believes partisan voting will bring him victory. On the other hand, the candidate who practices concept specificity will win the strong support of certain groups and alienate others. Furthermore, he is taking the risk of locking himself into an image from which he cannot escape if last-minute changes in issues or voters' moods should call for a change.

The second point is related to the first and it is that the candidate can assume a secondary product concept as well as a primary one. He could wear two images as long as they are not boldly inconsistent and as long as they do not confuse the best use of scarce resources. Thus a candidate might decide on being primarily a "law and order man" and secondarily a "fiscally responsible candidate." He may project the first concept at meetings of ordinary citizens and the second at meetings of bankers and business groups. It is important however that he avoid trying to be all things to all men.

As stated earlier, the concept he chooses and attempts to transmit is not necessarily the image voters will get of him. He controls only certain stimuli reaching them. The voters are also influenced by their peers, media commentators, opposition candidates, and fortuitous events which make his concept input, while quite important, less than perfectly determinant of the image that comes across.

Communication and Distribution Strategy

The candidate's concept becomes the basis for planning the communication and distribution program. His concept must be packaged into statements and actions that are matched and distributed to target voters. The candidate's ability to talk from prepared remarks versus extemporaneously, on television versus radio, in large mass rallies versus small home gatherings, are all factors to consider in the tactical development of his campaign. Everything the candidate does communicates something to the voters. He must rely on professional communication consultants to help him present the best possible image to the voters.

He and his campaign managers and specialists must lay plans for three important communication-distribution programs:

1. A paid advertising program
2. A personal appearance program
3. A volunteer worker program

Paid Advertising Program. Political advertising has come a long way from the days when the major media were billboards and posters. Today, all the media are used, including newspapers, radio, and television; and television in particular has transformed the nature of political campaigning. Copy can no longer be left to amateurs; the task of advertising the political candidate must be turned over to advertising agencies that handle them like any other product. The advertising agency participates with the other campaign managers in developing some basic principles for the advertising campaign, covering such matters as:

1. the basic message
2. the way the candidate will be photographed
3. the ad sizes that will be made for print and broadcast media
4. the allocation of the budget over the various media categories
5. the percentage of the budget that will be spent in each week up to election day

The candidate must rely on their professional knowledge about the effectiveness of different messages and media. He is in the same position as Nixon, who had to say in the 1968 campaign: "We're going to build this whole campaign around television . . . you fellows just tell me what you want me to do and I'll do it." [10]

The candidate should not, however, give up all his judgment. He must be comfortable with the advertising messages. He must avoid a too-slick campaign where voters get the feeling that he is being sold like soap-flakes or is spending too much on advertising. Advertising can turn people off as well as on. A bad ad can hurt his chances as much as a good ad can help his chances. He must exercise the final decision on matters of conscience.

A Personal Appearance Program. If a candidate is at all attractive, he would normally gain by achieving a personal exposure to every voter. Meeting a candidate personalizes and intensifies the voter's interest in the election and is normally worth a vote. The exception are candidates who do not make a good impression—who bore, confuse, or disappoint voters. Such candidates would do better to minimize their appearances or agree to them only under highly controlled and favorable circumstances.

The candidate who seeks voter exposure is rarely able to reach all the voters. His personal channels for reaching the voters consist of rallies, club meetings, coffees, and appearances at busy street corners. The *rally* gives him a chance to present his full case to the people who choose to come out to listen to him; and he can add *atmospherics* to the affair by featuring music and personalities from the entertainment and political world. The *club meeting* allows him to meet special groups of businessmen, church members, workers, and so on who might not have normally gone to see him at a rally. *Coffees* permit him the opportunity to meet friendly and curious neighbors in the intimate surroundings of a home where he can project a more personal quality. *Street corners* allow him to project himself into a crowd of strangers, many of whom might never have met him, and to communicate briefly but effectively with a smile or a handshake.

The candidate's time is severely limited and he, with his consultants, must carefully choose among all the possible functions he might attend. He must give some time to motivating his own party workers and committed voters. He must consider other opportunities in the light of their vote potential. He must estimate the number of uncommitted voters who might be there, the number of opinion leaders, and the chance that his appearance will be leveraged in the mass media. He must adjust his schedule as new trends and problems appear in the race. There are many factors to consider, and generally the task of scheduling the candidate's appearances is still a developing art.[11] It is not yet handled with the same analytical rigor as the analogous "sales call problem" in commercial marketing.

The candidate's organization must also think of specific promotional ideas to draw attention to the candidate. For he is competing not only against his specific opponents but also against candidates for other races, against detergent and soft drink commercials, against the soap operas, against the news reporting of thousands of other things happening in the world. The job is one of *event management*—that is, the staging of events designed to draw attention to the candidate. Examples include the announced plan to walk from one end of the city to the other meeting the voters, the calling of a special news conference to make an important announcement, and the appearance at a major sports event. At the same time, it is important not to create too many events and not to seem to be headline grabbing for its own sake.

A Volunteer Worker Program.   Although the candidate cannot distribute himself to reach every voter, he can achieve some of the effect by using agents, particularly speakers and volunteer workers. A speakers' bureau consists of various supporters who are articulate and individually effective with different types of groups. There should be every attempt to match the speaker to the audience: an older man should speak to the senior citizens, a woman to women's organizations, and a college student to college audiences. Studies of personal selling effectiveness indicate that effectiveness correlates with the degree of match between speaker and audience.[12] In addition, the candidate needs various volunteers who would carry out the multitude of tasks involved in an electoral campaign, including preparing mailings, canvassing and registering voters, providing transportation, and policing elections.

Managing the volunteers effectively has many similarities to the problem of managing a sales force effectively. The workers must be kept enthusiastic, work quotas must be set, accomplishments monitored. The organization must train these volunteers in what to say, when to call, how long to stay, and what to report back. Because the volunteers are a scarce resource, they must be managed as carefully as the money that the candidate commands.

Through the use of marketing research, product concept development, and communication and distribution planning, the candidate is prepared to wage a good fight for votes. These techniques do not guarantee victory, because increasingly candidates are resorting to modern marketing planning, and their efforts are somewhat self-cancelling. Conscious marketing planning only promises to maximize the candidate's potential. It cannot ordinarily sell a bad candidate; and lack of careful marketing planning will not necessarily harm a good candidate. It provides a form of insurance that the candidate's campaign planning is systematic, efficient, and voter-oriented.

GETTING REELECTED

The candidate who wins the office does not leave behind all of his promises, unless he is not interested in reelection. Most candidates will seek reelection and must fulfill the product expectations they generated during the campaign. They must live up to the concept they sold. The personality that the candidate sold early in his career tends, because of many forces, to stay with him afterward.

The reelection problem is analogous in marketing to the repeat sales problem. Business marketers who launch a new product are interested not only in first-time sales but also in repeat sales. It is only through repeat sales that the returns more than cover the investment. The key to repeat sales, in the marketer's mind, is the delivery of real satisfaction to the buyer. It is real satisfaction that will lead the buyer to pick the same product again in spite of new and possibly more colorful products vying for his attention.

But the delivery of customer satisfaction can mean a number of things. In the realm of commercial products, there are three types of satisfaction that can be offered to the buyers of a particular product, such as a particular brand of car. The first is to make sure that the car offers *good performance*—that is, it yields the functional benefits that were promised and expected. In the political realm, this is analogous to the elected official actually carrying out his campaign promises and doing the things he said he would. The second is to make the car and its service very accessible to the buyers, which is a problem in *good organization*. In the political realm, good organization means that the elected official builds an organization that carries out various services in the community, organizes the voters, and so on. The third is to keep the product salient and interesting to the public, the problem of *good rhetoric*. In the political realm, this means that the official must fashion symbols during his administration that constantly and favorably remind the voters of him. All of the three strategies for getting reelected can be pursued simultaneously, although many elected officials often emphasize one more than the others.

Performance

While in office, the elected official will build up a certain record that will come under scrutiny in the next election. This record provides some of the basis for his reelection theme and also for the opposition's attacks upon him. In general, he wants this record to be a good one. He wants to be able to say that he carried out, or tried to carry out, most of his campaign pledges. He wants to say that he has fulfilled the image voters had of him, that he met new issues as they expected the kind of man they elected to meet them.

Some elected officials do not attempt to fulfill the voters' expectations too soon. They want to generate a steady stream or a crescendoing stream of favorable news. They do not want to be a product that satisfies too soon and then bores for the rest of the time. They want to achieve peak effectiveness as the next election approaches.

Organization

Although some elected officials attempt to rest their major case for reelection on their performance in office, others decide to rely more on building an organization that will be effective in raising money and getting votes at the next election. While in office, they extend a lot of favors to various groups in exchange for future political support. The favors include legislative support, patronage jobs, and services that count in building future funds and supporters. They attempt to create a machine that reaches into every ward and is ready to pull in the votes during election day.

It cannot be settled in the abstract whether organization building or good performance will count more in the next election. In marketing terms, organization building is a "push" strategy and good performance is a "pull" strategy. Where the electorate is underprivileged and uneducated, a strategy of favors and organization may be superior to a strategy of performance. The reverse might be true in a voting district with a well-educated electorate.

Rhetoric

A third strategy open to the elected official is that of rhetoric with which he hopes to fashion the appearance of a favorable record and opposition to those who would thwart the people's interests. This might be used by the office-holder who lacks the skills to get legislation through or to build an effective organization but who will exploit his personal appeal to the voters. He trades largely on image and hopes to provide voters with the symbolic reassurance they need from the occupant of that office.

Hoping to win with superior rhetoric is the most tenuous basis for attempting to gain reelection. It may work because of an apathetic, ignorant, or cynical electorate or ineffectual opponents, but generally has higher risk characteristics than the other two strategies for reelection.

Conclusion

Throughout the chapter, we have examined the marketing approaches to getting elected and staying elected and not the moral questions that any of these methods may involve. None of these methods is illegal or unethical and indeed they constitute the standard of practice commonly found in political campaigning. It can further be argued that these methods deserve open discussion so that they are available to all sides in an election contest.

The ultimate question is whether the voters will get better elected officials or worse ones as a result of the growing marketing sophistication. Will the election go to the richest, the shrewdest, or the "best" candidates? Will the nation be better off if their elected officials simply mold themselves to the voters' wishes or if they promote independent views and attempt to bring the voters along? Whether politicians should lead or follow is a classic question in democratic theory and not to be resolved here. A marketing orientation means that even the politician who wants to lead must seek to understand his markets and their basic needs and aspirations. If he formulates benefits and promises in relation to their needs and delivers them after election, this should ultimately increase public satisfaction and the voters' sense of politically responsive institutions.

SUMMARY

Political campaigning for office has always had a marketing character, although in recent years much sophistication has been added in the form of scientific polling, computer analysis of voting patterns, mass advertising, and professional campaign management. The office-seeker who wishes to maximize his votes would do well to analyze the problem in marketing terms. He has to join a party, be nominated for office, win a primary, and win the election. He is essentially a new product looking for a successful launch in a voters' market. He must research the makeup and motivations of his market; develop an appropriate and effective product concept; and lay careful plans for the communication and distribution of his image. Once he achieves office, he must develop satisfaction for the voters through some blend of good performance, good organization, and good rhetoric. To the extent that office-seekers and office-holders orient themselves to voter satisfaction, better performance should occur in the political sphere.

NOTES

1. E. B. Weiss, "Political Advertising Blackens the Other Eye of the Ad Business," *Advertising Age*, February 12, 1973, pp. 35–38.
2. Theodore White, *The Making of the President 1960* (New York: Atheneum House, Inc., 1961).
3. Joe McGinness, *The Selling of the President 1968* (New York: Trident Press, 1969).
4. See Stanley Kelly, *Professional Public Relations and Political Power* (Baltimore, Md.: The Johns Hopkins Press, 1956); E. Glick, *The New Methodology* (Washington, D.C.: The American Institute for Political Communication, 1967); and Dan Nimmo, *The Political Persuaders* (Englewood Cliffs, N.J.: Prentice-Hall, Inc., 1970).
5. Glick, *The New Methodology*, p. 1.
6. Nimmo, *The Political Persuaders*, pp. 67–68.

7. For a discussion of these techniques, see David A. Aaker, ed., *Multivariate Analysis in Marketing: Theory and Application* (Belmont, Calif.: Wadsworth Publishing Co., 1971).

8. There are some exceptions. Some elaborate vote prediction simulation models have been built, usually in connection with presidential campaigning. See, for example, Ithiel de Sola Pool and Robert Abelson, "The Simulmatics Project," *Public Opinion Quarterly* (Summer 1961), pp. 167–83.

9. See Chapter 6, pp. 110–14.

10. McGinness, *Selling of the President.*

11. See "How a 'Scheduler' Plans His Candidate's Time for Most Efficiency," *Wall Street Journal*, March 1, 1972.

12. Franklin B. Evans, "Selling as a Dyadic Relationship—a New Approach," *The American Behavioral Scientist* (May 1963), pp. 76–79.

QUESTIONS

1. During the political campaign of Governor Dan Walker of Illinois, several campaign workers were asked whether they felt they were "marketing" Dan Walker to the public. For many, the word "marketing" seemed to have a dirty connotation. They were "not selling" Dan Walker for Governor. There was "no buying of votes" with payoffs of patronage jobs. They were instead presenting a human being to the people, showing them how he could cure the ills of Illinois government and give everyone a better life. What do you think of the workers' reaction?

2. How important are such things as a political candidate's name, sex, and occupation?

3. "Political advertising blackens advertising's other eye." Comment and discuss.

4. Where did George McGovern go wrong in his 1972 presidential campaign? Answer this question as a marketing consultant might answer it.

5. Compare the advantages that an incumbent candidate has over his rivals to those that an established brand of cereals, soft drinks, or razor blades has over its new competitors.

Case Studies

1. NORTHEASTERN ILLINOIS PLANNING
COMMISSION—MARKETING A REGIONAL PLAN *

In 1957 the Illinois General Assembly established the Northeastern Illinois Planning Commission (NIPC) to do the planning for the six county area surrounding Chicago and to insure "the welfare, health, prosperity, moral and general well-being of all the people of this state." The legislators further directed NIPC to "develop and adopt . . . a comprehensive plan . . . and to cooperate with various units of government in comprehensive planning for further growth and development."

In 1968 the NIPC finally published *The Comprehensive General Plan for the Development of the Northeastern Illinois Counties Area.* The comprehensive plan proposed a "finger growth concept" for the regional development of the area surrounding Chicago. New regional development would radiate out of Chicago in fingers and the area between the fingers would be open spaces in the form of farms, parks, and forest preserves.

* Case draws upon research by Scott Rutherford.

Having proposed this plan, the NIPC was not sure of what further responsibilities it should undertake. Most of the nineteen members of the commission saw their role as simply supplying the "facts" to the local governments and agencies who presumably thereafter would debate and hopefully adopt their recommendations. A few of the members, however, felt that the planning agency should be responsible for systematic advocacy and promotion of the plan. They felt that without advocacy and promotion, the citizens of Chicago would not know about the plan and it was not likely to be debated and adopted.

This small group defended a "promotional orientation" by citing the famous *Burnham Plan of Chicago* of 1909. Following the World's Columbian Exposition in Chicago in 1893, many citizens were impressed by the planning and development done for this fair and wondered if the same type of planning could be applied on a larger scale to the entire city. For fifteen years following the fair The Merchants Club and The Commercial Club (whose membership included the one hundred most prominent and influential figures in retailing, manufacturing, and banking) worked at various times on general plans for Chicago. However, it was not until 1907 when these two clubs merged, combined their plans, and enlisted the assistance of Daniel Burnham that real progress on a plan was realized. The Plan was published in 1909 by the Commercial Club and was well received both locally and nationally. It called for developing a beautiful lake front, many parks, wide boulevards, forest preserves, a railroad terminal, harbor facilities, and many other improvements.

The Plan's authors realized that they would necessarily have to have the backing of the city agencies and convinced the mayor to appoint a Chicago Plan Commission to administer the Plan. The Plan Commission consisted of the leaders of every influential group in Chicago (three hundred and twenty-eight citizens). Charles H. Wacker was appointed as chairman of the Chicago Plan Commission and Walter D. Moody was appointed managing director. Moody saw his job as chiefly "scientific promotion" and took the responsibility of marketing Burnham's plan to the citizens of Chicago. He contended that "there will be no marked accomplishment in city planning in the United States until promotional effort of the right sort is employed."

The Chicago Plan Commission attempted to rally the business, industrial, and financial groups plus the citizens as a whole, correctly assuming if these interests were satisfied the legislators would fall in line too. Because the Plan originated with the economic interests in the first place, the process of adding additional and maintaining existing support was relatively easy. Burnham and others appealed to the business leaders' sense of community and civic pride. In a speech before The Merchants Club Burnham said:

> You are the men who have made Chicago, who have fought her battles, who have never been content to pause and rest after deeds accomplished, but whose faces have always been turned toward the future, and whose motto has ever been "I will."

For the more economic-minded businessman, Burnham detailed the expected economic benefits of the Chicago Plan:

> You all know there is a tendency among our well-to-do people to spend much time and money elsewhere, and that this tendency has been rapidly growing in late years. We have been running away to Cairo, Athens, the Riviera, Paris, and Vienna, because life at home is not so pleasant as in these fashionable centres. Thus a constant drain upon the resources of the town has been going on. No one has estimated the number of millions of money made here in Chicago and expended elsewhere, but the sum must be a large one. . . . Thousands of people all over the country are becoming wealthy, and thousands are already so. These people go to New York to live, but many would come here if we should create conditions which would attract them. . . . Greece is still living on money brought there by visitors, who are attracted principally by the public improvements of Pericles 2300 years ago.

The most difficult task was to enlist the support of the general public, most of whom had neither the civic vision nor the financial stake in seeing the Plan implemented as did Chicago's leaders. Selling the Plan to the citizens was the responsibility of Wacker and Moody of the Plan Commission. This was critical, for without popular support to pass bonds the Plan had little chance of success.

Contending that "a well-grounded plan of operation, backed by wisdom and insistent endeavor, cannot fail," Moody and Wacker set out to insure popular support for the *Plan of Chicago*. Given their limited funds, most of their early efforts were concentrated on the press. They set out immediately to establish strong harmonious bonds with the editors and publishers of Chicago's newspapers. They supplied the newsmen with a never-ending supply of reports, projections, maps, drawings, and technical support. The newspapers responded well with countless day-to-day articles and numerous Sunday Supplement features. Any civic improvement related to the Plan was singled out and supplied as evidence that Chicago was indeed moving toward the "City Beautiful" described in the Plan.

In addition to the mass media effort, the Commission mailed special pamphlets (93 pages long) to *all* property owners and renters above a certain rent level. The planners also made members of their staff available to groups seeking speakers to explain the Plan in various meetings. Community meetings at schools were new at that time and drew as many as 1,500 people. To insure lecture attendance they mailed a circular to people in the community including *two free family tickets* to the lecture. In a seven-year period 400 of these lectures were delivered, reaching nearly 8 percent of Chicago's population. To supplement the lecture series, a movie entitled "A Tale of One City" was shown at sixty Chicago theaters. The movie contrasted the Plan proposals with existing conditions and reached another 8 percent of Chicago's population.

One of the most creative and effective tactics was a school textbook written by Walter Moody entitled *Wacker's Manual of the Plan of Chicago* which was adopted by the Chicago School Board in 1912. The book was used as a standard text in the eighth-grade curriculum to insure exposure to those not continuing to high school. The purpose of the text is best stated by Moody in his introduction to the book intended for the teachers:

> This book is intended to convince the child that he owes loyalty to the city that gave him his education and offers him an opportunity to enter any one of her great fields of industrial or professional activity. It seems advisable to give a number of questions at the end of each chapter to assist the child in this rather difficult subject. In seeking answers to these questions the school child will instill in his mind a permanent interest in the civic welfare of Chicago that will be an immense benefit to the future of our city. Proper emphasis has been given to the history of great cities of the past and to the causes that led to their power. It is the earnest purpose of the author to make the child feel that in him rests the responsibility of assisting Chicago to attain her future greatness. The cooperation of the instructor is earnestly sought for in teaching the child how he may lend assistance in this work. It is the firm belief of the author that the success of the Plan of Chicago depends on the hold it has in the hearts of the city's future citizens.

The book had thought-provoking questions at the end of the chapters such as:

> Why can the policies of the Chicago Plan Commission be relied upon as the right ones?
>
> Why is the Plan of Chicago superior to that of any other city, foreign or otherwise?
>
> What is one of the clearest lessons taught in the magnificent Plan of Chicago?

The text undoubtedly had an impact on the minds of Chicago's young as well as their parents.

The success of these efforts was measured by the people's support in passing bond issues to provide for implementing many facets of the Chicago Plan. It was the success of the 1909 Chicago Plan that led the minority of members on the Northeastern Illinois Planning Commission to feel that similar promotional activity was their duty and their right if Chicago was ever to adopt the "finger growth concept."

Questions

1. Was the Burnham Plan of Chicago brought to the people of Chicago under the sales concept or the marketing concept? Do you agree with the methods used by the Chicago Plan Commission?

2. How do you think the Northeastern Illinois Planning Commission should view its responsibilities and authority for the marketing of the "finger growth plan"?

3. Suppose the NIPC decides to undertake responsibility for marketing the Chicago Plan. Identify the main target publics and develop an overall marketing strategy.

2. THE BRIGHAM* FOUNDATION— DEMARKETING AN ART MUSEUM **

The Brigham Foundation, located in a fashionable, wealthy suburb on the "Main Line" of Philadelphia, operates the renowned Brigham Museum. The museum, once the private estate of the Brigham family (of patent medicine fame), houses perhaps the finest and most extensive private collection of impressionism in the United States and is an art lover's Xanadu. The finest examples of Renoir, Cezanne, Van Gogh, Picasso, etc., are on display and number in the hundreds.

Unfortunately, this museum actively "demarkets" in a number of areas with the expressed desire to keeping people from attending the museum. Originally the demarketing objective was apparently carried out by simply forbidding anyone from entering the museum who disagreed with the Brigham's views on art. (The family produced art critics whose books are notable in the art field.) Such undue harassment was brought

---

* Name disguised.
** Case was prepared by Louis W. Hirschmann under the direction of the author.

to an end when the Brigham Foundation was taken to court in order to force the museum to open to the public, which it presently is, to a limited extent.

Most recently, the foundation demarkets its museum in a number of interesting ways. First, taking color photographs of the paintings is forbidden in the museum, even by the Chairman of the Art History Department at the University of Pennsylvania. Second, lighting is generally poor in the museum, making some of the great canvases often hidden in shadow. Third, canvases are stacked high on walls rising up to 30 feet, and few of the paintings are identified, so one doesn't know what one is looking at unless one is knowledgeable. Fourth, tours are not given and there are no pamphlets available explaining where paintings are located, as is common in many museums. Fifth, there are no chairs on which to sit, and the museum is devoid of any resting places, furniture, etc.—again a situation uncommon in many museums. Sixth, nothing can be carried into the museum proper, including a coat, which must be checked in the basement. Seventh, only 100 persons by appointment 3 days per week are allowed to enter the museum for $1.50, and another 100, first-come first-served, are also allowed to enter on these days, an extremely unusual practice. Finally, there are no signs in town informing interested visitors of the locale of the museum.

In short, although the art is magnificent, and worth the visit, the difficulty associated with the visit makes the trip somewhat uncomfortable. However, positive aspects resulting from the demarketing effort include the privacy and quiet associated with so few visitors to the museum and the feeling that one is truly acquiring a rich experience limited to the few who are willing to put up with the listed unpleasantries.

The reasons for the demarketing effort can be only conjectured. Some possibilities include: an elitist family who, perhaps pressured into making their art collection into a foundation for tax reasons, wants to "punish the public" for their predicament; second, an overzealous staff which, attempting to preserve such a great collection, goes to absurd lengths to keep as many people as possible from visiting in order to avoid vandalism, damage, etc.; and finally, an overly protective security system that watches the art so carefully that its members get in the way of the viewing public.

Questions

1. Is the museum's management using demarketing in the most skillful way? Might their style of demarketing backfire? What social issues are raised by the demarketing effort?

2. What are alternative objectives that this museum might adopt?

3. Choose an alternative objective and propose museum marketing policies that would achieve this objective.

3. THE UNITED STATES ARMY—
ATTRACTING VOLUNTARY ENLISTMENTS *

In fiscal year 1974, the United States Army Recruiting Command (USAREC) failed to reach its enlistment objective of 125,000. Only 107,302 enlistments were recorded during this time period—about 86 percent of the objective. The Army was disturbed by the performance of USAREC and wanted to see it improved. It was especially concerned about how to recruit *more high school graduates* because Congress had dictated that funds for recruiting would only be appropriated if 55 percent of the enlistees had graduated from high school. The Army was also concerned about losing potential enlistees to the Navy, Air Force, and Marines.

In 1974, the management positions in USAREC were filled by career soldiers or Department of Defense civilians. There was a high turnover in personnel because the Army and Defense Department tend to transfer personnel approximately once every three years. Most of the marketing experience of the management personnel was of the "on-the-job training" variety.

The local recruiters of USAREC were competent, noncommissioned officers (staff sergeants and sergeants first class) selected for recruiter duty because they looked impressive, were articulate, and were judged capable of working independent of close supervision. New recruiters were put through a one-year probationary period before they were appointed to permanent recruiter duty. Turnover during this one-year period was high.

USAREC relied heavily on print advertising in a large number of publications to help it recruit high school graduates. Seven different *appeal categories* were used in the print ads and these categories were adjusted quarterly to take account of past results. The categories that were used in March 1974 and the percent of the advertising budget spent on each are shown below:

USAREC also supplemented its print campaigns with outdoor advertising.

---

* Case was prepared by Paul Bloom, based on research by Captain Albert R. Brownfield, III.

Appeal Category	Percent of Budget
Two-year option	31%
Jobs and skill training	24
Travel choice, unit of choice	18
Influencers (general)	12
Education	7
Challenge and adventure	6
Pay and benefits	2
	100%

USAREC continuously monitored the effectiveness of its advertising through seven different research programs. It compiled the following "cost per inquiry" figures for October 1973, broken down by type of appeal:

Travel choice, unit of choice	$110.39
Influencers	55.16
Challenge and adventure	40.91
Education	27.41
Jobs and skill training	21.19
Pay and benefits	15.93

The broadcast media was not used for advertising because of a legal restriction against the buying of broadcast time by any of the armed services.

Local recruiters were encouraged to develop their own recruiting techniques. Guidance on the "best" ways to contact high school students and graduates was supplied in annual plans issued by the USAREC Directorate of Recruiting Operations. The plans assumed that recruiters would be assisted willingly in their efforts by substantial numbers of school guidance counselors and administrators, and they therefore began with suggestions on how to gain access to these important influencers. They listed various national, regional, state, and local educational conventions the recruiters could attend. They also described procedures to be used in getting Army bands to support school social functions and athletic events, and gave advice on such interest-generating activities as tours of local Army installations by student prospects, Army films of nationally important sports events (complete with Army commercials), and demonstrations by the "Golden Knights" Army Parachuting team.

USAREC devoted considerable effort to acquainting itself with the characteristics of the high school graduate market segment. An annual survey of 3,000 subjects was conducted by the Army's civilian advertising agency, N. W. Ayer and Son, Inc., and information was continually accumulated from local recruiters, basic training centers, and independent research done by academicians and students. A short summary of the findings of this research follows:

1. The climate for enlistment of all categories of prospects was continually improving.

2. Thirteen percent of noncollege high school graduates age 17 to 21 were classified as reasonable prospects for enlistment. The group tended to contain disproportionate numbers at the lower end of the age bracket, blacks, Southerners, and men and women with no clearcut goals.

3. The opportunities offered by the Army for training and self-development ranked high among reasons high school graduates volunteered for Army service.

4. Army enlistment was unlikely unless the prospect was encouraged in his decision by someone important to him.

Questions

1. Formulate a marketing plan which would help USAREC recruit more high school graduates. Should USAREC try to "demarket" Army service to "less desirable" prospects?

2. What marketing goals should USAREC establish in relation to other key publics, such as Congress, the other services, and the general public?

4. TOWNSEND COLLEGE *—ATTRACTING STUDENTS IN THE FACE OF ENROLLMENT DECLINES **

In the spring of 1974, Allen Harris, Dean of Admissions of Townsend College, began his annual review of the Admissions Department's programs. The number of applicants to Townsend had been declining in recent years in line with the experience of similar institutions. The quality of the applicants as measured by College Board scores had also been dropping. The school was having difficulty balancing its budget, and all salaries had been frozen; tuition, third highest in the state, had been climbing moderately.

* Name disguised.
** Case was prepared by Steve Gregory and the author.

Townsend College was a private college of liberal arts and sciences; it had no graduate program, preferring to concentrate on quality undergraduate education. It was small, with about 1,000 students—the student-faculty ratio was 12 to 1. It was located in a parklike area near the center of a major Southern city. Townsend had a long and distinguished history of dedication to the concept of liberal education, and had earned a reputation for academic excellence in the five Southern states from which the bulk of its student population was drawn. Although it had won grants from the major foundations, and national acclaim for some of its faculty, it was little known outside of this region.

The recruitment of students had historically been a minor function at Townsend. Old-line administrators and faculty felt that anything more than a minimal effort was typical of a lower-status school, and preferred to rely on the attractions of the school's academic program. The position of dean of admissions was an academic position, reporting to the vice-president for academic affairs; Harris was a former professor of Religion. Much of the actual recruiting had been done by the wife of a faculty member until she was replaced by a specialist in student personnel activities. The school had typically offered a temporary nine-month recruiting position to one of its recent graduates to round out the complement of admissions officers.

The bulk of the recruiting program consisted of visits to high schools in selected areas by admissions personnel. Although these visits usually involved small groups of students in the counselor's office at the high school, presentations to large groups were made occasionally depending on the counselor's needs. Other contacts were developed informally through other sources, including current students and faculty, alumni, and the Protestant denomination with which Townsend was affiliated. Admissions officers acted as interviewers when these prospects visited the campus. Townsend possessed a uniquely attractive collegiate Gothic campus, and many felt this was one of its strongest recruiting attractions.

Overall admissions policy was set by a faculty committee on admissions and student aid. For example, the committee has narrowly approved a change in policy that resulted in the acceptance of the American College Test (ACT) as a suitable indicator of applicant quality. Formerly, only the Scholastic Aptitude Test of the College Entrance Examination Board (SAT) had been accepted, and critics in the school attacked the new policy as a lowering of standards. Proponents pointed out that the ACT was offered in more high schools than the SAT, and that this would increase the potential pool of applicants. Actual admissions decisions were made by a subcommittee of the larger body.

Members of the admissions committee were divided over the best way to reverse the declining trend in enrollment. Dr. Sam Chase, Chairman of the Department of Economics, said the college should keep its tuition rate down so that the college could be afforded by a larger number of students who want to attend a private college. He felt that students were highly sensitive to competitive tuition costs in times of inflation. To keep tuition down, he recommended larger classes, greater teaching loads for faculty, minimal pay increases, reduced administrative costs, and so on. Needless to say, his views were not appreciated by most other members of the committee.

Dr. Thomas Sharp of the business department argued that the solution lay in a program of more aggressive promotion. He said a college must not be ashamed to use the methods of promotion that industry used to stimulate customer interest. He cited other colleges that had recently adopted hard-sell merchandising techniques and enjoyed enrollment increases. St. Joseph's College, a 1,100-student Roman Catholic private school in Rensselaer, Indiana, put advertising in *Seventeen* magazine, bought commercials on Chicago and Indianapolis rock radio stations, and sent a mass mailing to students whose names were provided by the Student Search Service of the College Entrance Examination Board. Their freshmen class increased 40 percent in two years. The same school offered tuition rebates to students who successfully recruited other students—at $100 for each student who actually enrolled up to the limit of total tuition. (This was dropped later because of strong criticism from other colleges.) Another college distributed promotional Frisbees to students on spring break in Fort Lauderdale. Dr. Sharp summarized by saying that the name of the game was exposure and motivated selling.

Dr. Roger Alexander of the English department found all of this highly offensive. "Education is not a commodity to be sold like a common bar of soap. Gimmicks would debase education and attract people to college for the wrong reasons. There would be an endless battle to think up the next gimmick, which might one day include money-back guarantees and full refunds for courses and professors that you don't like. No, the answer is to improve education in the classroom, make our classes small, set a high academic standard, and let our quality speak for itself."

In addition to these different views, members of the admissions committee were split over whether Townsend College should confine recruitment activity to the Southern states which traditionally supplied most of its students or venture into the North and East in an effort to reduce its dependence on one region of the country and to diversify its student body.

Dean Harris pondered these issues as he faced the task of formu-

lating a coherent recruitment and admissions plan for Townsend College.
A report from The Carnegie Commission on Higher Education recently
came across his desk, estimating that national enrollment for the coming
September would be down 600,000 students from the 9.6 million who
were attending college the previous year.

Questions

1. What are the major marketing issues and alternatives facing
Townsend College?

2. Formulate marketing objectives and a recruitment strategy for
Townsend.

5. MINNEAPOLIS PARKS AND RECREATION DEPARTMENT—DECIDING AMONG RECREATIONAL PRODUCTS

The city of Minneapolis, Minnesota, is an attractive
modern city that boasts of 153 parks and 22 lakes. One of these parks is
Minnehaha Park, renowned for Minnehaha Falls mentioned in Long-
fellow's "Song of Hiawatha." The various parks have playgrounds, rose
gardens, golf courses, and swimming pools. Managing these parks is in
the hands of the Minneapolis Parks and Recreation Department.

The superintendent of the Minneapolis Parks and Recreation Department sees public parks as providing a product called *outdoor recreation*.
Outdoor reacreation yields three primary utilities. The first is *immediate
enjoyment*—that is, a sense of pleasure experienced immediately before,
during, and after participation in outdoor recreation. The second is *personal long-term benefits*, which consist of physical and mental benefits
associated with outdoor exercise and sport. The third is *benefits to the
community as a whole*, which consist of the conservation of the natural
environment and ecology.

Park administrators operate with severely limited budgets and must
make difficult choices among alternative projects such as playgrounds,
baseball fields, tennis courts, bicycle paths, and safety patrols. Too often
these choices are made on the basis of subjective judgment unaided by
any consumer research and responding to political pressures. For example,
an organized group of parents demanding a playground will probably
get it without any benefit-cost comparison being made to other possible
projects.

Fortunately, parks departments throughout the country are beginning to make more use of benefit-cost analysis to analyze competing
projects. The superintendent of the Minneapolis Parks and Recreation

Department found an opportunity to try out benefit-cost analysis for one of the small parks where two groups of citizens were pressing for two competing recreational projects. The superintendent felt that only one of these projects could be built and decided to use benefit-cost analysis as an aid in making a rational choice.

The two competing proposals were as follows:

1. *A four-court outdoor tennis court.* The total cost would be $30,000 to build and $1,000 a year to maintain. The courts would be usable from the beginning of April to the beginning of October. There were many people living near the park and about 200 persons presently played tennis.

2. *A bicycle path around the perimeter of the park.* This path would cost about $60,000 to construct and $600 a year to maintain. The path would be usable from April to October. There were many bicyclists in the area.

The superintendent turned the problem over to the recreational department director with the request that a quantitative analysis of the benefits and costs be prepared. The director worked on the problem during the week and finally turned in the following analysis to the superintendent:

Tennis Court

1. The tennis courts would be in constant use for 6 months (180 days) of the year. Each hour, 8 people would be playing (2 players per court times 4 courts). The court would be open for 12 hours a day (8 A.M. to 8 P.M.), which means 96 players a day (12 × 8). This means 17,280 players per year (96 × 180). Over 20 years, this means 345,600 users.

2. The total cost of the courts over 20 years consists of a $30,000 initial cost and a $20,000 maintenance cost ($1,000 a year). Thus the total out-of-pocket cost would be $50,000.

3. Therefore the cost per hourly user of the tennis court is 15¢ ($50,000/345,600). That is, the cost to society of producing the benefits of playing a single game is 15¢.

Bicycle Path

1. The bicycle path would be usable for 6 months (180 days) a year. About 20 riders would be found riding it per hour. The path would be usable for 12 hours a day (8 A.M. to 8 P.M.), which means about 240 riders a day. This means 43,200 riders per year (240 × 180). Over 20 years, this means 864,000 riders.

2. The total cost of the bicycle path over 20 years consists of a $60,000

initial cost and a $12,000 maintenance cost ($600 × 20), or $72,000 altogether.
3. Therefore the cost per ride is 8¢ ($72,000/864,000). That is, the cost to society of producing the benefits of a bike ride is 8¢.

The recreation director's report concluded:

If we make the assumption that the benefit one person gets from riding a bike is the same as another person gets from playing tennis, then the bicycle path is the superior social good. It costs only 8¢ to produce a bike-riding benefit whereas it would cost 15¢ to produce a tennis-game benefit.

Questions

1. Do you think benefit-cost analysis is the best way for a park district to choose between two competing social goods that a public wants? What alternative methods might be used?

2. Do you agree with the quantitative assumptions used in putting together the benefit-cost analysis in this case?

3. Can you think of some qualitative considerations that should be added to the analysis? Which project would you favor and why?

6. THE CHICAGO TRANSIT AUTHORITY—PRICING AND MARKETING URBAN MASS TRANSIT

The Chicago Transit Authority, a self-regulating municipal corporation with a board of directors appointed by the mayor of Chicago and governor of Illinois, operates the bus and primary mass transportation system within the city of Chicago. Under its service are 135 bus routes with 2,050 miles and six mass transit routes with 89 miles of rail rights of way. The CTA transports about 1.2 million people daily with 24 hours a day of service.

Over the years, the CTA has experienced a dramatic decline in ridership. In 1947, the CTA had 1,150 million originating revenue passengers; by 1961, ridership sank to 500 million where it stabilized until 1967; thereafter it fell another 20 percent to 400 million by the year 1973. The declining ridership came at a time of rising operating and capital costs. The CTA responded to the rising costs with fare increases, which only led to further declines in ridership.

The decline in ridership was occurring because of the movement of people and industry to the suburbs, the growth in automobile ownership, and the preference for auto travel. The CTA tried to reverse the decline by sporadic advertising campaigns, service improvements, and the like. These steps did not appear to be based on careful market analysis or marketing planning. Marketing research into the perceptions and preferences of actual and potential riders was minimal. In 1970, however, the CTA Research and Planning Department carried out a study to determine what factors would attract potential riders to mass transit. The following factors were identified:

1. More frequent, faster, dependable service
2. More comfort
3. More parking near the stations
4. Employee courtesy
5. Greater promotion—public relations

These factors, however, were not ranked in importance.

In its pricing policy, the CTA uses *standard fares* on all forms of transit and *exact fares* on buses. Both of these measures reduce collection time and costs. Standard fares are believed to reduce customer confusion. Zone fares have been considered as a means of generating more revenue but have been rejected because of the greater expense they would entail. Exact fare policy is a consumer nuisance, but it requires less standstill time by a driver to make change and it discourages would-be criminals from trying to hold up bus drivers.

CTA management does not like to resort to fare increases because they reduce ridership each time and generate great political and public opposition and hostility. From 1951 through 1964, the base fare stayed at 25¢. The fare was raised to 45¢ in 1970, and some zone fares were established in certain suburbs as high as 85¢. Fare increases generate slightly more revenue at the price of fewer riders. Milton Pikarsky, the CTA's current director, believes that *fare reductions* would be the greatest single stimulus to increase ridership, even more than improvements in service and equipment. In this spirit, CTA has experimented in recent years with selective fare reductions. Reduced fares for senior citizens and students in off-peak hours have stimulated demand somewhat and have reduced the economic hardship for these "captive" riders. An off-peak-hour "shoppers' special" is being implemented on the south side to see whether a lowered fare would lead a sufficient number of downtown shoppers to leave a little later and return home a little earlier. As many as 20 percent of the riders in rush hour are on shopping trips or errands that could be diverted to other times to reduce peak traffic loads. The CTA also experimented with 50 percent fare reductions for four Sundays in March 1974 and experienced an encouraging increase in Sunday ridership.

CTA policy makers, however, are quite divided over the best strategy for promoting mass transit in the long run. They all agree on the desirability of attracting more people to mass transit as a partial solution to the energy shortage and to environmental pollution. For example, a bus, which is equivalent in capacity to 25 autos, produces less pollution than a single automobile. But they differ on the best strategy to pursue. At least four different groups can be distinguished.

The first group would like to see more aggressive fare experimentation. They point to the city of Atlanta, which lowered bus fares in 1972 from 24¢ to 15¢, and traffic rose 20 percent, with 40 percent of the new bus passengers being former car drivers. They also cite the city of Seattle's one-year experiment offering free bus transportation in downtown Seattle. The number of riders doubled, business was stimulated, and downtown traffic and air pollution was reduced. The city of Seattle paid the deficit and feels that the benefits far exceeded the costs.

A second group within the CTA believes that selective fare reductions generate increased ridership only when these fare reductions are substantial, and that the price elasticity is still likely to be less than one which means increased deficits for the CTA. They strongly believe that demand elasticities are significantly greater for service improvements than for fare changes. They favor increasing the number of routes and frequency of service to reduce door-to-door travel time. They also favor better equipment as something that would draw more middle-class riders.

A third group favors increased investment in underground rail systems as opposed to buses. These systems can carry more people and may attract more riders because they are faster. Their costly construction is paid mainly out of federal funds. Cities like Atlanta, Baltimore, and Washington are digging these expensive systems in the hope that they will bolster the local economy and build local pride. These systems, however, are criticized by others who feel that buses make more sense. They are cheaper, more flexible, and perhaps less energy-consuming. Because travel needs shift, the bus routes can be readily modified whereas the rail systems represent frozen routes.

A fourth group feels that a major effort should be undertaken to influence employers to spread work hours in Chicago so that transit equipment could be used more evenly throughout the day. The CTA has to finance equipment to cover the traffic load at peak commuting time; if peak traffic could be reduced, equipment needs would be less. They see the solution as lying in approaching the largest employers in the Chicago downtown area (department stores, insurance companies, banks, and so forth), and trying to work out a plan for staggered work hours. If different jobs in the Chicago area would start between 7:00 A.M.

and 10:00 A.M., instead of all starting at 9:00 A.M., there would be less peak loading and more passenger comfort.

Questions

1. Formulate a marketing research proposal costing not more than $25,000 for learning about consumer needs, perceptions, preferences, and satisfaction as they relate to opportunities for attracting more commuters to mass transit.

2. How do you think mass transit should be promoted and financed? Formulate a coherent set of objectives and plans.

3. Appraise the present fare system of the CTA. Recommend a set of pricing objectives and a program for implementing them.

7. THE NATIONAL SAFETY COUNCIL— MARKETING AUTO SAFETY SEAT BELTS USAGE *

Motor vehicle accidents represent a major social problem that cost the nation more lives each year than the total Vietnam War battle casualties and more injuries than any other public health problem. The annual cost to the nation has been estimated at $15 billion. Although the death rate per 100 million vehicle miles has been decreasing during the last several years, the total number of deaths, which reached an all-time record in 1969, seems to have stabilized around 55,000 deaths a year. From this total, 23,000 deaths are due to collision between motor vehicles, 18,300 to accidents involving one vehicle only, and 10,600 to accidents involving pedestrians. At the same time, 2 million persons suffer injuries from nonfatal motor vehicle accidents.[1]

The National Safety Council and many other public and private agencies carry out continuous research and programs aimed at mitigating this problem. The *auto safety seat belt* is the best discovered solution to date. This statement is based on an analysis by safety experts of more than 30,000 real-life accidents and more than 3,000 simulated crashes. Massive evidence shows that lap belts are 90 percent efficient for accidents under 50 miles per hour, while lap and shoulder belts are 90 percent efficient up to 60 m.p.h.

Some years ago, safety belts were an optional purchase by motorists and most motorists failed to purchase them. In 1966, The National Highway Safety Bureau's *Motor Vehicle Safety Standard Act* was passed re-

* Case was written by the author based on research by Jean-Louis Chandon and Jean-Noel Kapferer.

quiring all American-made cars to have lap belts for front and rear seats; and in 1968, lap-shoulder belts for front seats became standard equipment.

In spite of the presence of these belts in most cars, seat belt usage has been disappointingly low. A 1971 study of 2,000 American motorists revealed the following levels of seat belt usage: [2]

	Type of Trip (miles each way)		
	Short (25)	Long (26–150)	Cross-country (+150)
Always use	17%	39%	44%
Sometimes	32	26	28
Never use	51	35	28

The data was based on verbal reports, which typically *overstated* actual auto seat belt usage. Furthermore, seat belts are less used where they prove most effective: in metropolitan areas where 95 percent of all trips take place.

Research has been carried on to determine the types of people that avoid using their auto safety seat belts. Safety belt usage appears to be correlated with higher education, nonsmoking while driving, and having a friend or relative who was injured but not killed in a crash. Safety belt usage does not appear to be correlated with sex, age, whether or not the respondent drove to and from work, reports of self-injury in a crash, or having a friend killed in a crash.[3]

Motivational studies have shed light on the potential causes of the low rate of seat belt usage:

> *Realistic causes:* inconvenience; it may wrinkle the clothes
> *Symbolic causes:* myth of the safe ejection; fear of being trapped in a submersion or fire accident.
> *Situational causes:* there are no danger cues in the environment of the driver while sitting in his comfortable car

To increase the rate of use of seat belts, two approaches have been taken in the United States: (1) promotional campaigns at the firm, community, city, state, and national levels; and (2) passive devices such as the *buzzer-light system* and the *starter-interlock belt system*. In the buzzer-light system, a buzzer rings and a light flashes for one minute when the driver starts his car to remind him to wear his belt. In the starter-interlock belt system, the driver cannot start his automobile until he connects his safety belt. All automobiles produced after January 1974 are required to have this system as standard equipment. Some drivers, however, regard these systems as nuisances and hire mechanics to detach them.

The problem of compliance with seat belts led the National Safety Council to hold a meeting with three academic experts who had quite different views on the problem. Below are excerpts from the meeting.

Professor Smith (a benefit-cost expert):   I think the essential problem lies in the assumption that seat belts should be required in the first place. The state, in my opinion, has no right to require persons to pay for and wear these belts if they choose not to. People are not harming anyone but themselves if they choose not to wear a seat belt and are injured. Furthermore, a substantial number of drivers never wear their belts and consequently the belts represent mostly cost without benefit. Nor will a public advertising campaign costing say $1,000,000 do much good. One measure of the benefit would be the *cost per life saved* through this campaign. Suppose we obtain the following results:

Estimated cost of the campaign	$1,000,000
No. of additional people who get into the habit of wearing their safety belt as a result of the campaign	10,000
No. who get into a potentially fatal accident	150
No. whose lives are saved by the seat belt	100
Cost per life saved ($1,000,000/100)	10,000

Now the question is whether this is a worthwhile investment. Certainly saving a life is worth more than $10,000 by any standard that one could name. One's earnings in one year often exceeds this amount. Any individual would gladly pay this amount to live. On the other hand, the proper way to view this expenditure is in relation to the cost of saving lives in other ways. For example, it is estimated that it costs $2,217 to save a life that would have been lost through cervical cancer; and $6,046 to save a life that would have been lost through breast cancer.[4] Public health agencies will want to make wider comparison between programs before deciding which are the most cost-effective in saving lives.

My colleague, Professor Schelling, has published a provocative calculation in which he concludes that seat belts hardly repay wearing them.[5] Suppose it takes the average driver one-half minute per day fastening and unfastening his seat belt. This amounts to two hours per year.

One thousand drivers would use up 2,000 hours in the aggregate, or one man-work year, just in fastening and unfastening seat belts. Now less than one driver in 1,000 is likely to be killed in an automobile crash. In fact, less than one in 10,000 people is likely to be saved by wearing a seat belt. Schelling therefore concluded that they are not an economic proposition on the basis of the time lost in fastening and unfastening them, leaving out entirely the cost of installing them.

Professor Jones (a public health expert): I take a completely opposite view from Professor Smith. People do not always know what is best for them. We have to label certain liquids as poison, we have to require safety features on many appliances and toys, and this is a matter of public responsibility. The person who gets hurt in an accident not only hurts himself but he hurts his family, he requires tremendous attention from others if he survives, and for these reasons, we cannot leave it to individual choice.

Promotional campaigns seem to be an alternative where we use open methods to inform and persuade people of the benefits of wearing belts or the costs of not wearing belts. Unfortunately, these campaigns have largely failed, considering the vast amount of money spent and the low levels of voluntary seat belt usage. Furthermore, these campaigns probably attract those persons who are the least likely to get into accidents in the first place. Those who resist belts are probably the most in need of wearing belts.

I see no choice but to require these belts in all cars in a starter-interlocking system so that the choice is not left to the individual. The ideal system would be "passive," where the driver gets into his car and the belt goes on automatically without human option. This solution has been used effectively in many danger areas. All milk is pasteurized, and drinking water is purified and fluoridated without leaving the choice to the citizen.

Professor Roberts (a marketing expert): I believe that both of you are too quick to write off the social marketing approach; that is, the use of public information and education campaigns, to accomplish the purpose of increasing seat belt usage. If you believe that the individual should have free choice, there is still a need to fully inform him of the benefits of wearing seat belts; otherwise he makes up his mind in ignorance. If you believe that the individual should be required to "harness" himself, there is still a need to convince him so that he does not feel anger and so that he does not hire a mechanic to disengage the equipment.

Actually there is insufficient information available on the effects of seat belt campaigns. The few well-planned studies seem to yield pessimistic conclusions but the fault, in my opinion, is that the messages used in the campaigns were inadequate in the light of the recommendations of the literature and research on communication effectiveness. There has been too much one-sided communication leaving the audience to silently counterargue. Fear messages have been too stark and many viewers have refused to attend to them. Few messages link up with the driver's pattern of entering and starting his car. I think that we should not write off persuasive campaigns until more work is done in the areas of message development and testing.

Questions

1. Which expert do you agree with? Why?

2. Assuming that past persuasive campaigns were not optimal, formulate a new approach to finding and using effective persuasive messages. How much additional seat belt usage do you think your campaign would generate for a given budget? Would this be of sufficient impact in terms of benefits and costs?

Notes

1. *Accident Fact Book, 1971,* National Safety Council, Chicago, 1971.

2. National Analysts, *Motivating Factors in the Use of the Restraint Systems,* Philadelphia, Pa., September 1971.

3. Leon S. Robertson et al., "Factors Associated with Observed Safety Belt Use," *Journal of Health & Social Behavior* (March 1972), pp. 18–24.

4. *The Analyses and Evaluation of Public Expenditures: The PPB System,* U.S. Congress, Joint Economic Committee, Subcommittee on Economy in Government, 1969.

5. Thomas C. Schelling, "The Life You Save May Be Your Own," in Samuel B. Chase, ed., *Problems in Public Expenditure Analysis* (Washington, D.C.: The Brookings Institution, 1968), p. 166.

8. NATIONAL ORGANIZATION OF WOMEN AND THE EQUAL RIGHTS AMENDMENT— MARKETING A SOCIAL CAUSE *

In 1963, Betty Friedan published her best seller *The Feminine Mystique* with its claims about the unhappy domestic lives of college educated, middle- to upper-middle-class married women. Her book spoke poignantly of college-educated women who had married young and found at the age of thirty that life was boring and without meaning.

---

* Case draws upon June Sochen's *Movers and Shakers: American Women Thinkers and Activists, 1900-1970* (New York: Quadrangle, 1973) and other sources.

In 1966, Betty Friedan and others organized The National Organization for Women (NOW). A major impetus was the disappointment of many educated, middle-class women with the lack of action on the Department of Labor's earlier Report of the Commission on the Status of Women. NOW was organized to lobby for "women's interests" in much the same way that the National Association for the Advancement of Colored People (NAACP) lobbied for "black interests." NOW would work within the system and lobby for legal changes in the status of women. The NOW Bill of Rights in 1969 listed the following seven points:

   I. Equal Rights Constitutional Amendment
   II. Enforce Law Banning Sex Discrimination in Employment
   III. Maternity Leave Rights in Employment and in Social Security Benefits
   IV. Tax Deduction for Home and Child Care Expenses for Working Parents
   V. Child Care Day Centers
   VI. Equal and Unsegregated Education
   VII. The Right of Women to Control Their Reproductive Lives

This organization, which started in 1966 with three hundred middle-class women and a few sympathetic men, reached a membership by 1970 of three thousand in sixty-two chapters.

Some women liberationists found NOW too conservative and newer organizations appeared in the late 1960s. One segment, the "politicos," saw the salvation of women to lie in New Left politics and joined with leftist men to fight for basic modifications of capitalism. Another segment, the "radical feminists," called for eschewing male coalitions in order to achieve a higher level of feminine consciousness and power.

The vast majority of women in the United States, however, belonged to none of these groups. Many women passively or actively opposed the women's liberation movement. They thought the women's place was in the home and could see nothing but trouble coming from efforts to upset the traditional relations and roles of men and women.

NOW placed much of its hope for women's rights in the passage of the Equal Rights Amendment to the Constitution. The amendment called for the ending of all discrimination on the basis of sex. In early 1972, Congress passed the Equal Rights Amendment and sent it for ratification to the states. Three-fourths of the states had to adopt this amendment for it to become the law of the land. Hawaii ratified it within hours and by April 1974, 33 states had ratified it with five more to go.

One of the states still to pass ERA is Illinois. The state's leading politicians, Senator Adlai Stevenson, Governor Daniel Walker, and Mayor Richard J. Daley all supported its passage; approving statements were made, such as "I never liked the idea of a subservient woman—that a woman was fit to be a nurse, not a doctor." At the other extreme were the remarks of State Representative Thomas C. Hanahan, who called ERA supporters a bunch of "braless, brainless broads." Even some members within NOW were opposed to the passage of the Equal Rights Amendment. They felt that women would lose the right to protective labor laws, alimony, and exemption from the draft.

NOW had carried on the marketing of ERA on a state-by-state basis. A "market survey" was conducted by the Illinois chapter of NOW to find the attitudes of typical Illinois women toward their roles as women. The findings are summarized below:

1. Women in general perceive discrimination on the job. They believe in equal pay for equal work.
2. Sex-role discrimination was not perceived as evident by these women. These women felt their most important role to be a mother or housewife (only 4.3 percent stated self-fulfillment as their most important role).
3. These women perceived men (their husbands) as rejecting women's groups and thus were influenced in their own rejection of active participation.
4. These women exhibited a high degree of self-confidence. It was felt that there was an underlying fear that new sex roles might threaten their position and consequently their confidence. Rejection of the movement was thus made.
5. These women lacked knowledge about the Equal Rights Amendment (ERA). It was felt that a low level of exposure and selective exposure contributed to this situation.
6. Finally, these women lacked any type of commitment and connection that is required or needed to join any of the aforementioned power groups.

Questions

1. Identify the various target publics to whom NOW should market the Equal Rights Amendment in Illinois.

2. Propose a marketing plan for the marketing of the Equal Rights Amendment.

9. THE FINNISH BUREAU OF TOURISM—
MARKETING A COUNTRY *

Until recently, Finland was a neglected area in the European travel market. It had been seen as too far away from the major

* Case was prepared by the author from notes provided by Heikki Paronen.

tourist centers. Its climate had been regarded as too cold. Its language was unfamiliar. As a result, Finland attracted only a few thousand foreign tourists a year.

During the last ten years, however, there has been a major change in European tourism patterns and tastes. Many travelers have already visited traditional tourist countries such as England, France, Spain, Italy, and Greece. These areas are overcrowded in the summer months. Their prices have been rising constantly. Tourists have shown a growing interest in exploring other countries in search of new experiences.

All these factors led to the discovery of Finland by tourists. Perhaps the most important factor has been the intensive information and marketing activity of the Finnish Bureau of Tourism. The Bureau has directed very heavy advertising campaigns in several countries; and it has made loans to hotel chains and other enterprises working with tourism.

The Finnish Bureau of Tourism, located in the Ministry of Commerce, was created in February 1971. Its responsibilities cover the promotion of foreign tourism to Finland as well as domestic tourism, tourist enterprises and their financing, tourist information, vocational training for tourism, and the surveillance of government tourist property. To carry out its responsibilities, the Bureau has to work effectively with several different publics: airlines, hotel and motel chains, all media, foreign travel agencies, branch offices of Finnish travel organizations abroad, and foreign governments.

The tourist market "discovered" Finland in the late sixties. The tourist growth-trend in recent years has been 30 to 40 percent annually, while in most other European countries it has been only about 20 percent. Tourism has become the third largest industry in Finland and has turned the Finnish balance of trade from a deficit of $31.3 million in 1963 to a surplus of $34 million in 1970.

Who are the tourists? Of the 2,300,000 foreign tourists, about half come from the other Scandinavian countries and the other half are non-Scandinavian. Of the non-Scandinavians, about 40 percent come from West Germany and the remainder are Americans, Englishmen, Dutchmen, Frenchmen, Swiss, Italian, and so forth.

It would seem that the Finnish people would feel pleased with the country's success in attracting foreign tourists. On the contrary, the people have very mixed feelings. The rapid growth of tourism has been accompanied by several problems.

First, the tourist influx is highly seasonal. Nearly 50 percent of the tourists come in the three months of June, July, and August.

Second, most of the tourists have come from lower- or middle-income classes with small travel budgets; they live in tents or trailers; they bring their own food; in a word, they spend very little money in Finland. Furthermore, they crowd the Finnish vacation spots at a time when the Finnish people are also on vacation and seeking rest and recreation. This has led to many complaints.

Third, Finnish environmental groups have complained that their scenic land, particularly the lake area and Lapland, is being threatened with ruin. The Lapps have complained about the litter and about tentfuls of tourists who camp next to their previously peaceful summer cottages.

The Finnish Bureau of Tourism recognizes that it has a new problem to solve. The earlier problem was to attract people to Finland. They succeeded but now are forced to adopt new objectives. Their major objectives must be to reshape the compositional and seasonal characteristics of the tourists. They seek to achieve the following specific objectives in the next few years:

1. They would like to attract fewer but wealthier tourists.
2. They would like to attract fewer tourists in the summer and more in the other seasons. This would leave more breathing space for the Finnish population during the summer.
3. They would like to attract more tourists who are motivated by wanderlust rather than sunlust. The sunlusting tourists want facilities like they have at home and this calls for much Finnish investment in new facilities. The wanderlust tourists, on the other hand, come to enjoy a different culture and live as people do in that culture.
4. They would like to attract tourists to areas in Finland that would not overtax or threaten Finland's best sites with pollution and ruin.

Questions

1. Are the new objectives of the Finnish Bureau of Tourism reasonable, consistent, and obtainable? Could you suggest any modification of these objectives?
2. Develop a marketing plan for the Finnish Bureau of Tourism that will accomplish the set of objectives you believe are reasonable.

10. LOUIS A. WEISS MEMORIAL HOSPITAL— RAISING FUNDS FOR A HOSPITAL *

Louis A. Weiss Memorial Hospital, a medium-sized 350-bed institution servicing the near-north section of Chicago, was opened in 1953 and named after the late Chicago philanthropist and industrialist. Since its inception in the early 1950s, the hospital has grown

* Case was prepared by Louis W. Hirschmann under the direction of the author.

steadily but carefully in the type and quality of services it has to offer: among them, providing more ambulatory, out-patient services; expanding the medical library; adding a new floor to the professional wing which houses doctors' offices; establishing a Cardiac Physiology Laboratory; increasing bed capacity, etc.

Although planning is one key to Weiss Hospital's steady growth, a concerted effort to market the hospital has also been employed in order to maintain the superior image of the institution, to keep the public aware of the services the hospital has to offer, and to acquire both large and small charitable donations from interested citizens.

There are a number of ways that the hospital's board of trustees goes about acquiring funds for Weiss. Each year, there is an annual charity affair at a cultural event (theater, ballet, etc.) which publicizes the good work of the hospital and also serves to acquire funds. For significant contributions to the hospital, the donor's name might be placed on a plaque and installed in a room, a laboratory, or a wing. Prominent interested citizens who show an interest in the hospital may be considered for membership on the board of trustees. Solicitations of $1,000 are requested every year from each member of the board. Possible donors are also presented by each member of the board in the form of lists. Such possible donors receive personalized letters describing the work of the hospital and asking for donations.

Weiss Hospital employs a full-time public relations man plus an assistant whose many jobs include seeing that the hospital receives coverage in the newspapers when a major hospital-connected event occurs, such as a large charity affair for Weiss or the opening of a new wing. However, the hospital does not rely exclusively on outside media to relay its news. "Word From Weiss," published quarterly by Friends of Louis A. Weiss Hospital, is a 15- to 20-page magazine that covers events and stories of interest to those who are connected with the hospital. There is also a movie, 15 to 20 minutes in length, which describes the hospital and its history. The film is used for any interested public gathering.

Finally, but importantly, the Women's Auxiliary provides an extremely valuable service to the hospital through its running of the gift shop. One of the largest gift shops of its kind in the U.S., its profits go to various hospital needs. Not only is this gift shop a significant marketing effort, but the Women's Board helps arrange benefits, charity affairs, and awards and tributes ceremonies.

Thus we can see that while Weiss Hospital has served the community and improved the services it has to offer over the years, it has also been engaged in a concerted marketing effort which sustains its reputation while simultaneously garnering charitable donations.

Question

Should Weiss Hospital move further into organized marketing? What steps might it take? What benefits would this bring?

11. MEDICAL ASSISTANCE PROGRAMS, INC.—
RAISING FUNDS FOR DISASTER VICTIMS *

Medical Assistance Programs, Inc. (MAP) is a voluntary international agency that sends medical help to missionary physicians who are meeting the health needs of people in eighty-two developing countries. The organization was founded in 1954 to serve as a catalyst between pharmaceutical firms and mission hospitals. Since its inception, over $110 million worth of donated supplies have been distributed through MAP in developing nations.

In recent years, the agency has expanded its services. Opportunities are offered to medical personnel and other qualified individuals to become involved in short-term mission assignments. These overseas assignments vary from supervision of relief projects such as a medical and house-building program in Bangladesh to helping in a critically understaffed hospital in Liberia.

The agency is funded mainly through private donors even though United States Aid for International Development (USAID) has partially funded several projects. Missionary doctors are asked to help finance transportation costs of supplies although MAP constantly seeks to reduce their burden. Only 2 percent of the total donations to the agency during the last year went for publicity and fund raising.

At the present time, MAP is heavily involved in distributing foodstuffs and medical supplies in the Sub-Saharan region of Africa. Twenty American volunteers have given three months of their time to help the people through their worst drought in history. About 90 percent of the population in the eight-nation region are starving. Several American corporations recently donated over 300 tons of foodstuffs for the disaster; however, over $100,000 is needed for transportation costs. MAP is unable to pay this amount without an appeal to the public. In the past few months, the donors and friends have received a letter of appeal for the starving Africans along with a stamped self-addressed return envelope. The letter included photographs of disaster victims and the agency's involvement. Another request to these individuals, churches, and foundations on behalf of the African situation may not be very effective.

* Case was prepared by David John Gotaas under the direction of the author.

The organization's staff is aware that most people feel harassed into giving financial support to nonprofit agencies and they have built up resistance to pleas. Bad publicity about poorly managed organizations by the news media has increased the resistance as well as demanding greater disclosure of sources and uses of funds because of lack of trust.

Dave Enlow, Director of Communications, has suggested to Dr. Raymond Knighton, President and Founder, that a letter be sent requesting help urgently for the famine. He has listed nine other credible agencies that are working in the disaster area. The appeal would be directed as an urgent plea to give to any of the organizations with the hope that MAP would receive a significant amount. MAP does not consider these agencies to be competitors, but rather co-workers. Dr. Knighton has asked for time to review the suggestion. All the other agencies listed in the letter are considerably larger and better known than MAP (i.e., Food for the Hungry, CARE, Lutheran World Relief, Billy Graham Evangelistic Assn., etc.). Sometimes the MAP personnel have referred to their organization as "the best-kept secret" because of the poor public awareness although it has received considerable praise from foreign governments and is well-respected by the United States Department of State.

Questions

1. Do you think a fund-raising letter from MAP mentioning other good agencies in the area of disaster relief would be effective in raising funds for MAP?

2. MAP has not conducted fund raising or publicity on a systematic basis in the past. Formulate a long-range marketing plan for MAP.

12. STATE PUBLIC ASSISTANCE AGENCY—A PUBLIC OFFICIAL COMMENTS ON MARKETING

A professor at a well-known private university in the Midwest sent a draft of a chapter he had written on Public Services Marketing to a high-placed official whom he knew in a large state public assistance agency. This official gave the draft a careful reading and then mailed the following letter to the professor:

Dear Professor:

I appreciate your sharing your article, <u>Public Services Marketing,</u> with me. Allow me to share a few of my thoughts with you. Your views are fundamentally valid, although not fully applicable to the realities of a state public assistance agency.

The major problem with the business analogy is that modern, effective marketing practices are expensive. The criterion of utility is where the customers are induced to buy enough of the product to generate more new profit than the costs of marketing. Modern selling policies do not necessarily produce the greatest benefit for the lowest cost to the consumer. Attractive and expensive advertising, public relations, salesmen, mass promotions, customer relations, etc., do not always maximize the public good.

Moreover, many people in our society view professional, aggressive advertising and selling with skepticism and resent the fact that the high costs are packed into the product price. At a time when government enterprises are underfunded and often subjected to political attack for being too costly and wasteful of tax money, a public agency would do well to avoid spending too much money on unnecessary and superficial promotion at the expense of substantive services. However, the kind of promotion which you are suggesting need not be unnecessary or superficial.

Public administration may borrow some business marketing approaches but we should not exaggerate the analogy with private business and salesmanship. Some marketing concepts are useful, but insufficiently applied in public programming. Others are already in use, but not conceptualized in marketing terms.

Allow me to look at some of the marketing functions identified by you. Market research is something we now do under the following labels: (1) needs assessment; (2) research; and (3) citizen participation.

Our system of community advisory councils, problem/goal/objective analyses, and target area resident participation in reviewing programs is actually a fairly sophisticated type of market research. The only type of consumer research we do not place much emphasis on is sample surveying of consumer attitudes, although we have done some survey work. The fundamental value of market research is in fact recognized and acted upon by this agency.

Advertising, including what you call design, communication, and promotion, is a function we should consider more fully than we currently do. The presentation of self to the public is done less effectively by government agencies than by most commercial products and services, even though the public service may be more important to the public and more deserving of public knowledge and acceptance than most brands of beer, soap, and new cars.

Government agencies should devote far more talent, effort, and resources to advertising than they currently do. Attractive interior atmospheres and exterior designs of public service facilities would be a worthwhile investment in gaining public awareness, confidence, and even pride in the activities of government. Mass communication and "public information" also deserve more concern. Few agencies hire the quality of talent and media space needed to really inform their user population or the taxpayer of the services available.

However, there is one feature of most government services that makes the need for advertising fundamentally different from that in free enterprise. A profit-making firm wants to increase public demand for its product whenever it can expand the supply and thus make more profit. But government is not-for-profit, users pay less than the cost of the service, many public programs are underfunded, and demand may already exceed supply.

Under such conditions, advertising may not be appropriate because it will simply increase demand even further. Then the only way to increase supply is through legislative or executive action; and administrators and legislators consider it inappropriate for agencies to take their cases to the mass public for the implied purpose of inducing political pressure for bigger agency budgets.

Generally, then, public agency advertising and promotion cannot be of the high-pressure variety employed by private enterprise. It must be more credible and generally informative. But there is no reason why it cannot be as skillful and attractive, and it certainly deserves more emphasis than is now the case in most agencies.

Distribution, pricing, and product management are other marketing functions which most modern public administrators recognize as necessary in public service. Your remarks appear sufficient in this regard.

Customer relations, user convenience, attractiveness of physical design are concerns which almost all government agencies need to take more seriously. Partly because they do not compete with others to attract customers, agencies often neglect to be pleasant, friendly, polite, and sensitive to their users as persons.

Government agencies should be concerned with their public image, the public dissemination of awareness and understanding about their services, and public confidence in the agency. Marketing concepts, selectively borrowed and selectively applied, do need greater emphasis in public administration.

Question

Discuss the reactions of the official with particular reference to whether he has a correct understanding of marketing and whether you agree with his qualifications about marketing's use in the public sector. Draft a reply to this official.

13. MODEL CITIES PROGRAM—
THE SEARCH FOR A CORPORATE IDENTITY

In recent years, various city governments set up new agencies to coordinate and facilitate the delivery of social services to people whose lives were marred by poverty and lack of opportunity. One such agency is Model Cities. The background and function of this agency is explained in its brochure:

Model Cities is a city government agency, operating as a part of the Mayor's office, dedicated to improving the quality of urban life. The agency was created in August 1971 through the consolidation of two programs . . . the Chicago Committee on Urban Opportunity, which was the city's anti-poverty agency and provided comprehensive services to residents of 14 inner-city areas, and Model Cities, which operated 12 Urban Progress Centers (UPC). These are neighborhood multiservice centers that bring together under one roof a variety of services, ranging from health, to education, to manpower, to housing. In these UPC's a breadwinner can get a job or training through a State Employment Service Counselor stationed in the center; a neighborhood resident can learn to read, using sophisticated electronic equipment; a high school dropout can get the equivalent of a high school diploma by attending weekly classes taught by city college personnel; a youngster may receive his basic inoculations and be tested for lead poisoning; the hungry can get food; youngsters and senior citizens can enroll in recreational programs; and taxpayers may receive help in preparing their income tax returns. . . . Secondly, Model Cities directly operates a wide range of programs that are not based in the UPC's. Included here is a city-wide Headstart program, a massive summer program, training activities, special health programs, and a wide variety of technical assistance. Model Cities also funds 254 programs serving residents of the 14 target neighborhoods. There are programs in health, housing, education, economic development, crime prevention, environment, child and family services, leisure time, manpower and transportation.

As a result of offering so many diverse services to the communities, Model Cities has failed to transmit a clear image to many of its publics. Many members of the general public have heard of Model Cities but have no concept of what it is; this is especially true of middle-class citizens in parts of the greater Chicago area who are not directly affected by Model City programs. Many prospective clients are unaware of the Urban Progress Centers and/or the many services provided by these centers. Some social service organizations in these communities feel threatened by this sprawling urban agency. There are some neighborhood leaders who see Model Cities either as a threat to their power base or as ineffective in changing the basic conditions that give rise to the plight of the poor. Finally, Model Cities is always being scrutinized by some legislators who think it may be misspending or misallocating money; they want more accountability. Model Cities provides a lot of ideas and help to other agencies that do not get sufficient recognition from legislators.

Increasingly, the directors of the agency have the feeling that their various publics need a clearer image of Model Cities. The publics get confused impressions because the agency has not worked out its own corporate identity. Its various employees communicate quite different messages about the agency. The directors prepared the following memo:

Model Cities is a management system which has to be accepted to
achieve its highest potential. What is our corporate identity and how
can we sell it? How can we appeal to the Chicago population in order
to develop the necessary leadership to make the management system
work? We must search for a solid identity, look at the advertising possibilities, and build our capacity to communicate an image which is
functional and understood by everyone.

Questions

1. Do you think this agency should take time to develop a corporate
identity? What possible ways can it go about searching for and formulating a corporate identity?

2. Suggest some possible alternative corporate identities for this
agency. Formulate a corporate identity statement. How would you communicate the corporate identity to the staff and later to the various
publics? What would be the cost? What would be the benefits? Who in
the agency should handle the development and dissemination of the
agency's corporate identity?

14. UNIVERSITY OF PENNSYLVANIA—
RELIGIOUS INDIFFERENCE ON CAMPUS *

The first Sunday at the University of Pennsylvania
finds many new undergraduate students attending the church of their
denomination. Yet by the end of the school term it has been noted that
nearly two out of three of these students are no longer present—a much
smaller percentage than attended when they lived at home with their
family.

Religious and church attendance has been declining all over the
country to a certain extent since the early 1960s. At the same time, a
smaller decline has been reflected on university campuses.

This downward trend in the university setting might be explained
in a number of ways, according to campus religious leaders. Rebellion
from previous parental coercion may negatively affect student church
attendance, because the individual now has a feeling of independence.
The students who attend because they get something out of it remain;
but the fringe students who attended in the past because it was "socially
acceptable" no longer attend because they do not feel this pressure. The
college curriculum is very demanding; and the competition for graduate
school is such that studying takes top priority over a number of activities,
including religion.

* Case was prepared by Robert E. Nissen under the direction of the author.

A focus group interview was conducted with eight undergraduate student members of a national fraternity chapter on the campus. Among the students were four Catholics, one Jewish student, one Greek Orthodox, and one nonpreference Christian. The purpose of the interview was to initially gain an overview of student attitudes toward religion and religious services on campus. It was also desirable to know the motivations and priorities involved in participation.

A number of ideas came to the surface as a result. "Hard-sell" religious groups were for the most part unacceptable to the participants. Equating religious beliefs and actual church attendance were not necessarily desirable; individuals should be able to practice religion in their own way. The attractiveness of folk-rock and other nontraditional services was met with mixed reactions. Finally, the association with friends and compatriots was helpful in encouraging students to attend. For the most part the group elicited many of the negatives associated with promoting religious attendance.

Obviously, the continuing decline has led many ministers and campus churches to initiate a number of changes. More relevant services, with the liturgy directed at the student audiences, have been attempted. Regular members have been encouraged to bring friends. Supplementary activities and outings associated with individual churches have been increased. Yet the impact these have had on averting a decline is hard to measure.

It is questionable whether religious attendance on this college campus will bottom out or whether there is any opportunity for reversing the trend. The problem—a case of declining demand within a declining industry—is one that requires considerable understanding.

Question

Should the concept of student religious participation be marketed more vigorously by religious groups on this campus? If so, how? If not, why not?

15. WINNETKA BIBLE CHURCH—A CHURCH TRIES ITS HANDS AT SYNCHROMARKETING *

While most churches were suffering losses in Sunday morning attendance, the Winnetka (Ill.) Bible Church enjoyed a steady increase in attendance throughout the late 1960s. Attendance climbed from an average of 358 people per Sunday in 1964 to over 500 per Sunday in 1970. Each year, peak attendance figures were reached during the

* Case was prepared by Paul Bloom based on notes by David John Gotaas.

spring and fall, while the summer months brought significantly lower attendance because people took vacations. Also, attendance fluctuated greatly because of the weather.

The church sanctuary is unable to seat more than 476 comfortably, although it can accommodate 550. For this reason, the church instituted a two-service schedule in October, 1970. One service began at 9:45 A.M. and the other at 11:00 A.M. Sunday School classes were run jointly at both hours for certain age groups, while other classes would only meet at one of the hours. The new schedule was designed to eliminate overcrowding and to allow newcomers to attend services. The church has a strong commitment toward attracting newcomers to the congregation.

During 1971, the year after the introduction of the new schedule, attendance began to decline. Neither service was filled, which gave people a feeling of emptiness compared to what they had experienced in the past. The choir was split in two and this hurt the quality of the music. Some families found they could no longer sit together because of the different Sunday School periods. Certain parents were bringing their children to Sunday School while they went to the church service and were then leaving immediately after the first service. Unity and fellowship among the members was strained because of the different services.

To make matters worse, the minister decided to go to another church in California in the spring of 1971. Following his departure, it was decided that the old, one-service system should be restored at least until a new minister was found. However, the return to only one service did not stop the decline in attendance.

In December 1971, a new minister was hired and within a few months attendance began to increase. Overcrowding again became a problem and the church decided to reinstitute a second service, 8:30 A.M. rather than 9:45 A.M. But attendance at the 8:30 service was poor. After about a year, the 8:30 attendance had not increased significantly over its initial level of 80 people. Many individuals walked in late and sat in the very back of the sanctuary. The service was described as "dead" by most people and few of the leaders of the church came at this time. The choir members did not enjoy singing at the first service and refused to do so. In short, most of the members continued to attend the overcrowded 11:00 A.M. service.

Questions

1. What goal should the Winnetka Bible Church set for Sunday morning attendance? What are the churchgoers' needs? What are the church's needs?

2. What "synchromarketing" techniques might be used to achieve the desired attendance goals?

16. THE OFFICE OF CITY CLERK OF EVANSTON— POLITICAL CANDIDATE MARKETING STRATEGY *

On January 11, 1973, Bonnie Hartenstein, a 32-year-old housewife, announced her decision to challenge Maurice Brown for the office of City Clerk of Evanston (Ill.). By entering the contest, Mrs. Hartenstein produced the first race for the post in 44 years. Mr. Brown had been appointed to the post 14 years before to fill a vacancy, and he had run unopposed in every election since that time.

At the time of the election, the city of Evanston had 49,000 registered voters. The maximum number of votes that would be cast in this election was judged to be 20,000. Thus, 10,000 votes could win the election. These votes would have to come from Evanston's nine wards, each of which had some distinctive characteristics. The first ward encompassed Northwestern University and, consequently, was heavily populated with students. But of the 7,000 students eligible to vote in this ward, only 1,500 were registered and only 1,200 had voted in the last election. The second and fifth wards were predominantly black (Evanston's 79,800 population was 16 percent black) and only 570 votes and 1,190 votes were cast in these wards during the last election. There were also wards with a high density of upper-middle-class whites. Some of these wards had a reputation for being predominantly Democratic or liberal, while about half were strongly Republican.

Mrs. Hartenstein had been very active in politics prior to this election. She had worked for presidential candidate George McGovern, Illinois Governor Dan Walker, and Chicago Alderman William Singer. In 1971, she served as campaign manager of the successful Evanston ninth ward aldermanic campaign of Maxine Lange. She was active in the League of Women Voters and the Women's Liberation Center of Evanston, and she belonged to the Independent Precinct Organization, the Independent Voters of Illinois, the Democratic Party of Evanston, and the Illinois Women's Political Caucus. In addition, she was the founder of a community organization in southwest Evanston that had 250 members and she was a member of the board of the Evanston Public Library.

Mr. Brown was 73 years old, with 14 years of experience as City Clerk and a powerful Republican organization behind him. Mrs. Hartenstein had not received the endorsement of the less powerful Democratic Party when she announced her candidacy but received it later.

* Case was prepared by Paul Bloom based on notes by John C. O'Leary.

The position of City Clerk carried a four-year term of office with a salary of $12,500. The annual operating budget was approximately $28,000, with an additional $28,000 allocated to the office every two years to conduct elections. The Clerk was responsible for taking minutes at weekly council meetings and for maintaining voter registration records and conducting elections. During the campaign, Mr. Brown pointed with pride to his ability to keep the expenses of his office at low levels.

Mrs. Hartenstein produced a campaign designed to give her a very broad appeal. She felt that she needed every vote possible and that she could not afford to alienate any one group in favor of another. She expected her universal appeal to reach the voters through a broad-based campaign organization with grass-roots volunteer support. Her positions on the issues were outlined in three "position papers," which were mailed to people who showed an interest in the Hartenstein campaign. Mrs. Hartenstein's main campaign pledge was that she would turn the City Clerk's office into an information-dissemination center which could help to get more citizens to participate in community affairs.

Mr. Brown's campaign was less vocal and it defended his record. Early in his campaign he gained the support of many community leaders, including the local president of the National Association for the Advancement of Colored People, the past president of the League of Women Voters, and a majority of local businessmen. Mr. Brown claimed that Mrs. Hartenstein's ideas for changing the Clerk's office were impractical and potentially expensive.

Questions

1. Do you agree with Mrs. Hartenstein's broad voter-appeal strategy? What other market positioning strategies were available?

2. Formulate the best possible campaign methodology for Mrs. Hartenstein. What are her chances of winning the election with this methodology?

17. THE NATIONAL JUNIOR TENNIS LEAGUE OF TOLEDO—MARKETING A SOCIAL SERVICE *

The National Junior Tennis League of Toledo is a chapter of a tax-deductible nonprofit organization which promotes tennis to youngsters between 9 and 16 who live primarily in the inner-city areas of Toledo, Ohio. In 1972, the year the Toledo chapter was founded, approximately 24 of these chapters existed in the United States. Toledo

* Case was prepared by Brian E. Engel under the direction of the author.

and Cincinnati were the first cities to introduce the NJTL philosophy of tennis instruction in Ohio. The NJTL philosophy of teaching tennis is radically different from traditional methods of tennis instruction. This approach, authored by some of the United States' greatest tennis stars and promoters, is particularly designed to satisfy the needs of the youngsters who have short attention spans and are perpetually restless. Psychologists have found that inner-city youngsters are particularly prone to these afflictions owing to their hectic environment.

The founder and first director of the Toledo chapter was Brian Engel, at the time a junior at the University of Toledo, who played varsity tennis and studied in the College of Business Administration. At the time, Engel viewed the organization to have four major publics: *donors, clients, watchdog agencies,* and a *nonparticipating public.*

The donors, by and large, consisted of the city government (facilities only), large financial patrons, small financial patrons, and volunteer personnel. The clients consisted of eligible youngsters (ages 9 to 16) and their parents. The public watchdog agencies were considered to be the media (local newspaper, television, and radio), the Chamber of Commerce, and the Better Business Bureau. The nonparticipating public consisted of groups such as eligible youngsters not currently participating, parents with eligible youngsters, noneligible youngsters, people concerned with helping others, tennis enthusiasts, and other service organizations (i.e., Boy and Girl Scouts, YMCA, YWCA, etc.).

The marketing themes Engel considered most important to be presented to these publics were resource attraction to the donors, goodwill generation to the nonparticipating public, fair-practice image generation to the watchdog agencies, and resource allocation and client attraction to the clients.

The plans for the first year's program called for a budget of approximately $10,000 to be used to benefit approximately 400 youngsters at five different locations. Criteria for evaluating success was based on both the total number of boys and girls "reached" and their consistency of attendance.

The strategy selected for fund raising was to acquire broad-based support as opposed to a few large sponsors solely from the private sector. This objective was adopted because it would more likely assure continued support in future years and also help in publicizing the new organization. The disadvantage to this, however, is the comparatively large amount of time and expenses required. Also, publicity cannot be given to any of the sponsors. This is because the media ordinarily does not like to mention sponsors of organizations and will especially not list twenty different ones. Also, twenty sponsors' logos will not fit on the youngsters'

T-shirts or other equipment. When an organization decides to seek a broad base of support, it must forego offering publicity to sponsors. This removes the organization from competing for the public relations dollar and places them in competition for the charity dollar, a much leaner and more difficult dollar to capture.

To the nonparticipating public, the marketing theme was based on the program's social impact. The nonparticipating public was very important to the long-range growth of the organization because it represented potential future donors and clients.

During the program's first year, the media gave a great amount of coverage to the organization's efforts. The coverage was mostly local; however, the world's leading tennis magazine did a feature on the Toledo program. The program was considered very successful and a viable contributor to inner-city life.

By the end of the program's first season, twenty donors were found among local businesses, organizations, and individuals. The largest of these were the Champion Spark Plug Company and the Questor Corporation, represented by the Goerlich Foundation.

As far as the clients are concerned, approximately 400 boys and girls benefited, of which approximately 52 percent participated regularly.

In the second year, much of the same type of marketing strategies were used with the central message that because of the first year's success, the program would be expanded to other local areas where requested. For the second year, the donors' list grew to thirty-four in number, generating an approximately $12,000 budget. Of this, one-tenth were nonmonetary contributions. During this second season, approximately 650 youngsters benefited, of which 61 percent participated regularly.

With the beginning of the third season, many questions confront the organization. A major question is where the leadership will come from. Engel no longer lives in Toledo; Vice-President Adams, who initially thought he could take over the leadership, suddenly had to change his plans. Because the organization was run in an entrepreneurial fashion, no one is very familiar with the administrative functions, particularly the marketing end.

Assuming new leadership can be found, NJTL has to maintain the participation of the donors. With small programs like the NJTL of Toledo, donors, particularly large businesses, like to spread their charitable support to many different organizations.

A further question is how to finance the program in terms of where the money comes from. Currently, financial support comes totally from the private sector. Should the public sector be asked to contribute money along with their permission to use public tennis facilities? Unlike the gift of property usage, a financial gift brings with it a very rigorous scrutiny, and at times, forces a relinquishing of administrative control.

Another question is how to continue to obtain good publicity from the media. A major story on the organization had already appeared in the Sunday Magazine Section of the only newspaper published in the city. More news coverage would not be forthcoming until NJTL could develop some fresh news about the program.

Question

Formulate a marketing strategy for NJTL-Toledo to use at this stage of the organization's life cycle.

Index

SUBJECT INDEX

NAME INDEX